To John

With f[illegible] wishes

[illegible]oofe

Life and Death of a Pirate

Reg Calvert

AUTHOR'S NOTES

REAL PEOPLE AND EVENTS

It has taken many years to research and write this book. In the process, I approached a number of publishers and literary agents who were very kind in their letters of rejection, their thought being that there would be no interest in this story. I hope, you the reader, will prove them wrong.

Life and Death of a Pirate is a biographical history, written as a novel. Life can be stranger than fiction and the narrative is based on real people and events. It is a poignant love story, full of twists and turns, sometimes shocking, often funny. The lives of many people, singers, musicians, disc jockeys and engineers are all woven into the tapestry of Reg and Dorothy's extraordinary lives. As the story unravels it comes to a tragic ending and even today, there are questions left unanswered.

You may like to dip into some of the **YouTube** recordings. Most of the singers and songs mentioned in these pages can be heard and seen on YouTube including Stately Strollers, (Clifton Hall Pathé film 1962). In addition, there are recordings and videos about pirate radio including Radio Sutch and Radio City. You can hear and see Reg Calvert, Screaming Lord Sutch and some of the disc jockeys who worked on the station.

The history of the Maunsell Forts, including Shivering Sands, is available on several websites including: **www.project-redsand.com**. There are some excellent websites with collections of pirate radio photographs, memorabilia and sound recordings, including Pirate Hall of Fame: **www.offshoreradio.co.uk** and **www.bobleroi.co.uk**

Life and Death of a Pirate was first written and performed as a stage play. The play is now available for theatre groups to perform from Fillongley Publications.

LIFE AND DEATH OF A PIRATE SPECIAL EDITION
Published 2017
Fillongley Publications CV7 8PB

ISBN 978-0-9515116-6-4
Printed in the United Kingdom

Dedicated to the memory of two extraordinary people

Reg and Dorothy Calvert

ACKNOWLEDGEMENTS

My sincere thanks to everyone who helped with the production of this book, to my friends and the many contributors. To Gerard McLaughlin for help with editing the books. My husband, Lyndon, for his help and patience. Paul Telfer for book cover design. Most of all, my thanks to the 'boys' who worked for Reg and Dorothy, the many musicians, singers, disc jockeys and engineers who told me their story and provided copies of photographs, newspaper cuttings and memorabilia.

PHOTOGRAPHS

Reg Calvert was an avid photographer and had a darkroom under the stairs at Clifton Hall. His photographs are identified by (RC), Susan Calvert (SC),
Eric Martin (EM), Eric Jay (EJ), Sheriden Street (SH), Alamy (AL). www.topfoto (TF)
The photographs and memorabilia in this book date to the 1950s and 1960s. Every effort has been made to contact copyright holders of images reproduced in this book and acknowledge them. Many visitors, including the press, asked to take photographs when visiting Clifton Hall or Shivering Sands and with the passing of time, we do not have all their names.

BOOKSHOPS and STOCKISTS

For a list of Bookshops and Stockists visit : www.regcalvert-plays.co.uk
Email: fillongleypub@btinternet.com
Paperbacks and eBooks also available to order from Amazon Books

FILLONGLEY PUBLICATIONS
The Old Granary, Fillongley, Nr. Coventry CV7 8PB

CONTENTS

Preface

POPCORN TO ROCK 'N' ROLL

Book One

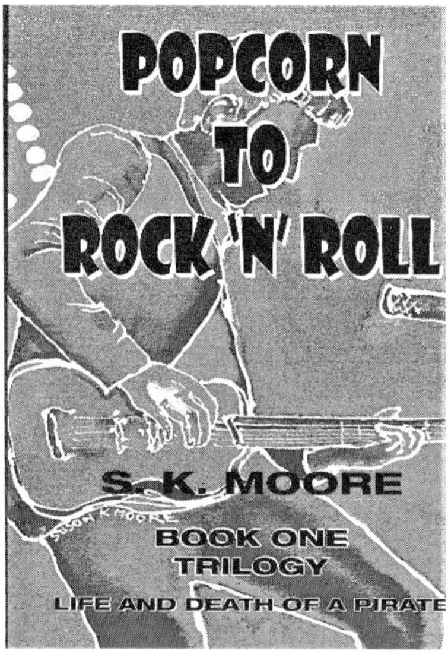

Biographical novel set in post-war England. Romantic, poignant, often funny, sometimes shocking. Adult reading – includes sex and drugs but not in the way you would imagine.

Reg Calvert is a dreamer, impulsive and determined to succeed. He falls in love with Dorothy and they marry at 18 with little thought of the consequences. Too soon, Reg feels trapped by marriage and children. With little money, he buys an old bus and converts it into a caravan and they travel south from Huddersfield to Southampton.

1950 Dorothy Calvert with Susan and pet goat in the apple orchard at Hedge End, near Southampton. (Behind) The old bus which becomes their home for three years until they can afford to buy a house (RC)

In post-war Britain, there were few opportunities and Reg tried many ways to make a living, including making popcorn and selling sweets on the markets, (top photo) having a sweet factory, then a sweet shop (bottom photo). He is fascinated by radio and for a short time, becomes a radio and television engineer. In the evenings he plays piano in a club and runs ballroom dances. Dorothy was often by his side, but with two daughters to bring up, it was hard for her as she never knew what Reg would do next. Full of ideas, he quickly became bored and moved onto new ventures leaving her to carry on and pick up the pieces.

Reg is a natural entertainer. When he first hears Bill Haley's *Rock Around the Clock*, he has a new dream. To bring Rock 'n' Roll to England. Few British big band musicians can 'rock' so Reg discovers young boys, musicians and singers who give up their day jobs to follow him. Reg puts together fabulous stage shows and is first to provide entertainment for the 'new' teenager. His boys tour the country as dancehall stars and soon, others are copying him and his ideas.

Left: 1953 Reg entertaining a street party to celebrate the coronation of Queen Elizabeth II
Below: c1957 Portland Terrace Southampton: Austin Sheerline loaded to go to the dances, Dorothy behind (RC)

Reg rents two houses in Portland Terrace, Southampton,.one as an office and the other as accommodation for his musicians to live. He persuades Dorothy to move to Portland Terrace temporarily while he establishes his dancehall business and suggests she runs her own print works on the ground floor.

The boys are given new stage names, Danny Storm, Eddy Sex, Buddy Britten, Rod Ace, Ricky Fever, Colin Angel etc. Reg dresses them in glamourous stage outfits and employs 'famous' stars to tour with them including Terry Dene, Billy Fury, Vince Taylor, Gene Vincent, Johnny Kidd, Rory Blackwell, Screaming Lord Sutch etc. There has never been anything like it!

Left: Danny Storm and Eddy Sex.
Below: Reg with Baby Bubbly. David Da Costa, Danny Storm, Ricky Fever and Glen Dale.

POPCORN TO ROCK 'N' ROLL

For bookshops and stockists visit: www.regcalvert-plays.co.uk
Paperbacks and eBooks also available from Amazon Books
Fillongley Publications, The Old Granary, Fillongley CV7 8PB
ISBN 978-0-9515116-7-1

CLIFTON HALL
School of Rock 'n' Roll
BOOK TWO

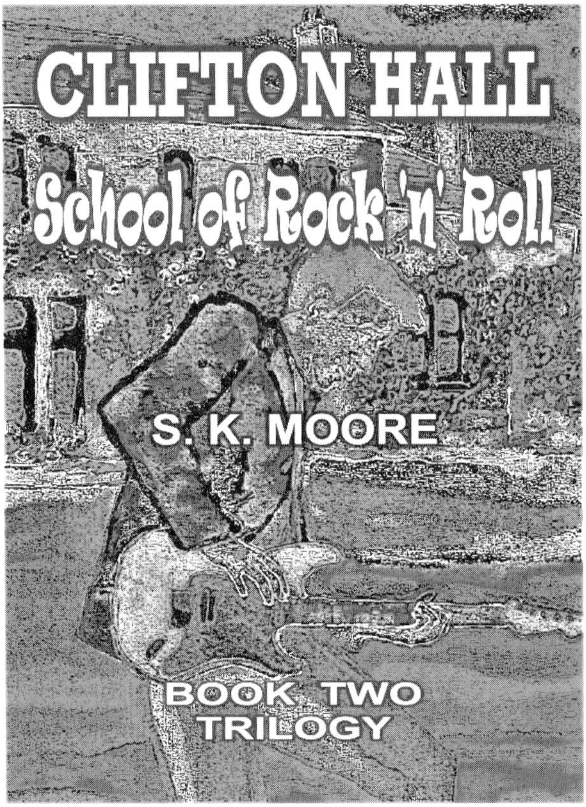

For bookshops and stockists visit: www.regcalvert-plays.co.uk
Paperbacks and eBooks also available from Amazon Books
Fillongley Publications, The Old Granary, Fillongley CV7 8PB
Email: fillongleypub@btinternet.com

1960 SOUTHAMPTON

'Training Session' posed for the press. Reg Calvert and Danny Storm, David Da Costa, Glen Dale, Ricky Fever (guitar), Tony Burnett (drums). (BIPS)

It was a dull grey afternoon and from the sea, salt winds blew, lifting and swirling the autumnal leaves and dropping them in neglected gardens. Reg Calvert gazed at the view from the bedroom window as he smoked a cigarette. It had been a good day and he was jubilant. His wife, Dorothy, came to stand by him and he impulsively put his arms about her to dance in a mad waltz around the bedroom before flopping down, pulling her on top of him. Dorothy giggled as she struggled to sit up.

"Not now, the girls will be home in a minute."

"Later then," replied Reg, lying back on the red satin eiderdown.

"I thought we were getting ready to go to the Chinese, or you can have the heart I was cooking?"

Reg grinned. Casseroled heart in orange sauce was his least favourite dinner.

"No, you can give that to the cat. Tonight, I want to celebrate."

Reg closed his eyes and relaxed. He was happy. Southern Television were going to make a film about his School of Rock 'n' Roll. At last, he was making his mark and this was just the beginning. Within a moment, he was asleep.

"It's time to go," said Dorothy, shaking Reg gently. "The girls are home."

The following morning, Reg was still in a good mood, pondering which dancehall he should book to stage the show for Southern Television.

"What do you think about Eastleigh Town Hall?"

"Should be good. Which boys will you have in the film?"

"It'll be up to the TV people to decide but I've told them about my main singers, Glen Dale, Danny Storm and Buddy Britten."

"Of course."

"And then there's Baby Bubbly, Ricky Fever and Carol Laine."

"I wouldn't have her in it," said Dorothy, dismissively. "She's not very good. How many pieces of toast do you want?"

"Two please," replied Reg, as he picked up the New Musical Express and started to flick through the pages.

While Reg was in a good mood, Dorothy decided to raise the subject of buying a new home.

"There's some nice houses being built near the Common. I thought we could take a look," smiled Dorothy, optimistically.

"Not now, I'm too busy."

"You always say you're too busy," muttered Dorothy, exasperated by his attitude as she placed two cups of steaming coffee and hot buttered toast on the dining table. "When are we going to move?"

"Soon, when I've some spare cash," replied Reg, flippantly. He did not want to argue and lit two Player's cigarettes, offering one to his wife. Dorothy inhaled deeply and started to splutter.

"You ought to give up, I'm sure the smoke is making you cough."

Dorothy ignored her husband's remark about smoking. They had both tried to stop and neither had succeeded for more than a few days.

"I've had some house details sent to me. Do you want to have a look?"

"Not at the moment. I'm too busy."

"When then?"

"I told you. When I can afford it."

"Oh yes. That'll be never then, won't it?"

They had had this conversation many times. Reg lifted his head from reading the paper and stared coldly at his wife.

"I wish you'd stop nagging me."

"I'm not nagging. You promised. You said we would only be here for a few months and four years later we're still no nearer to moving."

"The rent's not much," shrugged Reg. "And it's perfect for you to run the print works on the ground floor. It means you can work at night when the girls are in bed."

"So it might be, but I've had enough. I want to bring our daughters up in a nice house."

Reg could see his wife was near to tears. He disliked her telling him what to do and he particularly disliked being reminded of promises he had made. Stubbing out his cigarette on the glass ashtray, he stood up.

"I'll be going in a minute. My turn to run the dance at Worcester this week."

Dorothy, nodded her head in acknowledgement.

Their moment of joy was over. Dorothy knew she had ruined it and they were back to squabbling and arguing. She was disappointed with herself that she had not been able to persuade Reg to look at one of the new houses. She glanced at the estate agent details despondently. Everywhere, new homes were being built to replace the old and there was an air of optimism that the years of post-war austerity were almost at an end. She dreamed of moving into a modern, three-bedroom house with an upstairs bathroom and proper kitchen but realised, she had no chance of owning one if she could not persuade her husband to even talk about it. After clearing away the breakfast things, Dorothy went downstairs to begin her day's work of typesetting letter headings for clients and posters for the dancehalls.

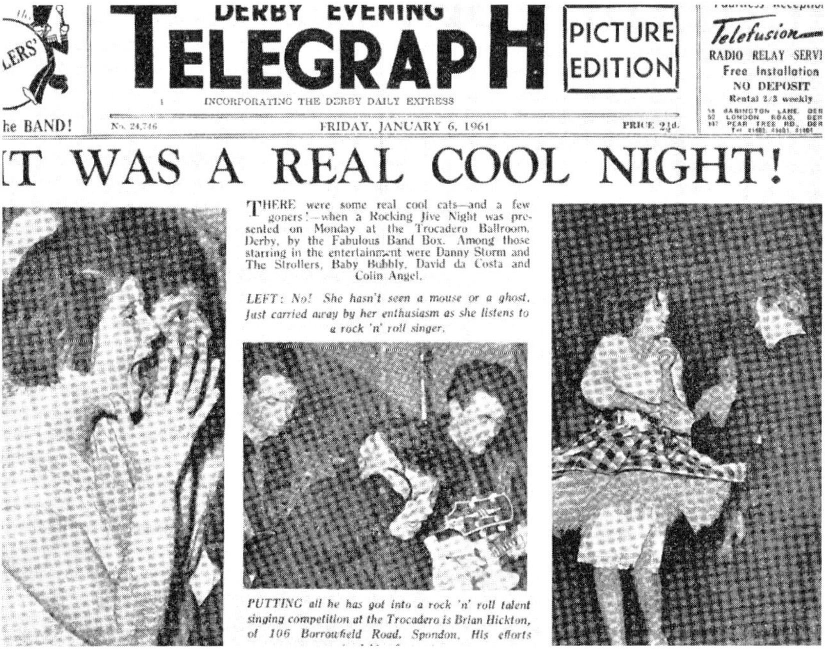
DERBY EVENING TELEGRAPH

PICTURE EDITION

INCORPORATING THE DERBY DAILY EXPRESS

FRIDAY, JANUARY 6, 1961

Telefusion RADIO RELAY SERVI Free Installation NO DEPOSIT

[T WAS A REAL COOL NIGHT!

THERE were some real cool cats—and a few goners!—when a Rocking Jive Night was presented on Monday at the Trocadero Ballroom, Derby, by the Fabulous Band Box. Among those starring in the entertainment were Danny Storm and The Strollers, Baby Bubbly, David da Costa and Colin Angel.

LEFT: No! She hasn't seen a mouse or a ghost. Just carried away by her enthusiasm as she listens to a rock 'n' roll singer.

PUTTING all he has got into a rock 'n' roll talent singing competition at the Trocadero is Brian Hickton, of 106 Borrowfield Road, Spondon. His efforts

Feature about the teenage dances Reg organised. Derby Evening Telegraph
(News cutting from Barney Peacock)

Reg was ambitious. He had chosen to reinvest most of his income on the business rather than pleasing Dorothy by buying her a house. He wanted his own recording studio and planned to expand his network of dances countrywide. His life was intertwined with his boys and he spent time training them and cared about their wellbeing, providing free accommodation, transport and amplification equipment. The boys were placed into groups of seven or eight and formed into fabulous stage shows. His best singers had something special, a charisma and star quality. He dressed them like stars to emulate Elvis, Cliff Richard, Buddy Holly and others and the girls went wild for them. Reg did not believe in tying people down with a contract and they were free to stay, and free to go. Added to the mix, he booked most of the famous stars of the day to appear with them on his shows.

With a busy day ahead, Reg parked his car outside the large, rambling premises he rented in St Mary's, Southampton. It was called the Bandbox and included a cellar nightclub, shop, office, ground floor flat and more accommodation on the first floor.

As Reg entered the building, he could hear the sound of guitars and drums coming from the cellar which doubled as a rehearsal room during the day. Dave Jay was in the shop, showing a customer various guitars and Reg nodded his head in greeting before entering the office. Mr Stennings, his secretary, sat working out the wages and filling small brown envelopes with pound notes and coins. Reg grinned and wished him 'good morning' as he sat down to discuss the day's work. By 3.30 p.m. he was ready to leave. It was Dave Jay's turn to run the dance at Eastleigh Town Hall, Dorothy would run the Bournemouth dance and he would go to Worcester.

Two years ago he had one show, then two, and now three. Each show consisted of seven or eight performers who had to be versatile and keep changing their acts. Soon he would have his fourth show on the road. It was like the chicken and egg. He could not expand his network of dancehalls without musicians but he could not afford to pay another eight wages without the dancehalls for them to perform.

When Reg arrived at Worcester there was a young boy carrying a guitar, waiting to see him. Reg gave an audition to anyone who asked and smiled warmly at the boy who had blond, wavy hair and a complexion recovering from teenage acne. He had a naïve innocence and was not the sort of boy to send girls wild but there was something about him Reg liked.

"Okay. I'll give you a spot at the end of the show to see what you can do."

The boy looked crestfallen.

"What's the matter?" asked Reg.

"No one will see me."

"Ah," smiled Reg. "I'll see you and if you're good, the crowd will stay behind and watch."

As a child, Roger James Scarrott had dreamed of owning a guitar. When he was thirteen his parents bought him an acoustic guitar and when he was fifteen, an electric one. This began his love of the instrument and he practised every spare moment, even sneaking out of bed in the middle of the night to practise some more! His friends had told him about a fantastic dance on Friday nights at the Worcester Corn Exchange, so he decided to go and ask for an audition. The first time he went, he was told by Dave Jay to come back next week when the 'boss' would be there.

All evening, Roger waited nervously as he watched the show. The penultimate number was slow and romantic for teenagers to smooch to and the finale, a fast rock number. As the curtains were drawn, Reg strode onto the stage.

"It's not the end of the show yet. We have one more act to see. Please give a big cheer for a local boy from Evesham. This is his first time at the Worcester Corn Exchange. So, come on, let's hear it. Let's have a big cheer for Roger."

Reg parted the centre of the curtains and waved Roger on. A gaggle of star-struck girls stood by the front of the stage and couples who were not in a rush to catch the last bus home, dallied, curious to see the new singer.

Roger began to sing *Down the Line*, a fast number by Jerry Lee Lewis. He was nervous. This was his first audition and big chance to prove himself. Next, he played Bert Weedon's instrumental *Guitar Boogie Shuffle* to show off his guitar prowess. The crowd whistled and clapped their approval.

"Well done my friend," said Reg, steering him away from the noise of musicians packing equipment away. "Would you like to come and work for me? Tour England, sing, play guitar and be part of a show?"

Surprised, overjoyed and for a moment, speechless, Roger considered the offer. The most he had hoped for was an occasional spot on the show.

"I'll have to ask my parents first."

"Okay. Come back again next week and let me know. If they say yes, we can make arrangements for you to start." Reg paused, observing the worried expression on Roger's face. "What's the matter, don't you think your parents will agree?"

"I've missed the last train. It went at nine thirty and it's a twenty mile walk home. Or I'll have to stay up all night and catch the milk train."

"Ah," smiled Reg. "Don't worry. I'll take you home in my car and talk to your parents."

Mr and Mrs Scarrott were surprised to see Reg, but greeted him warmly and invited him into their front room. Roger stayed in the back room and tried to listen through the walls to their muffled conversation. Eventually, his parents and Reg emerged, smiling genially and shaking hands.

"I'll see you next week," winked Reg.

Roger was very excited and spent most of his time practicing new songs. He caught the train to Southampton and Reg met him from the station and took him to a house he rented for his musicians in Derby Road. Once he had settled in, the other boys walked with him to the Bandbox.

During his first week, Reg explained he was to rehearse with the other musicians, Pete Mist on bass guitar and Tony Burnett on drums. He would support various lead singers and have his own spot as Rod Ace and the Fireballs.

Aged only sixteen, Roger had never had to fend for himself before and he missed his family. He spent his wage as a down payment on a new Gretsch guitar and arranged to pay the rest in weekly instalments.

On Roger's second week, he went with Reg and the other musicians to tour the dancehalls in the West Country. Monday night was at the Small Sidney Hall in Weymouth. Roger played guitar as part of the Strollers, backing Danny Storm, Eddy Sex and David Da Costa. When the interval came, he changed into his new jacket, combed his hair and returned to the wings to wait for his debut as Rod Ace.

Roy Phillips was on stage, singing and playing guitar. Roger had not seen him perform before and as he waited, he became aware that Roy was brilliant. He was a few years older than most of the Bandbox Boys and a true professional. Roger, by comparison, was a mere beginner.

"Go on. Now," instructed Reg urgently, as Roy left the stage. Reg did not like gaps between performers and the Fireballs had started to play the intro.

"I can't," replied Roger, who had become rigid with stage fright.

"Why not?" enquired Reg, impatiently as he observed the look of sheer panic on Roger's face.

"I can't go on after him! I'm not ready. The audience will boo me. I'm not good enough."

"Of course you are lad. Everyone has to start somewhere," insisted Reg, easing him from his frozen position by forcibly taking hold of his arm and leading him to centre stage.

Reg smiled at the audience and introduced Roger.

"Tonight, we have a new singer all the way from Evesham and it's his first time here in Weymouth. Let's welcome the fantastic Rod Ace and the Fireballs."

Reg turned to Roger and nodded for him to start. The show must go on. And it did.

When on tour, Reg and the boys frequented their favourite cheap cafes and Indian restaurants. Roger, very quiet, sat looking out of the café window as the other boys tucked into their meals.

"Are you not well?" enquired Reg, concerned.

"I'm okay."

"Have you stomach ache?"

"No, I feel fine."

"What's the matter, why aren't you eating?"

"I've no money," blurted out Roger, shamefaced.

"Did Mr Stennings pay your wages?"

"Yes, but I've spent it all on a down-payment for a new guitar."

"I see," said Reg, thoughtfully. "You need to learn to save your money to make sure you've enough to last the week. What's leftover, you can spend on extra things."

Taking pity on Roger, Reg took him to the nearest general store and walking up to the counter asked the assistant to give the lad a loaf of bread and a pot of strawberry jam. After paying for the food, Reg turned to Roger.

"This'll keep you going for a few days until you get your next wage packet."

Hearing of Roger's dilemma, the boys organised an initiation ceremony in the dressing room. With only moments to go before they were due on stage, with great hilarity, the boys caught hold of Roger and pulled his trousers down. No matter how Roger struggled, they forcibly removed his underpants and smothered his genitals with strawberry jam. Embarrassed and very sticky, Roger quickly pulled up his trousers and went on stage with jam in his pants!

1961 MUSIC TRENDS

Rock 'n' Roll was on its way out or so many pundits thought as soul, jazz and ballads topped the charts.

American music influenced the world and **Elvis Presley** was 'King' with a series of hits including: *Wooden Heart, Are You Lonesome Tonight? Surrender, His Latest Flame*, and *It's Now or Never*. **Jimmy Dean** with: *Big Bad John*. **Ray Charles:** *Hit the Road Jack*. **Matt Munro** British and **Danny Williams** American with: *Moon River*. **The Everly Brothers:** *Walk Right Back* and *Temptation*. **Jerry Lee Lewis** 'rocked' with *What'd I Say*. **The Shirelles** were the first American female group to have a hit: *Will You Love Me Tomorrow?*

British music was gaining popularity and **Cliff Richard** continued to be the UK's answer to Elvis. His hits included: *Theme for a Dream, A Girl Like You, I Love You*, and *Gee Whiz It's You*. **Marty Wilde** with: *Rubber Ball*. **Adam Faith** was encouraged to 'breakup' his vocals by Roy Young, a superb musician who was now working for Reg. With Adam's new voice, he had a series of hits with: *This Is It, The Time Has Come, Who Am I?* and *Don't You Know It?* **The Brook Brothers** who often worked for Reg, had a hit with: *Warpaint*. **Lonnie Donegan** 'skiffled' with: *Have a Drink on Me*. Comedian, **Charlie Drake:** *My Boomerang Won't Come Back*. A new music producer, Joe Meek, had his first hit with *Johnny Remember Me*, sung by **John Leyton**. It was banned by the BBC which helped its success and John Leyton's second hit was Wild Wind. Reg, when he was in London, sometimes visited Joe Meek's studio. He provided musicians for Joe, including Heinz Burt and Roy Phillips and Joe offered to help Reg set up his recording studio in the Bandbox.

British female vocalists were in the ascendant. **Shirley Bassey, Petula Clark, Cleo Laine and Helen Shapiro.** Helen, then aged 14, had a beehive hairdo and sang with a low voice. She had hits with: *Don't Treat Me like a Child, Walking Back to Happiness* and *You Don't Know*. Jazz was popular and **Johnny Dankworth**, a friend of Reg's since army days, married **Cleo Laine**. He made the charts with *African Waltz* and Cleo with: *You'll Answer to Me*.

The Allison Brothers were runners-up in the Eurovision Song Contest with 'Are You Sure', written by John Allison. It reached number one in the charts, selling millions of copies around the world. Unfortunately, they naively signed 'legal' contracts giving most of their rights away and only received a fraction of their earnings from record royalties and live performances!

THIS SCHOOL TEACHES ROCK' ROLES

Reg Calvert checks Danny Storm's song movements

Nobody escapes the job of loading the van

BOLDLY, in red and black, the posters announce ROCK 'n' JIVE SPECTACULARS and tell of faraway places like West Bromwich, and catchy names like Danny Storm, Ricky Fever and Rod Ace. A lot of these posters are on the walls . . . for this is the house that builds rock.

The house, of medium size, stands in a Southampton street that once knew better days. Step inside and the first impression is a sort of Liberty Hall, a no-rules playground for teenagers with long hair and jazzy clothes. An experimental free-expression school for character development, perhaps?

In fact, it is a school . . . a residential school for professional rock 'n' roll singers, and lessons here are known as rehearsals.

The curriculum is quite extensive. It covers voice training, posture, microphone technique and the art of loading a van full of clothes and musical instruments.

There is no school badge, but the symbols of rock—the guitar, the amplifier and the hand-held mike—are everywhere to be seen.

Monday will be the school's first "open day." Its work will be shown on *Southern Affairs*, devoting an entire programme to the business of rock 'n' roll. Included will be interviews with impresario Larry Parnes and top singers like Marty Wilde.

John Boorman, *Southern Affairs* director, sets the scene: "Rock has been on the wane for some time now, and we were surprised to discover, on our own doorstep in Southampton, this school for rock singers from which the proprietor puts on shows at dance-halls all over the country.

"Rock seems to have found its own level as a more or less permanent form of teenage entertainment. It may have fallen from the heights it once held, but the teenagers still want it."

Some of these teenagers who obviously still do want it were filmed by *Southern Affairs* at Eastleigh Town Hall, one of 23 halls throughout the country, as far north as Derby, where the school regularly presents rock nights, a hybrid form of entertainment which combines a dance with a stage show.

The school team of 18 rock artists, including one girl, are divided up to do shows in different parts of the country. "The smallest efficient 'packet' show we can put on the road is six," I was told by school "head,"

Buddy Britten gives advice on clothes to "recruit" Glen Dale

TV TIMES editorial 22nd January, 1961

"Boldly, in red and black, the posters announce ROCK 'n' JIVE SPECTACULARS and tell of faraway places like West Bromwich, and catchy names like Danny Storm, Ricky Fever and Rod Ace. A lot of these posters are on the walls ... for this is the house that builds rock."

On stage at Eastleigh Town Hall for Monday's *Southern Affairs*

Buddy Britten—the glasses are inspired by the late Buddy Holly

Marty Wilde

Reg Calvert. "This gives four different acts for an evening's show, and the audience can either watch or dance."

The artists are learning while they work; more formal training is given back at base. "Rock is stronger now because the business has become more organised," I was told. "At the same time, the style of singing has become more professional, so better singers are needed. We look for people who can not only act the part but have a voice as well.

"To start with, they are sent to a singing teacher in Southampton to learn breath control, musical scales, tonic sol-fa and voice projection. Then they are taught the ritual of movement that goes with rock singing, and about key changes, microphone technique and so on."

To the teenager, jiving or screaming in a dance-hall, the life of a rock artist must look wonderful . . . freedom to wear outlandish clothes, grow long hair and get paid for it, stay up late and live in constant, feverish noise.

There is not always much time for sleep, and meals are, at best, irregular. But the money pulls like a magnet. When they start at the school, pay is about £8 a week all found, and this increases as they progress.

A recent recruit who now spends about £5 a week on his clothes is Glen Dale, known to his family in Ashford, Kent, as Richard Garforth.

As a name, Richard Garforth sounded fine to me but only, I was told, for more mature audiences. Choice of a new name, therefore, was regarded as a top priority, and for thinking this one up Buddy Britten, one of the "seniors," was given the £1 prize by the boss.

"It helps to make us think," Buddy explained, modestly. The newly-named Glen Dale likes everything about the life . . . "the freedom, the clothes, the travelling, the autograph signing, the noise—and the money."

Ambition? "To make records and become somebody." He is 18, has not thought much beyond the next three years, but is determined to "get somewhere."

Naturally enough, this is true of them all. Danny Storm likes casual clothes, motorbikes and gramophone records.

His ambition? "To become a good singer, make a hit record and establish myself."

Buddy Britten sent to America for the heavy horn-rimmed glasses he wears—inspired by the late Buddy Holly. When the glasses arrived, Britten changed his Christian name to match them!

"Clothes are very important," said Buddy, "and they must be striking. I like suits either very light or very dark. And I like heavily buckled period-style shoes."

Odd-girl-out in this male society is 19-year-old Carol Laine, one of the few professional girl rock singers. Being the only girl is "all right really . . . the boys all treat me very well — in fact, they spoil me."

Her ambition is to "make records and do some TV," but meanwhile she helps the boys load up the vans—a duty from which nobody in this organisation escapes.

Finally, I spoke to Marty Wilde. Born Reginald Smith 21 years ago, he travelled fast from coffee bar guitarist to national stardom, and took in a Royal Variety Performance on the way.

"When I started," said Marty, "all the artists were copying Elvis Presley. Now the trend has changed, and people are developing their own styles. I think my own range in music has widened, and now I want to try all sides of show business, although I do not mind being stuck with rock, because I think it has a great future.

"I have grown up, and my tastes have become more mature. There is a danger of getting out of touch with teenagers, but this can be avoided by constantly listening to records to study the new approaches and devices.

"Yes, I would say it is tough at the top —but it is a terribly exciting life," said Marty.

Stewart Knowles

Rock singer Carol Laine tries a new hair style

7

TV TIMES editorial 22nd January, 1961

"The School Team of 18 rock artists, including one girl, are divided up to do shows in different parts of the country. This gives four different acts for an evening's show and the audience can either watch or dance. The artists are learning while they work."

2. A NEW START

Christmas Show: Tony Burnett, drums. Pete Mist and Colin Angel with guitars.
Front: Baby Bubbly, Glen Dale, Danny Storm and Dave Da Costa

Travelling from gig to gig in unheated vans was the downside of a musician's life and as winter arrived with icy roads, fogs and swirling sea mists, the boys rarely complained as they wrapped themselves in blankets and squeezed into the rear of the van, back between guitars, drum kit, loudspeakers and amplifiers. They took it in turns to sit in the relative luxury of the front bench seat, except when Reg or Carol Laine were with them as they always took priority.

A few days before Christmas, Dorothy packed her A 35 van for the long journey back to Huddersfield, with pillows and blankets for her daughters to keep warm, plus numerous small gifts for her relatives. When it was time to leave, Reg came to see his family off.

"I've left you some mince pies in a tin on the counter top. Your Christmas present is my side of the bed but don't open it until Christmas day."

"Thanks Doe Doe," smiled Reg, as he kissed his family goodbye.

"And don't forget to feed Katy."

"Okay. Have a good time and don't worry about me working my fingers to the bone."

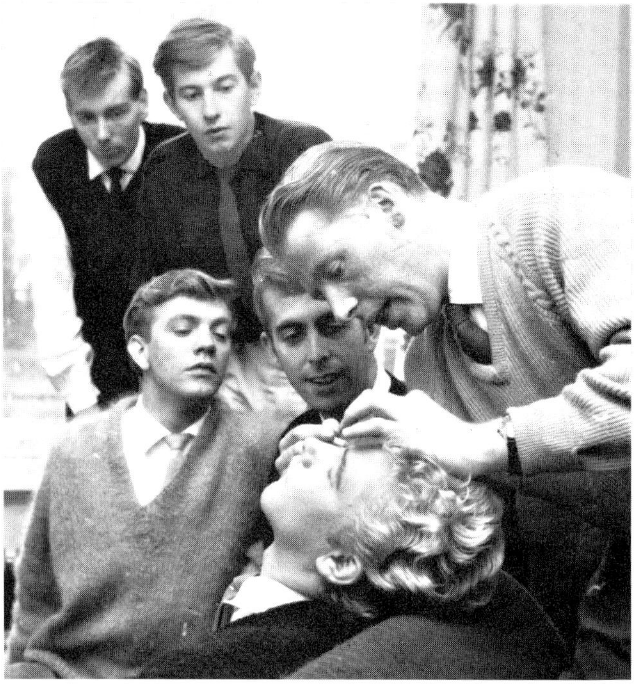

Left: Posed for the press. Reg Calvert demonstrating how to put on stage make-up with new recruit, Roger James. Watching: Tony Burnett, Pete Mist, Glen Dale, Roy Young. (BIPS press

Below: Picnic in the New Forest. Reg Calvert, Baby Bubbly, Carol Laine, Danny Storm, Eddy Sex, Dave Da Costa. On roof: Dave Jay

The festive season was the busiest for Reg with much to organise. He got a buzz out of making sure that his party-nights were the best. Each dance hall would be crammed to capacity; his musicians were well rehearsed and when Reg joined them on stage, his charisma and laughter spread through the crowd like a contagion. With ease, Reg encouraged everyone to join in with crazy party games and as a finale, he returned to the stage to do a crazy dance and sing, *Knees up Mother Brown* and the *Hokey Cokey*.

Reg and Dorothy had never spent a Christmas together in their own home. The Christmas and New Year dances were the most profitable and the extra income had to tide the business over during the quiet months of January and February. Most years, Reg did not mind Dorothy leaving, but this year was different.

Lazing in bed until late on Christmas day, Reg eventually rose and went down to the kitchen to make himself porridge and eat mince pies. He had two days to relax as there were no dances to run on Christmas or Boxing day. With only the cat for company, Reg was lonely but he needed this quiet time to reflect and consider. He had been leading a double life and knew he could no longer hide his deceptions. He needed to make a decision and knew he had to reveal all to Dorothy and face the consequences.

When Dorothy returned home, Reg was busy with little time to spend with his family. The first two weeks in January were hectic with rehearsals every day in preparation of the film. On the Thursday after filming, Reg arose early and hurried out of the house, lighting a cigarette as he walked briskly to the newsagents. On the counter lay a large stack of TV Times. Picking up a copy, he flicked through until he reached pages six and seven. A broad grin spread across his face as he read the headline, *This School Teaches 'Rock' Roles*.

Returning to Portland Terrace, Reg skipped up the stairs, two at a time and burst into the dining room.

"How many slices do you want?" asked Dorothy.

"Three will do," replied Reg, as he switched on the electric fire and spread open the paper on the dining table. "It's good, don't you think?"

"Good, good, good," replied Dorothy, laughing.

"We've made it Doe Doe. This is just the start."

Impulsively, Reg flung his arms around his wife and lifted her off her feet.

"Put me down," squealed Dorothy. "Toast is burning."

Simultaneously, they both sniffed the aroma of charred bread. Running into the kitchen, Dorothy saw flames flickering from under the grill.

"What a mess. We could have burnt the house down," exclaimed Dorothy.

"No good crying about burnt toast," laughed Reg.

A few days after the filming, Reg became moody and irritable again. Dorothy, matching his moodiness, ignored him as she held her tongue about buying a new house.

Friday nights, Dorothy ran the dance at the Holdenhurst Hall near Bournemouth and took her daughters with her, Susan aged 12, and Candy aged 10. It was the highlight of the girl's week, to be allowed to stay up late and go to a dance. By 11 p.m., the dance was over and the hall deserted, except for a few teenage girls who lingered in the hope of meeting the musicians after the show. The drive back through the New Forest was fraught with danger and Dorothy drove very slowly. The narrow country roads were only illuminated on clear nights by the moon and a million stars. At any point, there could be a deer or pony straddled across the way, or, even worse, black ice. There were no telephones and if she had an accident, they would be stranded with no one to help.

Reg waited anxiously for his family to return, not because he worried about the roads but because he knew he had to confront his wife about his duplicity. Hearing the front door open and footsteps on the wooden stairs, he lit another cigarette.

Holdenhurst Hall, near Bournemouth. Hall manager, Johnny Kidd, Dorothy, Susan and Candy Calvert

"Hi girls. Did you have a good night?" asked Reg, smiling as his family trooped into the dining room.

"I can nearly jive now," said Susan. She's hopeless," chipped in Candy. Her feet are all over the place."

"And I suppose you think you're good at jiving?"

"Better than you," boasted Candy.

"How do you jive Dad? Show me," asked Susan.

"Not tonight. It's too late. Some other time."

"Bed you two," instructed Dorothy.

The girls kissed their parents on the cheek and Susan picked up Katy, to take to bed with her.

"Peace," said Dorothy.

"Have they been arguing all night?"

"No, they've been good."

"Would you like a cigarette?"

"Not now. Looks like a fog in here," commented Dorothy, as she noticed all the cigarette butts in the ashtray. "Do you want a cup of tea and some toast?"

"Coffee please," replied Reg, as he began to nervously stir the sugar in the sugar bowl round and round while he waited.

Through the thin partitioned wall, he could hear Dorothy moving about, filling the kettle, placing it on the gas stove, striking a match and then the sound of a puff and a pop as the gas ignited.

A few minutes later, Dorothy returned with their drinks and buttered toast. He lit another cigarette while he watched her eat and they chatted pleasantly about the evening, the boys and the dances. January was never a good time and keeping numbers up during bad weather was difficult. Reg hesitated before deciding how to tell Dorothy his news. He had played the same scene over and over in his mind and now he had to act it out.

"I've something to tell you."

"Can you tell me in bed?"

"No. We have to talk. It's important."

"You could pick a better time, it's nearly one in the morning."

"It's quiet now, with no interruptions. I need to talk about Carol."

"Her?" queried Dorothy, dismissively.

"I've been trying to get rid of her."

"About time. Carol's okay but I never thought she was a good singer. You should have got rid of her years ago."

"We've been having." Reg paused before he could bring himself to say the words, "An affair."

"An affair?" repeated Dorothy, visibly shocked. "An affair with Carol?"

For a moment, they said nothing more. An icy chasm opened between them as Dorothy grasped the meaning of his words. Reg knew he was on the edge of a precipice and stared blankly into a frozen world where time stood still.

"It didn't mean anything. It just happened."

Dorothy studied her husband's familiar face, her eyes burning with anger and tears.

"Nothing just happens," replied Dorothy, sharply.

"She kept pursuing me. I was flattered at first. I know I'm not a good-looking bloke so I thought she would soon go off me and go with one of the boys. But she didn't. She only wanted me."

Dorothy heard his words like bullets piercing her heart and soul, her head throbbed and she felt as though she was falling, falling, falling. Her world had suddenly and violently erupted. Outwardly, she held herself stiff and proud. Reg was her husband and she had trusted him. Trusted him to be true. Slowly, she began to see how stupid she had been. The nights away. The tours. How she felt sorry for him spending Christmas alone. All the time, he had been with Carol.

"I'm sorry," said Reg, almost inaudibly, as he tried to hold Dorothy's hand in his.

"You can't blame her," snapped Dorothy, jerking her hand away. "You're just like your Dad."

It was the worst insult she could throw at him and it was as if she had slapped him across the face. He smarted and turned to look her in the eye, his face suddenly turning grey with anger.

"I'm not like my Dad. Never, ever, say that to me again."

For several moments, they both sat in silence while they each considered their next move.

"You've always had an eye for the girls. Remember when you played piano in the club with the singer with dyed blond hair?"

"No, I don't remember," denied Reg.

"I should have guessed. All my things that went missing. Did she have a key to the house?"

Reg lowered his head.

"You had her here, when I was away?" accused Dorothy, angrily.

"I told her to find someone younger and single but she said she'd tell you if I made her go. I tried again and again."

"That's no excuse."

"She wanted to be Mrs Calvert."

Everything was making sense as Dorothy recollected various incidents. More memories came flooding back but the words, she wanted to be Mrs Calvert, spun round and round in her mind.

"Why didn't you stay with her if she loves you so much?"

Reg paused. It was a question he was not prepared to answer.

"Carol told me she couldn't have children and then, she became pregnant. She thought I would leave you if she had my baby."

"Didn't you tell her you don't like babies? So, when is this baby due?"

"It's not."

"You mean you got her to sit in a hot bath and drink gin?"

"She tried but it didn't work," replied Reg, guiltily.

"So, what are you going to do now?"

"On the Friday I collected Billy Fury in London for the dancehall tour, I took her to a clinic."

Unable to control her anger any longer, Dorothy raised her voice and shouted.

"You mean you took her to an abortionist? She could have died and then where would you be? You've had your fun and now you're fed up with her. So why now? Why tell me now?"

"I'm being blackmailed."

"You mean other people know?"

"Lots of people want money to keep quiet and I can't keep hiding it any longer. I don't know what to do."

Reg paused, his face white with guilt and shame and Dorothy sat silent as she recalled various events during the preceding years. Her eyes narrowed and when she spoke, it was as a whisper, holding back her anger.

"The money you said was stolen from the Eastleigh Rock Festival. You promised me it would be for our new home. And Mr Cole, the money he embezzled. That's why you wouldn't go to the police?"

Slowly, Dorothy pieced together all the strange events like a jigsaw.

"My missing underwear. The children's savings books and other odd things. The brake wire on my van being cut. Did she do that?"

"She wouldn't have done it."

"But she could have got someone else to do it?"

"I don't know. I just know it had to stop. I had to tell you before someone else did."

"How long?" demanded Dorothy.

"I don't know."

"What do you mean, you don't know? Of course, you know."

"Three or four years."

"You mean all the time we've been living here, in this grotty house, you've been having an affair?"

"I couldn't help it."

"Of course you could help it," shouted Dorothy, letting out her anger. "I have men wanting to take me out and I ignore them. I make them call me Mrs C so they respect I'm married to you."

"But I'm just a man," replied Reg, meekly.

"And what does that mean, I'm just a man, what sort of reason is that? I'm just a woman, so what is it about being a man that makes you think you can have affairs and get away with them?"

"I'm sorry, so sorry," said Reg, hanging his head down and staring at the grains of sugar on the tablecloth. "It's over Doe Doe. I know I don't deserve it. But can we start again?"

Pulling a lace handkerchief from her cardigan sleeve, Dorothy blew her nose as her eyes filled with tears. Emotion swelled inside her chest and she trembled as she tried to quench the sickening feeling of disgust and betrayal.

"Sorry, what's the use of sorry? All these years I've trusted you. I can't believe you've done this to me. To us."

"I don't want her. I never wanted her. I've always loved you."

The awful truth was that he loved both women, in different ways. Carol, young and pretty, adored him and never criticised or shouted. Dorothy, his wife and soulmate was his equal and the bond that held them together, was strong, stronger even than love.

"How can you say you've always loved me? I don't believe you. I don't believe anything you say. You'll have to go. Go now," commanded Dorothy.

"I don't want to go."

"You should have thought about that before."

"What will you do?" asked Reg, looking at her intently.

"I'll find somewhere decent to live with the girls and make a new life. On my own."

Admitting defeat, Reg stood up.

"Will you tell the girls?"

"Candy's too young to understand. Susan will have to know. She'll guess anyway."

"What will you say?"

"I don't know." Dorothy paused while she considered her reply and then, looking Reg in the eye, said with finality, "The truth."

Reg packed his belongings into a brown leather suitcase and walked out. He drove to the Bandbox and found himself an empty bed in the flat above the nightclub and wrapped himself up in brown ex-army blankets to keep warm. The next day, he found a room in a cheap boarding house.

The cold bleak days of winter turned into weeks of loneliness. Both Reg and Dorothy sleepwalked through the pain of separation. They carried on working, not disclosing to family or employees they were now living apart. Dorothy tried to be positive and remained in Portland Terrace while she made plans for a new life. She had saved sufficient money for a deposit on a house from her print business and optimistically, made an appointment to see her bank manager.

The children were used to their father being away on trips but when he did not return after several weeks, Susan began to ask questions.

"Where's Daddy?"

"I've told you before, he's away," replied Dorothy.

"Where's he gone?"

"He's running dances like he always does.

"Is he coming back?"

"How should I know?" snapped Dorothy, as she cut pieces of potato into cubes and placed them into a large aluminium cooking pan.

"What are you making?" asked Susan, as her cat, Katy, jumped onto her lap purring loudly, easing herself up to wrap her sleek body around the child's shoulders like a stole.

"I thought we'd have stew."

"Can I make the dumplings?"

"If you like," answered Dorothy, as she started to peel carrots.

"Why are you crying?"

"It's the onions."

"But you haven't peeled any onions," observed Susan.

Dorothy sighed deeply. It was time to reveal the truth. She had been waiting for the right moment but realised now, there was never going to be a right moment. Susan was bonded closer to her father than Candy and she knew her words would hurt. Watching her daughter's face, she began to explain.

"Your Dad and I are splitting up. Daddy won't be living with us anymore and I've been looking to buy a house."

"Why?" asked Susan, puzzled, as she stroked her cat.

"I've found a nice house," explained Dorothy, biting her lip and trying not to cry. "It's big enough to turn into a guesthouse and I thought I could earn enough money to keep us by having lodgers to stay."

"With Daddy?"

"No. Just the three of us, you me and Candy."

"Where will Daddy live?"

Dorothy paused as she ignored her daughter's question.

"Yesterday I had an appointment with the bank manager to arrange a mortgage."

"What's a mortgage?"

"When you borrow money from a bank or building society to buy a house."

"And then you have to pay it back?"

"Yes, you do. But I can't. I can't borrow the money," blurted out Dorothy as her body began to heave with frustration, anger and emotion. "The bank manager said I cannot buy my own house because I am a woman. I have to have my husband or father act as guarantor."

"But your Daddy died?"

"Yes, and your Dad, my husband … won't act as guarantor. He's refused to sign the papers," replied Dorothy, bursting into tears. For several minutes, she sobbed, and Susan sat silently, stroking her cat. "I'm sorry Susie. I didn't mean to cry. I don't know what to do or where to go. It's really hard. I don't want to live in this awful house anymore. I want to make a better life for us."

"Not Daddy?"

"No, not Daddy. He's not coming."

"Why?"

"I need to make a new start. Just the three of us."

"But Daddy will want to come too, won't he? Where is Daddy?"

"He's gone away."

"Why?"

"Because I told him to."

"Is he coming back?"

"You've asked me that already. The answer is no. No, he's not coming back," replied Dorothy, quietly and firmly.

"Why? Why isn't Daddy coming back?"

Dorothy paused before blurting out the truth.

"Your Daddy's been unfaithful. He's been having an affair with Carol."

"Carol? But she's nice."

"Nice! To have an affair with your Dad and pretend to be friendly with you and Candy so she could take my place? That's not nice."

"But Daddy didn't want to marry her, did he?"

"No," replied Dorothy, as she started to cry again. "He said he didn't but I don't believe him. I don't know what I believe anymore."

Dorothy's tear-stained face had grey rivers of washed away make-up and with her handkerchief, she wiped her eyes and then her cheeks. Picking up a carrot, she began to peel and chop it, making a heap of orange chunks. Putting the knife down, she looked again at her daughter.

"When you get married Susie, you don't go with anyone else. You stay true to your partner. But your Dad, ... he didn't stay true to me."

"I don't want to go away without Daddy," responded Susan, sadly. "I want a Mummy and a Daddy."

"You can't always have what you want. Life isn't like that."

Gently, Dorothy tried to explain but her words tumbled out like wooden building blocks, crashing to the ground. Susan, with tears in her eyes, stood up and went into the lounge. Opening the piano lid, she began to play Beethoven's Moonlight Sonata and became completely absorbed in the music, her anxiety expressed in a torrent of angry notes, building to a crescendo, louder and louder, then falling, going down and down into a muted rippling.

Trapped by the unfairness of being a woman in an unequal world, Dorothy determined to be independent and buy her own house. It would take a few years of saving money from working in the printworks, but she would succeed.

After several more weeks, Reg tentatively began to call in to see Dorothy under some pretext or another, about the business or the boys. He bided his time and watched for any glimmer or sign that his wife might be warming towards him. There was none. Dorothy remained resolutely cold and distant. She was angry. Angry he had been unfaithful and angry he had not signed the mortgage to let her go.

"Guess what Doe Doe?" Reg asked, cheerfully.

Disinterested, Dorothy made no reply and stood with her back toward him while she continued working, taking letter by letter and setting them into a block in preparation for printing.

"I've just had a telephone call from Germany."

"So?"

"From a nightclub owner, Peter Eckhorn. He's opened a nightclub called the Top Ten Club in Hamburg and wants to book my boys.

"How did he hear about you?"

"He saw the article in the TV Times."

"Why doesn't he employ German bands?" asked Dorothy, coldly.

"The Germans like our British Rock 'n' Roll and the boys are keen to go. They're excited about having an opportunity to work abroad."

Reg paused, taking his time, he lit two cigarettes and handed one to his wife.

"I need to talk."

"I thought you were talking," retorted Dorothy, as she continued to work. Intuitively, she knew he had come to talk and try to win her back but Dorothy, stubborn and feisty, did not want to return to a marriage of inequality. She did not want to be a second-class citizen, forced by circumstances to do her husband's bidding and get nothing in return.

"I want to talk about us."

"There's nothing to say. I don't want you back. Let me get on with my work," replied Dorothy, sharply.

"We can't go on like this, ignoring each other, not speaking."

"It's over Reg. I'll find a way to manage, on my own, without you."

"I know you'd manage, but I won't. I can't live without you," said Reg, touching her shoulder as he tried to turn her round to face him.

Dorothy shrugged him off and continued to typeset.

"You should have thought about it before … before Carol," replied Dorothy bitterly, biting her bottom lip and swallowing the lump in her throat. Dorothy's instincts were sharp and realised she had bargaining strength. If only, if only, she could resist him long enough.

"Can we start again, make a new life?"

"No!"

"Everything's going so well. The dances and the boys."

Dorothy turned to look at her husband, her face contorted with anger and anguish.

"Four years I've been living in this grotty house with nothing but promises and as for money, yes you earn it but I never see it."

Reg stood silent for a moment, unsure. It was like playing a game of chess and he needed to consider his next move. He lit two more cigarettes and passed one to Dorothy.

"I know I've hurt you," he continued. "I know I've been stupid. I've had a lot of time to think. Weeks, living on my own. There's no one else for me. We can make a new start."

"It's too late," muttered Dorothy. "How can we start again when I could never trust you?"

"We could do it differently. You could manage the money and we could buy a house."

Reg had made his ultimate offer. Dorothy looked away so he would not see the flicker of pleasure on her face, but he knew, and reached out to take her hand.

"I love you Doe Doe. I've always loved you. Please, please give me one more chance. I'll make it better this time."

Dorothy pulled her hand away and said nothing as she held back her emotions. She had to play hard and make him wait. Tears stung her eyes and her heart was pounding in her chest. Should she stand firm and live her life without him? She loved Reg, admired his cleverness that sometimes bordered into genius, but, deep down she knew, he would never change. His promises were as nothing if he had a new idea or dream. All the time, at the back of her mind was the plaintive echo of her daughter's words. 'I want a Mummy and a Daddy'.

Reg and Dorothy understood each other like opposite sides of a coin, heads or tails, they were as one. Looking sideways out of the window, Dorothy stared vacantly into the brightness of the morning light and the emptiness of a life without Reg. Taking a long, deep inhalation of the cigarette, she slowly breathed out the hazy smoke.

"No Reg," replied Dorothy, firmly, shaking her head. "It won't work. We're better apart."

Dismayed, Reg felt hollow inside. He had played his trump card and was about to lose everything he held dear. He needed Dorothy to be there. Heads or tails? He could call Carol and she would come running. She had loved him and he felt pangs of remorse about the way he had hurt and rejected her. Now Dorothy was rejecting him. Taking a step closer, he gently gripped his wife's arms, pulling her close.

No Reg," insisted Dorothy, pushing him away.

Ignoring her words, Reg kissed her forehead, then her cheeks which were wet with tears, and then her lips.

"I love you and I promise I'll try to be better."

Reg moved back into Portland Terrace and for several weeks, he was the perfect husband, attentive and caring. He went with Dorothy to see various houses but his enthusiasm began to dwindle. After viewing one house Dorothy particularly liked, she grew angry when Reg refused to buy it.

It's not quite right.".

"It seemed all right to me," replied Dorothy, crossly. "It has everything I want. A good size kitchen, lounge, dining room, three bedrooms and an upstairs bathroom. It even has a garage and I like the walled garden."

"We'll find something better."

"I want this house. It's the best we've seen."

Reg shook his head as he got into the car.

"Promises," snapped Dorothy. "You make promises and then you don't keep them. I should have known you'd go back on your word. You're like a little boy, you'll never grow up. You don't like responsibility. You think having a mortgage will tie you down like a chain round your neck, instead of thinking of it as an investment for our future. When will you stop playing around and realise you're an adult. You're 32 and having a mortgage means we can buy a house instead of paying rent for a dump."

"I'm not 32 yet," grinned Reg.

"Nearly, and old enough to settle down," replied Dorothy, wearily.

"I will keep my promise. I said I'd buy you a house and I will. I was thinking we should move from Southampton and make a new start."

"We could move to Bournemouth."

"I was thinking about going further north."

"I like it in the South. We came down from the north and I don't want to go back."

"I've asked Dave Jay to look for properties in the Midlands when he's on tour up there. Somewhere more central to run dances from and I can expand the business in different directions. It makes sense to work from the centre."

Dorothy bit her lip and said nothing in reply. Reg, knowing he had made his wife angry, drove back to Portland Terrace in silence as Dorothy turned her face away from him and stared out of the car window. Never would she trust him again. She would bide her time and secretly save to buy her own house. When Dorothy was ready, she would have her independence.

October, 1960 Reg and Dorothy Calvert with some of the musicians and singers Reg employed. Front: Dowland Bros, Eddy Sex, Jeff Chalk, Danny Storm, Dorothy Calvert, Reg Calvert, Rory Blackwell, Dave Da Costa, Colin Wilsher, Carol Laine. Behind: Nevitt Bros.(?) Pete Mist, Buddy Britten Lucky Nelson, Tony Burnett

After the dances, Reg mixed a bucket of wallpaper paste and surreptitiously found places to stick his posters (Poster from Freddy Were aka Tony Rocco).

3. NEVER SAY NEVER

Clifton Hall, Clifton-upon-Dunsmore, near Rugby

When Reg handed his wife a large brown envelope, he watched her expression change as she slowly pulled the contents out and began to read.

"It's not far from Rugby," Reg explained. "And no one wants these old farmhouses nowadays, so it's not expensive. We can have a big house for not much more than a small one."

"We don't need six bedrooms, three would do."

"Let's have a day out with the girls and go and view," encouraged Reg.

Dorothy agreed and on Sunday, packed up a picnic and they drove towards Rugby and found the deserted farmhouse set back from the busy A5 road, hidden by a spinney of trees. Reg dangled a set of keys and after trying several, eventually opened the heavy oak door. Taking Dorothy's hand, they stepped inside the dark interior with their daughters following. The electrics were turned off and the entrance hall was gloomy.

"The kitchen's humongous," exclaimed Reg. "And it's got one of those cooker things."

"It's called an Aga but I prefer a gas or electric cooker. You don't have to keep feeding them with coke all day," replied Dorothy.

"This must be the lounge," said Reg, as he opened another door. "Very spacious. What do you think Doe Doe?"

"I like the oak floorboards and inglenook fireplace," commented Dorothy, trying to be positive. "It's a proper farmhouse, big, rambling and cold. But it's not where I want to live. I don't like it."

"Why not?" asked Reg, irritated by her refusal. It had to be better than living in a small house.

"Perhaps because I'm not a farmer's wife."

"There's lots of stabling and barns that would be useful to store speakers and amplifiers in."

"I don't like it. I don't want to live here," insisted Dorothy.

"Okay, I'll ask the estate agent if they've anything else."

Disappointed, Reg reluctantly accepted his wife's decision as he took one last look at the barns.

A few days later, Reg and Dorothy returned to Rugby and collected keys from an estate agent to view a 'Victorian Gentleman's Residence', just outside the village of Clifton-upon-Dunsmore.

Following directions, they found a long, narrow driveway off a country lane, and as they turned the corner at the top of the drive, they saw a substantial red brick house. There were no near neighbours and the house was standing in two-and-a-half-acres of gardens and woodland, almost as if it were on an island, surrounded by green fields instead of water. Set to one side and partly hidden by trees, were dilapidated stables and barns, featuring a tall steeple that had once housed a small wind turbine to pump water from the well below.

"Clifton Hall, sounds grand, doesn't it?" enthused Reg, as he pushed open the half-glazed front door for Dorothy to enter. Standing side by side, they surveyed in wonder the spacious hall. It ran the full width of the main house with another set of half-glazed doors at the other end opening out to the terrace and main gardens.

"It's big," said Dorothy, apprehensively. "We can't afford it. It's double the price of the farmhouse."

"Let's explore," grinned Reg, like an excited child, as he pushed open the door to the dining room. Tentatively, they opened each door and peered inside. Alongside the wide mahogany stairway was a quarry tiled passageway to the two kitchens and a scullery, and beneath the stairs, a door to the cellar which housed a large coke central heating boiler.

They continued their exploration and when Reg opened the door to the billiards room, his face broke into a grin.

"This is brilliant. I can buy a Scalextric."

"Not a train set?" laughed Dorothy.

"Boring. I've always wanted a Scalextric."

"You're like Peter Pan. You'll never grow up."

"Perhaps we could try for another Peter Pan?" said Reg, as he took Dorothy in his arms and kissed her passionately.

"Not here," laughed Dorothy, pulling her clothes straight. "And you don't like babies."

"I'm all grow'd up now," teased Reg.

"You could learn to play billiards instead."

"I could," replied Reg, squeezing her tightly.

Dorothy's face broke into a smile as they entered the last door off the main hallway. The drawing room was light and airy with high ceilings, wood parquet floor and full-length sash windows on two sides of the room. Holding hands, they walked to the windows and they stared at the view of the gardens, the spinney of trees and fields beyond. Saying not a word, Reg kissed his wife.

Upstairs they wandered from bedroom to bedroom. There were three in what would have been the servant's wing and five in the main house. As they entered the master bedroom they stopped again to gaze at the view. Green fields with grazing sheep and cattle as far as they could see, only interrupted in the distance by Rugby Radio Station with its tall radio masts reaching skywards.

"This house is perfect. I could run a radio station from here."

"You and your mad ideas."

"Sooner or later we'll have commercial radio stations and I want to be here, ready for them. We're always a few years behind the Americans and they have lots of local stations. This is the house, Doe Doe."

"It's way above our budget. There's no way we can afford it."

"It's been on the market a long time so they might be open to offers. The owners live in the new bungalow at the bottom of the drive. We could drop in on our way back and see if we can negotiate."

"I only wanted three bedrooms and one bathroom. What will we do with eight bedrooms and three bathrooms? We'll rattle around."

"We'll shake, rattle and roll, let's shake, rattle and roll…" sang Reg.

"And the gardens are enormous. How will we manage?"

"You worry too much. We'll get a gardener of course, and a home help. I've been thinking."

"Oh no," laughed Dorothy. "That means trouble."

"I've been thinking. The dining room would make a great rehearsal room."

"A rehearsal room?" repeated Dorothy, astonished.

"The boys can stay in the bedrooms in the wing, use the second kitchen and billiards room. We can have the main house."

Dorothy, was silent and thoughtful for a moment.

"There would have to be rules."

"What sort of rules?" asked Reg, puzzled.

"Rules of the house. No swearing in front of Susan and Candy. No alcohol and definitely no girlfriends here."

"Those sort of rules," laughed Reg. "I agree and if they don't like them, they can find their own accommodation."

"You and your big ideas. I don't know why we're even talking about it? This house is too expensive and we'll never be able to afford it."

"Never say never," grinned Reg. It was a phrase he often quoted when he was determined to achieve something against all the odds.

Single-mindedly, Reg set out on a plan to own Clifton Hall. First, he went to see the owners, Mr and Mrs White, and successfully negotiated a lower price. His next hurdle was to persuade his bank manager to grant him the large mortgage required. Nothing could be decided upon immediately, so they had to wait. In the meantime, Reg curbed his spending and Dorothy took over the management of the business banking. She stopped shouting at her children and instead, sang, laughed and smiled. Together, Reg and Dorothy worked as a team, and together they dreamed.

Telephone calls backwards and forwards to Germany secured a month's contract at the Top Ten Club in Hamburg. Reg decided to send Glen and Roger as lead singers with Pete Mist on bass and Tony Burnett on drums.

"Don't you think Roger's too young and inexperienced? He's only sixteen and seems very shy," said Dorothy.

"Green you mean," laughed Reg. "He'll soon mature when he's fending for himself. I've bought the boys new outfits. White shirts, black bow ties, red quilted jackets, white trousers and white shoes. For Glen, I've bought an evening dress suit so he looks super smooth when he sings. I've been thinking," said Reg, with a wide grin. "Can you imagine Roger as Robin Hood?"

"No, I can't," smiled Dorothy. "Has he got good legs?"

"How should I know?" laughed Reg. "One thing worries me. The club stays open until two in the morning during the week and four at the weekends. They expect our boys to play all night with only a ten minute break every hour."

"That's ridiculous," said Dorothy, astonished. "They should employ a minimum of two or three groups a night."

"The boys are up for it. They'll earn double the money. I'll phone Peter Eckhorn and tell him he'll have three acts. Rod Ace and the Fireballs, Robbie Hood and his Merry Men and Glen Dale and the Cliftones," said Reg, slowly, waiting to see if his words would cause a reaction.

"Cliftones?" queried Dorothy.

"Yep. Ready for when we move to Clifton Hall."

"You mean we've got it, we've actually got it? You horror," squealed Dorothy. "You kept it a secret."

"Only heard this morning for sure," replied Reg. "The bank agreed the mortgage and it's all signed and sealed. We should be in by the middle of May."

It was a warm spring day when the Calvert family arrived at Clifton Hall and a chorus of birds sang loudly from the trees in the spinney, as if to welcome the new inhabitants into their world.

Quietly, holding hands like young lovers, Reg and Dorothy went from room to room with their daughters running ahead and laughing, none of them quite believing, this was to be their new home. As they stepped outside to the gardens, Dorothy smiled, contentedly.

"I don't think I'll ever get tired of living here."

On the terrace, tumbling down the raised walls were masses of tiny purple aubrietia flowers intermingled with pink sedums and white-rock. In amongst them were faded daffodils and flashes of bright red and golden tulips standing erect with their faces to the sun.

"I wonder how old the oak tree is?" mused Dorothy, as she pointed to a large tree on the opposite side of the garden.

"Hundreds of years," replied Reg. "Maybe it was here before the house was built. I can make a tree swing from the branch over the ditch. It can be my first job."

"Oh no. First job is to make a partition across the back end of the kitchen so the boys don't have to walk through it to go up the back stairs. And it's not just a ditch, it's a ha-ha.".

"You and your posh education. What's a ha-ha?"

"It's a ditch to keep sheep and cattle out of the garden instead of a fence, so as not to interrupt the view."

"Ha ha," laughed Reg. "I think I'll apply for a Broadcasting Licence next week."

"And pigs can fly."

"No. Only birds," grinned Reg.

The family would never return to Portland Terrace and rarely to Southampton. Several days after their arrival, Reg received a telephone call with shocking news that their old house had gone up in flames. Not realising the family had moved, or where they were, neighbours thought Susan and Candy were in the house. Firemen did a frantic search of the blazing building but could not find the children. How the fire had started was a mystery. The fire brigade assumed someone had entered the house and 'accidentally' dropped a burning cigarette into machine oil in the print room. Reg and Dorothy could only guess who the person may be and were pleased to be away, safe in Rugby.

Top: Top Ten Club, Hamburg: Pete Mist, Glen Dale, Roy Young, Tony Burnett, Roger James (Hans Olof Gottifridsson)

Below: Benn Hall, Rugby: Danny Storm and the Strollers. A superb stage show. The Strollers were versatile and comprised of talented musicians and singers who all performed in their own right: Tony Clarke, Roger James and Glen Dale. Drums: Barney Peacock (RC)

4. TOP TEN CLUB – HAMBURG

1961 Top Ten Club, Hamburg: Roy Young, Glen Dale, Tony Burnett, Roger James, Pete Mist The group followed on from the Beatles (Hans Olof Gottifridsson)

The week before moving to Clifton Hall, Reg took the 'Cliftones' to Southampton railway station to see them off. They had not travelled abroad before and were very excited. With their guitars, drum kit, amplifier and loudspeakers safely stowed in the goods wagon, Reg waved them goodbye.

The Second World War had taken its toll on Hamburg, and, similar to Southampton, there were bombed out buildings to be seen everywhere. The city was being rebuilt and rising above the ruins, but it was a wild and violent place. Different ships docked in the port each day and transient sailors, of all nationalities, came into the city looking for a good time. Fuelled by alcohol, fights erupted for no more reason than someone disliked your face or wanted your girl.

The journey to Hamburg was long and when the boys arrived, they were tired and hungry. To their dismay, they discovered that not only had Roger's jacket with his wallet and passport been stolen, but their instruments and equipment were also missing. Fortunately, the owner of the nightclub was the sort of young man who took problems in his stride. Arriving at the Top Ten Club, he gave them cigarettes, and ten Deutsch marks each and introduced them to Horst Fascher, his right-hand man.

They had been booked to replace the Beatles and Peter Eckhorn, seeing Paul McCartney in the club, asked if he would mind taking the new boys to a café on the Reeperbahn for a meal. Paul was friendly and happy to help. After eating, he showed the boys to their sleeping quarters above the club. It was a long climb up many stairs and when they reached the top, the doorway was obstructed by the sleeping body of Tony Sheriden who lay straddled across the entrance. They gingerly stepped over him and surveyed the flat that was to be their home for the next month.

The Beatles had packed away their personal belongings but no one had cleaned the flat after them. Glen frowned, shook his head and angrily, returned down the stairs to find Peter Eckhorn.

"There's no way I'm sleeping up there. The flat is dirty and disgusting."

"Okay, okay, I will sort it out for you. I will have it cleaned. If not, I will put you in a hotel tonight," replied Peter, in broken English.

Glen waited in the club for the problem to be resolved while Roger, Pete and Tony, too exhausted to go anywhere, stayed behind in the room. A little while later, the door opened and a lovely old lady, called Mutty, smiled warmly at them. She carried a bucket, mop and cleaning materials and started to clear away the mess from the previous occupants. As she worked she complained and kept repeating under her breath, "Zose filtzy Beatles, zose filtzy Beatles."

The next day, the Cliftones were due to perform but having no equipment, Eckhorn borrowed the Beatles amplifier and loud-speakers and asked one of his friends who owned a music shop if they could borrow guitars and a drum kit. Fortunately, the whereabouts of their own equipment was discovered and retrieved the following day.

The Top Ten Club was situated in the 'red light district' and Teddy boys, sailors and prostitutes, frequented the club. The waiters doubled up as bouncers and were quick to deal with troublemakers. They protected themselves by carrying gas guns and knives. Some nights, without warning, the whole floor seemed to explode with young men hitting each other and falling to the ground, while others watched and cheered. Horst Fascher would call out to the musicians, "Keep playing, keep playing." The boys played on while Horst and the waiters physically threw out the troublemakers.

The boys found working in a night club very different to the dances that Reg organised. Admission was free except on Friday and Saturday nights. Every evening at 9.45 p.m., flashing orange lights accompanied by loud twanging sounds, reminded young teenagers, under 18, there was a curfew and they had to go home. At 10 p.m., the club resumed. By midnight, numbers in the club thinned out but the band had to play on, and on.

Their excitement at working abroad in a strange country soon diminished. During the day, club life was quite boring as there was little to do other than sleep or sit and drink. There was a profusion of friendly girls who frequented the club and Pete and Roger got entwined in innocent relationships but Tony and Glen had steady girlfriends in England and did their best to avoid them. Horst Fascher was their 'minder' and it was his responsibility to look after the 'nice' new English boys. He had been a Featherweight Boxing Champion but his boxing career had been cut short after he spent time in prison for killing a sailor in a street fight.

Roger, only 16 and very gullible, believed every word he was told. The waiters explained it was the custom to stay at a table all night with anyone who bought him a drink. One 'lady' took a particular interest in Roger and bought him a drink every time she saw him. Politely, he remained at the table but when she put her hand on his leg and started to 'play' with his genitals, he nearly jumped out of his skin. Worse was to come. She grabbed his head and pressed her lips onto his and kissed him, roughly. He had never kissed a girl before and having a snaking tongue forced into his mouth was repulsive. Roger's face took on an expression of startled embarrassment as his eyes nearly popped out of their sockets. The other boys and waiters, who had discreetly observed the 'goings on' with quiet amusement, were unable to contain themselves and burst out laughing as Roger disentangled himself and attempted to regain composure.

Other musicians frequented the club and the boys soon got to know them. Tony Sheriden often joined the group on stage. Stuart Sutcliffe and Astrid Kirchherr came to watch the shows and sometimes Tony and Stuart would offer to do a session to give the boys a break. It was exhausting working through the night and Tony Sheriden would ask, "Do you want some Prellies, they'll help you stay awake?"

Prellies was another name for Preludin, a drug legally available in Germany and used by long distant lorry drivers to keep them awake. If taken with beer, it gave a high. Dexedrine was another similar drug. When they looked exhausted on stage, a waiter would throw them some. The boys refused to take them, except for Glen who took the odd one. After the first week, they became acclimatised to the new routine and managed a little better with working long hours.

After two weeks in Hamburg, Roger celebrated his seventeenth birthday. No one seemed to notice he was working in the club illegally as you had to be 18 to have a work permit. He met another lady, Brigetta, who took pity on him and said he reminded her of a younger brother who had recently died. She was kindly, like an older sister and they talked and became good friends. Her mother ran a restaurant near the club and Roger was welcomed, like one of the family and could eat there anytime, so he never went hungry.

The week after the move to Clifton Hall, Reg, curious to see how the boys were getting on in Hamburg, impulsively decided to drive to Germany to visit them. When he told Dorothy, she was dismayed and tried to persuade him not to go as it was too far to drive on his own.

"You can come with me," grinned Reg.

"Don't be silly. I can't possibly go. There's so much to do and the lawns need mowing. You promised you would do them this week."

"I'll do them when I get back," smiled Reg.

In the adjoining boys' kitchen, Roy Young was eating breakfast.

"Have you got a passport with you?"

Roy looked surprised and thought for a moment. "Yes, I think so."

"How do you fancy a trip to Hamburg?"

"When?"

"In about half an hour," replied Reg, with a wide grin. "I'm off to see Glen and the boys."

Roy spluttered and nearly choked on his cornflakes.

"Half an hour? Okay. I'll pack my case," replied Roy, standing up. Nothing Reg did surprised him anymore.

Roy Young, in his mid-twenties, was older than the other boys and an exceptionally accomplished singer and pianist. He had previously toured with Cliff Richard, appeared on television shows Oh Boy and Drumbeat. Performed with the young Adam Faith and it was Roy who encouraged him to break up the words in his vocals which gave Adam his distinctive voice which led to stardom. For some reason, stardom had eluded Roy. He joined Reg the previous year in 1960, happy to be part of an established community, touring dance halls and receiving a regular wage in the uncertain world of show business.

After one performance, Reg had commented, "You're a good performer, but, and this is a big but, you look terrible on stage. You need to improve your appearance."

"I've always looked like this," replied Roy, taken aback by Reg's Yorkshire directness.

"It's time to change my friend. You need to buy a gold lamé suit."

"It'll be expensive," replied Roy, who never spent much on clothes.

"It will, but it'll be worth it. You have to look like a star to be a star."

Taking Reg's advice, Roy ordered a gold lamé suit. He knew he wasn't a good-looking guy so was surprised when the first time he wore it, girls began to scream at him. It was a life changing moment and Roy was thrilled. He remembered Reg's words. "You have to look like a star to be a star." From then on, he took a pride in his stage appearance.

Reg and Roy took it in turns to drive across the continent to Hamburg and on arriving at the Top Ten Club, they met Peter Eckhorn and his wife. Reg went into the office to discuss business with Eckhorn while Roy waited by the stage. Waving 'hello' to the boys, they beckoned him to join them and with little encouragement, he did an impromptu performance, playing piano and singing in the style of Jerry Lee Lewis.

"Your boys are like stars," commented Eckhorn, in his broken English. "They are the best and I like the new boy, what's his name?"

"Roy Young," replied Reg.

"I would like to book him."

"If Roy agrees, he can stay on if you like."

"Okay. That will be good."

Later in the year, Peter Eckhorn and Horst Fascher made a visit to England to see various groups perform and stayed at Clifton Hall before going onto Liverpool. Eckhorn re-booked Roy Young and Reg asked a Birmingham group, Danny King and the Royals, to be his backing group. They all gave up their day jobs to go, except their drummer, and a week later, Danny King, Tom Owen and Garth Quirke and a new drummer, Barney Peacock, went to Hamburg with Roy.

Arriving at the club, the new English boys soon realised they had 'minders' who acted as bodyguards to protect them. Sometimes, when they wanted to explore Hamburg on their own, they pretended to go to bed and then get up to venture out. On one excursion, they visited a different club and naively got 'rolled-over' by having a few drinks and a cuddle with a pretty girl. Unwittingly, they were drinking champagne and they lost all their wages paying for it. Back at the Top Ten club, they told Peter Eckhorn and the following day, he returned their wages.

With little to do, the boys chatted to girls who frequented the club. Barney Peacock fell in love with a 'big' girl called Heidi, who often brought him food to eat. It was an innocent affair; they ate, talked, held hands and kissed. He made friends with sailors from the H.M.S. Eagle and they took Barney on a tour of Hamburg. In one narrow street where only men were admitted, Barney was shocked to see on display in shop windows were naked women. To his astonishment he saw Heidi seated in a window. Until then he had not realised her occupation.

Eckhorn offered Roy a permanent job at the Top Ten Club and Roy accepted. Danny King and the Royals returned to England by train, boat and train, arriving back in Rugby only to discover their equipment, speakers, amplifier and drum kit were missing from the goods wagon. Back at Clifton Hall, Reg made a number of telephone calls and discovered that Customs at Harwich had dismantled their equipment and left it in a store without informing anyone.

Top: Rehearsal on the terrace. Graham Dunnett (Starliner), Dave Da Costa, Don Hawkins - drums, Danny Storm, 'Monk' (Starliner). Seated in Deckchairs: Glen Dale, Roy Young and Roger James
Bottom: Tree Swing - Barney Peacock, Roger James, Glen Dale, Danny Storm, Buddy Britten

5. LIFE AT CLIFTON HALL

1961 Reg and Dorothy Calvert in the office with a poster advertising: Teen-Beat June 1961, Majestic, Worcester. 7.30 – 10.30 p.m., starring Danny Davis with full supporting show: Admission 4/-

It did not take long for the inhabitants of Clifton-upon-Dunsmore to realise there were strange 'goings on' at the Hall. Rumour and gossip were rife. Who were these bohemian young men appearing in their village? What were they doing, and what was going on at the Hall? Soon, local and national press were intrigued by this unusual household and photographers and news reporters wanted to visit.

Dorothy posted advertisements in the local shop for a home help and gardener. In response, a young woman cycled to the house and asked for an interview. Mrs Muriel Podgson, widowed with three children, was perfect. Intuitively, Dorothy knew she would be trustworthy, reliable and discreet. More importantly, she was unpretentious and would be neither a distraction, nor attraction to her husband or the boys.

Jack, eighty years young, deaf, short-sighted but very sprightly, cycled three miles from Hillmorton to Clifton Hall to apply for the job as gardener.

Dorothy took an immediate liking to him and offered him the position working three days a week. Jack arrived most days for the joy of working in the gardens and not for the money he earned. He was cheerful with a ready smile and worked at his own pace, which was slow. The one job Dorothy was adamant he should not do was mow the lawns. This she reserved for Reg.

Articles began to appear in the press about Clifton Hall with a variety of headlines including, 'The School of Rock 'n' Roll' and 'The School of Pop'. More surprising was that a German magazine, Die Woche, ran a two-page feature about them. After this, more enquiries from abroad arrived for Reg to provide musicians for European clubs and US Bases. This resulted in his next booking to send boys to a US Army Base at La Rochelle in France and he decided to send, Buddy Britten, Glen Dale, Pete Mist and a girl singer from Southampton.

Clifton Hall was proving to be a happy and relaxed house with much fun and laughter. Living in the country with no neighbours, the boys could play music all night and no one complained about the noise. The house was quiet until midday when the boys got up, then the silence was broken. Most evenings were quiet until the boys returned from the dances when the cacophony of sounds, guitars, singing and records, resumed until the early hours.

Reg never stood still and with his increasing success, he wanted to expand his business. Dorothy was now, not just his wife but his business partner and she took an active interest in everything, picking up the pieces of each business as Reg moved onto another new venture. Before starting anything new, Reg liked to discuss his ideas with her. Often, she didn't agree and tried to put him off some of his more outlandish schemes.

"What do you think about me having a nightclub?

"No club," replied Dorothy, frowning. "You soon got bored with the Bandbox."

"The Bandbox was tiny by comparison. Nightclubs are the way forward. You should see the ones in Hamburg. They're enormous and stay open until the early hours."

"We've enough to do running dancehalls."

"And I think we need a London Agency."

"An Agency! Whatever for?" You should stand still for a moment and enjoy what we've got. We've only just moved to Rugby and you're thinking about having a nightclub and London agency."

"London's where it's all happening. With all these foreign clubs and US Bases wanting me to find groups, we would earn a commission on the bookings."

"I suppose it's possible," replied Dorothy, thoughtfully.

"And I've had another thought. Why don't you manage Buddy Britten?"

"Me, become a manager?" smiled Dorothy.

"You'd be a good manager and you get on well with him. Both of you having gone to snobby schools. It would make the news. You'd be the only woman impresario to manage a pop singer."

Barney Peacock was delighted when Reg offered him a permanent position, living at Clifton Hall and earning £3 a night. He was pleased to give up his day job as he loved playing drums and gladly accepted. Setting his drum kit up in the rehearsal room, he began to practice night and day and the house resounded to the beat of the drum.

"I can't stand it anymore. The drums are driving me mad. You'll have to do something about him," complained Dorothy.

"He's keen," grinned Reg.

"He's giving me a headache."

"Okay, I'll ask him to practise in the barns. We'll make a new House Rule. Drummers to practise outside, unless they're rehearsing with a group."

Behind the scenes, Reg and Dorothy were kept busy and mornings were spent in the office. With 21 weekly dances and shows to organise, promotions, advertising, accounts and wages to pay, they had little free time to themselves. The boys took it for granted that everything would be provided for them. The only one who offered to help was Pete Mist, a quiet, studious looking boy who wore glasses and had straight blond hair. He stoked the water boiler and Aga, cleaned the vans for which he got paid an extra pound per van and made loudspeaker cabinets for Reg in the barns. Dorothy really appreciated his help and often commented, "Pete will make someone a very good husband one day."

Food orders were telephoned to the local village Co-op store and delivered to the house. Boys, being boys, never thought to buy their own food, so Dorothy stocked their kitchen cupboard with basic provisions of bread, jam, butter, Kellogg's cornflakes, Force wheat flakes, milk, tea, coffee and sugar. She became proficient at cooking copious amounts of simple meals, stews, casseroles, sausages or pork chops with fresh vegetables.

The two kitchens adjoined each other and at mealtimes, a hubbub of conversation and laughter could be heard from the boys as they waited for their evening meal. Their food was served first and then the family sat down at the kitchen table to enjoy time together to talk and chatter.

Preparing dinner for the household, Susan, Candy and Dorothy Calvert

It was a happy time for the family and Reg and Dorothy were proud of their daughters. They were well-mannered, pretty girls but as different to each other as chalk and cheese. Susan was thoughtful, with fair hair and a face dotted with freckles. She was artistic and contrary to the rest of the household, enjoyed classical music. Candy was into pop music, more giggly, dark haired with big blue eyes like her mothers.

A few weeks after their move to Clifton Hall, Reg, full of ideas, suggested to Susan that she could start her own business. Dorothy sent Reg a look which said, 'don't be ridiculous' but Reg ignored her.

"You could keep chickens in the barns and become a poultry farmer.

"Keep chickens?" queried Susan.

"Yep. You buy them as little chicks and rear them," grinned Reg.

"Don't give her silly ideas, she's only twelve and too young to have her own business," said Dorothy, sharply.

"Nearly thirteen. I left school at fourteen," said Reg, ignoring his wife's remark as he winked at his daughter. "I'll take you to the Rugby Cattle Market on Monday and we'll buy some chicks. I'll lend you the money and you can pay me back when you start to make a profit."

Susan's face lit up; she was an ambitious girl and excited at the thought of running her own business.

"You're always giving her silly ideas. You make her think she can do anything," said Dorothy, irritably.

"And so she can. Girls are just as good as boys and everyone has to start somewhere," replied Reg, winking again at his daughter.

"Perhaps she'd like to earn her keep and help me do the washing up?"

"I always help with the cooking," replied Susan.

"I've an idea," said Reg. "Why don't you offer to wash-up for the boys? Charge them four shillings a week each. Most boys are lazy and I expect they'd rather pay you than do it themselves. Just ask and see what they say."

Dorothy frowned.

"Can I have a pony please?" asked Candy, smiling beseechingly at her mother.

"I expect so," replied Dorothy, reciprocating her smile.

"You can ride Mr and Mrs White's ponies, anytime you want to," said Reg.

"But I'd like my own," appealed Candy.

"There's a lot of work in keeping a pony," replied Reg, seriously.

"No more than keeping chickens," retorted Dorothy.

Rugby cattle market was a large bustling place, dusty with the smell of sweaty animals and manure permeating the air. Above the hullabaloo of cattle mooing and sheep baaing could be heard the amplified voice of the auctioneer as he called the bidding order in rapid succession. In one corner of the market was a quieter area with cages containing rabbits, turkeys, chickens, ducks, geese, puppies, kid goats and other small creatures. Reg and Susan studied the tiny fluffy chicks and Reg encouraged Susan to put her hand up and bid for the ones she wanted. When a small black and white kid goat came up for auction there was silence as no one wanted to buy him. Reg nudged Susan and whispered, "Put your hand up."

Bidding over, Reg paid for the animals and with great excitement they filled the back of the estate car with boxes containing twelve white Sussex chicks, twelve Rhode Island Red chicks, six white ducklings, six white baby turkeys, one white baby rabbit and a kid goat. When they arrived back at Clifton Hall, Dorothy came out to greet them, her face breaking into a smile when she saw the kid goat.

The chicks were kept warm for several days in boxes near the Aga cooker and then housed in one of the stables, with a layer of peat on the floor. When they were large enough, they were allowed to freely roam the grounds and soon established a daily routine. Only the turkeys, white, unpleasant natured birds, were kept in and housed in the hayloft.

Dorothy liked to see the birds and laughed at the ducks. She made a mash each day for the chickens with leftover potato and vegetable peelings and the ducklings were given a bowl of water with stale bread. The ducks quacked and splashed happily as they ate and once the scrabble for food was over, the chickens made a tour of the grounds pecking the soil and grubbing up insects. Where the chickens went the ducklings followed, quacking as they waddled along. As dusk fell, the birds returned on their own to the stable to be locked in for the night, safe from the fox.

When some of the chicks were heard to crow it became obvious they were cockerels and were segregated into a pen, their fate, to be fattened-up for a Sunday dinner. The turkey chicks were aggressive and when Susan went to feed them, they looked sideways at her with angry pebble-black piercing eyes, always mistrusting her and showing no bond of friendship to the person who fed them. When they were eight weeks old, Susan was shocked one morning to discover two birds lying dead with no obvious reason for their demise.

Dorothy feeding the chickens (RC)

Reg and Dorothy had invited their respective families to stay for a summer holiday but did not tell them they had purchased Clifton Hall. They wanted to keep it as a surprise and anticipated their arrival with proudness and pleasure.

"What d'you think your mother will say when she sees your new home?" asked Reg, with a twinkle in his eye.

"Don't know. She told me no good would come of marrying you. I remember her saying you'd come to a sticky end."

"Sticky toffee. Maybe she'll eat her words," laughed Reg.

"I can't imagine my mother ever eating her words."

When Reg received a telephone call from Ada, his mother, Dorothy tried to eavesdrop as she observed her husband's face become grey and serious. Ada, a professional musician, played clarinet and saxophone in many of the leading women's bands and orchestras and had continued her career after Reg's birth. He had been brought up by his grandparents, Lilla and Tom Calvert and Reg always referred to them as Mam and Dad. Lilla had died a few years prior and Tom now lived alone with his border collie.

"What's the matter?"

"You won't believe it," replied Reg, seriously.

"Trouble at mill?" joked Dorothy, lightly.

"Worse than that. Ada is coming with Tamara and Christian for a holiday."

"I thought you said that was bad news?" replied Dorothy, who disliked Ada, although she tried not to show it.

"And Dad's coming too."

"And?" asked Dorothy impatiently.

"Dad has gone and made his home-help pregnant!" explained Reg, as he chewed his bottom lip.

"You're joking," replied Dorothy, astonished.

"The woman is 40 and married."

"And he must be 75 if he's a day. Is she having the baby?"

"Don't know."

"Your Dad always had a reputation for being a philanderer but I wouldn't have expected a man in his seventies to behave like that. He should be ashamed of himself, but I don't suppose he is, and a woman of her age should have known better," muttered Dorothy.

Dorothy's mother, by contrast, seemed very straight laced and proper with a sharp tongue and as a widow, she chose to wear grey instead of black as was the tradition in Yorkshire.

Sarah Jane caught the coach from Huddersfield to Rugby and greeted her daughter with a cursory kiss on the cheek. Dorothy, with maturity, understood her mother had developed a hard exterior to mask her feelings and knew that underneath her shell was a soft and caring centre. During the 15-minute journey from Rugby to Clifton, Dorothy made polite conversation and enquired how her step sisters, Hilda and Edith were? How was John and his growing family and wasn't it a pity they couldn't have travelled down together.

Dorothy parked her van on the front drive under the shade of the Cedar of Lebanon tree and tried not to grin like a Cheshire cat.

"We're home."

"Thanks Dorothy. I could do wi' a sup of tea," replied Sarah Jane, in her broad Yorkshire accent.

"Come in, I'll put the kettle on. We'll go in the back entrance. That's the boy's kitchen," pointed Dorothy as they passed by the open door. "And this is our kitchen."

"Boy's kitchen?" queried Sarah Jane.

"Yes, the boys live with us now. They have their own kitchen and bedrooms in the wing above."

"Thou mean Danny Storm and th' others live int' house?"

"All of them but not all at the same time as some are away on tour."

"Do they do owt, cookin' or washin'?"

"No," laughed Dorothy. "They're boys and haven't a clue."

"Hello Grandma," greeted Susan, entering the kitchen and coming over for her peck on the cheek.

Sarah Jane glanced at her granddaughter with disapproval. "Thou look more like thee fartha every time I see thee."

Susan took this as a compliment and smiled. "Candy will be in shortly, she's just putting Shamie away. Would you like a rock cake? I made them yesterday."

"I'd rather have a sandwich, lass."

"We've got cheese, luncheon meat, fish paste or pork pie," offered Dorothy.

"Luncheon meat, ta."

"Or you could have Mum's new invention, a Mars bar sandwich," suggested Susan, pointing to some Mars bars on the counter.

"A Mars bar sandwich! Do I eckers like, whatever will thou be thinkin' of next our Dorothy?" smiled Sarah Jane warmly, at her daughter.

After lunch, Dorothy took her mother on a tour of the house. It was simply and sparsely furnished, mostly with the old dark oak furniture Mr and Mrs White had left behind and the few pieces of furniture they had transported from Southampton.

"What do you think Mother? Do you like the house?"

"It's grand. Have tha' bought it?" asked Sarah Jane, looking sideways at her daughter.

"Yes," beamed Dorothy.

For a moment, Sarah Jane said nothing. "I thought thee'd mak' it and end up wi' a house like this."

"I thought you said Reg was no good."

"I sed he'd lead thee a merry dance."

"And he does," laughed Dorothy.

Sarah Jane disliked Reg but with the passing of time she had mellowed and learnt to keep her sharp tongue quiet. Reg, in return, paid her due deference and ate kippers with her for breakfast but afterwards, avoided her company using any excuse to be out of the house and away.

Different relations came to stay and Reg and Dorothy took immense pride in showing them their new home. They had grown in the esteem of their family from being as poor as church mice and living in an old bus, to being comparatively rich and owning a beautiful country house.

Reg, full of fun, bought some heavy rope to make a tree swing and when he saw the boys lazing on the terrace one warm sunny afternoon, asked for a volunteer to climb the oak tree. The boys looked at each other and shook their heads and agreed that it was too dangerous.

"Okay, I'll climb it myself," replied Reg, with bravado.

It was not an easy climb and as Reg set about scaling the wide trunk the boys assisted him by pushing him up from behind.

"This ditch is called a ha-ha," laughed Reg, as he clung to the first large branch.

The boys watched in awe and cheered their boss as he balanced himself on top of the branch and wrapped the rope round and round. He then secured it with a knot, leaving a good length of rope to fall to the ground. Grinning, Reg slid round the underside of the bough and shimmied down the rope. A little red in the face with all the exertion, he stood laughing with the boys before making a loop in the bottom of the rope as a foot hold. Putting both feet in, he tentatively jumped up and down.

"Okay, it's good. Who wants to have a go first?"

The boys looked at each other impishly and shook their heads.

"You go first Reg. Show us how to do it."

"Okay. Give me a good push and with any luck, I should swing over the ha-ha and back again."

"Ha-ha," laughed the boys, as they pushed.

Reg swung across the ditch, spinning round several times and swung back again. He laughed and chuckled. This was fun. Every time Reg swung towards them, the boys pushed again, and again.

"That's it boys, let me off," laughed Reg, seeing the funny side of his predicament. "My arms are aching."

The boys ignored his appeals and uproarious with laughter, they kept on pushing and the more Reg begged them to stop, the harder they pushed.

Dorothy, sensing something amiss, went into the garden to see what was happening. Suppressing a smile, she watched her husband being pushed back and forth and then called out loudly in her school mistress voice.

"Don't you think you ought to be getting ready to go out?"

Turning to look at her guiltily, the boys stopped their revelries. Within minutes, the quiet of the house was filled with jollity as the boys returned to sort out stage clothes and equipment in preparation for the evening shows. Reg, red faced and laughing entered the kitchen and gave Dorothy a kiss.

"Little things please little minds," smiled Dorothy.

DANCEHALL SHOWS - SUMMER 1961

With the move to Clifton Hall, Reg no longer had a personal secretary. To plan the dances, he made a chart on a large sheet of paper so he could see at a glance who was where. Below is a compilation of this plan which is not a complete listing. Summer 1961, there were four touring shows to manage: The Danny Storm Show, Buddy Britten Show, Roy Young Show and Mike West-Robbie Hood Show. In addition, local groups and stars were booked to appear at the dances.
Letts Desk Diaries were used 1962-1965 to keep a record of the dancehalls.

SATURDAYS

COVENTRY Centre Ballroom:
3rd June 1961: Barry James, Johnny Neal & the Starliners

ANDOVER Drill Hall:
3rd June: Dave Antony, Falcons // 10th June: Johnny Panters plus local group £9.
17th June: Roy Young show // 24th June: Danny Storm show

WEYMOUTH Small Sidney Hall:
3rd June: Danny Storm show // 17th June: Dowland Bros. // Fri 23rd June: Dave Antony, Falcons

HEMEL HEMPSTEAD:
3rd June: Roy Young, Glen Dale, Rod Ace, plus group.

TIDWORTH:
10th June: Danny Hunter. The Semi-tones. Danny Storm show. The Falcons.

ERDINGTON BRS:
17th June: Danny Storm show // 24th June: Crestar's, Grasshoppers

SUNDAYS

LYE:
28th May: Buddy Britten show // 4th June: Danny Storm show
18th June: Roy Young show

MONDAYS

RUSHDEN Co-op Hall:
29th May: Buddy Britten show // 5th June: Danny Storm show // 12thJune: Toreadors // 19th June: Danny Storm show

BURTON ON TRENT Town Hall:
12th June: Danny Storm and Mike West/Robbie Hood show // 19th June: Roy Young show

MELKSHAM Assembly Hall:
12th June: Roy Young, Glen Dale show, Falcons

TUESDAYS

TAMWORTH Assembly Rooms:

2nd April: Johnny Kidd & the Pirates // 5th May: Danny Storm, Baby Bubbly, David Da Costa, Mike West and the Silhouettes // 15th May: Cuddly Dudley with Red E Lewis & the Red Caps. Admission 4/- // 30th May: Glen Dale and Buddy Britten show // 6th June: Danny Davis, Mike West-Robbie Hood show // 13th June: Roy Young show // 20th June: Teen Beat Rock - Danny Storm show

OXFORD Carfax Assembly Rooms:

30th May: Danny Storm show // 6th June: Roy Young and Glen Dale show // 13th June: Danny Storm show // 20th June: Roy Young show

WEDNESDAYS

NEWBURY Corn Exchange:

7th June: Roy Young and Glen Dale show // 14th June: Danny Storm show // 21st June: Roy Young and Danny Storm show

SOLIHULL Assembly Rooms:

28th June: Roy Young show

THURSDAYS

WASHWOOD HEATH BRS:

1st June: Grasshoppers. Glen Dale // 8th June: Danny Davis
15th June: Roy Young show and Atlantics // 22nd June: Danny Storm show

LYE:

1st June: Barry James. Cresta's // 8th June: Grasshoppers // 15th June: Danny Storm show // 22nd June: Cresta's, Johnny Neal & Starliners

CAMBERLEY Agincourt:

1st June: Danny Storm show // 8th June: Roy Young and Glen Dale show
15th June: Barry James, Lin Treasey, Semi-Tones // 22nd June: Roy Young show

FRIDAYS

WORCESTER Corn Exchange:

9th June: Danny Davis, Mike West/Robbie Hood show // 16th June: Roy Young show // 23rd June: Danny Storm show and Dominoes

NUNEATON Co-op Hall:

2nd June: Barry James, Johnny Neal & Starliners // 9th June: Roy Young show
16th June: Danny Storm show // 23rd June: Colin & Whirlwinds, Johnny Neal & Starliners

EASTLEIGH Town Hall:

2nd June: Dowland Brothers // 9th June: Danny Hunter, Johnny Neal & Starliners, Lin Treasey, Brian Fisher // 16th June: Dowland Brothers, Falcons // 23rd June: Roy Young show

BOURNEMOUTH Holdenhurst Drill Hall:

2nd June: Danny Storm show, Falcons. // 17th June: Falcons, Dave Antony
24th June: Roy Young show

Calvert family: photo by Reg Calvert. He mounted his Rolleiflex twin-lens camera on a tripod, set the timer and ran 'into' the family picture. Susan with rabbit, Dorothy with Quacker Barney, Reg, Candy with rabbit (RC)

6. THE RELUCTANT GARDENER

Clifton Hall: Lawnmower - Rod Ace -Roger James, Roy Young and Glen Dale.
Behind – rehearsing on the terrace, the Starliners

Dorothy loved her garden and spent her free time weeding, planting and deadheading the profusion of roses that clung to the south facing walls of the house. Her vegetable plot had been a mixed success. The beans had done well, but no one wanted to eat her cauliflower or cabbage even though she covered them with thick brown gravy to disguise the abundance of wildlife, caterpillars and insects that had thrived on them.

Sundays were a day of 'rest', with only one dance to organise. Dorothy cooked a large Sunday dinner with roast potatoes and Yorkshire puddings. Each week, she reminded Reg, a reluctant gardener, that the lawns needed mowing.

"Do you want a cup of tea before you mow the lawns?" prompted Dorothy.

Reg nodded his head in reply. At the end of the kitchen counter was a pile of comics, Superman, Batman and Forbidden Worlds. Most of the boys enjoyed reading them and the pile formed a library for anyone to borrow. Reg picked up a comic and put his feet up on a chair as he relaxed.

"Have you heard they've invented the Pill? It's a tablet to prevent women from becoming pregnant?" mentioned Dorothy.

"Really? Could mean the end of the human race as we know it. I can't imagine many people in their right mind wanting to have babies."

"Is that so, and what planet do you live on, and did you know that grass keeps growing if you don't mow it?" replied Dorothy, smiling.

"I thought we had a gardener? You could ask Jack to mow the lawns," suggested Reg, lazily.

"He's eighty," retorted Dorothy, exasperated. "Much too old to mow our lawns. When you finish drinking your tea, perhaps you'd like to get off your backside and twist and shake while I cook the Sunday dinner. You need to mow them at least once a week to keep them down."

"You could get a younger gardener. Or we could have some sheep."

"Do they have sheep on Mars or is it Venus, I can't remember?" asked Dorothy as she pulled a bag of potatoes over to the table.

"The Americans will try to land on the moon next. Just you wait and see," said Reg, with a smile as he put his Forbidden Worlds back on the pile.

"I don't care about men landing on the moon. I do care about our lawns. If you don't cut them today, the grass will be too long."

"Okay okay. I never get any peace," replied Reg, giving Dorothy a mischievous grin as he made his way to the rehearsal room.

"Your Dad's up to something," Dorothy said, as Susan entered the kitchen. "I can tell by the silly look on his face."

"The boys are all following Dad to the barns," remarked Susan, as she looked out of the kitchen window.

"I told you, he's up to something. He'll do anything to get out of gardening."

The barns contained various broken down and unwanted items that had been left behind by the previous owners, including old lawnmowers and prams. Reg had repaired two of the mowers and, with great merriment, got the boys to push them along with two old prams to the main lawn.

"Come on guys, this could be the next Grand Prix. The fastest lawnmower in the west. Who wants to go first?" enthused Reg, as he securely tied a pram to each of the mowers. "First to the spinney is the winner."

Setting the mowers in a line, Reg encouraged his dubious retinue of boys to climb into a pram. Not one of them volunteered but all eyes were on Baby Bubbly, the smallest person. Laughing, they chased him round the lawn. Catching hold of him, they picked him up and sat him in a pram with his legs dangling out. A new drummer, Gary Fletcher, had just been recruited and Reg encouraged him to join in the fun.

"We need another volunteer. What about you Gary?"

"Not me man. It doesn't look safe," grinned Gary.

"We'll help you," said the boys, as they gave chase.

"I'm too big," laughed Gary, as he succumbed and climbed into the other pram, with a little help from his colleagues.

"When I say go, pull the starter cord. On your marks. Get ready. Go," shouted Reg. The starter cords were pulled, the spark plugs ignited and the lawnmowers came into life, trundling at full speed to the other side of the lawn. The boys followed, laughing and cheering.

Gary, seeing the spinney of trees looming ahead, started to shout. "Help. Help. Let me out...." A few seconds later, there was a crash. The lawnmower stopped, the pram tipped over and Gary tumbled out.

Bubbles' lawnmower kept going a little longer, cutting through the spinney until it came to a sudden jolt as it hit a large tree.

"That was great man," said Gary, picking himself up.

"I won," giggled Bubbles. "Because mine kept going longer."

"I got there first, so I won," said Gary, laughing.

The lawns needed cutting every week and when the boys bored of the lawnmower race Reg offered to pay them a pound to take a turn. None of them volunteered so Reg experimented with other ways to get the job done. He decided to sit in the larger pram himself, legs outstretched. It made mowing the lawn good fun until the inevitable happened. First, the spindly wheels buckled under his weight and then the wheels fell off and he found himself unceremoniously being dragged by the lawnmower and thumping along the ground in a pram with no wheels. His next idea proved little better. Carrying a heavy garden fork, he placed it in the centre of the lawn and jumped on it to ensure the prongs were deep in the ground. He attached a long rope between the mower and fork and started the mower and it began to chug round and round the fork in ever decreasing circles. Smiling smugly to himself, he sauntered off to a deckchair to watch the mower circumnavigate the lawn. After a few successful turns around the fork, the mower stuttered and the fork jerked out of the ground. Reg jumped up. He was quick off the mark and raced to the mower and caught it, just before it crashed into a tree.

Few people ventured up the long drive to Clifton Hall unless they had a reason to visit. The boys felt safe from aggressive young men and adoring girls but not from pigs. One afternoon, a wandering sow with eight baby piglets took up residence between the barns and vehicles in an unkempt part of the garden under low-hanging trees. When the boys went to load the vans, the sow became agitated and started to snort loudly and stamped her trotters in readiness to charge anyone who came near her or any of her piglets. The boys beat a hasty retreat and looked on helplessly from the house windows. They were terrified to go outside. After making numerous telephone calls, Dorothy managed to contact the farmer who eventually sauntered up the drive holding a big stick. "Go pigs, go," he called and the pigs obediently walked back down the drive with the farmer following behind.

Dorothy did her best to maintain some sort of order and calm in a household of testosterone-fuelled boys. Girlfriends were prohibited but then, one day, she noticed how puberty was rapidly transforming her eldest daughter. Both parents realised the potential for trouble. Dorothy did her best to keep Susan looking as young as possible with badly cut hairstyles and unfashionable clothes. Reg thought carefully how he could best protect his daughter and decided it was time to educate her into the ways of the world and men.

They were right to be concerned as one of the new recruits, only three years older than Susan, had begun to make advances towards her. Roger, when he returned from Hamburg, saw Susan for the first time and fell in love. Realising she went out each morning to feed her animals, he waited for her to appear and then, casually sauntered over to see her in the privacy of the barns.

"You look a lot like Hayley Mills, you could be her twin sister."

"Do I?" replied Susan, surprised.

"Whistle Down the Wind is my favourite film," added Roger, smiling broadly at her.

"I haven't seen it yet," replied Susan, returning his smile. She was flattered by the attention and happy to make a new friend. She thought of the boys in the house as older brothers and rarely had a proper conversation with them, other than in passing when she helped to carry in their meals or to ask for payment for doing their washing up. Susan knew her parents would be angry if they found Roger was secretly meeting her and tried to put him off.

"Why won't you let me kiss you?" asked Roger, as he tried to put his arms around her.

"You'll get the sack if my parents find out," giggled Susan, pushing him away. She had always been a tomboy, caring little about her appearance until recently, thinking herself plain, as no one had ever told her she was pretty. No matter how Roger tried, Susan refused to be kissed. It was a game, an important part of growing up but Susan knew, as the 'bosses' daughter, she was out of bounds and intuitively began to develop an aloofness with the other boys in the house.

Top: Backstage before the show at the Benn Hall, Rugby: Danny Storm, Susan Calvert, Roger James, Glen Dale (RC)
Bottom: Johny Washington, John Wileman, Jane Price, Dave Spence, Andy Brown

Top: Danny Storm, Pete Mist on bass guitar (RC)
Bottom: Tommy Bruce with Roy Young, Danny Storm and Glen Dale. Tommy was touring with the Clifton Hall boys and had a hit record, *Ain't Misbehavin'*

7. MORE NEW RECRUITS

ROBBIE HOOD AND HIS MERRY MEN (RC)
Rod (Bainbridge) Allen, Gary Fletcher, Mike West, Barry Pritchard.

The transition from Southampton to Clifton Hall had gone smoothly but not everyone had made the move, including singers Eddy Sex and Ricky Fever. Guitarist, Geoff Chalke, returned to Southampton after a short while as did drummer, Tony Burnett. When David Da Costa was offered work in France at a US Army Base, he persuaded his wife to become a singer and asked Colin Angel to join them. This left Reg with vacancies to fill.

Gary Fletcher had recently been recruited from the Alpines, a Burton-on-Trent group. His father and uncle were in the building trade but Gary had always dreamed of being a drummer, not a builder. He found life away from his family quite hard and it took him time to develop his confidence. The other new drummer, Barney Peacock, took him under his wing, gave him advice about drumming and as they were both early risers, they cooked egg and bacon for breakfast while the other boys were still sleeping.

Rod Bainbridge and Barry Pritchard had known each other since childhood, attended the same schools and like brothers, they bickered. They both had the same interest in music, played guitar and sang together. Reg auditioned them at the Nuneaton Co-op Hall dance and offered them the opportunity to turn 'professional'. They accepted and Gary was placed with them to make a trio.

A Coventry group, the Vampires, had a young, good looking singer called Johny Washington, with a mass of blond hair, loads of personality and cheeky confidence. Reg and Dorothy both liked him and asked him to audition on his own the following week at the Nuneaton dance so they could check his versatility. Johny agreed and with no rehearsal, he went on stage and performed with Alvin Jay and the Jay Cats. Undaunted by the occasion, he sang well and when he came off stage, Reg complimented him, put his hand in his pocket and gave him three, £1 notes. This was more than Johny earned in a whole week as an apprentice. On the Sunday afterwards, his parents were invited to visit Clifton Hall and were shown around the house. Johny stayed in the boys' kitchen, getting to know Glen, Danny and Roger. Two days later, he moved into Clifton Hall and began his musical career.

Reg and Dorothy were having a competition to see who could give up smoking the longest and did not encourage their new recruits to start. Most boys smoked, except for Pete Mist, who had a £5 bet with his aunt that he wouldn't smoke before he was 21. Roger smoked but on his return from Hamburg, realised he couldn't afford to buy cigarettes and pay hire-purchase on his Gretsch guitar. At night, he sneaked into the kitchen and rolled his own from dog-ends but after a few days, decided to give up. When Dorothy saw Johny Washington smoking, she reprimanded him.

"Johny, did I just see you smoking?"

"Yes," replied Johny, honestly, entering her kitchen.

"Well don't smoke anymore," instructed Dorothy, sharply.

"All the others smoke, so why can't I?"

"Because you're only 15 and too young, for heaven's sake. Now go away and stop bothering me."

The other boys took every opportunity to tease the new recruit.

"No cigarettes for you Johny, you're too little to smoke." Each time he lit a cigarette, the boys would call out, "Mrs C, he's smoking again."

Candy, aged eleven, fluffy headed and giggly with the boys, blushed bright red whenever Danny or Bubbles entered the same room. She was easily star-struck and with the arrival of Johny Washington, her affliction became worse. Each time Candy saw him, she blushed even more and her older sister delighted in teasing her.

"You're blushing again."

"Leave your sister alone," rebuked Dorothy, sharply.

"She's silly. I don't understand why she does it. He's just a boy."

"She's normal," replied Dorothy, protectively. "Most young girls get crushes."

"I don't."

"You're not normal," responded Candy, glaring angrily at sister as her red face subsided to its normal colour.

Barney Peacock practised drumming on the front lawn when the weather was good and seeing Reg outside, he asked if he could have a quiet word.

"I thought I'd be working five or more nights a week but I'm only working three. I wondered if I could have a pay rise."

"Ah," said Reg, taking time to consider his reply. "You see the drive over there? At the bottom are lots of drummers all waiting for you to leave so they can take your place. It's up to you Barney. You can continue working for £3 a night or you can look for another job."

A look of disappointment flickered across Barney's face, realising what Reg had said was true and £9 was more than his father earned for working a 40-hour week.

"Okay. I'll stay," agreed Barney.

Reg made regular trips to London and often visited the 2i's Coffee Bar in Soho. On one visit, he recognised Mike West, a tall young man, rugged in appearance with blond hair and a squint. He had formerly been a member of both Johnny Kidd's and Billy Fury's backing groups. Reg greeted him and ordered them both a coffee and apple pie. Mike was out of work and after chatting for a while, Reg offered him a job.

Reg was late returning home and Dorothy was sitting in bed reading a Woman magazine.

"I wish you'd telephone me when you're going to be late. I was worried," said Dorothy, closing the magazine.

"I've found a new Robbie Hood," replied Reg, grinning widely. "I saw Mike West in the 2i's and offered him a job. I took him to a costumier and bought the original gear from the Robin Hood film that Richard Greene wore. It fitted him perfectly."

"So that's what taken you so long," replied Dorothy, as Reg began to chuckle.

"On the way home, we stopped at Watford Gap Service Station and I asked Mike if he'd like to be noticed? He said he would, so I suggested he put the outfit on. You should have seen everyone's astonished faces. For a moment, there was complete silence in the café as they all stopped eating and stared."

Mike was a lively personality and soon settled into Clifton Hall. He enjoyed being the centre of attraction rather than a musician in a backing group and did two spots on the show, one as himself and the other as Robbie Hood. When dressed in costume, he delighted in teasing the girls by flaunting his sexuality, moving green clad hips and shapely legs in time to the beat of the music. Robbie Hood was a singer whom no one forgot but

Mike's squint was unattractive and he often wore an eye patch to hide it. Reg, realising it was a problem that could be resolved, arranged for him to see an eye specialist and have an operation to straighten his eye.

Bookings came in for Robbie Hood, including a long tour of Scotland. This posed a problem for Reg as Mike was an integral part of one of the shows and did not have his own backing group. To accept the Scotland tour meant he needed to form another new group of Merry Men.

The Lawmen were a good Birmingham group and Reg recruited drummer, Andy Brown, bass player and singer, John Wileman and guitarist, Dave Spence, to become Mike's backing group. They all readily agreed and gave up their day jobs to become professional musicians.

Reg also needed a girl singer to appear in the show as Maid Marion. Jane Price, an attractive girl with black bouffant hair was engaged to John Wileman and often accompanied him to the dances. Without first auditioning Jane, Reg offered her the job.

The group rehearsed, working on two different shows. Robbie Hood, Maid Marion and the Merry Men. With a change of outfits and Stetson hats, the second show featured Miss Jane and the Lawmen.

They set off for Scotland and Jane proved an unexceptional singer and before each show, she was so nervous, she was sick. The tour was lengthy and although Mike could drive, he preferred to sit in the rear of the van and let John do most of it. After a while, those travelling with him in the back were embarrassed to see Mike and Jane holding hands. At the end of the tour, Jane broke off her engagement with John. By the time they returned to Clifton Hall, Robbie Hood no longer had any 'Merry Men'.

Reg put together another set of Merry Men, placing his new singers, Johny Washington, Rod Bainbridge and Barry Pritchard with Gary Fletcher on drums. Dorothy made more tunics and when Reg took the finished outfits into the rehearsal room for the boys to try on, he suggested, mischievously, they put socks in their underpants to make large codpieces to emphasise their 'contour'. The rehearsal room was in uproar as the boys dressed up in their outfits and strutted around like ballet dancers. On stage, however, modesty prevailed as Mike refused to wear socks in his underpants.

Dorothy liked Mike West but did not trust him. He was a 'merry man' who did not follow rules or regulations. After one dance at Washwood Heath, Dorothy's sixth sense was prickling. Covertly, she followed the dorma van Mike was driving and after a few miles, flashed her headlights for the vehicle to pull over. Mike ignored the flashing lights and continued to drive on. Dorothy eventually made him stop by overtaking the van and slowing down to a stop.

"What's the matter Mrs C?" asked Mike, with a cheeky grin.

"Can you open up the back door please?"

"Why Mrs C., everything's okay, isn't it?" replied Mike, trying to steer Dorothy away from the van as he realised they could both hear sounds of muffled laughter and giggling.

"Let me have the keys. I'll open the door if you won't," insisted Dorothy, in her school mistress voice as she held out her hand. Mike submitted and gave her the keys. Dorothy opened the rear door and through a fog of cigarette smoke could see the van was packed full of teenage girls sitting on the boy's laps.

"Get out," ordered Dorothy, coldly.

The girls looked at Dorothy but did not argue. Closing the door, she handed the keys back to Mike.

"Drive home please. I will be following."

"What about the girls?" asked Mike, as he looked at the forlorn girls standing in a cluster on the pavement.

"What about the girls?" repeated Dorothy. "They'll have to make their own way home. They're not my responsibility but you and the boys are and so is the insurance on this van."

Back at Clifton Hall, Dorothy related the episode to Reg and he went into fits of laughter.

"It's not a laughing matter," said Dorothy primly, trying to be serious and then she burst out laughing. "You should have seen Mike's face, it was a picture."

Candy Calvert with Robbie Hood - Mike West (RC)

Robbie Hood - Mike West (RC)

Baby Bubbly had always been popular with everyone but his personality was changing from happy-go-lucky to a more serious young man. His choice of repertoire had also altered to ballads and blues. At the dances Dorothy was running, she became exasperated as she repeatedly had to remind him to sing upbeat numbers. Dorothy appealed to Reg to speak to him but he was reluctant to do Dorothy's bidding as Bubbles always sang rock numbers when he worked for him. Eventually Reg complied and talked to Bubbles.

"You have to sing numbers the kids can dance to. It is a 'dance' and you kill the atmosphere by singing slow numbers."

"I want to develop my own singing style."

"You can include one slow number near the end of the show but the rest of the time, you have to sing upbeat numbers."

"I don't want to do rock anymore. I want to sing ballads."

"You have a choice my friend," said Reg. "You can stay, working for me and earn a good wage or you can go your own way. And remember, it's a hard world out there."

"I'll think about it," replied Bubbles, sullenly.

Bubbles and Danny shared a room together at Clifton Hall and Danny could sense something was wrong with his companion.

"What's the matter man?" asked Danny.

"I keep getting these headaches. Sometimes I think my head's going to split," replied Bubbles, holding his head in his hands.

"Do you want me to ask Mrs C for an aspirin?"

"They don't help," replied Bubbles, sitting up. "I've decided to go back home. Try and make it on my own."

"You can't man. You can't leave Clifton Hall."

"I want to sing ballads and Reg told me I can't do them," replied Bubbles, miserably.

"No man, you have to sing upbeat songs at the dances. But you can't leave. You're part of our show."

"I don't want to go but I have to find a way to do my own music"

It was a sad day when Bubbles left and as Reg predicted, he found difficulty obtaining work as he had no backing group or transport. He became a shadow of his former self, no longer happy or bubbly. He lived near Banbury and Reg and Dorothy continued to give him occasional work, when they could.

Why Reg recruited Tony Clarke, a young musician from Coventry, no one was quite sure though he did look good on stage strumming away on his large double bass. He had been to Art College and had an eclectic knowledge of music and encouraged the boys to listen to jazz and the blues. Fortunately, the audience could not hear his playing above the sound of guitars and drums, but Roger could and he spent time showing him how to play an electric bass guitar.

Larry Reddington, wrote to Reg on the off chance, asking for work. He had been the drummer in the Alphabeats, an Oxford group, and they had split up. He was lucky. Reg received the letter and a phone call later, it was agreed Larry, along with the guitarist from the group, Mike Richards, could start the following week.

Larry and Mike became part of the Strollers, backing both Danny Storm and Roger. They were paid eight pounds a week for up to four nights and extra if they played more gigs. Rehearsal began, learning new numbers and how to move. While performing, Reg insisted they were not to stand motionless but had to move and step in time with Danny and the music.

Becoming a professional musician was very different to doing local gigs around Oxford. Now, they had to travel the country in the back of a cold uncomfortable van and the work was not without danger. While on stage, they felt safe but once they finished, anything could happen. Boys in the audience were sometimes hostile towards Danny and at the end of each show, the group were careful in case a gang was waiting outside to pick a fight.

During one show, a young man heckled Danny from front of stage and annoyed him so much, that when they did the 'Shadows' walk, Danny put his foot on the face of the heckler and pushed him backwards in time to the music. The heckler crashed onto the floor. His face was red with anger as he picked himself up ready to jump onto the stage and fight for his honour. Fortunately, his mates thought it was hilarious and calmed the situation. The Strollers played on, nervous of the consequences. At the end of the show they were relieved to see the hecklers had gone and only star-struck girls were waiting by the stage door for autographs and more!

Danny Storm and the Strollers were booked to play at the Black Cat Club in Plymouth. They arrived early and after setting up, went for a drink in a nearby pub. Mike Richards did not drink alcohol and the boys mischievously suggested he try West Country cider as an alternative. Danny bought him a pint but as it tasted different from ordinary cider, he asked the other boys to taste it. They all unanimously agreed, as they stifled grins, there was nothing wrong with it. Naively, Mike drank the cider not realising how strong it was. When he stood up, his legs were like jelly and as they walked to the club, he hung onto bus signs and lamp-posts.

The show had to go on and Mike managed to walk, unaided, onto the stage and strummed his guitar. He had no sense of feeling in his fingers and no idea what he was playing. After a short while, he realised he needed the toilet but in his drunken stupor knew he should not leave the stage. There was nothing he could do but play on. The next moment, he felt the warmth of urine travelling down his legs to his feet and a large puddle appeared on the floor where he was standing. The group started to laugh uncontrollably. Danny, seeing his predicament, quickly moved the electrical wires and microphone out of the way while he continued singing with a big grin on his face.

The subject of employing another girl singer was never discussed but when Mary Day won a talent competition with the Dominators at the BRS

Ballroom at Washwood Heath, Reg immediately offered the attractive blonde a job. Unfortunately, he neglected to inform his wife. The next day, the telephone rang in the office and before Dorothy could answer it, Reg had picked up the receiver.

"Mr Calvert?" queried a girl, with a broad Black Country accent. "I'm Mary Day, the girl who sang in last night's talent competition. Do you remember me?"

"Yes, of course."

"I've decided to accept your offer and hand my notice in at work today."

"That's grand," replied Reg, smiling. "If you can catch a train to Rugby next Monday, let me know the time and I'll pick you up from the station."

"Who was that?" asked Dorothy.

"A new singer I've found," answered Reg, evasively.

"It sounded like a female voice on the phone?"

"Yes, it was, Mary Day," replied Reg, in a matter-of-fact voice.

"You mean you've invited a girl singer to come here?" asked Dorothy, incredulously. "I thought we'd agreed. No more girl singers and no girls in the house."

"We need a girl singer to balance the shows and provide entertainment for the boys in the audience."

"Over my dead body," shouted Dorothy, as her temper flared. "I'm not having a girl singer staying here. After all we've been through Reg Calvert, you've invited a girl to come and stay without even asking me."

Dorothy stood up, glared angrily at her husband's blank expression and stormed out of the office, banging the door behind her. Reg ignored his wife. He was used to her temper tantrums and knew that if he was quiet and reserved, she would calm down, eventually.

Mary Day was 'born to sing'. She lived in Blackheath, near Birmingham, the youngest of eleven children and had led a sheltered life, rarely travelling far from home. Mary worked in a factory office where she sang all the time and on her twentieth birthday, went to a pub with a few friends where the Dominators were playing. One of her friends, as a joke, told the group that Mary wanted to sing and they beckoned her up. Mary was so embarrassed, she had to be pushed onto the stage. With the crowd cheering and whistling, she reluctantly sang *Whole Lotta Shakin' Goin' On.* Afterwards, The Dominators asked if she could sing with them on a regular basis and two weeks later, they won a talent competition at the BRS Ballroom.

When Mary arrived at Clifton Hall, Reg introduced her to the boys and his wife. "Mrs C. will show you to your room," said Reg, smiling at Dorothy, who responded by glaring back, stonily.

Dorothy led Mary in silence up the back stairway and through to the main part of the house. She opened a bedroom door and ushered Mary into a large and simply furnished room, with a double bed and dark oak wardrobe. Mary put her bags down and turned to thank Dorothy but found she had already left, clicking the door closed behind her. After hanging her clothes in the wardrobe, she tentatively made her way downstairs to the rehearsal room where she could hear guitars playing. Reg was there and explained that new singers were given a stage name. With much laughter, banter and discussion, the 'naming game' began and Buddy Britten was awarded a pound note for suggesting her new name, Tanya Day.

Tanya had to spend her first week rehearsing with the Strollers, learning new songs by listening to records Reg gave her and also sing two songs in a duo with Glen Dale. Once Tanya had settled, Reg took her to London to kit her out with glamourous stage clothes.

Tanya was a natural performer and Reg placed her in the Danny Storm Show. She was much admired by the boys in the audience but not the girls. Some of them would stand at the front and annoyingly thump the stage with their fists and call out, "We want the boys. We want the boys." Tanya, in response, would smile sweetly and reply, "You've got me," and continue singing.

The one thing Reg disliked about Tanya was her Black Country accent and instructed her not to speak to the audience as it would spoil her persona. In the middle of one show, the power supply failed and the musicians were silent. Tanya explained to the audience what was happening and afterwards, Reg was cross and told her not to speak on stage again. The next time there was a power failure, Tanya kept the show alive by encouraging the audience to clap while she carried on singing without the group. This time, Reg was pleased and praised her.

Having Tanya in the show did not always mollify the males in the audience. One night, they were booked to perform at an army social club. A gang of intoxicated soldiers became jealous of the way the girls screamed at Danny and plotted revenge. They waited outside for the group to emerge at the end of the show and as soon as they saw Danny, they took him by surprise, punching and kicking him to the ground. Tanya screamed at them to stop and tried to run inside for help. Several soldiers turned on Tanya, trapping her against a tree and threatened to beat her up as well. The Strollers came out and seeing Danny on the ground, fought back. After a few minutes of aggression, fists flying, punching and kicking, the soldiers scattered. They had had their satisfaction and left Danny and the Strollers to nurse their bruises.

Tanya fitted in well with everyone and dressed modestly when not on stage. The boys treated her with respect and were pleased to have a girl around. Wherever they went, people stopped and stared at the gang of fashionable young men with one girl.

Some evenings, Dorothy, with bad grace, gave Tanya a lift in her car to the dances but rarely said a word during the whole journey. This puzzled and upset Tanya as she could not understand what she had done to cause so much hostility. Tanya queried this with the boys and they explained about Reg's affair with a singer in Southampton. With new understanding, Tanya took her opportunity to speak plainly the next time she was travelling in the car.

"Mrs C. I'm not interested in your husband. He's a very nice man and I'm sorry if you don't like me."

After this conversation, Dorothy did her best to be civil. It was hard to come to terms with having an attractive female singer in the house and she remained nervous. She moved Tanya to share a bedroom with Susan and the two girls got on well together. Dorothy also gave permission for Tanya to relax in the family lounge with her daughters on the nights she was not working and watch the only television in the house, a small black and white set. This was a privilege the boys did not enjoy. Instead, they had the rehearsal room and billiards room to relax.

Rehearsal for stage show: Glen Dale jiving with Tanya Day. Buddy Britten behind

Dorothy Calvert became Buddy Britten's manager. She enjoyed the challenge and worked hard to promote him and make his name. Above: Publicity photograph taken in the front hall of Clifton Hall by Reg (RC)

8. RECORDING CONTRACTS

Reg and Dorothy Calvert (RC)

When Reg first set out on his quest to bring Rock 'n' Roll to England and put together fabulous stage shows, he had not considered making his boys into stars, but he realised now, it was a natural progression. Clifton Hall had become a hothouse for young musicians, all ambitious to make a record and become famous. Reg, however, was wary, realising that few would make the 'big' time and he particularly disliked the way some managers abused young boys, pushing them into the limelight before they had served what he called, an apprenticeship.

When he considered his own retinue of boys, there were two he thought were ready, Danny Storm and Buddy Britten as they both had that something special. He hoped that once they had recording contracts, it would open the door for his other boys. Glen Dale, Rod Allen and Barry Pritchard, all had superb voices. Tanya Day had excellent potential and was one of the few female singers who could 'rock'. Johny Washington and Roger James were very young and just needed more experience, and there would be others to follow, all in good time.

Reg spent time in London, going to different recording companies, chatting to various A&R men and getting to know them. People were just beginning to hear about Reg and his school of 'rock' but most of the record companies were not interested in what he had to offer. Returning home from one expedition, Reg looked particularly gloomy.

"What did they say? Have you managed to get any of the boys a recording contract?" asked Dorothy.

"Nope. They like our boys but it's no good. I won't agree to their terms."

"What terms?"

"The gist of the conversation is that they want me to find young, good looking boys who can sing, and they'll give them a recording contract."

"Brilliant," smiled Dorothy.

"But, there's a catch. They have to be willing to bend over."

"Bend over. That's disgusting," replied Dorothy, shocked.

"If the boys don't do it, most of their managers do," explained Reg. "Not only that, the amount the singer receives in royalty payments is peanuts. They're lucky to get half a penny for each record sold. The only way to make money is for them to write their own songs."

Reg was not the sort of man to take no for an answer and kept returning to the record companies. On one trip to London, Reg took Danny with him and left him in a studio café eating apple pie while he went to talk business. Reg was away a long time and while Danny was waiting, a dark-haired young man came up and asked if he could join him at the table.

"Are you a singer?" asked the young man, smiling warmly at Danny.

"Yes, I'm hoping to get a recording contract soon."

"I'm Lionel Bart."

"Danny Storm. Pleased to meet you," replied Danny, who did not recognise the man or the name.

"I can help you. I'll write you a song. I've had quite a few hits," said Lionel, enthusiastically.

"Really?" replied Danny, incredulously.

"You've heard of *Living Doll*?"

"Yes, by Cliff Richard."

"That's one of mine and I've got the musical, 'Oliver!' showing in the West End."

"That's great man," enthused Danny, who had never heard of 'Oliver'.

Before the conversation could continue, Reg returned and seeing Lionel, walked briskly to the table, his face showing signs of anger.

"Leave him alone," said Reg, very quietly.

"I don't know what you mean?"

"You know exactly what I mean," replied Reg, with a piercing look. Lionel stood up and walked away. "Have you finished your apple pie?" asked Reg, abruptly.

“Yes,” replied Danny, astonished by Reg’s abnormal behaviour.

“Let’s go.”

“He promised to write me a song,” explained Danny, crestfallen to lose such a good contact.

“You don’t want anything to do with that kind of man.”

“What kind?” asked Danny, innocent of Reg’s insinuation. “He seemed very nice to me.”

“He would be.”

“I’m sure he was genuine. He wrote *Living Doll* for Cliff Richard.”

“Too bad. It’d be better if you had a go at writing your own songs.”

Getting nowhere with his male singers, Reg decided to try a different route and obtain a recording contract for Tanya. He arranged an audition at Pye Records with an A&R manager who was interested in meeting her. First, he took her to have her hair styled and then to Max Factor to be professionally made-up.

Tanya looked glamorous and the A&R Manager, handsome and charming, with dark hair, was pleased to meet her. His role was to find singers with potential and match them with suitable songs and songwriters. They talked together for a while, making polite conversation but then he asked her to sit and wait in the studio while he talked business with Reg.

The two men moved to the other side of the room and while they were talking, often glanced at Tanya. This made her feel very uncomfortable and the longer they talked, the more incensed she became. Tanya did not like being excluded. It was her future they were discussing. Eventually, Reg came over and sat down beside her.

“It’s been agreed. This is your big opportunity,” smiled Reg, encouragingly, as he tried to show confidence. “He will make records for you but first, he would like you to join him for a two-week holiday on the Norfolk Broads. He has his own boat there.”

For a moment, Tanya said nothing. She sat in shocked silence while she comprehended the words and their meaning.

“He’s a married man and what would we do for two weeks?”

“He would expect things, of course,” admitted Reg, shamefacedly. “But when you get back you would have a recording contract and make records.”

“No way.”

“This is your big chance to become a star. It’s like this Tanya. You can give yourself to some boy for nothing. Or you can have a holiday with someone who will make records. This may be your one opportunity. It’s up to you.”

“I’m not doing it,” replied Tanya, stubbornly.

The journey back to Clifton Hall was in almost total silence. Tanya could see Reg was very angry. Not only was he angry, he was exasperated. She had thrown away her golden opportunity and at the same time, wrecked his chances of obtaining recording contracts for the boys with a leading record company. Reg blamed himself for not foreseeing the price she would have to pay and felt remorse for asking her to do something he would not have asked his own daughters to do. When they reached Clifton Hall, Reg found Dorothy in the lounge reading a House and Gardens magazine.

"How did it go?" enquired Dorothy.

"Not well," answered Reg, quietly, as he explained what had happened.

"It's a rotten, sordid business," said Dorothy, sympathetically.

"I haven't given up yet," replied Reg, without much optimism. "Pye has a new offshoot company, Piccadilly Records, and they're looking for people. Maybe they'll listen to our boys without expecting anything extra. First, we must find good songs.

It was unusual for singers to write their own songs but Reg persisted in encouraging his boys to try, explaining how composers earn more in royalties than singers. Even if their song did not make the A-side, it would earn an equal amount on the B-side. Buddy, Barry, Roger and Danny were all trying to compose their own songs, but it was Danny who succeeded first. In high spirits, Reg almost skipped into the kitchen to tell Dorothy. She turned to smile at him as he spun her round and began to sing.

"I love you, h-h-honest I do. Oh how I need you. H-h-honest I do."

"Your poached egg is nearly ready."

"I love you, h-h-honest I do. Oh how I need you, h-h-honest I do." Reg stopped singing and asked, "What do you think?"

"Think of what?" asked Dorothy, puzzled.

"The song, *Honest I Do*. Danny has written a song. We're working on it now in the rehearsal room. Come and listen."

Having words and melody was just the start. *Honest I Do* needed an arrangement with guitars, piano, harmonica, percussion and backing singers. Reg, with his musical training, helped to put it all together and asked Johnny Neal and the Starliners, a good Birmingham group, to do the backing tracks. *Sad But True,* by Les Vandyke, was agreed as the B-side.

The Starliners made frequent visits to Clifton Hall, rehearsing hour after hour as the music arrangement developed. Reg recorded the songs onto acetate discs in the rehearsal room so they could hear them played back and when he was satisfied, booked a London recording studio. Everyone was excited as they had never been in a proper recording studio before. When the big day arrived, they were so well-rehearsed, the recordings were completed early and with the remaining studio time, Reg offered to let Johnny Neal and the Starliners record several of their own numbers.

Piccadilly Records liked the recordings and agreed to give Danny a contract with 'no strings' attached. Reg asked his new recruit, Tony Clarke, to do the artwork for the record sleeve and he created a simple design, with a photograph of Danny looking from a window at a girl by a lamppost, in a moonlit street.

Buddy Britten was an integral part of a stage show but Dorothy, who was now his manager, wanted to give him more experience and book him out to other venues. To do this, he needed to have his own backing group and Barney Peacock and Pete Mist were placed with him to form a trio.

Buddy was next to write a song, *The Beat of My Heart,* so Dorothy followed in her husband's footsteps and arranged a London recording studio to do a professional demo disc. For the second song, they chose a number composed by Jim Dale, *Don't Spread it Around.*

Dorothy and Reg were very competitive and when Dorothy managed to get Decca, one of the top four recording companies in the UK to agree to release the record, she and Buddy were thrilled, even though Decca selected *Don't Spread It Around* as the A-side. The release date was planned for February, 1962, the same as Danny's first record, *Honest I Do*.

BUDDY BRITTEN AND THE REGENTS

Pete Mist, Buddy Britten, Barney Peacock (Card from Barney Peacock)

Top: Clifton Hall: having fun, Dorothy Calvert and Buddy Britten (RC)
Bottom: On the road, stopping for afternoon tea (RC)

9. FIREWORKS AND BIRDS

Clifton Hall: Loading the vehicles for the dances

The cool winds of autumn brought a change in the garden as trees turned from green to gold and then to auburn. Dorothy harvested the fruits and vegetables she had grown with great satisfaction. The chickens, ducks and turkeys were getting fat but when Susan entered the hayloft one morning, she discovered two more dead turkeys on the floor. Bursting into tears, she ran to the house to tell her mother.

"It must be the explosions," said Dorothy.

"Why do they die in pairs? When I go up to feed them they look at me with their little black beady eyes as if they hate me. They give me the creeps. Can you ask Old Jack to take the dead birds out? I don't want to touch them."

"They're just birds," said Dorothy, sympathetically. "I keep telling your father to grow-up and stop playing with fireworks. It's too dangerous but he won't listen to me and the boys are just as bad. They're all making tubes and things to fire rockets."

“Dad says he’s trying to make the biggest bang ever. He showed me the jars in the storeroom and how he puts the powders in the tubes.”

Dorothy shrugged her shoulders. She had resigned herself to the fact that there was nothing she could do or say to make her husband, or the boys, be sensible about fireworks.

The bedraggled vegetable plot had been partially taken over by the erection of a large bonfire in preparation of 5th November. The boys had divided to form two teams and were preparing, with great excitement, for the firework battle and plotting strategy. Reg’s team were to be in the spinney and Glen’s team behind the billiards room.

On the night, all contenders were dressed in multiple layers of clothing, including several hats or balaclavas. Reg had Dorothy wrap his body with layers of newspapers for extra protection. At eleven, the Guy Fawkes Susan and Candy had made was hoisted to the top of the pile and the bonfire lit.

The females of the house stayed indoors and peered through the hall and lounge windows to watch the spectacle outside. In the dark of the night it was difficult to make out what was happening as shadowy figures darted about, lit for a brief moment by flashes from exploding bangers, or stream of sparkling stars from rockets whooshing through the air.

Yells of pain, shouts and laughter rang out as the boys hit their targets or made near misses. The person they aimed at most, was of course, Reg. He jumped out of the way, hid behind trees and tried to avoid being hit. Then, the inevitable happened. A rocket smacked him straight on the forehead and the next second he collapsed in a heap and lay on the ground.

“Halt. Ceasefire. Reg is hit,” shouted one of the boys. They all ran to the spinney to see Reg sprawled out under a tree, unconscious. With some concern, they checked him and saw he was breathing. For a moment they hesitated, discussing what action to take next. As they stood over his body, Reg began to regain consciousness. With relief, the boys let out a whooping cry and circling him, began to do a war dance like Red Indians, hooting and howling as they ran round and round.

Sitting up slowly and rubbing his forehead, Reg saw the funny side of his situation and began to chuckle. The battle resumed. A rocket fired at Glen just missed him and landed in the large box of fireworks stored behind the billiards room. Everyone ran for their lives when they saw the glow of sizzling touchpapers all coming alive. With one enormous whoosh, the whole box of fireworks simultaneously ignited. Rockets flew in all directions, bangers exploded, Jumping Jacks cracked and jumped over the ground. For the finale of the display, the Catherine Wheels twirled, sparkled, whizzed and whirred. Everyone stood at a safe distance, laughing at the spectacle. It was a terrific display and when it ended, Reg shared his remaining fireworks out but the battle was soon over. Reg’s team were triumphant and announced themselves the winners.

The bonfire, blazing brightly became the next focus of the evening as potatoes wrapped in tinfoil were poked into the ashes and sausages, stuck on long sticks, were held up towards the burning embers. It had been a fantastic night.

The two remaining turkeys survived Bonfire Night and in December, were transferred to live in the scullery kitchen so they would not die of cold. Diligently, Susan fed and cared for them along with her ducks, chickens, rabbits and cat. Her goat had been sold after he had annoyed Dorothy by eating the bark off the Victoria Plum tree. Shortly before Christmas, Reg decided to make a game of 'despatching the turkeys. He cut straws into varying lengths. Each of the boys had to pull one straw out from his tightly clenched fist. Laughing and joking, they were relieved when they compared lengths to see that Buddy had picked the shortest straw.

The 'turkey despatch' game was arranged a few days before Christmas. At midnight, after the dances, the boys congregated in the walled courtyard by the kitchen entrance and the large double gates were closed to make an enclosed area. The night was cold and frosty and everyone was shivering as Reg handed Buddy a scythe and went to fetch a turkey. Buddy waited nervously. He had never killed anything before.

Reg emerged, holding the bird tightly by the legs and neck before letting it free. The turkey flapped its large white wings and weighed up its options of escape. There was a small gap under the gates and it proceeded to charge at the space. Buddy followed, scythe held high, ready to make the chop. The bird soon realised it was too big to squeeze through the gap and began to run around the courtyard, squawking and flapping its wings madly as it tried to take off. Unable to fly, it ran between the legs of the shivering boys.

"Come on Buddy, off with its head," heckled the boys, who were really not enjoying the spectacle.

Eventually, Buddy managed to catch the exhausted turkey and he pinned it to the ground with his knees. Holding the scythe aloft and with both hands, he brought the blade down, chopping off its head.

Having done the deed, Buddy stood up, tall and erect but definitely not triumphant. His face was as white as the turkey's feathers and he eyed his victim with revulsion. The bird lay on the ground, blood spurting from its severed neck, turning the white feathers red. As Buddy stared, the headless creature picked itself up and began running round and round the yard in a final ghoulish burst of life. Buddy freaked in terror, let out a scream and began to do a St Vitus dance. A moment later, the headless bird fell to the ground, dead.

Reg offered to let anyone else kill the second bird but the horrific game was over and all bystanders, shivering with cold, declined. Reg despatched the second turkey more humanely. In the morning, Susan, who was unaware of their demise, went into the scullery to feed them and seeing the two headless birds hanging upside down by their feet, ran out of the room in shock.

Reg and Dorothy made plans for the festive season. For the first time, they would have Christmas together and invited their relations to stay with them so they could have a big family gathering. All the boys were to return to their own homes with only Roger requesting to stay on at Clifton Hall. Dorothy refused. She made a point of encouraging the boys to return to their own family whenever they had a few days off, especially at Christmas. This year, everyone had three days holiday as Christmas Eve fell on a Sunday and there were no more dances until Wednesday.

Reg arrived early on Saturday night at Nuneaton Co-op Hall and encouraged everyone to help blow up several hundred balloons. They were then stowed in a net and hung from the ceiling. As soon as the entrance doors were opened, the crowds poured in. The cashier, a silver-haired lady called Mrs Thomas, sat in the kiosk and took the money, while the doorman, Jim, checked the tickets as happy teenagers made their way up the winding stairway into the dancehall.

The evening's competition prize was to be one of Susan's ducks. She had kept her favourite one which was smaller than the others, and named him Quacker Barney. Reg paid her £1 each for the other five ducks. One of the ducks was in a cardboard box, quacking by the side of the stage. Buddy Britten and the Regents were the stars of the show and when the drummer, Barney Peacock, realised the duck was to be given away, he pleaded with Reg to let him buy it.

"I can't let you have it Barney. What else am I going to give as a prize?"

"You can't give the duck away. Someone might kill it and eat it for Christmas dinner," replied Barney, looking forlorn.

"I'll tell you what," said Reg, smiling mischievously. "I've an idea. When I start the competition, you have to enter it."

"Me, in a competition?" What will I have to do?" queried Barney, suspiciously. He had heard about Reg and his mad games.

On the dancefloor, girls danced in clusters around their handbags. Mistletoe was hanging above doorways and streamers and hats were given out. Almost everyone was dancing the 'Twist', a new dance which entailed gyrating the hips and twisting to the music. When the bar closed, intoxicated young men started to arrive on the dance floor, breaking the circle of girls in a quest to find one they could take home at the end of the night. Just after 10.30 p.m., Reg stepped onto the stage with his trousers rolled up and wearing tartan slippers.

"Are you having a good time?"

The crowd cheered and whistled in response.

"I can't hear you. Are you having a good time?"

The crowd cheered louder.

"Then let's hear it for Mother Brown," chuckled Reg, as he started to sing with the group.

"Knees up Mother Brown! Knees up Mother Brown! Under the table you must go, Ee-aye, E-aye-oh! If I catch you bending, I'll saw your legs right off. Knees up! Knees up! Don't get the breeze up. Knees up Mother Brown. ..... Oh my! What a rotten song! What a rotten song. What a rotten song! Oh my! What a rotten song. What a rotten singer too! ...."

"It's party time girls and boys. I want ten young men to volunteer for this competition."

Within a moment, ten boys had scrambled up, onto the stage and Reg arranged each of them to stand by a chair.

"Take your seats, gentlemen. Are you sitting comfortably?" laughed Reg. "Good. Now take off your shoes and socks and hold your feet out. Oh my, what a pong." Reg, held his nose and began speaking in a funny voice. "Next, I need a young lady to volunteer as my assistant."

Reg smiled at a girl standing by the stage and leaning down, gave her his hand to help her up. Whispering instructions, he handed her a large white turkey feather.

"Let's welcome our first contestant. And your name is?" asked Reg. Before the young man could reply, the girl began tickling his feet with the feather. "Do you have ticklish feet?" enquired Reg. The contender, trying to remain poker faced, could hardly stay seated on the chair and wriggled as he burst out giggling and jiggling about, pleading for mercy.

The game continued, with all the contestant's feet being tickled. Reg thanked the girl and helped her down from the stage. The next part of the game was to find the person with the smelliest feet. Reg went along the line of feet, sniffing and making various rude remarks about the 'pong'. The winner of the contest, without a doubt with the worst set of smelly feet was Barney. Reg fetched the large brown cardboard box from the side of the stage and asked, "Do you want to take the box or would you like a £5 note?"

"I'll take the box," replied Barney, grinning.

"Are you sure you want the box? It might be empty."

Reg put the microphone up to the box and from within came the sound of quacking. "Should he take the box or the money?"

"Open the box!" shouted the audience.

"They say you should open the box," laughed Reg, handing it to Barney who made a pretence of cautiously lifting the lid and looking surprised as he carefully lifted out the duck. The crowd cheered and laughed as Barney cradled the quacking duck in his arms.

"We all know what you'll be eating for Christmas dinner," beamed Reg, as Barney left the stage, proudly holding his prize.

After the show, Barney travelled home with his duck and woke his parents to give them their surprise Christmas gift. They were delighted and Duck lived a long life as a pet in their garden.

Dorothy and Reg were both excited as they prepared everything for the arrival of their families which included Dorothy's mother, stepsister Edith, brother John, his wife Mary and four children, and Reg's Dad who was bringing his border collie. Reg managed to stoke up the big old coke central heating boiler. Every room in Clifton Hall was warm but to keep the boiler going, Reg had to 'feed' it every few hours. Dorothy erected a green imitation Christmas tree in the lounge and underneath, piled numerous small gifts she had lovingly wrapped in brightly coloured festive paper.

Christmas morning, the weather was cold with a leaden grey sky and in the bare oak tree, sat the crow. All the family congregated in the lounge, eating chocolates and sweets while they opened their presents. It was a joyful occasion and the house echoed with the laughter of children instead of the usual guitars. The rehearsal room was returned to a dining room and tables were laid with cloths, candles, Christmas crackers and wine glasses. Dorothy cooked dinner on the Aga and complained when the Yorkshire puddings came out flat. Everyone complimented Susan on her turkeys and how delicious the meat was but she could not bring herself to eat them.

When the family departed after Christmas, Reg stopped stoking the boiler. It was one chore too far! The boys returned and the house became alive once more with a cacophony of sounds, guitars and singing. Outside, the fields and gardens took on a magical appearance with the first fall of snow. Milder westerly winds blew in for the New Year and the melting snow became a grey slush. The boys gingerly loaded the vans for the New Year's Eve dances, trying to avoid standing in the puddles. Fashionable, thin-soled pointed toe shoes were not made for winter weather and no one thought to wear wellies or buy sensible shoes.

1962 MUSIC TRENDS

From the USA, Elvis had a string of hits including: 'Can't Help Falling in Love', 'Good Luck Charm', 'Return to Sender', 'Rock A Hula Baby' and 'She's Not You'. **Ray Charles**: 'I Can't Stop Loving You' and 'You Don't Know Me'. **Brian Hyland:** 'Sealed With a Kiss'. **Marty Robbins:** 'Devil Woman'. **Neil Sedaka:** 'Breaking Up Is Hard To Do'. **Everly Brothers:** 'Cryin' in the Rain'. **Nat King Cole:** 'Ramblin' Rose'.
Pat Boone: 'Speedy Gonzales'. **Jimmy Rogers:** 'English Country Garden'.
Cliff Richard continued to be the British answer to Elvis and had hits with 'The Young Ones', 'Do You Want to Dance?' 'I'm Looking out the Window', 'The Next Time' and 'It'll Be Me'. **Adam Faith:** 'As You Like It' and 'Don't That Beat All'.
Miki and Griff: 'A Little Bitty Tear'. **Frank Ifield:** 'I Remember You' and 'Lovesick Blues'. **Mike Sarne and Wendy Richard:** 'Come Outside'. **Bernard Cribbins:** 'Hole in the Ground'. From Australia, **Rolf Harris** with 'Sun Arise'.
Female singers were few. **Helen Shapiro** with 'Tell Me What He Said?' and 'Little Miss Lonely'. **Brenda Lee:** 'Speak To Me Pretty' and 'Rockin' around the Christmas Tree'. **Carol King:** 'It Might As Well Rain Until September'. **The Vernons:** 'You Know What I Mean'. **Susan Maughan:** 'Bobby's Girl'. **Ketty Lester:** 'Love Letters'.
The 'Twist', a new dance anyone could join in with became popular.
Chubby Checker: 'Let's Twist Again' and 'The Twist'. **Petula Clark:** 'Ya Twist'.
Sam Cooke: 'Twistin' the Night Away'. **Chris Montez:** 'Let's Dance'.
Little Eva with another new dance: 'The Locomotion'.
Instrumental recordings included the **Tornadoes** with 'Telstar'. The bass player, **Heinz Burt**, had previously worked for Reg and asked permission to record with Joe Meek. Telstar became a massive hit both sides of the Atlantic. **The Shadows** with 'Wonderful Land'. **Duane Eddy:** 'Dance with the Guitar Man'. **B. Bumble & the Stingers:** 'Nut Rocker'. **Kenny Ball and His Jazz Men:** 'Green Leaves of Summer' and 'Midnight in Moscow'. **Acker Bilk** with 'Stranger on the Shore', another great success both sides of the Atlantic.
Stars booked to appear at the dances included: Joe Brown with 'A Picture of You'. **Karl Denver** with 'Never Goodbye', and 'Wimoweh'. **Eden Kane:** 'Forget Me Not', and 'I Don't Know Why?' **Mark Wynter:** 'Venus in Blue Jeans'. **Billy Fury** with 'Once Upon a Dream', 'I'd Never Find Another You' and 'Last Night Was Made for Love'. Other 'stars' to visit Clifton Hall and play at the dances included **Tommy Bruce, Johnny Kidd, Gene Vincent, Screaming Lord Sutch and the Beatles.**

Top: Danny Storm, Buddy Britten and Pete Mist, all very nervous about riding a horse for the Pathe News film
Bottom: Rehearsal in the lounge in preparation for filming day: Reg Calvert holding *Honest I Do* sheet music, Danny Storm, Roger James, Tony Clarke, Barney Peacock (Behind settee watching rehearsal: Susan and Tanya)

10. THE BIG FREEZE

Clifton Hall in the snow (RC)

The New Year was a time of celebration, a time to look forward and Dorothy revealed to Reg that she was pregnant. Reg was delighted and hoped that this time they would have a baby boy.

With 21 dances on the go, Reg and Dorothy were working very hard and earning a considerable income. Dorothy paid extra off the mortgage and planned to buy new cars and an oil central heating boiler. She also put money aside in her private savings account for a 'rainy day', which she knew would surely come.

Few houses in England had central heating and Clifton Hall, being larger than most homes, seemed exceptionally cold. From hardy Yorkshire stock, Dorothy and Reg were used to freezing northern winters and did not complain. Dorothy disliked the grime and soot from coal fires so never ordered coal. In the lounge, she had the lovely fireplace boarded up and hidden by a sheet of fashionable, grey Formica and a coal-effect electric fire was placed on the hearth.

Electricity was expensive and Reg installed electric fires into the boys' bedrooms with a one shilling slot meter. If the boys wanted the luxury of warmth, they had to pay for it! All the bedrooms had fireplaces but no one thought to buy themselves any coal to keep warm. The two bedrooms above the kitchens were first choice with the boys as they were a degree or two warmer than the other bedrooms. The new 'Strollers', Larry and Mike, were given the bedroom above the scullery and as the weather froze, a gale blew through a cracked window pane.

There was friendly rivalry between Reg and Dorothy as to which of them would make their protégé a star first. Dorothy spent hours posting out editorials to various newspapers and Reg succeeded in obtaining television appearances for Danny on Scottish, Tyne Tees and Yorkshire television, and began to rehearse Danny on how to perform in front of a television camera.

"The Television producers have all said that they consider the speaking part of the song too sexy to broadcast, so you have to cut it out," explained Reg. "And don't forget, when they film you, look into the eye of the camera as if it were a beautiful woman. All the girls will be watching as you make eyes at them through the lens."

At the end of January, Dorothy offered to drive Danny to the television studios and when it was time for them to leave, Reg came out carrying a spade and old carpet he had found in the barns.

"I'll put these in the boot, just in case you get stuck. It looks like snow again."

"Thanks," said Dorothy, with some irony in her voice as she looked at the gunmetal grey sky.

Reg kissed her and waited to wave her off while she removed her fur-lined boots and put on her slippers to drive in.

Travelling north was like going to the arctic, with hedge-high snowdrifts on both sides of the road. Dorothy drove slowly and they arrived safely, and on time. The filming went well and on their return journey, while they were in Yorkshire, Dorothy took the opportunity to visit her mother and other relatives.

Tom Calvert, not expecting visitors, was unlike his previous self. He was cheerful enough, with his black and white collie for company but he looked like a tramp, unshaven and unwashed. With no home-help, the cottage was dirty. To save him climbing the stairs, he kept a bucket in the scullery kitchen to use as his toilet. Dorothy and Danny were both shocked. On her return to Clifton Hall, Dorothy nagged Reg to do something about it.

"Dad's gone right downhill since your Mam died."

"He seemed fine when he stayed at Christmas. I'll speak to Ada."

"Ada won't do anything," retorted Dorothy. "You'll need to organise it. He's the one who brought you up. The house is disgusting. It needs stripping out, redecorating and cleaning. You can't let him continue to live like that."

Reluctantly, Reg agreed and when he had a few days free, he made the journey to Yorkshire to see his Dad and decorate the house. He also called in to see one of his old friends, Arthur Addy. He and Arthur had known each other since they were ten-years old and they talked and laughed about their childhood antics, how they were always up to mischief and the time they secretly experimented with radio links between their houses and upset the radio reception in the area.

Dorothy continued to work as normal during her pregnancy and ran the dance at Banbury Winter Gardens on Saturday nights. There were often brawls between warring youths and the Swallow Gang were easily identified as each member had a swallow tattooed on the back of his hand. It was a large square shaped hall and the gap between the stage and the side was where girls went to sort out their differences. The catfights were often vicious as girls tore into each other, stripping off clothes, even down to bras and pants. Fearlessly, Dorothy would separate troublemakers and no boy would think to hit a woman but with the girls, she had to be careful.

Most of the aggression was between the gangs but one night the Swallow gang turned on Danny Storm and the Strollers. Danny had sung his new record, *Honest I Do*, whilst making eyes at the screaming girls in the audience. At the end of the evening as they packed up and carried their equipment through the hall, a mob attacked without warning. The whole floor seemed to be writhing as they fought, hitting, punching and kicking. Dorothy ran over and screamed at them, pushing her way in to stop the fight. Glen, completely unaware, was sitting with his back to the trouble as he chatted up some girls next to the stage.

The fight was over as quickly as it had begun and the aggressors dispersed, running out of the hall. Danny and the group had received a good beating, receiving black eyes and punched in teeth. The police arrived too late to catch the culprits, so Dorothy and the boys had to spend most of the night in the police station making statements and giving descriptions.

When they arrived home in the early hours, Reg put his arms around Dorothy and gave her a hug.

"We'll have to get more bouncers. I'll find some ex-boxers and wrestlers. We can't have our boys being attacked again," said Reg, concerned. He could sort out troublemakers when he was at the dances but realised it was too much for Dorothy.

The fame of Clifton Hall had travelled far and out of the blue, in February, 1962 Pathé News requested permission to make a short documentary to be shown in cinemas across the country. Reg was elated. It was perfect timing to fit in with the release of *Honest I Do*.

Life was now more hectic than it had ever been and the excitement in the house was almost tangible, with everyone preparing for the Pathé film crew to arrive. Clifton Hall was to be portrayed as a stately house with country pursuits for boys who were training to become Rock 'n' Roll singers. The weather was grey and chilly but it did not dampen spirits and the outdoor shots were filmed in the morning.

Candy's pony and the White's horses were prepared and Danny and Buddy, who had not ridden before, nervously mounted their steeds and slowly rode around the gardens of the house. Susan's hens, pecking in the undergrowth near the barns, were included in a shot with the boys throwing bread to them. Archery was another country pursuit that the boys were supposed to take part in and Danny was filmed with a bow and arrow.

The final scene included everyone in the lounge with Danny Storm singing *Honest I Do*. Johnny Neal and Tanya Day were shown twisting to the music while Reg made a recording on an acetate disc. The filming was going well, until it was brought to a sudden halt by two of the Starliners who shouted out they had forgotten to bring their mouth organs. Reg hurriedly improvised. He found two nail brushes and covered them with black paper. The filming resumed, this time with the Starliners 'playing' nail brushes instead of mouth organs!

To further promote Danny's record, Reg asked everyone to write postcards with fictitious names to radio request programmes on the BBC and Radio Luxemburg. These were then posted from various towns and villages as the boys toured the dancehalls. When *Honest I Do* reached the bottom of the charts, everyone was thrilled. This was a real achievement for a first record. More surprising, was that *Honest I Do* became one of the most requested songs of all time on Sunday lunchtime's 'Two Way Family Favourites'. This had nothing to do with fictitious requests as you had to be part of the Armed Forces to get a record played.

A new oil-fired central heating boiler was installed and everyone enjoyed the luxury of a warm house until the boiler had 'drunk' a tankful of oil in only two weeks. Clifton Hall proved too costly to heat and the house returned to being very cold as the weather continued to freeze.

To keep warm, the boys wore their coats and hats all day and even to bed. Mike Hopcraft, fed up with feeding the meter in the bedroom with one shilling pieces, drilled through the ceiling to the scullery below and plugged in his own electric fire. Going on a weekend tour with Danny, he forgot to switch it off. On his return Reg was waiting for him. Very quietly, Mike was reprimanded for his stupidity and asked to leave, immediately! Larry left shortly afterwards and the two boys returned to Oxford. Their places in the Strollers were filled by ex-Lawmen, John Wileman on bass guitar and Andy Brown on drums.

Dave Jay had become Reg's right-hand man, helping to run dances and assisting with any other jobs. He had recently passed his driving test and Dorothy loaned him her small Austin A35 van to drive to the Newbury Corn Exchange on Wednesday nights to run a 'disco'. Returning one night, he hit a pocket of thick fog and being unable to see the road ahead, stamped on the brakes, lost orientation and ended up the wrong way around and upside down. The heavy equipment, loudspeakers and records, tumbled and bounced around in the back of the van, gradually settling as it juddered to a halt. Dave crawled out and passing motorists helped to lift the van up and point it in the correct direction and then took him to a telephone box.

"Is the van okay?" asked Reg.

"It's a bit dented and the windscreen has fallen out."

"Can you drive it?"

"I suppose so."

"Well get in and drive it back," instructed Reg, unsympathetically.

In shock, Dave drove very slowly. A bitterly cold wind tore through the open windscreen and his face felt as though it was being cut by icy knives. He screwed up his eyes, watching every cat's eye glow in the headlights. After a while a vehicle flashed from behind. Reg had sent a rescue party! When Dave arrived back, he heard Dorothy say in a loud voice as she stood by the back door. "That's the last time we allow *him* to drive one of our vehicles."

Dave understood that Dorothy held a grudge against him as he had helped to conceal Reg's affair with Carol. The little van had been her pride and joy and she did not soften her resolve. Dave had been loyal to Reg and now he felt betrayed and undervalued, doing odd jobs and rarely working with the boys. After a few weeks, he gave notice and returned to Romsey.

Dorothy had grown in confidence as a manager and tackled the problem of promoting Buddy as best she could but she did not have Reg's flair or charisma. Small editorial features appeared in many newspapers but had little impact. In March, 1961 she managed to get him on ITV's *Thank Your Lucky Stars,* but even with this, the record did not make the charts or sell the two thousand copies required for Decca to agree to a second recording. It was disappointing but on the positive side, Buddy Britten was becoming known and would go on to earn a good income as a 'recording star'.

Danny Storm, Glen Dale and the Strollers were booked to tour with Jerry Lee Lewis, the Allisons, the Bachelors. Jerry Lee Lewis had been top of the charts with *Great Balls of Fire* and other songs but had caused a scandal by marrying Myra, his thirteen-year-old cousin. He was a brilliant performer, much admired by other musicians and as Glen stood in the wings to watch him, Jerry asked if he could look after Myra and catch his jacket each evening, when he threw it off stage.

Reg, who was a big fan, took his family to see the show and afterwards invited Jerry and his manager back to for supper. Jerry accepted the invitation. Reg was thrilled and very proud that one of the most famous performers in the world had come to visit Clifton Hall.

When Dorothy reached the three-month stage in her pregnancy she told their daughters the good news. The two girls were surprised and not knowing what to say, accepted it with less excitement than if their parents had told them they were about to have a new kitten or a puppy. Dorothy had lost weight and looked hollow-eyed but she was happy and Reg was thrilled. He wanted a son and Dorothy knew intuitively, she was carrying a boy.

Candy and Susan Calvert with Candy's pony, Shamie (RC)

11. LESSONS IN LOVE

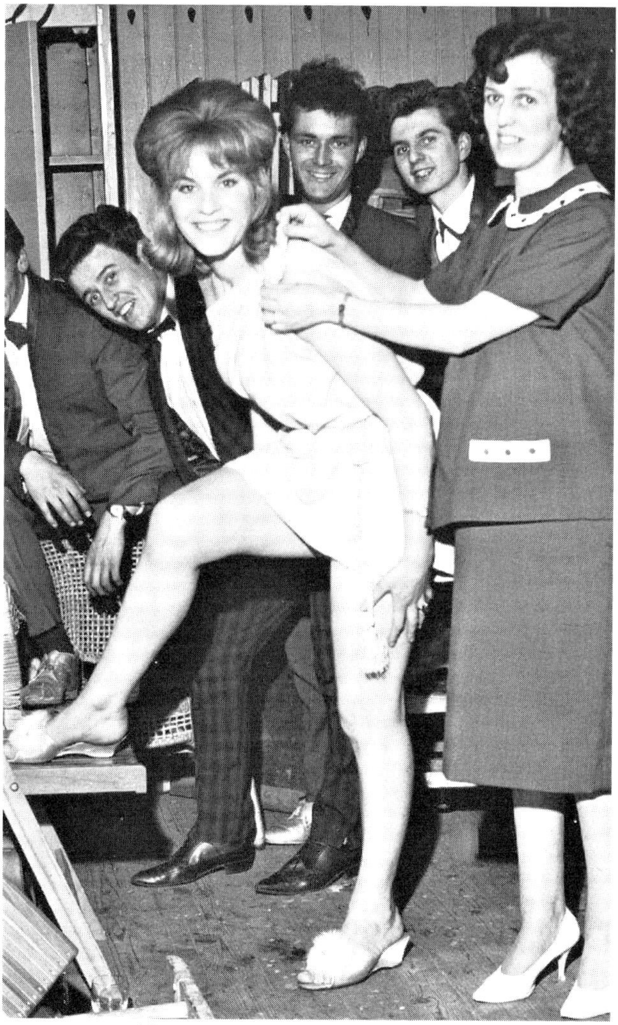

Tanya Day, 'dressed' in a towel at the Trocadero, Derby
(Dorothy, showing her pregnancy) Behind Dowland brothers and Alpines

Reg's love of big old limousine cars had not diminished and he paid a deposit on a second-hand Jaguar and arranged to have it delivered to Clifton Hall. Dorothy was not pleased when he presented her the bill.

"But it's beautiful, with real leather seats."

"It's no good Reg. Tell the garage you've changed your mind."

"I've always wanted a Jag."

"It's time we had new cars, not big old ones," insisted Dorothy.

"I don't like new cars," replied Reg, stubbornly.

"I've seen a car you may like. The new Ford Zephyr. They're the replacement for the Consul, big and comfortable. Why don't you come and look?"

Reluctantly Reg relented and Dorothy had her way. The Jaguar was cancelled and they ordered a Zephyr 6 for her and a Zephyr 4 for him, in a matching lime-green body colour.

With the loss of Dave Jay, Reg needed more help. Susan, now aged thirteen and a half, was a sensible girl, trusted by her parents to be cashier at Rugby Benn Hall on Wednesday nights. When Reg asked if she'd like to learn how to run dances, Susan was delighted. The following weeks, he took his daughter to the Nuneaton Co-op Hall and showed her how to set up the sound system, organise and introduce the groups and all the while, observe the crowd for their reactions. It was the best dancehall on his circuit and he booked it for both Friday and Saturday nights. To keep numbers up, he often featured famous stars and ran an early show for pre-teenagers on Fridays where he was known as 'Uncle Reg'.

The journey from Clifton to Nuneaton along windy lanes took about forty minutes, which gave father and daughter quality time together without interruption from everyday distractions in the house. Reg took the opportunity to talk to his daughter about politics, religion, the universe, the supernatural, love and marriage. He wanted to prepare his daughter for life, forewarning her of some of the difficulties she may have to face being a girl in a man's world.

The car journeys each week, often involved a different topic with heated discussions. They laughed and chatted and Reg set his daughter mental arithmetic games to help with her school work. 'Sex' was a word never spoken, but implied. He wanted Susan to be prepared and not taken in by the boys and men who would surely want her.

"All boys have one thing on their mind. They'll try to get you to go to bed with them. Some boys will say they love you and insist that if you love them you should let them have their way. That sort of boy is only thinking of himself. If a boy really loves you, he'll respect your wishes. Other boys will get engaged and buy the girl a ring. If it's a long engagement, you'll know he's getting what he wants!"

"I prefer older boys, young boys seem very silly," confessed Susan.

"Girls grow up much faster than boys," agreed Reg. "But if you go out with older boys you'll have to be much more careful. They'll know how to treat you and spoil you but they'll be difficult to control and much more demanding. Younger boys are easier to handle as they are less experienced."

Susan said nothing in reply as her father continued.

"The trouble is, if you marry a boy who's too young and inexperienced, by the time he's 30, he'll think he's missed out. A boy needs to sow his wild oats while he's young or he'll do it later, after he's married. And have you noticed how single girls wear pretty clothes and make themselves look good but most married women look dowdy. Have you ever thought why?"

"Not thought about it," replied Susan. "I suppose single girls have more money to spend on clothes.

"There is that," agreed Reg. "But psychologically, a husband does not want his wife to be attractive to other men. He will tell her that he prefers her without make-up. The trouble is, he'll see lots of pretty girls. A wife needs to keep herself more attractive after she's married. Do her hair, wear make-up and pretty clothes, just as she did when she was single. It's important to become her husband's mistress, so he looks forward to coming home. Most men are fickle. If temptation's put in their way, it's in their nature to stray."

Drinking too much alcohol and getting drunk was something Reg didn't approve of. His employees were not allowed to drink while they were working and no alcohol was permitted at Clifton Hall. When he was walking around the dancefloor, doing a sound check, Reg discreetly pointed to a girl who had too much to drink and was making a fool of herself.

"Tomorrow, she won't remember anything. There's many a girl who gets pregnant, and afterwards, doesn't know who the father is. If a boy tries to get you drunk, he's not the sort you want to go out with."

Susan nodded in understanding as she watched the giggling girl with legs like wobbly jelly, and a boy each side, holding her up. There was no way she ever wanted to be like that.

Reg knew his daughter had already had several boyfriends, young boys from the village who walked up to see her and he and Dorothy had set strict guidelines to try and keep her safe.

"Never tempt providence by being on your own in a house with a boy," explained Reg. "It's too easy to be tempted, get carried away and find it difficult to stop. If you don't know the boy or you're unsure, there's safety in numbers, stay in a crowd or go out with another couple, and don't get separated."

Travelling in the car, the conversations continued with Reg's observations on love and marriage. Like all parents, Reg wanted his daughter to marry well.

"It'd be better to fall in love with someone who has money than someone who is poor."

"I don't think I want to get married," replied Susan. "But if I do, I'll marry the man I fall in love with."

"If you've no money and your love dies, life will be miserable and a struggle. If you've money, at least you can be miserable in comfort."

"I'll marry the man I fall in love with," insisted Susan.

"The main problem with marriage is having no money and getting pregnant too soon. It's natural for a girl to want a baby. Some people think having a baby will make a bad marriage better. It won't. It will only make it worse."

Another much discussed topic was the mystery of life.

"For all we know the Earth could be a miniscule atom in a cluster of atoms making up a table leg in a much larger world and universe. How do we know how small or large we are?" asked Reg.

"Do you think the world was formed over millions of years?"

"Millions and millions."

"We had a scripture lesson about the first chapter of the Old Testament. In break time, all the girls in my class discussed it and agreed the world couldn't be made in six days. We had to write an essay and I couldn't believe it when I found out I was the only girl who said it would have taken millions of years and not six days."

"Really," laughed Reg.

"Mrs Biggs made me stay in after school and see the headmistress. She told me the bible version was true. I don't understand why my friends didn't write down what they really thought?"

"Sheep and shepherds. The world is made up of sheep and shepherds," explained Reg. "Most people follow their leader without thinking. They don't want to stand-up or stand-out. If their leader says 'baa,' then they say 'baa'. It's up to you to decide whether you want to be a sheep or a shepherd."

Life itself was a mystery and Reg often talked about it and his lack of understanding.

"The only thing in life we know for sure is we're going to die. No one knows how long they will live. You know you are here now, in this second of time but you don't know what will happen in the next moment or the next day."

"That's morbid," replied Susan.

Reg was an optimist and he loved life but the fear of going blind haunted him.

"When you're young, you think you'll live forever. But no one does. You have to live life for today as there may be no tomorrow."

Over the weeks and months, from conversations with her father, Susan began to absorb a better understanding of life, love and marriage. She realised that her father had explained to her, in a roundabout way, why he'd been unfaithful. He hadn't tried to justify his actions, but wanted to pass on his knowledge so that the same would not happen to her. Most of all, she began to realise that both parents worried about her simply because she was a girl. It was all right for boys to have a 'good' time, but girls had to be 'good'.

Glen Dale had lost interest in the many girls who waited for him after the shows. He had been seeing a beautiful Rugby girl, Sylvia, and decided to settle down. To his surprise, his proposal of marriage was rejected. Sylvia, although very fond of Glen, had grown up in a family, strictly controlled by her domineering father and observed how it had affected her mother's life. She was determined the same was not going to happen to her, so instead, chose to have a career and freedom.

Everyone sympathised with Glen, particularly Dorothy, though disparaging of girls who 'gave themselves away', she was now critical of a girl who had chosen not to. She could not help feeling protective towards her 'boys' and did not like to see Glen moping about the house with a broken heart.

Susan's lessons with her father had not come a moment too soon. Another boy in the house started to pay her attention and she was, of course, flattered. He was tall with dark hair, very handsome, intelligent and fun. They enjoyed each other's company, talked and laughed a lot and he sought her out when her parents were not in. One evening, when they were alone, he surprised her when he took her in his arms and kissed her passionately. In his fervour he was forceful, moving his hands over her body as he tried to feel her breasts and then between her legs. Susan restrained his passion, firmly, removing his hands. She had never been kissed before and he was older and demanding. Remembering her father's words and as young as she was, remained in control. Not quite fourteen, she felt grown-up in her mind but had the sense to know she was still a child. The thought of telling her parents did not cross her mind. It was something she had to keep secret as she knew he would instantly get the sack if they found out.

Dorothy continued to be very cautious about having Tanya living in the house. Her first concern was her husband and she kept a careful watch for signs of attraction, but there were none. One morning, when Dorothy was working in the office, she heard noises and a knocking sound coming from the billiards room. Standing outside the door she listened and then opened the door quietly. In the dim light, she could see two bodies on the green baize top of the billiard table. Without saying a word, she banged the door shut and walked quickly down the quarry tiled corridor and into the kitchen.

Dorothy was both shocked and pleased. Her instinct about having a female singer living in the house had been proved right. Making herself a cup of coffee, she sat down to compose herself, then made a drink for Reg and went upstairs to wake him.

"You'll have to speak to Glen," said Dorothy.

"What's he done now?" asked Reg, sleepily.

"I've just found him .... and Tanya .... on the billiard table."

“You what?” said Reg, sitting up in surprise and grinning at the humour of it.

“It’s not funny,” snorted Dorothy, primly.

“No, it’s not,” replied Reg, still laughing.

“She’ll have to leave.”

Reg took his time, washed, shaved, ate breakfast and ignored his wife’s impatient glances. When he was ready, he went to find Glen. He did not want to lose either of his best performers so picked his words carefully.

“I understand that you and Tanya were on the billiards table?”

Glen nodded guiltily.

“It’s like this Glen. We can’t have that sort of behaviour at Clifton Hall. You have two choices. One, you get married to Tanya and I’ll buy you a trailer and you can live together. Or you can pack it in. What’s it to be?”

“I’ll pack it in,” replied Glen, shamefacedly.

Tanya placed an advertisement in the Rugby Advertiser to rent a flat. A few days later, she heard the communal telephone ring and answered it.

“Can I speak to Mary Day?”

“Speaking.”

“Good. I’m glad I’ve got hold of you. I kept phoning and another woman said you weren’t there and put the phone down on me. I was ringing to tell you I’ve got a little flat on the first floor of my house in Temple Street. Would you like to see it?”

Writing down the address, Tanya went to see Dorothy.

“That’s good,” replied Dorothy, bluntly. “Go pack your bags and I’ll take you to Rugby to see it.”

Dorothy, wearing her slippers, drove Tanya to Rugby and dropped her off outside the house. As Tanya stepped out of the car with her case, Dorothy drove off abruptly, leaving Tanya on the pavement with little doubt in her mind that she had no option but to accept the accommodation. An elderly lady answered the doorbell and after viewing the flat, Tanya accepted it and moved in.

Tanya’s new landlady, in contrast to Dorothy, was friendly and took an interest in her career. They shared meals together and she encouraged Tanya to open a bank account to save for a ‘rainy day’.

One evening, they went together to a spiritualist meeting and as the clairvoyant leading the group went around the room, she stopped at Tanya.

“Someone wants to make contact with you. He’s an elderly man.” The clairvoyant then went on to describe the spirit to Tanya.

“That’s my father,” replied Tanya, startled by the description as she was dubious about spirits and the other world.

“He’s worried about you and the life you’re leading. He says you must take care and you’ll be going on a journey soon, travelling overseas.”

Dorothy happened to see Buddy looking at her eldest daughter with more interest than he should have and her sixth sense prickled. She kept a wary eye open and decided to mention her concern to Reg.

"I think Buddy is interested in Susan."

"Can't be. He can have any girl he wants," replied Reg, sceptically.

"It's my sixth sense. I'm sure he's attracted to her."

"It won't be the first time an older man is attracted to a young girl," commented Reg, thoughtfully. "Jerry Lee Lewis got himself into a lot of trouble by marrying his thirteen-year-old cousin."

"Forget about Jerry Lee Lewis. What are we going to do about Buddy?"

"Are you sure?"

"Ninety per cent."

"What do you want to do?" asked Reg, throwing the question back.

"I don't know. If we interfere or say something, we might make the situation worse and push them together."

"A bit like your Mum did in criticising me?" winked Reg, as his wife frowned in response. "You can ask him to leave but you'll be losing a good singer. I've an idea," added Reg, looking thoughtful. "Roy Young has asked if Buddy can go out to Hamburg as part of the big opening festival at the Star-Club. When he returns, we can say we've no space at Clifton Hall and find him somewhere else to stay, either in Rugby or the village."

"Good idea. But he'll guess if we move him on his own."

"We could move Pete as well. Barney stays most of the time in Rugby so it won't affect him. If he's not living in the house it puts temptation out of his way," said Reg, thoughtfully.

Through her pregnancy, Dorothy continued to work and went with Reg to the dance at the Trocadero Ballroom in Derby. The press arrived just as Tanya was due to go on stage. Reg, who never missed an opportunity for some extra publicity, whispered instructions to Tanya.

"Pretend to be locked out of your dressing room and say you've nothing to wear. It'll be good publicity."

Dorothy found a large, pale blue towel and dressed Tanya in the skimpy outfit. The following week, a photo of Tanya in the towel made the news!

Top: Glen Dale singing to the crowds at the Trocadero, Derby
Below: Rehearsal: Reg asked Tanya and Glen to do a duo and sing two numbers together, *Doctor Doctor* and *Twist and Shout*

12. ZANY ROCKERS

Mike Everest and the Alpines: Front: Mike Everest (Banks)
Ken Ratcliffe, Tony Tipper, Doug Perry and Bob Bishop (RC)

Mike Banks had seen a feature in a local newspaper, 'Burton-on-Trent 'Rocked' on Monday Night at the Jubilee Hall'. He went along with his bass guitar and asked for an audition. He met Reg, who saw him play and was amiable but made no offer of work. When Mike returned a few weeks later with the Alpines, he asked for another audition. The Alpines were a lively lot of lads from Burton on Trent, home of the brewing industry and they considered themselves 'registered' drinkers. Their singer had a motorbike accident and they asked Mike Banks to stand in for him.

"I thought you were a bass player?" queried Reg, who remembered him from before.

"I am but the Alpines' singer is injured."

"You're good," said Reg, smiling. "I could do with a bass player who can sing. How do you fancy working for me?"

"I'm not sure," hesitated Mike.

"I'll pay a starting wage of £5 a week with everything all in. You'd stay with us at Clifton Hall most of the time," coaxed Reg.

Mike was very tempted. £5 a week was more than he was earning but after some deliberation decided to be 'sensible' and keep his steady job rather than live the life of a 'rock' musician.

Reg didn't permit his own groups to drink alcohol but he could not prevent freelance musicians from having a pint. He insisted, however, that alcohol didn't improve anyone's performance and when the Alpines worked for Reg, they kept their drinking to a minimum.

They retained Mike Banks as their lead singer and changed the group's name to 'Mike Everest and the Alpines'. Jealous boyfriends were a recurring problem. After one incident, Reg suggested they should be friendly with the boys in the bar when they were having a drink so they wouldn't want to fight them. This psychology worked and the Alpines had no more trouble.

The Alpines were paid £12 a night and they bought a big old Humber Super Snipe Estate to travel to the gigs. The car had a chequered history. First, as a hearse to carry coffins and then an armoured vehicle with a floor-safe. The Humber drank petrol like they drank beer and it cost more to run than they earned.

Reg liked zany groups and went out of his way to develop their potential, suggesting they wore leather Alpine outfits. With Reg's encouragement, they ordered specially made lederhosen. On another occasion, he suggested they introduce comedy into their show.

"You could make people laugh. You're naturals. You're always larking about. I'll increase your wages from £12 to £15 a night if you can do it."

With the incentive of increased wages, the Alpines started to experiment and adapt other comedy acts to create their own shows. Reg and Dorothy were booking them into most of their dances and they became one of their favourite feature acts. Reg realised it was important for them to keep their act fresh with new ideas and often made suggestions.

When Reg was in London, he found the sheet music to an old Hoagy Carmichael song and gave it to Mike. Together, they went into fits of laughter as they sang the words and Reg suggested the visuals.

'I gotta girl that's mighty sweet, with blue eyes and tiny feet.
Her name is Rosabelle Magee. And she tips the scale at three o three.
Oh gee, but ain't it grand to have a girl so big and fat that when you hug her
You don't know where you're at.
You have to take a piece of chalk in your hand,
And hug a way and chalk a mark, to see where you began.
One day when I was huggin' and a chalkin'. And a chalkin' and a huggin' away.
When I met another fella with some chalk in his hand.
Comin' around the other way,
Round the mountain. Comin' around the other way......'

On another occasion, Reg suggested to Mike that he buy a haversack and put a smoke bomb in it.

"You're joking!" replied Mike, astonished.

"No, it'll be a scream. You light the smoke bomb just before you go on stage and continue singing as the smoke gradually seeps out of your haversack. The crowd won't know what to do as you ignore it and pretend not to realise you're on fire."

The new act went down very well. The group found it hilarious as they watched the faces of the startled audience while they sang. They performed it successfully at various dancehalls until the night they were booked to perform at the 76 Club, Burton-on-Trent. It was a very small venue with a tiny stage. Mike did the smoke bomb act but within minutes, a cry of 'Fire! Fire!' was heard as smoke began to engulf the audience. Panic ensued with a hasty mass exodus. The crowd pushed, screaming, as they ran for their lives out of the club and assembled in the car park waiting for fire engines to arrive. The band ignored the audience and played on....

Another zany person Reg often employed was David Sutch, otherwise known by his stage name of Screaming Lord Sutch. The two men were attracted to each other like magnets. David became a regular visitor to Clifton Hall, driving up in his white Cadillac or when touring nearby, be 'dropped off' by his backing group, the Savages. David would walk into Dorothy's kitchen and politely ignore her black looks as he drank tea and chatted to Reg for hours, often through the night, about the entertainment business, the mystery of life and the universe.

David was a quietly spoken, intelligent young man, who wanted to make a name for himself. On stage, he was an outlandish punk rocker before punk was invented and he valued Reg's 'off the wall' ideas. Most singers had one or two stage outfits but David had a large trunk containing many different costumes. When he lifted the lid, the smell of stale body odour was so foul the other guys in the dressing room opened a window or left the room. Musicians with any experience of his shows, cleared the stage of their equipment as he could 'accidentally' destroy anything in his way. He appeared to go raving 'mad' but knew exactly what he was doing. He would leap out of a coffin, carry a real axe, throw a knife, scream and do crazy things to terrify the audience.

Unlike other performers, David Sutch was neither fashionable nor good looking. Rather surprisingly, he began to take an uncharacteristic interest in Reg's new singer. When David started to flirt with Tanya, she laughed and pushed him away. He was quite definitely not her type. He tried to persuade her to join his act. To have a girl wearing a leopard skin who could 'rock', would greatly enhance his show. Tanya refused his entreaties and could not be persuaded to join him, preferring to keep Reg as her manager.

1962 Hamburg: (? Horst Fascher) Gene Vincent, Roy Young and Reg Calvert
Car belonging to Manfred Weissleder who owned the Star-Club (RC's camera)

13. BEATLES, STAR-CLUB

1962 The Beatles, John Lennon and Tanya Day at the Star-Club, Hamburg (RC)

Roy Young remained at the Top Ten Club in Hamburg for several more months until he was 'headhunted' and offered employment with a company car, his own apartment and excellent salary. Manfred Weissleder was in the process of planning the opening of the new Star-Club and it was to be much larger than the Top Ten Club and cater for up to two thousand people.

It was Roy's responsibility to plan and book performers for a spectacular opening season, beginning Friday 13th April, 1962 with a 'Rock and Twist Festival' to last for several months. Gene Vincent was more popular in

Germany than Elvis and he was pleased to book him for the first two weeks at a low rate.

Horst Fascher also transferred to the Star-Club and asked Roy if he could book Tanya Day. Horst had seen Tanya the previous winter when he stayed at Clifton Hall with Peter Eckhorn. Roy agreed and Reg arranged for Johnny Neal and the Starliners to go as her backing group. Other groups to perform included: The Graduates, The Beatles, Tony Sheridan and Davy Jones, Gerry & the Pacemakers, Tex Roberg, The Big Three, Glen Dale, Buddy Britten and the Regents.

Tanya was met at the airport by Roy who flirted with her all the way to the club. She was the first female singer to appear there and for the first few days, it was arranged for the Beatles to be her backing group. Roy had collected them from Liverpool, driving them to Hamburg in his new car.

Tanya rejected Roy's amorous attentions, preferring Horst Fascher, but she was impressed by Roy's musicality. He was superb and she enjoyed watching him perform, either on his own or with various groups, including the Beatles. He was the best pianist and singer she had ever seen. When the Starliners arrived, she introduced them to the Beatles. Johnny Neal did not look like a 'rock' star, being older and stouter but with his experience, he got the shows warmed up by including novelty songs in his repertoire, such as, *I'm Henry the Eighth I Am.*

Johnny Neal quickly took to club life, relishing the attention of numerous girls. He also enjoyed a drink and was invited to go with the Beatles, Gene Vincent and others, to a 'drinking den' next door.

Tanya had led a sheltered existence before becoming a singer and had never been exposed to the seedier side of night life. Working in the Star Club was full of little incidents. There was not much to do when not performing and sometimes she would remain in the club. One day, when Tanya was sitting with a pretty girl, a singer came up to them and began to smack the girl around the face.

"She's a dirty bitch and she's given me the crabs!" he shouted, angrily.

Tanya, taking it literally, could not understand why he was angry about crabs. On another occasion, a singer collapsed on stage and was rushed to hospital. Later, she heard whispers that he had syphilis and his genitals had greatly enlarged.

After one performance, a man approached Tanya and asked if she would like to make a record. He explained he was from Polydor Records and needed a singer or he would lose his budget. Tanya was sceptical but the Starliners said they would escort her to ensure her safety. She had to learn a new song by the Shirelles, *His Lips Get in the Way,* but there was little time for rehearsal and the recording was rushed. Tanya, dispirited with the quality of the record, refused to return for a second recording.

Drugs were prevalent and Preludin was easily available from a coin slot machine in the gent's toilets. Many of the musicians took one tablet to keep them awake during the night but John Lennon was sometimes seen taking four or five at a time.

Frequent drinking sessions were affecting Johnny Neal. On more than one occasion, he became legless and unable to get up on stage and sing. Manfred Weissleder, gave him notice to quit and asked the Beatles to back Tanya again. They refused. Manfred, unhappy with their attitude, gave them a choice. They could either back Tanya or pack their bags and leave. Reluctantly, they agreed and a rehearsal was arranged for the following morning.

Tanya was living in a hotel room and went to the club next day for the rehearsal and waited. After half an hour or so, she decided to go up to their flat and see where they were. Tentatively, she knocked and opened the door. Inside, she could see the flat was in a mess and not smelling good. As she entered, the stench increased.

The Beatles were in bed, each with a girl and their grubby feet were sticking out of the bedcovers. Someone had been sick on the floor and in the vomit, cigarette butts had been stubbed out and left there. Tanya, shocked to see the flat, reminded the boys politely, they were supposed to be rehearsing.

Performing with the Beatles was not a pleasure. John Lennon behaved as though he was superior and could be particularly rude and sarcastic to her and others he met. Tanya tolerated John's behaviour as the others in the group were polite enough and George Harrison, always pleasant.

Buddy, Glen, Barney and Pete were the next group from Clifton Hall to go to Hamburg. After speaking to Roy several times, Reg realised they needed really good amplification in such an enormous club. He purchased Geloso amplifiers and Celestian G12 speakers from Benn Radio in Rugby and with Pete's help, made large speaker columns in the barns.

Pete Mist was sensible with money and had saved to buy a new Ford Consul car. He offered to drive to Hamburg rather than go by train and his car and roof rack was loaded with drum kit, guitars, speakers, amplifier and clothes. With little space remaining, the four young men squeezed in like sardines and began their long journey. Arriving in Hamburg, they were given tickets to exchange in the club for drinks and food. Accommodation was provided in flats across the road and their 'minder' was Horst Fascher.

Heidi, a girl Barney had met on his previous stay in Hamburg, visited the club to continue their friendship. She brought him food and they sat, held hands and kissed.

Tanya introduced the Clifton Hall boys to the Beatles. It was a sport for the experienced musicians to show the new innocent boys around town with all its delights. After the groups finished at four in the morning, they often took a stroll to have breakfast in the lively market area where prostitutes were still working. It did not take the boys long to realise Hamburg was a wild place, like no other they had visited.

John Lennon and Buddy Britton struck up a friendship and got on well together. John's nickname for Buddy was 'Bliddy Button'. John and Paul decided to 'educate' Buddy and took him on a stroll down the Herbertstrasse where prostitutes sat naked in shop windows. John encouraged Buddy to make a choice and select one of the girls. Laughing, Buddy declined. He had no inclination to go with a prostitute.

Unsure of Buddy's sexual preference, John and Paul hatched another plot. They invited Buddy to the nightclub next door, saying an attractive girl had seen him perform and wanted to meet him. The four of them sat at a table talking and the girl seemed very nice. Buddy asked her to dance and while they were on the floor, he saw Paul and John sniggering and realised they must be playing a joke on him. He continued to dance, wondering what the joke was. After a while, he realised he was dancing with a man!

The Big Three, a Liverpool group, had made enormous loudspeakers nicknamed 'coffins' to give them a powerful sound. Adrian, the guitarist, bought a cute pet pig and it lived with him in the flat, leaving its excrement around the place. John put the pig in Buddy's bed where it curled up and went to sleep. When Buddy finished working, everyone thought it hilarious when he found he was sharing his bed with a pig. The pig, of course, grew larger and after a while, was 'despatched'.

Reg liked to check out the nightclubs and made a trip to see Tanya and the boys in the new Star-Club. He photographed Tanya with her new backing group and Roy suggested he might think about becoming their manager.

"No, I don't think so," replied Reg. "I don't want to manage a scruffy Liverpudlian group."

Each time Reg travelled abroad, he returned with small gifts for Dorothy and his daughters. In Hamburg, he purchased two 'fountain' pens, one blue and one pink. Instead of holding ink they held a small cartridge of CS gas. It amused Reg and when he got back to Clifton Hall, he gave the pink one to Dorothy.

"I don't want this. What will I use it for?" asked Dorothy, who without thinking, immediately pressed the release and let out a small amount of gas towards the boys who had come to have a look.

"You're not supposed to let it off," said Reg, as the boys ran away laughing. "It's to use if anyone attacks you when you're carrying money from the dances or to the bank. It's not dangerous. It's just tear gas and makes a person's eyes sting so they can't see for a few minutes. They sell all sorts of gadgets like this in Germany for personal protection."

"Okay," shrugged Dorothy, smiling. "I'll keep it in my handbag."

When the Beatles were preparing to leave Hamburg, they tried to persuade Roy to return to England with them and become the 'fifth' Beatle. Roy declined. He was doing well in Germany and had just signed a three year contract to be resident at the Star-Club. Back in London, the Beatles were looking for a drummer and asked another of Reg's former employees, Johnny Watson, to join them but he also declined.

1962 Star-Club, Hamburg: Tanya Day backed by the Beatles, Paul McCartney and George Harrison behind (RC).

1962 Star-Club: Tanya Day and the Beatles (RC)

1962 Star-Club: Gene Vincent and Tanya Day (RC)

14. THE BLUE BABY

When Buddy Britten returned to Clifton Hall, Reg tactfully explained they were short of space in the house and had arranged for him and Pete Mist to stay in the village with Mrs Podgson and her family. No mention was made of Dorothy's suspicions and she continued to do her best to promote him and to obtain a second recording contract with another record company.

Buddy had written several times to Susan during his stay in Hamburg but was careful to send no news of what he was doing. The letters contained only song lyrics but on his return, he gave her a silver St Christopher on a chain. They were still attracted to each other but the new regime meant they had little opportunity to meet on their own.

Dorothy reached her fifth month of pregnancy feeling unwell. Instead of gaining weight she was losing it. When she started to have stomach pains and diarrhoea, she went to see her doctor and explained she thought she was losing her baby. He disagreed, diagnosing gastroenteritis, and told her not to worry. The following day, she felt worse.

"Stay in bed, have a lazy day," suggested Reg. "I'll bring you breakfast. Do you want toast and coffee?"

"No thanks. I'm not hungry. I've got pains and it feels like labour contractions," replied Dorothy, grimacing, her eyes large in dark hollows and her face ashen with worry.

"Can't be," said Reg, concerned. "It's far too early."

"I know it's early. But I'm sure. You'd better call the doctor and the midwife," said Dorothy, holding onto her stomach and breathing deeply between each contraction."

Reg made the phone call and did his best to remain calm. He could see Dorothy's condition was deteriorating.

"Can you get some old towels out of the cupboard and put them underneath me," asked Dorothy, quietly. She feared what was to come and looked anxiously at Reg as he gently lifted her up and placed towels underneath her body. A few minutes later, her waters broke.

"It's over Reg," said Dorothy, looking at him apologetically through frightened, tear-filled eyes. She was losing their baby and she felt the pain of loss more than the physical pain from the contractions. Reg tried to comfort her as he placed more towels underneath her and threw the soiled ones in the bath.

Together they waited. Reg held her hand and wiped her forehead, not knowing what else to do as the contractions became stronger. He wished he believed in a god he could pray to. 'Please save my baby boy.' But he knew his prayers were unheard. There was no one listening and nothing he could do but wait and hope.

With relief, they heard the sound of a car and Reg went to greet the midwife. She immediately assessed the situation, sending him for hot water and more towels. A few minutes later, the doctor arrived and after examining Dorothy, realised there was nothing he could do but stand back and wait for nature to take its course. Dorothy's final contractions were strong and she held onto the scream she wanted to make as the midwife encouraged her to push.

"Push. Push now. Push. The head is through. Now, big breath. One final push." The baby emerged, the midwife caught it and after cutting the umbilical cord, gently wrapped it in a towel and handed it to Reg. A small, blue, baby boy. Reg showed it to Dorothy as he cradled it in his arms."

"I'm so sorry. I'm so sorry," said Dorothy, crying softly and holding out her hand to Reg. He squeezed it as they both looked at their son. Reg lifted her hand to his lips and kissed it while she cried.

The doctor glancing at Reg said briskly, with no sensitivity, "Wrap it in some old newspapers and burn it in the boiler."

Reg left the bedroom in shock. He walked quietly into the boy's kitchen where Danny was seated at the table eating a large bowlful of Force wheat flakes, milk and sugar.

"What have you got there?" asked Danny, as he saw Reg carrying something in a towel.

"My son," blurted out Reg, his face a ghastly white as he looked down at his baby. "It's my baby son - and he's dead."

Danny, in shock, stopped eating and came and stood by Reg and looked at the dead baby, the blue baby boy that Reg cradled in his arms. They both stood frozen for a moment, a static wall of emotion between them and then Reg broke the silence, his voice cracked and almost inaudible. "Can you leave me alone, please?" Danny nodded and left the room.

Reg had to force himself to do what the doctor had instructed. Making a space on the table, between dirty bowls and plates left from breakfast, he lay down the motionless warm body of his son. He collected several old musical papers and gently wrapped his baby round and round in the paper. Pausing for a few moments to find the inner strength and courage to do the final act, he opened the lid to the boiler and placed the paper bundle inside. He heard the newspaper catching light and the whoosh of the flames. He stood staring at the boiler. It was over.

Returning to the bedroom, Reg saw the ghastly scene of Dorothy haemorrhaging and lying in a pool of blood. The doctor was speaking in an urgent voice on the telephone, calling for an ambulance.

“It will be here soon,” said the Doctor. Turning to Reg, he said in a loud whisper, “It’s fifty-fifty whether your wife will pull through. If she does, she should never, never, have another baby.”

Reg went over and sat on the bed and took her hand. She turned her head to look at him with large scared eyes. She had heard the doctor’s whisper. As they waited, she bled more and her face became porcelain white and her hand lay limp in his grip.

The ambulance arrived and Dorothy was lifted onto a stretcher. Reg stood back and silently watched as she was taken away to hospital. The doctor and midwife packed their bags and said their farewells, not looking him in the eye as they left the bedroom. Reg closed the door and shut out the world. A feeling of hollowness overwhelmed him and he threw himself onto the bed.

Dorothy had given Reg one last look and tried to smile as he squeezed her hand before she was lifted onto the stretcher. Her life blood haemorrhaging from her, she lost consciousness. When she awoke it was with a strange sensation that her mind, or was it her soul, had detached itself and Dorothy was now floating above her lifeless body. Below her, doctors and nurses were rushing around, giving her a blood transfusion and trying to resuscitate her. She watched all that was happening, dispassionately, with no will or desire to return to her body. In that split second, she knew with certainty, there was for her, no God. No God and no Heaven.

Reg lay on the bed staring blankly at the white ceiling above, for a minute, or was it an hour? As he emerged from his stupor, he had an overpowering desire to get away. He needed to escape from the overwhelming pain of grief and disappointment. He had always been responsible for his destiny but now he was out of control and helpless. Dorothy was dying and there was nothing he could do or say to bring her back or block the memory of wrapping his baby boy in paper and burning him. It was too much! Too much for any one person to bear. Hastily, he packed a small suitcase and went downstairs. As he passed the rehearsal room he heard the guitars playing and thought to say to the boys that he was going to London on business.

Sometime later, Dorothy struggled with the effort of opening her eyes and when she did, she saw lights floating somewhere above her. Someone was squeezing her hand. She blinked, trying to focus, unsure where she was as she recollected her earlier vision.

“Are you all right Mrs Calvert?” asked a nurse.

“Yes. Yes, thank you,” acknowledged Dorothy weakly, turning her head to look at the nurse. But she was not all right. She had lost their baby boy.

Susan and Candy returned from school and Candy changed to go out and ride her pony. Susan, sensing something was wrong, searched for her parents. Normally when they went out, they left a scribbled note on the kitchen table but today, there was none. She went into the rehearsal room and the boys explained what had happened. One of the boys drove her to the St. Cross Hospital in Rugby and waited outside while Susan made her way in. When she found the right ward, it was not visiting time and the nurses refused her entry but then relented when Susan explained she could not come later.

"Hello Mum," said Susan quietly, as she took hold of her mother's pale white hand and squeezed it gently.

Dorothy remained silent for several minutes and then, opening her eyes to look at her daughter, said almost inaudibly, "I lost the baby."

"I know."

"Is your Dad here?"

"No, he's gone to London on business."

"It was a baby boy. Your dad always wanted a boy and I lost him," murmured Dorothy, as tears began to run down her face. "He should be here. Here with me."

Dorothy began to cry, her hand limp in her daughter's hand. When Susan returned home, her heart was laden with sadness. She explained to Candy what had happened and realised it was now her responsibility to carry on and look after the house without her parents.

Two days later, Dorothy was permitted to convalesce at home. Mrs Podgson cared for her during the day and Susan after school.

"Where's your father?" asked Dorothy, when Susan went to see her.

"In London."

"Is he coming home?"

"I don't know. I haven't heard from him."

"Has he telephoned?"

Susan shook her head in response.

"He's a coward. He never could bear pain. When I need him most, he's not here," said Dorothy, turning her head away so her daughter would not see her crying.

"I've cooked the boys some sausages, mashed potatoes and baked beans. What do you want to eat?"

"Nothing."

"You have to eat or you won't get better."

"You're a good girl," said Dorothy quietly. "Where's Candy?"

"She's out with Shamie and her friends."

"That's good."

"You have to eat Mum."

"I don't want anything. What's the point?"

Susan decided to change the subject and try to cheer her mother by chattering about her pets, trying to make her mother smile.

"Katy was waiting for me at the top of the drive when I came home from school today. She waits for me most days. She must know the time and yesterday, she caught a crow and brought it into the kitchen. It was an enormous bird."

"The crow that lives in the oak tree," said Dorothy, listlessly. "Your Dad was always taking potshots at it."

"And I'm sure Quacker Barney thinks he's a hen. He follows them everywhere. He was trying to lay an egg today and cluck instead of quack. He looked really funny."

"Oh Susan. What am I to do?" burst out Dorothy, sobbing.

"What do you mean?"

"When you get married, make sure you marry a man who goes out to work, nine to five each day. Not someone like your Dad."

"Boring, boring," replied Susan, smiling. Her mother had told her this on more than one occasion.

"You don't understand what it's like. I should have listened to my mother. She warned me but I took no notice. It's better to be bored and know where you are than live with a man like your Dad. I never know what he's going to do next."

On Friday afternoon, five days after the miscarriage, Reg returned from London and behaved as if nothing untoward had happened. Dorothy was in the lounge and he greeted her with a cursory kiss and asked how she was, with seemingly less concern than if she was recovering from a cold.

"I'm feeling a little better. Not that you care," responded Dorothy bitterly, as she glared at him with large, angry eyes in her pale face.

Reg said nothing, acknowledged her anger with a flick of the head and walked away. He needed to forget. He had no wish to relive the anguish or pain and pushed it to the back of his mind. A chasm so deep had developed between them, pulling them apart as they bottled up their emotions to make a bitter spirit. Dorothy was grieving for their lost child and angry at Reg's rejection. She needed his love and reassurance. Reg had become matter of fact, cold and distant, his mind in another place.

Pop goes the school for the teenage hopefuls of tomorrow

GOOD NIGHT YOUNG SINGERS

CLIFTON HALL is Britain's strangest private school. Only three miles from Rugby, it has about as much in common with the famous public school for boys as a pickled walnut with a porcupine.

Grooming

Mrs. Calvert says goodnight to a combo with guitars, drum ... and hot-water bottle.

Love flies in for Blind Jack

'STAY AT HOME OR GET OUT'

for the dog who's one of the family

is talks

Daily Sketch feature, 14th March, 1962: *"Clifton Hall is Britain's strangest private school. Only three miles from Rugby, it has about as much in common with the famous public school for boys as a pickled walnut with a porcupine. Its pupils are plumbers, fitters and apprentice engineers, instead of sons of peers. It has no desks, no inkpots, no prspectus, no fees. In fact, the 33 year-old headmaster, Reg Calvert, has turned the whole education system inside out. He PAYS his pupils. Bluff, blue-eyed and business-like, he has been a hairdresser, TV engineer, clarinet player and popcorn maker. "You name it, he's done it," his wife, Dorothy said."*

NEWS FEATURE written by Bob Driscoll:
"Clifton Hall is an 18th century mansion built from solid rock. ... But it is rock of a different kind that has given the 23-roomed house a new lease of life – rock of the twangy type! For Clifton Hall is now a cool school for young 'pop' artists. ..... When I paid a visit to this country seat for singers I was told by the principal, Mr Reg Calvert, that this was no place for beginners. ..... "I'm only interested in boys who have done some singing around the dance halls and who have some idea how to approach a large audience. The same goes for instrumentalists."
Let me quote just the basic rules which must be adhered to if you want to enrol in this show biz academy. 1. No girls. 2. No drinking. 3. No holidays. 4. No shirking under any circumstances. Smoking is allowed although it is very much frowned upon. ....." *(Newspaper cutting from Barney Peacock)*

15. PAIN AND LAUGHTER

THE FORTUNES. Comedy with Tony Britnell, Rod Allen, Glen Dale, Barry Pritchard, Gary Fletcher (drums), Chris Capaldi (piano). Reg encouraged all his performers to do a comedy act (RC)

During the summer of 1962, Reg and Dorothy kept themselves busy and did not display their inner feelings to the outside world. Inwardly, their lives had been inextricably altered and would never be the same. It was now no longer enough for Reg to have all the success in the world. His restless mind tried to grapple with the meaning of life and often retreated into himself, sitting alone in the kitchen where Dorothy would find him, stirring sugar round and round in the sugar bowl. Dorothy knew it was just a matter of time before he would be away, starting something new and leaving her behind once more.

Dorothy and Reg had been having a competition for several months to see which of them could stop smoking the longest. Picking up a cigarette, Reg began to smoke again and Dorothy reminded him, he had lost the bet. Reg conceded and took her shopping in London to buy the fur coat she had always dreamed of. To possess such a coat made Dorothy feel immensely proud. It was an outward sign which said she was no longer poor but rich and successful. Owning a mink coat did not, however, bring her happiness and within a few days of buying it, she began to smoke again.

The house, the dances and the boys needed to be organised and Dorothy did her best to focus on everyday things. Keeping busy, she worked through her heartbreak and fears. Optimistically, she obtained another recording contract for Buddy, this time with Piccadilly Records. The search was now on to find a really good song with the potential to become a hit.

Dorothy's mother came to stay for her holiday and was concerned when she saw her daughter. Dorothy smiled and chatted, pretending all was well but Sarah Jane could see through the trivia. She recognised deep pain and understood, her daughter was still grieving.

"Tha' looks jiggered lass. Tha' need t' tek it easy."

"I've too much to do," replied Dorothy, endeavouring to smile.

"Thee'll work thy sen into an early grave."

"I'll be all right, don't worry Mum."

Sarah Jane did worry and busied herself doing whatever she could to take some of the load off Dorothy. In the quiet times of the morning she did the washing-up, tidied the cupboards and wiped down the shelves. One morning, she heard an unusual bellowing sound from just outside the kitchen window. A bull was joyously running around on the front lawn. Sarah Jane picked up the first implement she could find and went to chase the bull back through the gap in the fence.

Hearing a commotion in the garden, Reg awoke with a start and got out of bed to look through the window, calling to Dorothy, "Come and see what your mother's doing. It's the funniest thing I've seen in years. Only your mother could do this."

Dorothy, blinking sleep from her eyes, made her way to the window, staring for a few seconds, taking in the scene of her mother holding onto a sweeping brush and yelling at the top of her voice as she chased after a large black and white bull.

"If she got on the brush it might take off and fly," chortled Reg.

"Stop standing there like a gormless idiot. Get some clothes on," snapped Dorothy. "The bull could attack her."

In fits of laughter, Reg was bent over holding his sides as Dorothy passed him some clothes.

The terrified bull, instead of having the sense to return through the gap whence it came, tried to jump over the six-foot fence. Sarah Jane looked on in horror as the bull became impaled on the fence and blood seeped from his wound. Her mood altered from fierce warrior to gentle sympathetic woman, full of remorse. The bull, oblivious of her soothing words, bellowed loudly in fear and pain.

Standing by his mother-in-law, Reg relieved her of the sweeping brush and tried to disguise his amusement by changing his facial expression to one of concern.

"Thee'll have t' get tha' poor creature down," said Sarah Jane, looking sharply at Reg.

"You must be joking. The bull's much too dangerous. I can see the whites of his eyes and I'm not going near it."

"Reg Calvert! Thee are neither use nor ornament. Thou canno' leave tha' poor creature stuck up there."

"I didn't put it there. Come on in. Dorothy will find the farmer."

"Aye and leave it sufferin'. I'll nay go in till the farmer comes to fetch it," rebuked Sarah Jane.

"This'll teach you to chase bulls with a broomstick," teased Reg, as he waited with her for the farmer to arrive.

Summer was not a good time for the dancehalls as it was usually too hot to dance and many teenagers were away on holiday. Needing a new project to keep himself occupied, Reg booked Wembley and Hornsey Town Halls in August, to put on two 'showcase' performances of all his artistes in the style of a cabaret. He enjoyed planning big events and Dorothy helped with the budgeting and organisation.

New acts were created and the boys rehearsed and rehearsed. Microphones on fixed stands were a disadvantage to singers who also played guitar as it limited their free movement on stage. Roger James and Tony Clarke were to do a duo act as Rog and Ton. Reg ingeniously resolved the problem, Heath Robinson style, by contriving a wire necklace from coat hangers which held the microphones, so they could sing, play guitar and move about the stage at the same time.

On the night Reg stood in the wings, co-ordinating the running order. The show was going really well to a packed audience. The only freelance group was Mike Everest and the Alpines as Reg wanted to include a good comedy act. As Mike waited to go on stage, Reg fiddled about in his haversack.

"What are you doing?" asked Mike.

"Wait and see," replied Reg mischievously, as they both heard the refrain of *The Happy Wanderer.*

There was no time for Mike to explain he no longer did the smoke bomb act. Taking the microphone, he danced and frolicked as he sang:

I love to go a wandering, Along the mountain track, And as I go,
I love to sing, My knapsack on my back.
Val-deri, val-dera, Val-deri, Val-dera-ha-ha-ha-ha-ha

Little by little, thick black smoke began to seep out of his haversack. Mike totally ignored the smoke as the audience began to show concern and carried on singing, seemingly oblivious to the fire as members of the audience tried to tell him. By the end of the song, the smoke was so dense everyone on stage was coughing and spluttering. Reg stood in the wings, laughing and coughing as he watched the drama unfurl. With it being a large venue, he had purchased a large smoke bomb. A bank of smoke drifted down to cover the first few rows of the audience and everyone was coughing and laughing but thankfully, no one called the fire brigade.

The show continued with Glen Dale who wowed the audience with his superb voice. Johny Washington was featured as the 'Sensational 15year old Star of Tomorrow'. He did his solo act and then reappeared later with sword in hand to fight Robbie Hood. Buddy Britten and the Regents sang rhythm and blues including their signature song, *Money (That's what I want).* The finale and star of the show was, as always, Danny Storm and the Strollers, singing *Honest I Do*.

The Wembley and Hornsey Town Halls were booked in August to present a spectacular show of Reg's artists with the addition of the Alpines for a comedy act

(Poster from John Allison, Allison Brothers)

Reg was pleased with the success of the shows. Johny Washington was a natural and performed well. The sword fight had gone down so well, Reg decided to place him with the 'Merry Men' to make a singing trio and Dorothy made another outfit. Shortly afterwards, Mike West gave notice to leave. Reg and Dorothy were not surprised. He had always been a free spirit who disliked house rules and discipline. They parted on good terms and Reg let him keep the Robin Hood outfit which had become so much part of his act.

"What shall we do with the 'Merry Men?" asked Reg.

"You could ask Rod and Barry to leave. We don't need them anymore."

"They're too good to lose, the best singers I've got, apart from Glen."

"Good or no good, I'd ask them to go."

"What's for dinner?" asked Reg, looking up.

"Pork chop, fried potatoes and baked beans for the boys. Pork chop, mashed potato, cauliflower and gravy for us," replied Dorothy, with a sigh. "I think it's time to stop cooking for the boys. It's too much work and I'm sure they could cook for themselves."

"Oh yes and what planet do you live on?" laughed Reg.

"Well they've two choices, cook their own or starve."

"I was thinking," said Reg. I need to find a London Agency."

"You and your London Agency. And pigs can fly Reg Calvert. Why aren't you satisfied with what you've got?"

"You have to keep moving," smiled Reg. "What do you think about keeping Johny, Rod and Barry together as the Cliftones. They'll make a really good backing group for the big stars coming over from America."

"Sounds okay but I think Johny would prefer to sing on his own rather than be part of a trio."

"He can, some of the time but it will be good experience for him."

Reg began to rehearse the Cliftones but Dorothy was right, Johny did not like being part of a trio. He was very young and impatient to make a career as a solo singer and he succeeded in obtaining a recording contract with Fontana records. When he told Reg and Dorothy of his plans, they were supportive and wished him luck.

"Anytime you need work, let us know and we'll book you into the dances," said Reg, amiably.

On the day of Johny's departure, Dorothy came out of the house to see him off. As he got into the car, Dorothy called after him. He turned to see her smiling as she waved and reminded him, "Johny, be good."

Dorothy suggested again that Rod and Barry should leave but Reg ignored her advice and instead, put Glen with them to form a trio. With Glen's ability to sing falsetto, he realised they would form a really unusual vocal group. Glen did not want to be part of a harmony group and went around saying so to everyone. "I don't want to be in a trio. I don't want to be in a trio." Reg ignored his complaints and rehearsals began. Soon, Reg was proved right. As he walked by the rehearsal room one afternoon, he stopped and listened. The sound of them singing a cappella, sent shivers down his spine, their harmonies were amazing. He continued to the office and beckoned Dorothy to come and listen.

"What do you think Doe Doe?"

"Very good," agreed Dorothy, reluctantly.

"They're not just good. They're exceptional," said Reg, his mind immediately turning over new ideas. "I think I'll rename them the Fortunes and get them a recording contract."

"They'll be nothing but trouble," replied Dorothy, shrugging her shoulders and returning to the office.

Reg opened the rehearsal room door and complimented them on their singing. "From now on I want you to widen your repertoire to include classics, standards and ballads. In fact, anything you want to learn that will appeal to a wide range of audiences."

"You mean we don't have to do rock music anymore?" queried Glen.

"Exactly. I want you to become more of a cabaret group. What do you think of the Fortunes as a name?"

Glen, hardly believing what Reg was saying, glanced at Rod and Barry for approval. "Okay, we'll give it a go."

"I'm going to make you into a six-piece group and put Gary Fletcher on drums and Tony Britnell on saxophone."

"That's five," commented Rod, smiling.

"I need to find a pianist. Do you know anyone?"

The following week, a pianist Roger James recommended came for an audition at the Evesham Public Hall. Chris Capaldi could sight-read music so Reg presented him with the sheet music of *Honest I Do*. It was easy and Chris played it well, then he played some 'blues'.

"Pack your bag my friend and be here next week. Tell your girlfriend you're going to be away for some time," said Reg, smiling broadly. He had found his sixth musician.

Chris had no electric piano so Reg bought one, to be paid back in weekly instalments from his wages. Chris shared a room with Barry but soon discovered his roommate had an overactive mind and was writing songs half the night. He transferred to Glen's room until he realised that Glen was a late riser. If woken suddenly, Glen's natural reaction was to immediately hit out. When Barry woke him one morning for rehearsals, he received a black eye. Chris decided to change rooms again and ended up sharing, more amicably, with Rod.

Day after day, week after week, the Fortunes were made to rehearse. If they slacked or thought a piece was okay, Reg would insist they improve, and play it again, and again, and again. If they disagreed or argued, he would bring his hand down hard on the table top making a loud bang and quietly say, "It's not good enough. Practise it again."

When the Fortunes were alone, they joked they would string Reg up to the apple tree outside if he asked them to play the same song again. He had become a perfectionist. When a song was almost right, he recorded it on an acetate disc so they could hear it, then he made them rehearse it, again.

After several weeks of rehearsals Reg announced to Dorothy he was going into Rugby to order the Fortunes matching suits.

"Can you buy four pieces of fillet steak from the butchers while you're in town? Make sure it's good," smiled Dorothy.

"Okay Doe Doe," replied Reg, giving her a kiss on her cheek.

Rod, Barry, Glen, Gary, Tony and Chris all squeezed into the lime-green Ford Zephyr. Reg went first to the butchers with his entourage following.

"My wife has asked for some fillet steak and told me it has to be good," grinned Reg, in good humour. "Can you cut me a small piece to try?"

The Butcher knew Reg and grinned back as he handed him a small piece of meat on the end of his butcher's fork. Reg took it and ate the raw meat.

"Yes, it's good. I'll have four slices please."

The Fortunes looked on in amazement.

"You have to try it first. It's the only way to tell if it's any good," explained Reg, as he paid the butcher.

The clock tower in the centre of Rugby said five twenty nine and the sales assistant at Burton Tailors was closing the shop door.

"Sorry sir, we're closed."

Reg put his foot in the door and looked at the assistant with steely determination in his eyes. "No, you're not. You're not closed to measure up for six new suits, are you?"

"I suppose we're not sir," replied the flummoxed assistant, opening the door widely to let his customers in.

"Good," replied Reg, smiling. "Do you think I can look at the pattern swatches while you measure these young men for jackets?"

Reg, who did not work nine to five, had no consideration for staff working late and after some time going through fabric swatches, decided upon a bold blue check cloth so the Fortunes would look both smart and a little different to other groups.

Brian Epstein telephoned Clifton Hall and spoke to Dorothy. He explained he had taken on the management of the Beatles and wanted to give them more experience. He asked if she would book them into some of the dancehalls and Dorothy agreed and told Reg.

"I know the Beatles, they backed Tanya in Hamburg," commented Reg. "So they've got a manager now. Roy Young suggested I should take them on but I didn't want to manage a scruffy Liverpudlian group. They're a good group and it'll be interesting to see what their new manager has done with them."

"I've done a swap on Thursday 4th October. Booked Buddy into the Cavern in Liverpool and the Beatles and the Alpines to Washwood Heath. On Friday night, I've booked the Beatles into Nuneaton with the Avengers and Buddy.

"Good. How much did you agree to pay them?"

"£25 but they've got their accommodation and travel to pay for."

"By the way, I saw Bubbles at Newbury," said Reg, thoughtfully.

"How was he?"

"Not good. Didn't look well. Penniless. He hasn't been able to find regular work since he left Clifton Hall."

"It's a shame."

"I said we'd give him a few more bookings to help him out. He doesn't live so far from Banbury," said Reg, thoughtfully. "And guess what? Remember Freddy Were? He's changed his name to Tony Rocco and released a song he's written himself called *Stalemate*."

"Brilliant," smiled Dorothy. "I hope he does well. It seems a long time since he worked for us in Southampton."

"Those were the days," chuckled Reg.

In October, there was more excitement in the house as Buddy Britten and the Regents released their second record, *Long Gone Baby* with the B-side, *My Pride, My Joy*, written by Buddy. When Dorothy heard the final version she was disappointed. She thought the songs were poorly produced and that her own demo discs were better. Buddy had onstage charisma, but this was not projected into his recordings. Regardless, Dorothy continued to do a large amount of work to publicise him but to no avail. The record did not reach the bottom of the charts.

Many groups visited Clifton Hall and often stayed for a free night's accommodation, sleeping anywhere they could find a bed. Reg and Dorothy never minded who was in the house, providing they abided by the 'House Rules' and did not encroach upon their private family rooms.

The Beatles arrived unannounced at Clifton Hall with their driver. They had heard much about the avant-garde lifestyle of the residents from conversations in Hamburg. They made their way through the back door entrance to the rehearsal room, where they could hear guitars playing and were soon chatting with the boys and offered tea and coffee.

John Lennon, who was wearing glasses the same design as Buddy's, joked, "I just play the maraca and carry the gear."

Gary's drum kit was set up on one side of the room and Ringo asked if he could play it and the two drummers discussed one of Gary's unusual cymbals.

Love Me Do, the Beatles first record, was due for release the next day. John and Paul had written it between them and were very excited and asked if they could play it on the record player. The Clifton Hall boys listened and were a bit nonchalant, preferring the B-side, *P.S. I Love You.*

Brian Epstein travelled to the dance at Washwood Heath to watch his protégés and chatted to Reg while they were setting up. Reg was interested to see how Brian had worked on the Beatles and radically transformed their appearance so they were now a 'smart' Liverpudlian group. There was no dressing room so all the boys had to change behind screens in one corner of the hall. Mike Everest and the Alpines were also setting up and when Mike asked them what the very large boxes were for, they joked, "It's our bass cabinet and our bass player lives in it."

While the Beatle's were performing, Reg stood in the audience with Mike to watch them, commenting, "They've got a different line-up to most groups as all four musicians sing."

The Beatles introduced their new record, enthusing the audience to go out and buy a copy. As they started to play, John Lennon waved his hand to pause. He had forgotten to take his mouth organ out of his pocket. Finding it, they continued with the introduction before starting to sing, *Love, love me do, you know I love you, I'll always be true, so please, love me do.* A couple of girls screamed but most of the crowd were indifferent as they returned to dancing, jiving and twisting.

Friday afternoon, the Beatles made their way to Clifton-upon-Dunsmore to visit Buddy in the cottage where he was staying. The four boys came running up the path, knocking on windows and the front door, shouting, "We're the Beatles. We're the Beatles. Let us in." Muriel Podgson was used to unconventional pop groups and invited them in and made cups of tea and brought out homemade cake. Pete, Buddy, the Beatles, Muriel and her elderly mother, all sat in the small sitting room chatting and joking before they had to leave to go to Nuneaton for the early show for young teenagers.

Arriving at the Co-op Hall, Ringo and Barney set their drum kits up alongside each other on the large stage and before the start of the show, the two drummers had some fun, 'jamming' together. Soon John Lennon joined in playing guitar. The evening went well with good crowds. The Beatles received no more interest than other groups and the 'star' of the show was Buddy Britten. Afterwards, Buddy suggested they visit Clifton Hall again before returning to Liverpool.

Roger was curious to hear their new record and had walked to Rugby during the day to buy a copy. After the shows, the boys were together in the rehearsal room and Roger picked up his record to play it on the Dansette record player. As he held it in his hand, the Beatles walked in. John Lennon casually strolled over to see what Roger was holding and smiled when he saw it was their record. He took the disc off Roger, lifted the arm of the record player and lowered the disc onto the machine's slip mat.

They all listened politely to *Love me do*. It had been written mostly by Paul and had simple lyrics. As the song concluded, Roger commented, "I wouldn't pin your hopes on that one. You might be lucky to sell 2,000." Roger compared the Beatles to Danny Storm and the Strollers, whom he considered, far superior. Everyone knew that 2,000 records were the minimum number you needed to sell before a record company would agree to make a second recording.

George Harrison, seeing Roger's Gretsch guitar, asked if he could play it. Roger agreed and George complimented him on the guitar's quality and sat on the window ledge, happily strumming away. Drinking coffee and tea, the boys exchanged banter and jokes until the early hours of the morning, when the Beatles decided it was time to leave and return to Liverpool.

Impatient to make a name for himself and bored with touring the dancehalls, Roger decided to leave and went to see Reg to give him notice.

"You've a good job with regular money. Believe me, it's really tough to make it on your own. There's plenty of time to do that when you've more experience. If I were you, I'd stay a bit longer. Think about it."

"I've made up my mind," replied Roger, stubbornly

"Okay. We'll be sorry to lose you. You'll always be good Roger, in fact, you'll be very good and always able to make a living as a musician. But you'll never be brilliant."

Reg was honest and to the point with his performers and Roger was very young and like so many before him, left on a dream. When he arrived in London, the reality was harder than anticipated. Tito Burns, who managed a number of artists, including Cliff Richard, signed Roger up with a two-year contract which restricted him from working for anyone else. Roger hoped to be developed as a singer songwriter but after being told to go home and wait, he became disillusioned. The phone call never came. When he went back to see Tito Burns, he was ignored. Having signed a contract which prevented him from performing, Roger decided to run dances. Naively, he enquired about renting the same hall as Reg but on a different night. When Reg saw him, he was furious.

"Are you trying to put me out of business?"

Apologetic, Roger explained he was broke and out of work. Reg, more calmly, put his hand in his pocket and gave him a ten shilling note. Later, when Roger found his own backing group, Dorothy and Reg gave him work again, at the dancehalls.

16. TIN PAN ALLEY

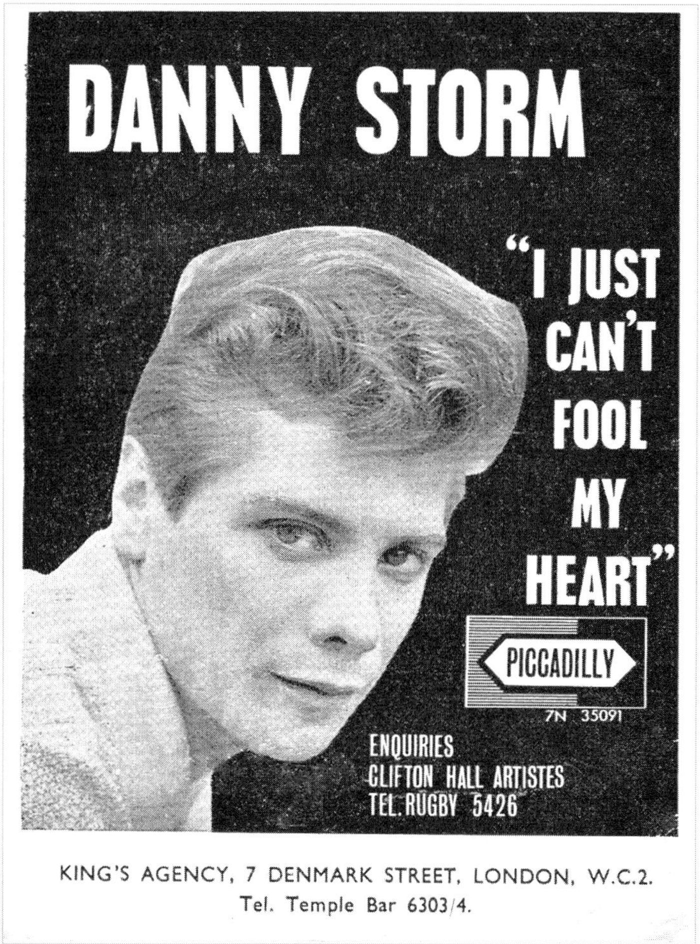

Danny Storm promotional card (from Mike Hopcraft)

The desire to have an office in Tin Pan Alley kept Reg returning to Denmark Street. It was a short, shabby street, just off the busy Tottenham Court Road and close to the Soho district. The street consisted mainly of cafes, music shops and the offices of various music publishing agencies. Eventually, Reg found what he was looking for and returned home pleased with himself. Whistling merrily, he went to find Dorothy to tell her the good news.

"No Reg. Not in Tin Pan Alley. You and your big ideas. We can't afford the expense. You need to keep your feet on the ground and live within your means. You're spending money like water. Do you have any idea how much it's costing in setting up the Fortunes, paying wages, buying them new suits and equipment? And have you thought when you might get your money back?"

"You have to invest money to earn money," replied Reg. He enjoyed teasing his wife and making her cross, so he ignored her question.

"I've agreed to go to the agent's next week and sign the lease."

"We can't afford offices in Tin Pan Alley."

Reg's eyes twinkled in response as he suppressed a grin.

"They're not expensive. They're on the 2nd and 3rd floors above the Tin Pan Alley club and a bit run down. It all needs re-plastering and a lick of paint. I've agreed a rent of £350."

"£350 a week!" exclaimed Dorothy.

"No, a year," grinned Reg. "On a seven-year lease although they may kick us out with six months' notice if they want to demolish the building. And I've found a man to run it for me. His name's Terry Meacher and I've invited him to stay at Clifton Hall this weekend with another chap, Kenny Bell, who'll work with him. You'll be able to meet them both. Terry looks a bit like Buddy Holly. He's got dark hair and wears Buddy Holly style glasses. We're thinking of changing his name to Terry King and we'll call the agency, King's Agency. What do you think Doe Doe?"

Dorothy took a deep breath and let it out slowly as a sigh of relief.

"Sounds okay. How will you make any money out of it?"

"I'll receive 10% commission on the groups and bookings I put through."

"I trust you'll get a proper signed contract and not work with just a hand shake? You know how people diddle you."

"I will. That's all in hand," smiled Reg.

"Do you know what Old Jack did today?" laughed Dorothy, as her mind wandered to her garden. "He weeded out my wallflower plants thinking they were weeds. I found them on the compost heap. He's so short-sighted he can't see what he's doing."

"Perhaps you should buy Jack some glasses or you could find a younger gardener. Someone who can mow the lawns," chuckled Reg.

As the weather grew colder and the winter nights drew in, the village could hear loud explosions emanating from Clifton Hall. It was that time of year when Reg liked to experiment with making the loudest bang.

"You'll blow yourself up one of these days," said Dorothy, exasperated. "And you shouldn't be encouraging the boys to have firework battles. Someone could get badly injured."

"You worry too much."

"Worry, why should I worry? Shields," said Dorothy. "Where did the boys get their shields from?"

"Shields. What do you mean?" asked Reg, innocently.

"You know what I mean. Dustbin lids. All the lids in the village have disappeared."

"Ah. How did you hear?"

"The hairdresser. I hear all the gossip at the hairdressers. Everyone in the village can hear your explosions and they've put two and two together and guessed that Clifton Hall is where their bin lids are."

"Mm," smiled Reg, trying to be serious. "I'll get the boys to take them back after Bonfire Night."

The boys spent weeks preparing for battle except for the pianist, Chris Capaldi. He considered it stupid to try and blow each other up and went home to Cheltenham. The fireworks this year had become more outlandish and much louder. Reg bought Crow Scarers, Thunder Flashes from the army with no fuse paper so the boys had to make their own and Air Bombs containing five or six rockets which said clearly on the label, *'do not hold'.*

The boys were given a large bag of fireworks each and the cost was docked from their wages at the end of the week. They made bazookas from empty carpet tubes and had various other aids for the battle. In the spinney, Reg built himself a kind of fort as a shelter and at 11 p.m. on Monday night, 5th November, the firework battle commenced.

Reg had the largest arsenal of fireworks and wore three woolly hats and a thick layer of newspapers around his body for extra protection. He only had a couple of boys on his side. Everyone else was against him. Reg thrived on excitement and danger, running backwards and forwards, avoiding rockets and fireworks aimed directly at him, retreating to his fort to recharge his bazookas.

Various boys limped off to the kitchen to recover from their injuries before going back to resume the battle. Barry was hit in the head and temporarily knocked unconscious. Gary's shoe was blown off but fortunately, his foot remained intact. A few minutes later, the Air Bomb he was holding did not fire all its rockets and they exploded in his gloved hand. The pain was excruciating. For weeks, his hand remained numb. When the battle came to an end, no one was seriously injured, and the madness ended in calm with everyone laughing as they ate their charred jacket potatoes and sausages around the bonfire.

There was more excitement in the house when Danny released his new record, *I Just Can't Fool My Heart*, written by Alan Klein. A lovely romantic song. It was well produced with good orchestration. Everyone was optimistic it would reach the top of the charts. The B-side, *Thinking of You*, was jointly written by Danny and Reg.

After weeks of Reg working to promote the record, it came as a huge disappointment when it did not make the bottom of the charts or sell as well as Danny's first record. Music trends were on the cusp of change and good looking singers were going out of fashion. The Beatles and new groups, especially those from Liverpool managed by Brian Epstein, were just beginning to make their name and taking over the top of the charts.

Reg's mother, Ada, rarely telephoned as phone calls were expensive. When she did, it was usually to relay bad news. Reg listened in almost silence. Dorothy knew Reg was deeply upset by the expression on his face and the way he chewed his bottom lip.

"What did Ada say?" coaxed Dorothy.

"Dad was found in bed with the neighbour's little girl. She was only six."

Reg felt so ashamed that his grandfather, the man who had looked after him and brought him up, could be so abhorrent. Dorothy was not surprised. Her sixth sense had warned her of his unnatural tendencies from the first time she had met him.

When Susan returned from school, she picked up Katy and carried her into the kitchen.

"I wish you wouldn't put your bags down in the middle of the floor for everyone to trip over," snapped Dorothy. "Why don't you take them straight up to your bedroom?"

"I will, in a minute, when I've made a drink," replied Susan, warming herself by the Aga. "What's up Mum?" Susan could see by the black look on her mother's face, something serious was troubling her.

Dorothy was quiet for a moment as she deliberated whether she should reveal the news to her daughter.

"It's your Granddad."

"Is he all right?" questioned Susan, fearing the worst.

"Yes, he's all right. He would be," replied Dorothy, sardonically. "He's always all right." Pausing, she then blurted out the news. "Your Granddad was found in bed with a six-year-old girl from the cottage next door."

Susan said nothing, shocked by the revelation as she gathered together her own childhood memories. "He did the same to me.".

"When?" Dorothy's face flickered with shock and anger, hardly believing what her daughter had said as she had always tried to protect her children.

"When he came to stay with us in Southampton and was sleeping in the lounge."

"The dirty old man," said Dorothy, venomously. "He'll never, never, come to stay with us again. Never!"

Picking up her school bags, Susan left the kitchen, regretting she had told her mother. The episode had not physically damaged or hurt her but with maturity, she understood that what he had done was very wrong. Now she carried a much heavier burden. One of guilt. He was never to be invited to Clifton Hall again and she felt responsible for him being ostracised from the family he loved.

The mid-December weather was dreadful. London was covered in a blanket of noxious smog and the rest of the country had both fog and snow. Clifton Hall grew colder as the outside temperature dropped to below zero. With Christmas not far away, Reg put his mind to the festive season's dances and how to organise them.

"What shall we do for prizes this year?" asked Reg. "I want something really different. Any ideas?"

"What about a slap-up dinner for two?"

"Old hat."

"My mother, John and his family are coming again for Christmas. What meat do you want? Pork or turkey?"

"Pork," replied Reg, grinning. "Pigs. That's it."

"Pigs," repeated Dorothy, surprised.

"Yes, baby piglets for prizes. They would get the kids laughing."

Reg purchased two piglets from a local farmer and kept them in a stable and each night before the shows, he went to catch them and put them in boxes to travel with the boys to the dances. The larger piglet was quite tame and easily caught. The little pig was lively and squealed loudly as it ran around and round the stable and between Reg's legs. Eventually, with the help of several boys, Reg caught him and put him in a box.

"You take Little Pig," said Reg, grinning at Dorothy. "It won't be as much trouble as Big Pig."

"No," smiled Dorothy, knowingly. "You take Little Pig."

The boys were not impressed with transporting a smelly pig inside a box but they did it with good humour, making many jokes about the aroma. At the respective dances, Reg and Dorothy organised a competition and the contestants had to line up and take it in turns to hold the pig and sing to it. Dorothy's pig behaved himself perfectly but Little Pig did not.

Reg asked for 10 volunteers and within a moment, boys and girls had jumped onto the stage and he stood them in a line.

"Close your eyes," instructed Reg to the first contestant. "Put your arms out so you can hold what I have in the box but first you must guess what it is." The audience roared with laughter as Reg lifted out the pig and placed it in the girl's arms. "It's pink, warm and quite heavy. Keep your eyes tightly shut. Can you guess what it is?" The girl did as she was told but when Little Pig began to wriggle and squeal, she opened her eyes and immediately dropped the pig. Little Pig made his escape and ran full speed, scuttling away to hide behind the drum kit and speakers.

The stage soon became a shambles as Reg took chase. Contestants and musicians were almost falling over themselves with laughter as Little Pig ran between their legs as they tried to catch it. The audience watched in uproar. Nothing so funny had been seen on the stage before.

Little Pig, squealing loudly, was cornered and caught by Reg who quickly put him back in the box. "Now Little Pig," laughed Reg, as he stood by the microphone. "We are going to sing to you."

The competition continued with Reg holding tight to the pig as each contestant sang a song of their choice. The winner was chosen by the audience who received the loudest cheer and they were presented with the pig. After Reg had escorted the winner off stage, he offered a £5 prize instead and Little Pig was placed securely in the box. Two minutes later, Reg was back on stage with his trousers rolled up to lead the audience in a song and dance. Kicking his legs, he began.

Knees up Mother Brown, Knees up Little Pig,
Under the table you must go, Ee-aye, Ee-aye, Ee-aye-oh.

The piglets were returned to the farmer and a large pork joint purchased for Christmas day lunch. The house was peaceful, warm and quiet as the boys had all returned home and the central heating was switched on. Dorothy's family arrived, but Ada could not come and Reg's Dad was not invited.

Dorothy wrapped numerous small gifts and placed them under the Christmas tree. Realising she could no longer dress her eldest daughter like a child, she surprised Susan by taking her shopping to buy her first pair of high heel shoes, lipstick and blue eyeshadow.

On the day after Boxing Day, Dorothy answered the phone and looking somewhat bemused, passed the receiver to her daughter. When Susan finished speaking, Dorothy could not contain her curiosity.

"Who was that?"

"Andrew Simpson, the vicar's son."

"Do you know him?" asked Dorothy, raising her eyebrows at Reg.

"No, I've never met him but he wants to take me out."

"How does he know you?" asked Reg, surprised.

"He saw me in the choir on Christmas Eve at Midnight Communion and asked his mother who I was. He's coming to see me on his motorbike."

"That's good, we'll be able to meet him. You can invite him to the dance in Nuneaton on Friday night if he'd like to come," suggested Reg pleasantly, disguising his concern about his daughter going out alone with a boy he did not know, even if he was a vicar's son.

"Okay," replied Susan, happily, leaving her parents in the kitchen to go to her bedroom so she could comb her hair, put on her new shoes and pink lipstick, in readiness for her mysterious visitor.

1963 MUSIC TRENDS

THE LIVERPOOL SOUND and Beatlemania began to dominate the charts. **The Beatle's** hits included: *She Loves You, From Me to You, Please Please Me* and *I Want to Hold Your Hand*. **Gerry and the Pacemakers:** *You'll Never Walk Alone, How Do You Do It* and *I Like It*. **Freddy & the Dreamers:** *You Were Made For Me, I'm Telling You Now* and *If you Gotta Make a Fool of Somebody*. **Billy J Kramer and the Dakotas:** *I'll Keep You Satisfied* and *Bad To Me*. **The Fourmost:** *Hello Little Girl*. **The Searchers:** *Sweets for My Sweet* and *Sugar and Spice*. **Dave Clark Five:** Glad All Over . **The Bachelors:** Charmaine.

REG CALVERT booked top stars to appear at his dancehalls, including: **The Rolling Stones:** *I Wanna Be Your Man*. **Joe Brown:** *That's What Love Will Do*. **Mark Wynter:** *Go Away Little Girl*. **Johnny Kidd and the Pirates:** *I'll Never Get Over You*. **The Hollies:** *Searchin*. **Brian Poole & the Tremeloes:** *Do You Love Me* and *Twist and Shout*. **The Ronettes:** *Be My Baby*. Also: **Ketty Lester** and **Gene Vincent**.

SOLO SINGERS were unfashionable, but **Cliff Richard** stayed at the top with: *The Next Time, Bachelor Boy, It's all in the Game, Don't Talk To Him, Lucky Lips* and *Summer Holiday*. **Adam Faith:** *The First Time*. **Billy Fury:** *In Summer, When Will You Say I Love You* and *Like I've Never Been Gone*. **Frank Ifield:** *Confessin* (*That I Love You*), *The Wayward Wind* and *Nobody's Darlin But Mine*.

FEMALE SINGERS to make the charts included **Dusty Springfield** with: *I Only Want To Be With You*. **Kathy Kirby:** *Dance On* and *Secret Love*. **Shirley Bassey:** *I Who Have Nothing*. **Brenda Lee:** *All Alone Am I*. **Lesley Gore:** *It's My Party*.

FOLK MUSIC had gained popularity. **The Springfields** reached the top with: *Island of Dreams* and *Say I Won't Be There*. **Peter, Paul and Mary** with: *Blowing In the Wind*. **Rooftop Singers:** *Walk Right In*. **Tommy Roe:** *The Folk Singer*.

INSTRUMENTALISTS included: **Jet Harris & Tony Meehan** with: *Diamonds, Scarlet O'Hara* and *Applejack*. **The Shadows** with: *Atlantis, Foot Tapper* and *Dance On*. **Heinz and the Tornadoes** with: *Just Like Eddie* and *Globetrotter*. **Duane Eddy** with: *Dance with the Guitar Man*. **Kenny Ball & His Jazzmen:** *Sukiyaki*.

THE AMERICANS were no longer the trendsetters. **Elvis** succeeded in topping the UK charts with: *Return to Sender*. **Paul and Paula:** *Hey Paula* and *Young Lovers*. **The Four Seasons:** *Walk like a Man*. **Roy Orbison:** *In Dreams, Blue Bayou* and *Mean Woman Blues*. **Ray Charles:** *Take These Chains From My Heart*. **Jim Reeves:** *Welcome to My World*. **Buddy Holly:** (died 1959): *Wishin'* and *Bo Diddley*. **Steve Lawrence and Eydie Gorme:** *I Want to Stay Here*. **The Crystals:** *Then He Kissed Me* and *Da Doo Ron Ron*. **Del Shannon:** *Little Town Flirt* and *Two Kinds of Teardrops*.

Top: Fortunes wearing their 'new' blue check suits (RC)
Bottom: Jimmy Stevens and the Jackpots: Tommy Pratt, Stu Brown, Roger Chapman, Rick Grech, Derek Diamond (RC).

17. THE DANCE GOES ON

The Fortunes: Rod Allen, Barry Pritchard, Glen Dale (RC)

Roger James had been wrong about the Beatles. *Love Me Do* surprised everyone by reaching 17 in the charts. The Beatles were booked to tour Scotland in January, 1963 and the Barron Knights, at the last minute, had cancelled the tour. The promoters contacted Reg and asked if he could find someone to replace them. He recommended his new group, the Fortunes.

As the Fortunes set off on their journey to Elgin, weather conditions deteriorated and when they arrived they found all the hotels were full. Fortunately, on each night of the tour, various people offered them Scottish hospitality. The Fortunes had developed into a brilliant six-piece group and the Beatles stood in the wings to watch their show. When it was the Beatles turn to perform, the girls in the audience screamed ecstatically and the four young men were barely audible even with their enormous loud speakers. They were on the brink of making it big and the audience loved them.

January, 1963 was the coldest month anyone could remember. Colder than the 'great snow' of 1947. It seemed as if it would never end as rivers, lakes and even the sea off the Kent Coast, began to freeze over.

The dances had to go on and musicians at Clifton Hall went out regardless of weather conditions. Returning late one night after struggling through snow blizzards, vehicles were abandoned at the bottom of the drive. Tired and cold, everyone had to trudge the last quarter of a mile to the house, forcing their way through hedge-high snow drifts, wearing fashionable clothing and unsuitable footwear.

England was almost at a standstill as railways and roads were closed. This time, there was no choice but to cancel dances and advertisements were placed in local papers to inform teenagers. Dorothy fretted. She had wages to pay even if the boys had no work. Conditions became worse when the village had a power cut and tap water froze. Clifton Hall was isolated and everyone congregated in the two kitchens to keep warm. Fortunately, Dorothy had provisions to feed everyone and a store of white wax candles to dimly light the rooms. At first, it was fun, but the reality of living a frugal life in extreme cold with water carried in buckets from the well, became tedious. When the lights flickered on a few days later, everyone was relieved.

The vehicles remained 'parked' at the bottom of the driveway for most of January and into February. Keeping numbers up at the dancehalls was a constant effort and once a dance closed, even temporarily, it took time to re-build a regular audience. Other promoters had copied Reg's ideas and teenagers now had a choice of venues to go to. Reg allowed the dances in the South and West Country to close, instead, he expanded his network in central England. The Cheltenham dance on Saturday nights was in decline so in one last effort to try and boost the numbers, he decided to let Susan run the Nuneaton dance on her own.

Reg had taught his daughter well. She understood how to do soundchecks, stage lighting, observe the audience and manage the groups. The most important aspect was to maintain the atmosphere in the hall and ensure changeover between groups were no longer than a two record break. Reg and Dorothy graded the groups: A, B or C and paid them accordingly. The A group received £15, the B group £12 and the C group £10. Each group played two sets, with the C group starting the show and the A group ending the evening.

Restrictive licensing laws were relaxed and dancehalls were permitted to stay open to 11.45 p.m. The Co-op gave Reg permission to organise a bar in the tea room and he employed a Rugby couple, Mr and Mrs Jackson, to manage it for him. This made a big difference to the dance, as boys who routinely went to a pub first, now came earlier and drank in the bar.

On Saturday night, Susan was escorted to Nuneaton by Frank, one of their regular stewards who lived in Rugby. Before she left, both parents gave final instructions.

"You've a new group auditioning tonight called the Demons. Put them on first and let me know whether they're good enough to book again. Here's my shopping bag with the admission tickets and a cash float to give to Mrs Thomas. At the end of the show you'll have to pay the groups. Put their money out of the takings in these brown envelopes with the group's name on," explained Dorothy, as she put three envelopes in the shopping bag.

"Okay," replied Susan, whilst screwing her nose up at the large old-fashioned leather bag her mother gave her.

Reg smiled at his daughter to give her confidence.

"Mrs. Thomas will give you the takings. Hide them in the shopping bag in the back office behind the desk. You'll be okay, you know what to do. But remember, if someone attacks you don't try to be brave. Give them the bag. You're far more important than all the money."

It was after midnight when Susan returned home. Both parents smiled at her as she joined them at the kitchen table to eat a late supper.

"How did you get on? Did you have a good crowd?" asked Reg.

"The groups were fine and did what I asked them."

"And the Demons, were they any good?" asked Dorothy.

"Not very but okay as a C group."

After a few weeks of going to Cheltenham, Reg found he was unable to revitalise the dance and it was closed. He looked around for a replacement venue and arranged to book the new Memorial Hall in Atherstone. It was only a short drive from Nuneaton which meant he could take Susan to the dance and collect her at the end of the shows. Their one-to-one time in the car resumed and they continued to enjoy their conversations about love, life and the universe.

The contract for offices at 7 Denmark Street was signed and Reg began to organise their refurbishment, enlisting the aid of the Fortunes to help with the decorating.

"We've got a lot of gigs lined up," they protested.

"No, you haven't. I've cancelled them for two weeks," grinned Reg.

Reg was persuasive and each night, after their day's labour, they returned to the guest house covered in white dust. The building was dilapidated and the stairway rickety. All the lath and plaster had to be removed. Gary did not mind as his family were in the building trade but the other boys complained to no avail. They were musicians and did not expect their 'apprenticeship' to include building and decorating.

Spring arrived late but when it came, it was as though winter had never been. The birds celebrated the awakening by singing loudly from every tree. Dorothy looked each day at the terrace to see snowdrops and crocuses break through the frozen earth. Next came the yellow daffodils shimmering gold in the warm sunshine, followed by red tulips and purple aubrietia tumbling down the walls. She loved her garden but Reg could no longer be persuaded to mow the lawns so she had taken on a second gardener. His name was also Jack and they called him Young Jack.

Gene Vincent had a large following of British fans and his song *Be-Bop-A-Lula* had become a rock classic, sung by most of the groups. Reg booked him to tour the dancehalls and on the Friday after Easter, he was due to be on at Worcester Corn Exchange. The audience, excited with anticipation, waited for him to perform. When he did not arrive the atmosphere in the hall changed. The audience became impatient and agitated. Dorothy was running the dance and she did not have Reg's charisma to run impromptu competitions to fill in time, so the supporting group, Mike Everest and the Alpines, played on, and on.

Near the end of the evening, Gene arrived with his 'minders' holding him up, one each side, apologising in their American drawl, "Sorry ma'am, he's too ill to perform."

"Don't be ridiculous," stormed Dorothy. "He's not ill, he's drunk and he will go on. Get him to the dressing room and I'll see you there."

The minders did as they were instructed and waited apprehensively for a very angry lady to reappear. When she did, it was with a large plate of bread rolls and a jug of black coffee. After being force fed by Dorothy, he became coherent and able to stand on his own. Dorothy led him to the stage and introduced her star guest, the audience none the wiser as to the reason for his delay.

Gene, dressed in sleek black leather with his distinctive stance, left leg held back, started to sing. He had injured his leg firstly in a motorbike accident and then a second time in the fatal car crash with Eddie Cochran. He was one of the few singers the males in the audience enjoyed. Gene was good, even when he was drunk, his slurred speech put down to his American accent!

More stars were booked during the year. Rising and falling stars were less expensive than those currently at the top of the charts. The maximum Reg would pay was £125 but most were paid between £25 and £60. He listened to new record releases and took a gamble by advance booking relatively unknown groups in the hope they would become famous by the time they appeared at his dances. In this way, he held ticket prices at an affordable amount. In June 1963, he booked Eden Kane, the Chantels, Billy J. Kramer, Billie Davis and Ketty Lester.

Ketty Lester had achieved worldwide recording success with a beautiful ballad, *Love Letters*. Reg had agreed to provide accommodation for her and knowing Dorothy's dislike of female singers, telephoned the best hotels in Rugby. After several calls, he angrily slammed the phone down.

"What's up with you?" asked Dorothy, startled by the thud.

"Would you believe it? The hotels won't accept my booking for Ketty Lester because she's black."

"That's ridiculous. I've seen signs in London saying, 'No Blacks and No Irish' but I've never seen anything like it in Rugby."

"Can she stay here?" asked Reg, appealing to his wife.

Reluctantly, Dorothy agreed and when Ketty Lester arrived, she did her best to be pleasant and polite. Reg, by comparison, was courteous and treated her like a lady. He was proud to have a world famous singer staying in his house and invited her for lunch on Saturday to the Andalusian restaurant in Rugby. Dorothy declined to go, saying she was too busy. Instead, he took Susan with him as chaperone so as not to agitate his wife.

Reg had become well known in the music business and when he took the Fortunes demo discs to Decca Records, they agreed to a recording contract with no 'strings' attached. Barry had written a good song for the B-side and Decca chose *Summertime, Summertime,* for the A-side, a song with catchy lyrics previously released in the USA.

Reg was in demand as a manager but declined to take on many groups. He knew how much work was involved and was against tying them down to a worthless contract unless he could promote them personally. He mentored young musicians and if they were good enough, helped them turn professional by offering long contracts to work abroad in nightclubs and US army bases. The best musicians, he signed up to King's Agency.

He accepted the management of the Rockin' Berries, an exceptional Birmingham harmony and comedy group. Reg knew the group well and they often came to Clifton Hall to rehearse. There was no contract to tie them down and after six months, they changed their minds and changed their manager.

The Exciters, a good Leicester group, often worked for Reg and he suggested they change their name to Jimmy Stevens and the Jackpots. They looked at him in surprise.

"There's already an American group called the Exciters who've made a record," explained Reg. "And if you wear caps you'll stand out from the other groups."

They agreed and changed their name. Soon, they began to earn more money so were able to give up their day jobs and Reg enlisted them with King's Agency. He took an interest in their progress, suggesting various crazy ideas to attract attention and gain free publicity. One idea was to roll around in the road to make the news for press photos but they declined, preferring to concentrate on their music.

Since the loss of their baby, Reg was restless and spending more time away from Dorothy and Clifton Hall. Quite often, he would be in London for two or three days and other times, fly to Europe and Jersey to meet nightclub owners. When he returned, he always thought to bring Dorothy a small gift.

"Perfume, lovely," smiled Dorothy.

"Clubs are the way forward Doe Doe. Dancehalls are going out of fashion."

"Dinner won't be long," replied Dorothy, ignoring his remark. She did not want to encourage him to have a night club.

When the family were together, Reg, holding a paper bag in his hand, beckoned to his daughters.

"I've bought you a little surprise from Germany. Stand over there with your backs turned and keep your eyes closed until I say open."

The two girls giggled. Out of the bag, Reg took two large, grotesque, hairy plastic spiders and placed one on each of the girl's shoulders. When they opened their eyes, they screamed in unison as they shook them off.

"They're not real," chuckled Reg. "You'll be able to have fun frightening your school friends."

"Really Reg. Whatever will you bring back next? Just keep them away from me, they're horrible," laughed Dorothy.

It was accepted boys would come and go and when Tony Clarke gave notice to leave, Reg and Dorothy wished him luck. He had an ambition to become a record producer and it came as no surprise when he was later offered a job working for Decca Records.

18. VOTES FOR TEENAGERS

Screaming Lord Sutch campaigning for votes for teenagers (RC)

Buddy, continued to come to Clifton Hall to rehearse and meet up with the rest of the boys. One afternoon he saw Susan in the passageway and smiling, asked if he could borrow her mother's address book, explaining he had lost a telephone number. Susan fetched the small red and black book from her mother's desk drawer and was surprised when he took it and said he would return it in a couple of hours.

Impatient for success, Buddy was planning his future. He often asked the boys, "What are you going to do when the war's over," meaning, what career plans have you made? Most had no idea. Living at Clifton Hall was a dream come true, something to be enjoyed in the moment. Being a rock musician was for the young and sooner, or later, they would grow old and have to move back to the real world.

Dorothy had not foreseen Buddy's departure and felt betrayed and bitterly disappointed when he told her he was leaving. She had worked hard for him and succeeded in obtaining recording contracts, features in newspapers and an appearance on television. Buddy, well-mannered and charming as always, thanked Dorothy for all she had done, while explaining he had found a new London agency to manage him. Barney and Pete had also agreed to go with him. With no contract to tie them down, Dorothy held her tongue and said little in reply. Grudgingly, she wished them luck.

News and current affairs rarely filtered into the consciousness of the Clifton Hall residents. The only television in the house was in the lounge, a small black and white set occasionally watched by the family. No one listened to the radio and newspapers were rarely bought.

Spring 1963, the Profumo affair was making headline news. It was a sordid story involving sex and a Russian spy. John Profumo, Secretary of State for War, had denied in the House of Commons his relationship with Christine Keeler. Many well-known establishment figures were embroiled in the saga and when the truth was revealed, it rocked the British government.

Profumo's resignation meant that there would be a by-election in Stratford-upon-Avon. Reg knew the press would be there in abundance and he had a 'brainwave'. Picking up the telephone, he rang David Sutch.

It was generally accepted that Reg had become David's manager. There was no contract, nothing on paper and no management commission paid. The two men simply enjoyed each other's company and at every opportunity, David travelled to Clifton Hall and spent hours talking to Reg and drinking tea.

"How do you fancy standing for parliament?"

"You're joking?" replied David.

"No, I'm serious. You could stand at the by-election in Stratford."

"No one will vote for me."

"No. You won't get elected but you'll get fantastic publicity."

"You're right man, what a fantastic idea."

Reg did not reveal his plans to Dorothy, immediately, and when she heard, she was, as he expected, annoyed.

"What's the point in promoting him? He's not one of our boys and you're not his manager," said Dorothy, dismissively.

"It'll be good fun and exciting," replied Reg, grinning.

"It's a waste of your time. He pays you nothing and you'll probably end up out-of-pocket paying his election costs."

"We'll need a manifesto. What do you think David should stand for?"

"Teenagers. Teenagers should get the vote," replied Dorothy, glibly.

"Brilliant idea. Why didn't I think of that? Will you write the manifesto?"

"No, you can write your own stupid manifesto."

"Come on Doe Doe. You're much better at writing than I am," said Reg, smiling, as he handed her a pen and notepad.

"If," said Dorothy, thoughtfully, "You can get married at sixteen and have babies, why can't you get the vote at eighteen?"

"If you can go to war at eighteen and die for your country, why can't you get the vote at eighteen?" added Reg, enthusiastically.

In July, Susan had her 15th birthday in July and neither parent thought to ask her what career she wanted. She was a 'girl' and it was usual for girls to leave school and find a job. Most girls in her class were looking forward to leaving but Susan was more ambitious and asked her mother if she could stay on until she was 16 and study to for her O-levels. Dorothy, who had always assumed responsibility for her children's education, would not agree.

"Complete waste of time, you're not clever enough to get any O-levels."

"I want to go to Art College and I need 'O' and A-levels," explained Susan.

"Don't be ridiculous. Art College is for beatniks and drop-outs and you're not going. You're not even artistic," added Dorothy, as an afterthought.

"Please Mum," pleaded Susan.

"I've said no and that's the end of the matter," replied Dorothy, sharply.

"But it's what I want to do."

"It would be a complete waste of your time and my money for you to go to college. You'll be sixteen next year and you've so many boyfriends, you'll be getting married in no time."

"I don't want to get married. I want to go to Art College."

"Pigs can fly. You need to live in the real world and realise what life is about. Your father gives you silly ideas and makes you think you can do anything, but you can't."

"If I were a boy, you'd let me stay on at school and have a career."

"That's it," shouted Dorothy. "I've had enough. Get a job. Any job. You need to keep your feet on the ground and earn your own money. Not have airy-fairy ideas like your father."

"That's not fair. What am I supposed to do? Get a job in a factory?" shouted Susan, storming out of the room, banging the door behind her.

Dorothy was used to ruling the house, the boys, and her daughters. Her word was the 'law'. She would never relent or reconsider her decisions. Having a rebellious teenage daughter who had the audacity to shout back was a new phenomenon. Reg would not interfere with his wife's authority so there was nothing Susan could do.

Danny Storm posing for a photo on Andrew Simpson's Norton motorbike (RC)

When Susan came to talk to her father, he would not take sides and instead, changed the subject.

"Is Andrew coming to see you in the summer holidays?"

"I expect so," replied Susan, smiling.

"Don't go off on his motorbike this time. Motorbikes are dangerous."

"Didn't you have one when you were young?"

"Yes. But it didn't go that fast and when I married your Mum, I had a sidecar fitted so it was more stable"

"Andrew's really fed up with being at boarding school. He wants to leave and get a job."

"How old is he now?"

"17 but his parents won't let him leave. They want him to take A-levels and go to university."

“I left school at 14 and was married at 18. When you’re young, you’re impatient to grow up.”

“I’d like to stay on at school and go to Art College.”

“You’ll have to find another way to follow your dreams,” replied Reg, sympathetically, as he lit a cigarette and inhaled smoke. Slowly, laying the cigarette down on the ashtray he looked at his daughter.

“You don’t want to do this Susie.”

“Do what?”

“Smoke. It’s not good for you and this is what you do with your money,” said Reg as he took a ten shilling note from his wallet. Striking a match, he put the flickering flame up to the note. “All you do is burn your money and once you start smoking, it’s hard to stop.”

In August, Sarah Jane arrived for her summer holiday and as the family were sitting together in the kitchen having a late breakfast, the door swung open and David Sutch entered without knocking or invitation. This annoyed Dorothy immensely. All the boys respected her kitchen and knocked before entering. David ignored Dorothy’s glare and sat down to talk to Reg about the election. Dorothy held her tongue and politely asked if he would like some kippers.

“No thanks Mrs C.”

“I’m flummoxed as t’ why you’re wearin’ a top hat? Are th’ going t’ be wed?” asked Sarah Jane.

“No Ma’am,” replied David. “Have you heard about the Profumo affair? I’m standing for Parliament at the Stratford by-election.”

“David’s going to be a politician. That is, if anyone votes for him,” chuckled Reg.

“No one will vote for me. They’d have to be mad,” laughed David.

“We know he won’t win but everyone will hear of Screaming Lord Sutch. It’ll make his name,” explained Reg.

“Great,” retorted Dorothy, under her breath.

“Can I come?” asked Susan.

“And me?” asked Candy.

“You can all come and support us. I’ve booked an office for our headquarters and we’re getting loads of newspaper interest. I wouldn’t be surprised if David doesn’t get on the tele,” said Reg, enthusiastically.

“And who’s paying for the office and all the publicity material?” asked Dorothy, pointedly, to which neither Reg nor David replied.

“You could help us with the campaigning. Hand out leaflets to people while you do some shopping in Stratford,” suggested Reg.

“Seeing you two pretending to be serious about politics and making speeches is not my idea of a day out,” replied Dorothy, irritably. “It’s as if you haven’t got enough to do.”

“I am serious about politics. I wouldn’t mind being Prime Minister one day,” replied Reg, grinning.

“Thee’d be as ‘appy as a pig in muck,” commented Sarah Jane, smiling sympathetically at her daughter.

“Mrs C wrote our manifesto. I’m standing for Teenagers,” grinned David. “Teenagers should get the vote at eighteen.”

“Oh Aye,” said Sarah Jane, incredulously. “Thou must be kiddin’. It were not so long since I was a lass and suffragettes were chaining themselves up t’ lamp posts.”

“Why shouldn’t teenagers get the vote?” asked Susan.

“You can marry at sixteen and have children. Fight for your country at eighteen. So why shouldn’t teenagers get the vote?” asked David.

“And we want to campaign for free radio,” said Reg. “It’s about time we had free radio, like the Americans. We’re always one step behind.”

“The BBC have refused to play *Jack the Ripper,*” said David, grinning.

“I’m not surprised,” interjected Dorothy, as she glared at Reg to show disapproval of an intruder in her kitchen. “I shall be glad when the election is over and we get back to normal life.”

Reg and David were enjoying themselves. Each day, they travelled to Stratford and took part in the razzmatazz of electioneering. Screaming Lord Sutch created so much interest, he was featured in newspapers, on television and radio. He provided light relief from the other more serious candidates and when Polling Day arrived on 15th August, 1963, both Reg and David were delighted with the result. 209 people voted for him and overnight he was a household name. It was the best publicity stunt Reg had ever devised and he had loved every moment.

With his new fame, David began to earn much more money for his bizarre stage performances. He often became reckless, breaking musician’s instruments that were left on the stage and one evening, in a frenzy, he smashed Chris Capaldi’s electric piano. Chris, very angry, stormed into the dressing room.

“I know what you want,” said David, not looking Chris in the eye. “How much was the piano?”

“£102.”

“Here you are,” said David, taking a wad of notes from his pocket and offering Chris the money.

Sarah Jane stayed at Clifton Hall until the end of August and one afternoon, Susan and her grandmother were in the kitchen together. On the counter under the comics was one of the spiders and for fun, Susan placed it on her grandmother’s shoulder.

“Look Grandma,” giggled Susan.

Sarah Jane turned her head and seeing the ghastly creature, gasped in horror as she collapsed to the floor.

Not knowing what to do, Susan ran from the kitchen shouting for help as she searched for her mother. The house was unusually quiet and empty of residents. Running back to her grandmother, she knelt beside her and tried to make her more comfortable by putting a cushion under her head. It was a desperate situation. Susan was terrified she had killed her.

For what seemed like hours, but in reality was only a few minutes, Sarah Jane lay motionless. Slowly, flickering her eyes, she looked about as she recollected what had happened.

"I'm sorry Grandma," said Susan, crying. "It was only a toy spider."

"It's nay your fault Susan. Thou weren't t' know I'm terrified of spiders. Help me up and promise, thou'll nay tell thy mother, promise me Susan."

Susan shook her head, knowing she must tell her mother.

"Promise me Susan. I don't want tha' mother to be worried. Promise me," insisted Sarah Jane.

Susan again shook her head in reply. She had expected her formidable grandmother to be angry and scold her for her stupidity, but instead, she spoke gently and kindly. In the end, Susan made the promise.

Dorothy bought the latest records each week and left them in the rehearsal room for the boys to sift through to decide which ones they wanted to learn. Out of curiosity, she had bought Buddy Britten's new record, *If You Gotta Make a Fool of Somebody*. It was a good song and she wondered whether his new manager would be more successful than she had been. The song climbed the charts, reaching number three. A great success for a new singer but it was not Buddy's version which became a hit, but one recorded by Freddy and the Dreamers. Having a new manager did not improve Buddy's fortune. After a while, he reinvented himself, stopped wearing Buddy Holly style glasses and changed name to Simon Raven.

The Fortunes' record, *Summertime, Summertime,* was a cheerful, catchy number but for some unexplained reason, Decca delayed its release until 23rd August, 1963 much too late for the summer. Not surprisingly, the record sold very few copies.

Reg considered how he could get more publicity for the Fortunes and make them stand out. Rod had a superb voice but continued to be quarrelsome and often wore dark sunglasses, not to be fashionable, but to disguise the black eyes he received as a reward for his behaviour toward other musicians.

"You could be angry young men on stage, kick guitars and speakers. Throw things around and Gary could fall off his drum kit."

The Fortunes shook their heads in disagreement. Their onstage persona was of perfect young gentlemen, charming and well-mannered.

"Why don't you have your ears pierced?"

"Only girls have their ears pierced," replied Rod, with the others agreeing.

"Just one ear," coaxed Reg. "Gypsy's have one ear pierced and it'd be different and good publicity. You could set a new trend for boys."

"No way man," they all agreed. "We don't want our ears pierced."

There was nothing Reg could do to make them change their appearance but their stage shows and vocals were so good, they passed every television audition and were booked to appear on three different networks, Granada, Westward and Grampian Television. It was a great achievement for a new group who had not yet released a successful record. Reg felt proud of himself as a manager as few other pop groups were of a standard to appear 'live' and had to mime to their records.

With the Beatles writing their own music, it had become acceptable for musicians to think about composing their own songs. Danny and Barry collaborated to write an upbeat song for Danny to record, with catchy lyrics, quite different to his slow, romantic ballads.

Say You Do was released by Piccadilly Records in September, 1963. Everyone was optimistic it would become a big hit and Reg did his best to promote it. Sadly, it didn't reach the bottom of the charts. Pop culture, fashion and music trends are fickle. Liverpudlian groups were on the rise and good-looking singers, like Danny, were falling stars.

Reg and Dorothy kept in touch with their 'old' boys and helped them when they could by giving them work. Mike West, aka Robbie Hood, received the occasional booking but his show was now out of fashion. He married the girl singer, Jayne, and had a little boy to support and was finding it hard to survive financially. Roger James was with a Bristol group, the Cyclones and Johny Washington, was backed by the Congressmen before moving on to sing with the Applejacks.

Tanya Day continued to be managed by Reg although he no longer tried to obtain a recording contract for her. She was happy to receive regular bookings, working in England and abroad as one of the few female rock singers. When Reg saw her one night, he joked that he needn't have worried about her Birmingham accent. He had heard Cilla Black speak with her broad Liverpool accent and it hadn't affected her career.

Baby Bubbly had last appeared at the Banbury dance in January but had not seemed his normal 'bubbly' self. Bubbles had left on a dream and found life very hard. Then the dreadful news came through which left everyone in shock. He had died suddenly of a brain tumour.

19. MONKEY BUSINESS

Dorothy with William, the monkey Reg had bought for a Christmas prize. (RC)

Johnny Bev was booked to appear at the Atherstone Memorial Hall on 28th September, along with Mike Everest and the Alpines. Johnny Bev had achieved success as a songwriter with *A Picture Of You*, recorded by Joe Brown. Mike rated him very highly and invited his parents down from Blackburn to see the show.

The wiring-up of electrical equipment was primitive at many of the dancehalls and most systems were not earthed. When Johnny Bev was singing, he accidently touched the microphone with his lips and the electrics shorted out. Johnny collapsed, falling to the front of the stage. The musicians stopped playing and the hall went silent, except for a gasp of horror.

Shocked, the audience watched helplessly as Johnny Bev began to turn blue. It was obvious he was going to die.

Reg, realising the seriousness of the situation, ran to the office and dialled 999 for an ambulance.

Mike's father pushed his way through the audience and climbed onto the stage. He was a St John's Ambulance first aider and took immediate action. He knew what to do and began to resuscitate Johnny. The audience stood in hushed silence as the singer came back to life. A few minutes later, the ambulance arrived and Johnny was lifted onto a stretcher and carried away. The show resumed but the subdued atmosphere meant no one felt like dancing and most of the crowd did not stay to the end of the dance.

The craze of Mods and Rockers was constantly in the news headlines. They separated teenagers into two conflicting and distinctive groups. The Mods were fashionable and smartly dressed and their choice of transport was the scooter. Rockers wore black leathers and rode motorbikes. At weekends, the two opposing gangs of Mods and Rockers sometimes met and clashed violently, making headline news as the police came out in force to deal with the troublemakers.

In October, 1963, Candy reached the magical age of 13 and Dorothy now had to worry about having two teenage daughters living in a house full of boys. Dorothy found her younger daughter more pliable and worried less as she did not seem to attract boys in the way her older sister did. Candy was a follower of pop music and fashion and wanted to be a 'Mod.' Dorothy, happy to help, sewed her Mod dresses in small flower prints, gathered from above the bust and free flowing like a tent.

"Looks really good," said Dorothy, smiling as Candy twirled around with her new dress on.

"Those dresses make Candy look fat and very unattractive," commented Susan, when Candy had left the room.

"They suit her," smiled Dorothy, knowingly.

"No they don't. They make her look fat and frumpy."

"Don't you dare say anything to your sister," instructed Dorothy. "Candy has little enough confidence as it is and she's happy wearing them. It's hard for her being your younger sister, always following in your shadow."

Not long after Candy's birthday, Dorothy received a phone call from her brother with news that their mother had died. Sarah Jane had recently written to Dorothy, telling her how much she was looking forward to the completion of a new bathroom being built onto her cottage bungalow. Years of going down the yard to the toilet and filling a tin bath with hot water were nearly over. Sarah Jane had caught a bus into Huddersfield to withdraw cash from her building society account to pay the builder. When she returned home, the money was missing from her handbag. The shock was too much. Sarah Jane collapsed and died of a heart attack.

Dorothy travelled to Huddersfield several times to organise the funeral and sell her cottage. When she returned to Clifton Hall, she was full of regret, wishing she had persuaded her mother to live with them at Clifton Hall. Susan was also full of remorse and told her mother about the incident with the spider.

"You should have told me before," said Dorothy, quietly.

"I wanted to, but she made me promise," explained Susan, in tears. "Grandma said she didn't want to worry you and she made me promise."

Dorothy nodded.

"If I'd have known, I would have stopped my mother from going home. She must have known she had a weak heart, but it's too late now. We can't turn back the clock and it's not your fault. She would never have wanted me to worry," said Dorothy, sadly. "I wish I could have made her life a little easier. My mother worked so hard all her life and just when she should have been able to enjoy herself." Dorothy's voice trailed away as her eyes filled with tears. "Life isn't fair Susie. It's not fair."

Cold foggy nights and damp dreary days meant that November had arrived and Reg and the boys were once again preparing for Guy Fawkes Night, making more fireworks. Dorothy shrugged her shoulders and ignored their antics. November 5th was a Tuesday and Reg booked the Demons and the Rockin' Berries into the Evesham dance, leaving his own boys free. The battle was planned in fine detail and everyone, apart from Chris Capaldi, looked forward to it with great enthusiasm. When the battle was over in the early hours of the morning, Reg and the boys came into the kitchen laughing and joking about the near misses and frights. Dorothy was relieved. It was over for another year and no one had been seriously hurt.

On Friday nights, Reg left Clifton Hall early to run the shows at the Nuneaton Co-op Hall. Having two shows on the same night meant he could book big names and keep the ticket prices low. To boost numbers, he sometimes organised a coach from Rugby to transport teenagers to the dance. On 8th November, 1963 the Fourmost were booked for a fee of £125. They were under the management of Brian Epstein and their first record, *Hello Little Girl*, written by John Lennon, reached No. 9 in the charts.

The following week, 15th November, the Liverbirds, the first all-female rock band were booked, costing £20 and the Rolling Stones for £60. It was not often that Reg suggested to his daughters to come and see a new group but he recommended they see the Rolling Stones. He thought they were going to make it big and had recently released a record, *I Wanna Be Your Man*, written by Lennon and McCartney.

The Beatles had become incredibly famous and almost everything they wrote made the top of the charts. Susan and Candy, curious to see what the Rolling Stones were like, did as their father suggested and caught the coach to Nuneaton. When they arrived, they went backstage to say hello to him. The Rolling Stones were setting up their equipment and the girls stood to one side to watch.

"Do you think that's a boy or a girl?" asked Susan, looking at a tall thin person with shoulder length hair and large lips. It was the first time she had seen a boy with long hair and it made him look very effeminate.

"I don't know," giggled Candy. "Could be either. What do you think?"

"Perhaps we'll know when we hear them singing."

Susan and Candy made their way into the hall and joined the small crowd that had gathered near the front of the stage. The Rolling Stones were no better than the local groups and they wondered why their father had recommended them. They did not look as though they would become stars as they were the scruffiest and most unkempt group the girls had ever seen. In the junior session, young teenagers had shown their disapproval by throwing cakes at them. When Mick Jagger introduced, *I Wanna Be Your Man,* the audience watched in bemused silence. Reg had booked them early in anticipation they would be famous by the time they appeared at the dance, but this time he had misjudged his timing and barely covered his overheads.

In the late afternoon of Friday 22nd November, 1963 news of President Kennedy's assassination reverberated around the world and was repeated on television. Never before had viewers seen an actual murder take place and this was far more appalling than any horror movie. Everyone was in shock and for a moment, time seemed to stand still.

Reg had booked Mike Sarne for £135. He was the most expensive singer he had ever booked and famous for gimmicky songs *Will I What* and *Come Outside*, produced by Joe Meek. Also on the show were Danny Storm and the Strollers and the Size 7. No one expected the dance to be cancelled and teenagers made their way to the hall, talking in hushed whispers about what they had seen, whilst at the same time, looking forward to a good night out.

As Christmas drew near, Dorothy became depressed. She was in mourning and not looking forward to the first year without her mother.

"How do you fancy a day out at the zoo?" suggested Reg, cheerfully.

"The zoo?" queried Dorothy.

"You're always saying I don't take you out enough. We can have a fun day out. It would do you good."

"You're up to something. I can tell by the silly grin on your face."

"Prizes," replied Reg.

"No thanks. I've a lot to do. You ought to look for an animal importer rather than a zoo and don't bring back anything stupid. Remember, you have to look after whatever you buy and please, don't bring back any spiders."

The cold winter sun had turned to a fiery sunset when Reg returned in the late afternoon with his prizes. The sky had darkened and the lights from the house glowed, making Clifton Hall look warm and inviting. Reg parked his green Zephyr by the back door and took a large cardboard box out of the boot, whistling merrily as he carried it into the kitchen.

"What've you got there?" asked Dorothy, with feigned boredom.

"Wait and see and no peeping," grinned Reg, as he put the large cardboard box on the floor and returned to the car. Carrying a cage with a blanket over it, he placed it on the kitchen table and smiled at Dorothy.

"Come and see what I've bought."

Reg removed the blanket from the cage and inside was a baby Capuchin monkey who immediately began to screech and do a war dance.

"A monkey!" exclaimed Dorothy. "Really Reg. He looks wild and I don't think he likes you."

"And see what's in here," grinned Reg, as he put his arm into the box and lifted out a large snake.

"How could you? It's revolting," said Dorothy, stepping back in revulsion. "You can take the snake to the dances and I'll take the monkey."

"They won't hurt. Quite harmless. I bought two. They'll make good prizes and I don't expect anyone will want to take them home. They don't bite. See how it curls around my arm. The monkey will be more trouble," chuckled Reg. "He's been screeching all the way home."

"I expect he's hungry. What does he eat?"

"Fruit, bananas, oranges and things. The snakes eat dead mice but they don't need to be fed every day."

Dorothy shook her head in amazement and took a deep breath. "Where are you going to get dead mice from?"

"I thought the cats could catch a few," grinned Reg. "Katy's always bringing them into the kitchen or leaving them by the back door."

"If *you* want to be fed tonight, you'd better take them into the lounge," said Dorothy, arms folded in disapproval. "Do they need to be kept warm? You ought to leave the electric fire on and you can take this banana and orange for the monkey. I don't know what you're going to do about the snakes. You'll have to put some traps out and catch a few mice."

Grinning mischievously, Reg carried the animals into the rehearsal room to shock the boys, before taking them in the lounge. The little monkey did a war dance making everyone laugh. Reg carried him into the lounge and poked pieces of banana and orange through the cage wires but the monkey continued to shriek. Slowly and carefully, Reg opened the cage and put some fruit on the cage floor. The monkey, taking his opportunity, bit Reg with razor sharp teeth and Reg swiftly withdrew his hand. As quick as a flash the monkey darted out of the cage, ran across the floor, climbed up the curtains and onto the pelmet.

Dorothy opened the lounge door to see her husband running around the lounge trying to catch the monkey. The chase was on but as soon as Reg got near, the monkey shrieked and scampered away.

"I think you'll need to take him back tomorrow. He's too wild to keep and he can't stay on the pelmet all night. I dread to think of the mess."

"And how am I going to catch him?" asked Reg, raising his eyebrows as he sucked his bleeding hand.

"You'd better put antiseptic on that and wear some leather gloves next time," laughed Dorothy. "I've old net curtains we could throw one over him. But dinner's ready. I think if we leave him quiet, he might settle down."

Sometime later, the monkey was caught and returned to his cage. He refused to eat, even when they left him alone. It became obvious the monkey was so distressed at having left his monkey family he was on a hunger strike. Dorothy couldn't help feeling sorry for him as his large brown doleful eyes watched her every move.

"Leave me on my own with him," murmured Dorothy, sitting down on the settee with the cage beside her. "I'll see what I can do."

For several hours, Dorothy talked soothingly to the monkey and her patience was rewarded. The monkey began to chunter in reply and when she offered him a piece of orange, he snatched it and started to eat.

Dorothy arose early next morning and wearing thick gloves, sat quietly and talked to the monkey as she pushed small pieces of fruit through the wire cage. In response, he chuntered back. Slowly, she opened the cage door and put her gloved hand in and gently stroked the back of his neck. His eyes looked up at her, nervous and appealing.

Reg opened the lounge door and as he did so, the monkey let out a screech, jumped out of the cage and onto the top of the curtain pelmet where he continued to shout and do his war dance at Reg.

"Look what you've done," said Dorothy, crossly. "I had him eating out of my hand."

"I was going to take him back to the importers."

"You'll have to catch him first," smiled Dorothy, wryly.

"Come and help Doe Doe," appealed Reg, as he picked up the net and tried to throw it over the monkey. Dorothy declined and sat smiling as she watched the baby monkey outwit her husband.

"He's too clever for you. I think he might come back to me if you leave us alone."

"Better you than me, Gunga Din," grinned Reg.

Dorothy stayed perfectly still, talking to him in quiet soothing tones and waited patiently for the monkey to become calm. He murmured in reply and after a while, came closer and nervously sat on the back of the settee. Dorothy stretched out her hand and offered him small pieces of fruit which he snatched and ate eagerly. As he became more confident, he came close enough to allow Dorothy to stroke him.

Dorothy with William. (RC)

Reg advertised the Party Nights at the various Christmas and New Year dances. The halls were packed to capacity and the atmosphere became hot and steamy as bodies danced to the music, twisting or jiving close to each other. Reg gave out free paper streamers, balloons, party hats and mistletoe and did his party songs. The highlight of the evening was when Reg presented the competition prize to the unsuspecting girl winner. Reg asked her to close her eyes as he took the snake out of the box and draped it around her neck like a stole. Girls in the audience screamed and the winner, when she opened her eyes, almost fainted in horror. Unsurprisingly, no one wanted the prize and accepted money instead.

Susan and Candy were dismayed when their mother told them she was not taking a snake but the monkey to her Party Nights.

"You can't give him away," they appealed. "You've got to keep him."

Dorothy replied by smiling her enigmatic, Mona Lisa smile. "We'll see what we will see."

Dorothy organised her competition but when the girl winner insisted she wanted to keep the monkey, Dorothy's heart dropped and composing herself, she tactfully explained how wild and vicious he was. The girl absolutely refused to take the prize money of £5 and it was only when Dorothy bribed her by increasing the amount to £35 that the girl relented and Dorothy took home her prize.

"You're a daft thing," laughed Reg, when Dorothy explained what had happened. "He only cost me £15 and I could have bought another one when I take the snakes back."

"I think I'm going to call him William," replied Dorothy, smiling. She had fallen in love with him and within a few days, the monkey and Dorothy were inseparable. To keep him warm, Dorothy knitted small jumpers and toilet trained him. He liked being in the warmth of the kitchen and would sit high on the clothes airer that hung from the ceiling. He hated Reg with a vengeance. His other enemies were Screaming Lord Sutch and the two cats. If he took a dislike to anyone who walked into the kitchen, he screeched to tell them so. If by chance, they stood under the clothes airer, he took aim and urinated on them, chuntering and laughing as he sprayed them.

Christmas day was on a Wednesday which meant a two-day break for the boys before the dances resumed on Friday. On Christmas morning, the weather was cold, wet and dismal. The family ate their dinner seated around the kitchen table, making merry as they pulled crackers and laughed, but it was not the same. The house was empty and quiet.

Boxing Day, Reg invited a family from Rugby to join them, thinking that having guests would brighten up their festivities. He employed Mr and Mrs Jackson to run the bar at the Co-op Hall in Nuneaton and had become friendly with them. They also had two daughters, similar ages to Susan and Candy. After lunch, the girls went upstairs to their bedrooms while Reg brought out the snakes.

"I'm taking them back to the importer tomorrow. Can't see why no one wanted them as a pet," chuckled Reg, as he let them coil around his arm. William, who was sitting on Dorothy's shoulder, screeched and ran to the top of the curtain pelmet where he did a war dance making everyone laugh.

"I wonder if I can straighten it out?" said Mr Jackson, taking the snake off Reg and holding it out as he slowly unravelled the long body and smoothed it with his hands. When he finished, the snake was smooth and straight - and dead. He then picked up the second snake and proceeded to do the same. Reg and Dorothy looked on, speechless and disgusted, hardly believing what they were witnessing as he let the second dead snake drop into the box.

"Ah," murmured Mr Jackson, unconcerned. "Don't think you'll need to take them back now."

GROUPS BOOKED AT THE DANCEHALLS

EXTRACTS FROM THE 1963 DIARY

DANCEHALLS: Atherstone Memorial Hall. Banbury Winter Gardens, Washwood Heath BRS, Evesham Public Hall, Nuneaton Co-op Hall. Rugby Benn Hall

SEPTEMBER 1963

5th Thursday - Washwood Heath: Rockin' Berries. Fortunes
13th Friday -Nuneaton: Screaming Lord Sutch. Demons. Scotty Wood Combo
17th Tuesday - Evesham: Robbie Hood. Roger James and the Cyclones. Alpines
18th Wed - Rugby: Mark Allen. Alpines. Jet Blacks. Audition: Lee Christian & Singers
20th Friday - Nuneaton: Strollers. Roger James and the Cyclones. Jackpots
21st Sat - Banbury: Roger James & the Cyclones. Travellers. Johny Washington
21st Saturday - Atherstone: Rocking Renowns. Astranoughts
21st Saturday - Nuneaton: Evergreens. Matadors. Size 7
24th Sat - Evesham: Danny Storm & Strollers. Brian Gulliver & the Travellers
25th Wednesday - Rugby: Barry Nobel & Sapphires. Danny Storm & Strollers
26th Thursday - Washwood Heath: Rockin' Berries, plus four more groups
27th Fri - Nuneaton: Johny Washington & Congressmen. Alpines. Danny Storm
28th Saturday - Atherstone: Alpines. Johnny Bev. Impicks
28th Saturday - Nuneaton: Emperors. Demons. Roger James and the Cyclones
28th Saturday - Banbury: Evergreens. Sunspots

OCTOBER 1963

4th Fri - Nuneaton: Fortunes. Tanya Day & Tremors. Russ Sainty & the Nu-Notes
29th Tuesday - Evesham: Brook Brothers. Fortunes
30th Wednesday - Rugby: Fortunes. Danny Storm & Strollers
31st Thursday - Washwood Heath: Beatmen. Rockin' Berries

NOVEMBER 1963

1st Friday - Nuneaton: Lee Christian & Sinners. Fortunes
2nd Saturday - Atherstone: Barry Noble & Sapphires. Cyclones
2nd Saturday - Nuneaton: Beatmen. Demons
2nd Saturday - Banbury: Working Kind
8th Friday - Nuneaton: The Fourmost £125. Fortunes. Danny Storm
15th Friday - Nuneaton: Liverbirds £20. Rolling Stones £60.
22nd Friday - Nuneaton: Mike Sarne £135. Size 7. Danny Storm
29th Friday - Nuneaton: Big Three £65. Size 7. Carl & the Cheaters

DECEMBER 1963

6th Friday - Nuneaton: Emile Ford & Checkmates. Midnighters £15.
7th Saturday - Atherstone: Emile Ford & Checkmates. Unit One
7th Saturday - Banbury: Size 7. Demons
7th Saturday - Nuneaton: Travellers. Stormbirds. Zephyrs (Decca)
11th Wed - Rugby: Emile Ford & Checkmates. Fortunes. Tickets 4s 6d.
12th Thursday - Washwood Heath: Emile Ford. Fortunes

1964 Music Trends

THE SWINGING SIXTIES - EASTER 1964. Radio Caroline began broadcasting from a ship at sea, soon followed by Radio Atlanta and Radio Sutch. They broke the BBC's monopoly, hoping that one day the law would change and there would be 'free' radio. Along with playing the latest discs, they promoted their own records and musicians. Teenagers bought transistor radios, carrying them around like handbags so they could tune in and listen to pop music.

BRITISH POP MUSIC AND BEATLEMANIA spread around the world. **The Beatle's** hits included: *A Hard Day's Night, I Feel Fine, Can't Buy Me Love, I Wanna Hold Your Hand* and *She Loves You*. **Rolling Stones:** 'It's *All Over Now, Not Fade Away,* and *Little Red Rooster*. **The Animals:** *House of the Rising Sun*. **The Kinks:** *All Day and All of the Night. You Really Got Me*. **Manfred Mann:** *Do Wah Diddy, Diddy, Sha La* and *5-4-3-2-1*. **The Hollies:** *Just One Look, Stay,* and *Here I Go Again*. **The Swinging Blue Jeans:** *You're No Good* and *Hippy Shake*. **Wayne Fontana & the Mindbenders:** *Um Um Um Um Um*. **Barron Knights:** *Call Up the Groups*. **Searchers:** *Needles and Pins, When You Walk In the Room* and *Don't Throw Your Love Away*. **Mersey Beats:** *Just One Look*. **Freddie & the Dreamers:** I Understand. **The Four Pennies:** *Juliet*. **Peter & Gordon:** *A World Without Love* and *Nobody I know*. **Brian Poole & the Tremeloes:** *Someone, Someone* and *Candy Man*. **Gerry & the Pacemakers:** *Don't Let the Sun Catch You Crying*. **The Fourmost:** *A Little Crying*. **The Bachelors:** *I Wouldn't Trade You for the World* and *Ramona*. **The Rockin' Berries:** *He's In Town*. **The Fortunes** reached the lower charts with *Caroline*. Ex-Clifton Hall 'boy', **Johny Washington** joined the **Applejacks** and had a hit with *Tell Me When*.

UK FEMALE SINGERS to make the charts included: **Marianne Faithful:** *As Tears Go By*. **Petula Clark:** *Downtown*. **Cilla Black:** *You're My World, It's For You* and *Anyone Who Had a Heart*. **Millie:** *My Boy Lollipop*. **Mary Wells:** *My Guy*. **Lulu and the Luvvers:** *Shout*. **Sandy Shaw:** *There's Always Something There to Remind Me*. **Dusty Springfield:** *Losing You, I Only Want To Be With You* and *I Just Don't Know What To Do With Myself*.

UK MALE SINGERS were fewer and included: **Cliff Richard:** *The Twelfth of Never* and *On the Beach*. **Georgie Fame:** *Yeh, Yeh*. **Frank Ifield:** *Don't Blame Me*. **P.J. Proby:** *Together*. **Matt Munro:** *Walk Away*. **Val Doonican:** Walk Tall.

FROM THE USA: **Jim Reeves** with romantic ballads: *I Love You Because, I Won't Forget You* and *There's a Heartache Following Me*. **Roy Orbison:** *Oh Pretty Woman and It's Over*. '**Gene Pitney:** *I'm Gonna Be Strong* and *Twenty Four Hours from Tulsa*. **Louis Armstrong:** *Hello Dolly!* **The Four Seasons:** *Rag Doll*. **The Beach Boys:** *I Get Around*. **Elvis:** *Kissin' Cousins*. **The Supremes:** *Baby Love and Where Did Our Love Go?* **Doris Day:** *Move Over Darling*.

20. CAROLINE

Reg and Susan Calvert (Photographs by Mike Burnett)

The Searchers were booked into the Nuneaton Co-op Hall on Friday 3rd January, 1964. They were a nice group of boys that fame had not spoilt. The previous year they had knocked the Beatles off the number one spot with their hit, *Sweets for My Sweet.* Reg watched them with satisfaction as they played a preview of their next record, *Needles and Pins*. The supporting groups were the Cheaters and the Travellers. The hall was full and it was a good start to the year.

The Nuneaton group, the Demons, had been booked regularly during 1963 and had improved since their audition with Susan. They were taken by surprise when Reg asked if they'd like to turn professional. He was looking for a group to work in Germany, to back Sonny Stewart to replace the Dynamos who had left to join up with ex-Clifton Hall boys, Dave Da Costa and Colin Angel. Only the pianist, Geoff Wright, was remaining.

John Roberts, John Beeby and Herbie Prestidge were thrilled to give up their day jobs but their singer, Max Hollyman, was not required and he was left behind to find a new set of 'Demons'.

The Demons: Herbie Prestige, John Beeby, John Roberts and singer Max Holliman. Reg offered the musicians work in a German nightclub enabling them to turn professional. On returning to England, they formed the Ram Jam Band

17th January, the boys set off on a journey that was going to change their lives. On the first night, they slept uncomfortably on the floor of King's Agency, so they could catch the early morning flight to Germany. None of them had flown or been abroad before and were very excited. On arrival in Germany they were met at the airport and taken to a hotel. Not realising what duvets were for they searched for sheets and blankets but found none. In the morning, they were woken by loud rumblings and went to the window to watch a convoy of British tanks passing their hotel. It made them realise that Germany was still occupied by the British and US military and had been since the end of the Second World War.

The Demons, now called the Dynamos, were given basic accommodation in grotty rooms above the Arcadia Club in Frankfurt. As lads together, they accepted it and the English boys soon discovered they were in demand with the pretty German girls.

It was a great life and they did not have to work so late into the night as in the Hamburg clubs. Sometimes, they were booked to appear in other clubs and US Air Force Bases. The black GI's welcomed them and they played them James Brown records on their jukebox. The Nuneaton boys had never heard anything like it. They were so excited by the sound, they formulated a plan to start their own 'funk' music band when they completed their contract in Germany.

14th February, Valentine's Day, an Interflora van stopped outside Clifton Hall and a man delivered a large bouquet to Dorothy. Reg had been away all week and Dorothy, glowing with happiness, carried the flowers into the kitchen. Placing the bouquet on the kitchen table she picked up the envelope and read, '*Flowers to Miss Suzanne Calvert'.* Disappointed, she put them in the scullery kitchen to remain cool. Later, when Susan returned home, Dorothy gave her the flowers and watched her daughter's face light up with pleasure.

"Who are they from?"

"I don't know," replied Susan, puzzled as she read the card. *Roses are Red. Weekdays are Blue. Weekends are lovely. And so are you.*

"I can't keep up with your boyfriends. We'll soon get you married off when you're sixteen."

"I wish you wouldn't say that. It's not funny," retorted Susan.

On leaving school, Susan had found it difficult to find work in the small town of Rugby and in the previous October, had reluctantly accepted a job as a Trainee Comptometer Operator, earning £3.12s, a week. It was mindlessly boring but on one day a week, she was sent to the Further Education College where she studied for O-levels in Art, English and Maths. In the meantime, she continued to apply for other jobs and in February, was offered a position as telephonist at The Rugby Advertiser earning £4 a week.

Shortly after joining the newspaper, the photographer, Mike Burnett, met her from work and asked if he could take photographs of her for a competition. Susan told her parents and they reluctantly gave their permission. He had taken Reg's photograph for the paper and they remembered him, a tall young man, rugged in appearance, in his late 20's.

"Be careful," advised Reg, looking at his daughter intently. "He may be after more than taking photographs."

Susan modelled one sunny spring morning and several weeks later, Mike presented her with a large yellow Kodak box filled with a set of photos. She proudly showed them to her parents but was disappointed when they only looked at a couple and closed the lid with disinterest. Again, they cautioned her to be careful.

Reg was always looking to the future to plan his next project. He realised dances were going out of fashion and he needed to find another way to entertain teenagers. Dorothy was so set against the idea of running nightclubs, he surreptitiously looked for suitable premises by himself and found the Essoldo at Loughborough. It had been a cinema and Reg signed the lease to rent it. He returned home like a naughty schoolboy and reluctantly confessed to Dorothy what he had done. She was furious! He knew she would be and sat quietly, ignoring her torrent of words like rain on a windowpane. When the first invoice arrived, Dorothy waved the paper at him and shouted in frustration.

"What am I supposed to do with this?"

Reg shrugged his shoulders and ignored her question.

"Do you think money grows on trees? Have you thought how we're going to manage to pay this amount of money each month? Did you stop and think there will be council rates, heating and wages to pay? Did you sit down and work the sums out before you signed the lease?"

Reg looked blank and waited for her to finish.

"When are you going to have time to run a club? Don't you think you've enough to do with the dances, managing the boys and King's Agency?"

Reg remained silent.

"How long will it be before it starts to earn money?"

"Not sure," replied Reg, in a matter-of-fact voice. "Probably mid-March if all goes well. I need to spend some time making a few alterations and fitting it out."

"Everything costs money and fitting out a club will be expensive. Just when I think we're on our feet and comfortably off for the first time in our lives, you go out on one of your mad-cap schemes and sign a lease on an old cinema."

"The new dance at the Camp Hill Club went well this week," commented Reg, as he endeavoured to change the subject.

"We're supposed to be a team. A partnership."

"We are," agreed Reg.

"It doesn't feel like it, when you're away all the time and you sign a contract for £4,000 a year without first discussing it," snapped Dorothy. "You'll need to open more dancehalls. If we don't pay our bills we could go bankrupt. It could be several years before the club starts to show a profit and in the meantime, you need to earn more money."

Over the ensuing weeks, Reg travelled most days to Loughborough to work on the fitting out of the old cinema. He wanted a groovy, intimate place for teenagers to congregate and the walls were painted dark colours and lighting kept low. One room was converted into a coffee bar that also sold soft drinks and beef burgers. A larger room was made into a discothèque with spotlights and a good sound system. The main theatre would feature shows and have a dance and seated area.

The opening night of the club was planned for 21st March, 1964, the Saturday before Easter. Danny Storm and the Strollers along with the Confederates were booked for the launch. The opening night went well and Reg was satisfied that, given time, his gamble would pay off. Planning ahead, it was possible he could have a number of nightclubs around the country. Dorothy had no choice but to wait and see. She knew Reg well enough to know that when he got bored, she would be left to pick up the pieces and carry on. This time, she had made it clear to her husband, that under no circumstances did she want to run a nightclub.

To earn more money, Reg reopened the dances at Evesham on Saturdays and Washwood Heath on Tuesdays but both were closed after a few weeks. A new dance at Kettering was started and this was successful. Altogether, there were now only seven dances a week, plus Loughborough to organise, compared to 21 just three years earlier.

The Fortunes were all systems go and recorded their second disc, *Caroline*. It reached the bottom of the charts and television appearances were booked in Glasgow and London. Chris Capaldi was singing with them to make four-part harmony and Reg tried to get him to perform front-of-stage with the others but Chris refused as he could only sing when he was behind a piano!

The more famous the Fortunes became the more nonchalant Rod and Barry were towards Dorothy. The other boys all knew how to charm her but Rod and Barry did not and she resented them living in her house. She grumbled to Reg but he shrugged off her criticisms as they always showed great respect to him.

In April, the Fortunes were booked to tour various German nightclubs. To make the journey more comfortable, Chris Capaldi found old bus seats in a junkyard and fitted them into the rear of the Austin J2 van. Chris did most of the driving with Rod taking a turn but they refused to let Tony Britnell take the wheel as his driving was erratic. In Hamburg, they met Cliff Bennett in a café and Rod and Cliff began to argue. Cliff got so annoyed by Rod's arrogant attitude, he picked him up and carried him to a fountain and threw him in. It soon settled the argument and made everyone laugh.

The Rolling Stones were now famous and Glen, being a good mimic, did an interpretation of Mick Jagger in the show that greatly amused the German audiences. They went on to a nightclub in Frankfurt but after a few days, they all had laryngitis and could not sing. A doctor examined them and suggested a simple remedy that worked. They should not drink ice cold orange juice in the breaks but have drinks at room temperature.

The Cologne nightclub proved to be their most scary performance. In an interval, Chris was standing by the bar when a man came up to him and pushed a gun into his side. Shocked and terrified, Chris followed the man's instructions as he beckoned him to sit down at a table with four other men. In broken English, they told him to play a Jerry Lee Lewis number. Shaking his head, Chris explained they did not know any of the songs.

"You play it," said the man with the gun.

Chris returned to the stage and nervously, told the group. Looking at each other, they began to do an impromptu compilation performance of all the Jerry Lee Lewis numbers they could vaguely remember.

Their new record *Caroline* was well received but had not made the charts, until the events that followed, gave it a life of its own.

Life at Clifton Hall was good and may have continued much the same for years, with Reg starting new ventures and Dorothy picking up the pieces when he got bored. Reg had always dreamed of having his own radio station but it seemed an impossibility and he had put it to the back of his mind. What brought it to the forefront was a 'pirate' radio station named Caroline out at sea off the Essex coast.

News spread rapidly. There was so much excitement that at last, the BBC monopoly had been broken and Radio Caroline was playing pop music, including the Beatles and Rolling Stones and using the Fortunes record as their signature tune.

Reg had never considered buying a ship and was excited by the prospect until Dorothy reminded him they did not have enough money. Heedless of Dorothy's warnings, Reg searched for a way to pursue his dream.

THE END

Is just the beginning

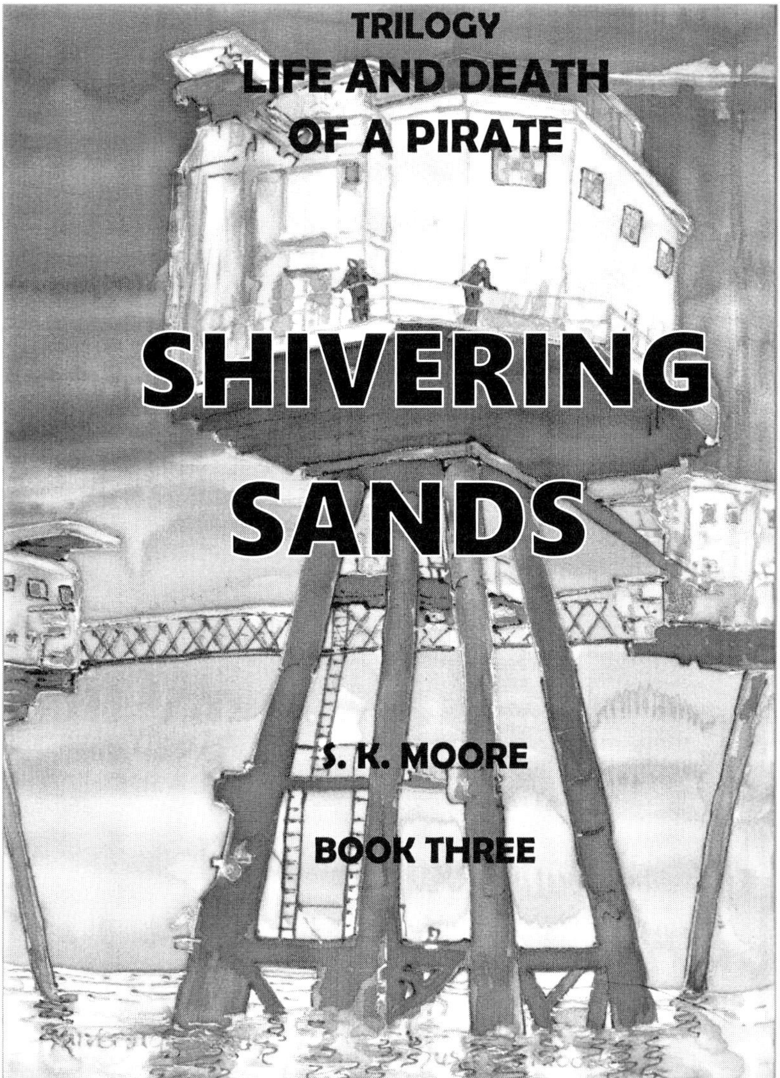

For Bookshops and stockists visit: www.regcalvert-plays.co.uk
Paperback and eBook also available from Amazon Books

Fillongley Publications, The Old Granary, Fillongley CV7 8PB
Email: fillongleypub@btinternet.com

Dorothy and Reg Calvert, Clifton Hall, near Rugby (RC)

1. THE MUSIC CONTINUES

Clifton Hall, Clifton-upon-Dunsmore, Near Rugby

Dorothy Calvert awoke with a start and elbowed her husband. "Doorbell Reg."

"Uh."

"Someone's at the door. You go."

Half asleep, Reg rolled out of bed, pulled on some trousers, a sleeveless jumper and slipped his feet into tartan slippers. Unshaved, with tousled hair, Reg made his way down the wide mahogany stairway to the glazed front door. Rubbing sleep from his eyes, he saw a tall, good looking young man.

"Mr Calvert?"

Still in a daze, Reg nodded his head in confirmation.

"I'm Tony Newman. I've come to ask for an audition."

"Haven't you heard of such a thing called a telephone?" asked Reg, irritably.

A look of surprise crossed Tony's face. Reg's annoyance at having his sleep disturbed at ten in the morning was obvious. Tony had never asked for an audition before. He now felt stupid. Of course, he should have called first, but his parents didn't own a phone and he hadn't thought to go to a coin box.

Seeing how nervous the young man was, Reg asked him more kindly, "Where are you from?"

"Rugby. I've just joined a group and we were hoping to have an audition."

"What's the name of your group?"

"The Solitaires."

"Okay, I'll book you into the Benn Hall on Wednesday night. Come into the office, I'll write down your details. I won't be there but my wife will," smiled Reg. "You'll know it's her because she has a pet monkey."

After chatting for a moment, Tony left and Reg returned to bed.

"Who was that?"

"A local lad asking for an audition. I've said you'll see the group on Wednesday night."

"We may as well get up now we're awake. What d'you think William?"

William, sitting up on the doll's bunk bed by Dorothy's side, chuntered in response as she turned over to stroke him and got out of bed. Climbing into her arms, she carried her pet monkey into the bathroom, placing him on the rim of the toilet bowl. "Be a good boy," murmured Dorothy, as she waited for him to do his business. After he had finished, she washed his hands and face with a damp flannel, then dressed him in a brightly coloured red jumper.

Clifton Hall was an unusually relaxed household. Reg and Dorothy lived there with their two daughters and the groups he managed. Their main business was running teenage dances but they were going out of fashion so Reg was looking around to develop new ventures. There were no longer dances to run on a Sunday, Monday, or Thursday, but Reg rarely stopped working and was spending all his free time converting the old Essoldo cinema in Loughborough into a nightclub. He was convinced nightclubs were the way forward to replace dancehalls but Dorothy strongly objected to this idea. She didn't want to run a nightclub and worried that when Reg got bored, she would be left to manage it.

Tuesday 24th March, 1964 was Reg's birthday. When he returned from Loughborough in the late afternoon, he found Dorothy preparing dinner. As soon as she saw him, she smiled as William screeched, leaping off her shoulder to climb the rope to the ceiling clothes airer where he swung upside down by his tail. Laughing, Reg put his arms around his wife, hugging her as he gave her a sloppy kiss.

"What are you cooking? It smells good."

"Your favourite, fillet steak. Can you call the girls for dinner please?"

Reg went to the main stairway, calling out, "Dinner time." A moment later, his daughters, Susan and Candy, emerged from their bedrooms to make their way down to the kitchen.

On birthdays, Dorothy made a special effort, serving up a delicious meal of fillet steak coated in a little salt and flour, fried in butter with onions, mushrooms, chips and cauliflower cheese. A birthday cake followed and everyone sang *Happy Birthday* as Reg blew out the candles.

"Sorry, I couldn't fit 36 candles on the cake," laughed Dorothy.

“That was lovely Doe Doe,” said Reg, appreciatively. “I suppose I’d better get ready to go to Washwood Heath.”

“I’ve booked the Emperors and Delmont Four,” reminded Dorothy.

“Won’t be long before we have to close this dance. No matter what I do, the numbers keep going down,” shrugged Reg.

“The Benn Hall is going the same way. Soon we’ll have no mid-week dances.”

“When I’m in London tomorrow, I’ll book a star group to give them a boost.”

“Worth a try, might keep them going a bit longer,” agreed Dorothy.

The previous year, Reg had started King’s Agency and he was in the routine of driving to London on Wednesdays and staying over until Thursday. Dorothy felt lonely on her own even though Clifton Hall bustled with the boys who lived with them, their music filling the house with a cacophony of sound as they practiced in the rehearsal room.

Dorothy spent Wednesday on her own and was pleased to see Candy when she returned from school, windswept and pink cheeked as she propped up her bicycle in the carport and headed off to see her pony.

“Don’t forget to change out of your school uniform first before you see to Shamie,” reminded Dorothy.

“It’ll be dark in a minute,” complained Candy, turning back to do as she was told.

Susan arrived later. She had recently started work as a telephonist at the Rugby Advertiser and it was a long cycle ride from the centre of Rugby to Clifton Hall. Dorothy was in the kitchen preparing their meal as Susan entered and warmed herself by the Aga cooker.

After eating, Dorothy quickly cleared the dishes into the sink and prepared to go out, taking Susan with her to be cashier. The Benn Hall was their local dance in Rugby and Dorothy expected a good crowd as it was advertised as an ‘all-star’ night with Danny Storm and Nicky James on the show.

Nicky James had been fortunate to have a record produced by Tony Hatch called, *My Colour is Blue,* and even though it didn’t make the charts, he could now promote himself as a ‘recording star’. Nicky had been lead singer in a Birmingham group, the Lawmen, until Reg asked his bass guitarist, John Wileman, and drummer, Andy Brown, if they would like to do a tour of Scotland backing Robbie Hood (aka Mike West). When they came off tour, Reg offered them a permanent position in the Strollers, backing Danny Storm and living at Clifton Hall. Nicky, with no group, joined Denny Laine and the Diplomats, and for a short time, the Moody Blues 5.

The changeover between acts had to be slick, completed within the time of two records being played. When the Solitaires were due on, they were in disarray. Both their rhythm and bass guitar players had decided to leave the Solitaires to form the Mighty Avengers. Tony Newman, who had only just learnt guitar, had to step in as a replacement. The drummer, Rex Barton, was so nervous, he began to be sick on his drums and rushed off stage while they were setting up. Tony could only apologise as they anxiously waited for him to return. Eventually, the curtains were pulled back and as they started to perform, the guitarist, Chris Pottle, broke a string and went off to replace it. The group continued playing as best they could, cheered on by a crowd of local enthusiasts who knew the lead singer, Sam Kempe.

When Chris got back on stage, his guitar was out of tune and Dorothy called out from the wings, "Tune up." Mishearing her instructions, Chris turned up the volume. As soon as there was a lull in their playing, Dorothy called again, "I said tune up, not turn up."

The audition had been a fiasco and the Solitaires left the stage, embarrassed by their performance.

"I'm sorry, Mrs Calvert. We weren't very good. It was the first time we'd all played together."

"Never mind," replied Dorothy, smiling as she took pity on them. "Everyone has to start somewhere. I'll arrange another audition next Saturday with Reg at Atherstone Memorial Hall."

She could see they were a nice group of boys and made a note in her book. *'Very good equipment but not much idea about playing it'.*

The following weekend was Easter, the weather was cold and dreary but Reg was in high spirits.

"Would you like tea or coffee?" asked Dorothy.

"Coffee please. As it's Easter, I wouldn't mind some toast and a chucky egg with a face on it."

"Easter egg day was yesterday."

"It's Easter Monday." Reg grinned as he caught his wife's hand and pulled her down to sit on his lap, making her giggle while he kissed her.

"Have you remembered it's my birthday tomorrow?"

"Is it?" teased Reg.

"You know it is. It comes exactly a week after yours."

"Mm, 36 this year, we're getting old Doe Doe. I'll take you to the Spanish restaurant for lunch."

The telephone rang and Reg quickly reached out to answer it.

"Hello David. Thanks for calling back. …… Yes, I've heard the news. It's fantastic. Can you pick it up where you live? ..... Okay. I'll see you Saturday."

"What was that all about?" frowned Dorothy, instinctively knowing her husband was up to something.

"Guess what? There's a ship anchored out at sea playing pop music all day. They've called it Radio Caroline. There's never been anything like it. Commercial radio, it's brilliant."

"Yes there is. Radio Luxembourg's been doing it for years."

"But not from a ship and you can only hear Luxembourg at night. I told you we'd have commercial radio sooner or later. You only have to be three miles off the coast to be outside the legal limit."

"Don't get any ideas, they won't let you start a radio station from Clifton Hall and you can't afford to buy a ship," cautioned Dorothy.

"Maybe not, but we can have some fun."

"No Reg, you need to stay focused on the nightclub. You've only just opened it and it's costing money."

"The nightclub will be fine."

"Not if you go off on another harebrained scheme."

Dorothy passed her husband a steaming egg with buttered toast, cut into soldiers.

"You haven't put a face on it."

"No, here's the pen."

Concentrating, Reg began to draw two eyes, nose, scribbly moustache with smiley mouth. A moment later, he cut off the head, then sprinkled salt over the yellow dribbling yolk.

"I think I'll go to King's Agency tomorrow."

"Not tomorrow," smiled Dorothy, sweetly.

"Why not?"

"It's my birthday. Remember? You said you were taking me out. Don't forget, you've booked Wayne Fontana and the Mindbenders into the Washwood Heath and Rugby dances."

"So I have."

Dorothy put her arm out for William to jump down from the clothes airer so she could feed him small pieces of fruit.

"Never mind. I'll go on Wednesday. I can hear Radio Caroline while I'm down there. I wonder what the government will do?"

"I expect they'll close it down."

"Don't you think it's ridiculous to have so many petty laws and red tape?"

"Not really. We need laws and boundaries to keep everything in order. And you need to keep your mind in order and not think about having a radio station. There's no way we can afford it."

"This egg tastes good," commented Reg, changing the subject.

For several weeks, Dorothy had dropped hints she would like a gold necklace for her birthday and had even let slip which Rugby jewellers Reg could find the one she liked. On her birthday, however, she was disappointed.

"I don't know why I bother. I always buy things for you."

"Come here, give's a kiss and don't be grumpy," smiled Reg. "You know I don't bother about birthdays. Anyway, I'm taking you out for lunch."

"Then can we go to the jewellers?" asked Dorothy, optimistically, although she soon realised by the blank expression on her husband's face, he was in no mood for shopping.

On Wednesday morning, Reg left for London in good humour, kissing his wife goodbye. "See you later, alligator."

"In a while, crocodile. You drive carefully."

As Reg drove down the M1 motorway towards London, he tuned his car radio to 199 metres in the hope of picking up Radio Caroline. The signal was weak with a lot of interference but when he reached Denmark Street, he could hear it better. For a while, he sat listening before reluctantly turning the radio off. Locking the door to his lime green, Ford Zephyr, he crossed the road and opened the unimposing dark green Regency style door which now had a new plaque outside saying 'King's Agency'. He bounded up the two flights of rickety stairs to the offices and as he burst in, everyone smiled. They looked forward to Reg's weekly visits to enliven their day with his ideas and exuberant character.

"Good morning Reg. Coffee?" asked Terry King, smiling as he greeted Reg with a handshake.

"Please," replied Reg, smiling, as he sat down at his desk. "Have you any news."

"We've been quite busy with an enquiry from a nightclub in Italy."

"Good. What about Radio Caroline? Have you heard it?"

"Yeah. I've listened a few times," replied Terry.

"I've just managed to tune in. It's not a bit like the fuddy-duddy BBC."

Terry King was Reg's partner in King's Agency. He had chosen him the previous year when he started King's Agency as he had some experience in agency work and he could talk the talk. Terry was a slick, well dressed Londoner with dark hair who wore Buddy Holly style glasses. He changed his name from Terry Meacher to Terry King so most people thought the agency belonged to him, not realising Reg was the brains behind the organisation. Reg didn't mind, it suited him to have a reliable front man to do the administration work. Reg found the groups and the agency arranged bookings, supplying British performers to German and European nightclubs, US army bases and UK gigs. Reg didn't expect to earn much money from the agency, his main interest was to get work for his own musicians and to receive 10 per cent commission from the groups he found work for.

Reg spent time listening to Radio Caroline while in London and made enquiries to try and find out who was behind the station. It was all a bit secretive but he learnt that an Irish man, Ronan O'Rahilly, had started it with some rich sponsors. Back at Clifton Hall, Reg kept his interest in pirate radio to himself as he knew his wife would not approve.

Friday afternoon, Clifton Hall became quiet as the Fortunes left to go to Milford Haven and Danny Storm went to Bristol. Dorothy stayed at home as Reg left early to go to Nuneaton Co-op Hall. He had two dance sessions to organise, the first for youngsters mostly aged between 10 and 13, followed by the normal dance at 8p.m. Four local groups were booked to perform, the Dynamic Sounds, Cheetahs, Cascades and Unit 4. Reg particularly enjoyed the early show as he had fun entertaining the kids with new and spontaneous competitions and was affectionately known as 'Uncle Reg'.

On Saturday nights, there were three dances to run. Dorothy went to Banbury Winter Gardens, Reg to Atherstone Memorial Hall and Susan to Nuneaton Co-op Hall.

Reg had trained his daughter how to run a dance and drove her to Nuneaton before continuing his journey on to Atherstone. Arriving outside the Co-op hall, Reg flashed his car lights at a white Cadillac parked opposite and David Sutch hurried over to take Susan's place in the front seat. The two men were both excited about Radio Caroline and wanted to spend the evening discussing ideas about starting their own radio station.

Since their first audition, the Solitaires had reformed, changing their name to the Liberators. Their new line-up comprised Sam Kempe, Tony Newman, Barry Bernard, Tom Long and Johnny Wallbank. They had been rehearsing all week in anticipation of their second audition. As they finished their spot, Reg smiled, saying, "Well done".

After two records, the 'stars' of the show were ready to perform, Reg walked to centre stage as David pulled open the curtains.

"Hello girls and boys, ladies and gentlemen. I hope you enjoyed our new group, the Liberators from Rugby. Now, all the way from London, we have our star group who have just released a new record. Let's welcome, the one and only, the fantastic, Wayne Gibson and the Dynamic Sounds."

An explosion of sound erupted from the loudspeakers as guitars and drums began to play. A few couples danced and jived but most stood in a large crowd near the front of the stage to watch the show.

Reg knew Wayne well as he sometimes worked in King's Agency. His record, *Kelly,* produced by Shel Talmy, was a cover of a Del Shannon song. On the B-side was *See You Later Alligator*, a cover of Bill Hayley's hit. At the end of the evening, Reg talked to the Liberators, confirming he would book them again. They were chuffed with their success. It was generally acknowledged that Reg ran the best dances in the Midlands and to be accepted by him was an accolade.

Reg and David made their way back to Nuneaton and continued their almost non-stop conversation about pirate radio. Stopping outside the Co-op Hall, David drove off in his Cadillac as Reg went to find his daughter.

The groups were packing away their equipment, the dancefloor deserted except for a few girls who lingered by the stage in the hope of attracting one of the boys. Susan was backstage in the office, waiting with the hall manager, Mr Buckby, and cashier, Mrs Thomas, who beamed with delight when she saw Reg. She was a slim, silver-haired lady and Reg gave her a hug as she kissed his cheek. Their fondness for each other was obvious and at the end of each dance, he made a point of giving her a lift home.

Father and daughter chatted all the way back to Clifton Hall. When Dorothy returned with Candy from Banbury, she sniffed the air.

"It smells like old socks in here."

It had become a Saturday night tradition for father and daughter to eat Gorgonzola cheese, pickled onions and cracker biscuits together while Dorothy and Candy preferred toasted teacakes.

"Have you had a good night?" asked Reg.

"So so. Numbers are going down," replied Dorothy. What do you think of the new group?"

"They've got potential and could be good. They've changed their name to the Liberators and are keen to rehearse. By the way, I've booked Dave Sutch for next Friday."

"Why? I've already booked three groups. Dave Kaye and the Dykons, the Unones and the Midnighters."

"He'll attract a good crowd," replied Reg, evasively.

The following week, Reg began to spend time investigating the alternatives to buying a ship. After the dance on Friday night, David returned with Reg and annoyed Dorothy by resuming their never-ending conversation about pirate radio.

The boys who lived at Clifton Hall had their own kitchen and did not think to enter Dorothy's domain without first knocking the door and waiting for permission. David had become a regular visitor and always took the liberty of sitting in the family kitchen, seemingly oblivious to her pointed remarks and black looks.

"Hello Mrs C," greeted David, smiling his toothy grin at her.

Dorothy grimaced and tried to be polite. William, sensing her disapproval was less than polite. He ran screeching to the top of the clothes airer and did a war dance.

"He doesn't like you," muttered Dorothy.

David ignored Dorothy's comments and grinned mischievously. "Fantastic news."

"What is?"

"Pirate radio."

"Do you think so?"

"Pop music all day. We can pick it up in London. Everyone's tuning into Radio Caroline, even my Mum listens and they're playing the Fortunes *Caroline* song as their theme tune."

"That's good for the Fortunes," agreed Dorothy, with a touch of sarcasm.

"It's time for change," observed Reg. "I've always said the Government would have to relax their broadcasting laws and allow local and commercial radio. We're at least ten years behind the Americans."

"They're starting a third television channel soon. BBC 2," commented Dorothy.

David grinned cheekily. "They won't play pop music. It's like living in a police state. Can't do this, can't do that."

"There has to be a way we can start our own radio station. We'd need to buy a ship, a transmitter, an aerial, pay staff and so on," added Reg.

"Don't be ridiculous," snapped Dorothy.

"It would cost thousands," remarked Reg, casually.

"Could you get a bank loan?" asked David.

Reg raised his eyebrows and looked sideways at his wife. "Afraid not. I've still got the nightclub at Loughborough to sort out."

"Are you coming to bed tonight? You've got a busy day tomorrow with a new dance at Kettering to sort out."

"Okay Doe Doe, I won't be long."

Dorothy looked despairingly at the two men as she left the kitchen.

The following day, as Dorothy expected, Reg stayed in bed until two in the afternoon. When he surfaced, he met David in the kitchen and they resumed their conversation. Dorothy was angry, but held her tongue, giving them both very black looks.

"We've got an idea. We're going to hire a boat on the Thames."

"Have a Rock 'n' Roll party and say it's Radio Sutch. Cruise up and down playing Rock 'n' Roll as we pass the Houses of Parliament. That'll shake up the old fogies."

"It'll be great publicity," agreed Reg.

"Yeah man," nodded David.

"And who's going to pay for hiring a boat?" Dorothy asked, looking directly at David.

"We'll sort something out, it shouldn't cost much," grinned Reg. "There are offshore radio ships in other countries who are proving very successful."

"I don't care about other countries. We've bills to pay from the nightclub so "shouldn't cost much", is still too much," reminded Dorothy.

Top: Cornucopia fishing boat hired from Colin Knapp, Southend-on- Sea (RC)
Bottom: Launch of Radio Sutch, Rock 'n' Roll party on the Thames

2 RADIO SUTCH

24th May, 1964 Rock 'n' Roll Party on the Thames in the Cornucopia
Terry King, Screaming Lord Sutch, Brian Paull, Candy and Reg Calvert,
The Savages: Pete Philips, Geoff Mew, Paul Nicholas (and his friend,
Ronnie Harwood) (Colin Dale out of picture) (TF)

Reg surprised Dorothy by casually suggesting they had a family day out at the seaside on Whitsunday, 17th May, 1964. Dorothy, unsuspecting an ulterior motive, agreed to makeup a picnic and invited Eddie, Susan's latest boyfriend to join them. When they arrived at Southend-on-Sea, the day was warm and sunny with a gentle sea breeze. In good humour, Reg strolled up to the seawall and spent a few minutes scanning the horizon. Disappointed not to see what he was looking for, he casually suggested to his family that they go for a boat ride and sauntered off to find a boat. A short time later, he returned, whistling cheerfully, *We're off to see the Wizard, The Wonderful Wizard of Oz.*

"I've found a fisherman who'll take us out and he'll pick us up by the wall in a few minutes."

"I'm not going in that," protested Dorothy, when she saw the small open-top fishing boat. "You know I don't like boats."

Taking his wife's arm, Reg began to walk her towards the boat while Dorothy obstinately pulled back, protesting, as William shrieked at him.

"Come on Mum, don't be chicken," called Susan and Candy, as the fisherman helped them step aboard.

"No, I'll wait behind with William," insisted Dorothy, her hair blowing across her face as William chuntered and clung firmly to her shoulder with his tail tight around her neck.

Reg walked unsteadily to the front of the boat to stand by the helm with the fisherman. "Do you think we could go out to Knock John Fort?"

The fisherman looked thoughtful for a moment, then nodded in reply. The boat chugged into action and they waved goodbye to Dorothy who soon became a dot in the distance. The boat headed out to sea with Reg chatting cheerfully to the fisherman. Candy sat one side of the boat and Susan and Eddie on the other. To drown out the monotonous drone of the chug, chug, chug of the engine, they began to sing sea shanties, very loudly.

As they journeyed further out with no sight of land in any direction, the weather changed as dark grey storm clouds scuttled across the sky forewarning of a squall. The light breeze became a turbulent wind that lashed the sea into waves of icy water which gushed over the gunwales. The skipper beckoned to the girls and Eddie to pull the dirty grey canvas tarpaulin, attached to the side of the boat, over the top of them. Already drenched to their skins, they sat shivering, half crouched in the canopied gloom, feeling every pitch and roll in the base of their stomachs. They had long since stopped singing and took it in turn to pass a bucket as they vomited the remains of their breakfast.

Up and down the boat rose, one moment high on the crest of a wave, then with a sickening lurch, it dropped into a trough before ascending again. Wave after wave crashed over the top of the tarpaulin and onto the decking. All the time, Reg stood steadfastly by the helm, doggedly determined to see Fort Knock John.

Thinking her family were on a short boat trip, Dorothy found a tea shop to while away the time. When she saw the thunderous sky, she became anxious. A grey sea haze had descended and the fishing boat was nowhere to be seen. For more than an hour she scanned the sea, looking for her family. When she caught sight of the little boat struggling to make way through the turbulent waters, she became terrified as it rose on the swells and disappeared into the hollows. Each time it was out of view, her heart pounded as she held her breath.

Eventually, the boat made it back to shore. The passengers alighted, dripping wet and white with cold. Reg dared not meet his wife's eyes as he paid the fisherman and endeavoured to be nonchalant.

"What do you think you've been doing? You could have got yourselves drowned," hissed Dorothy, angrily as she protectively put her arms around her shivering daughters to usher them away. "Boat trip! Fun! You're the limit Reg Calvert! There's a men's bath house over there. You go in with Eddie. I'll take the girls to the ladies for a hot bath while I dry their clothes."

The failed boat trip had not dampened Reg's determination to find what he was looking for. A few days later, he returned to Southend-on-Sea. After studying naval charts and talking to local fishermen, he learned more about the wartime forts that were designed by architect Guy Maunsell in the early 1940s to protect the Thames estuary from German bombers and mines.

The forts had been abandoned in the mid-1950s, the only inhabitants now were seagulls. There were two designs. Naval forts had two very large round tubular legs with a flat platform on top, built to house up to 100 men. These were at Rough Sands, Sunk Head, Tongue Sands and Knock John. The army forts comprised of seven towers supported by Meccano style legs with interconnecting walkways. These were at the Nore, Red Sands and Shivering Sands.

Without telling Dorothy, Reg arranged another boat trip to view the Knock John Fort and the Shivering Sands Towers. This time, the crossing was pleasant with the sun sparkling on a slightly choppy sea. He stood alongside the skipper, trying to glean more information. Most of the local fishermen knew of the forts and there were rumours that some were used as a base to smuggle illicit goods into the country. After a while, the skipper pointed to the dark shape of Knock John Fort.

The boat tied up alongside partly collapsed scaffolding next to one of the legs. Reg leapt from the boat to the ladder. Cautiously, he climbed up the outside of the scaffolding until he reached a small hatch. Pushing his way through, he quickly explored a couple of the dark interior rooms before emerging into the daylight. On the top, standing sentinel, were wartime guns still in their fixings and in the centre of the platform were more rooms with portholes. It was brilliant. With great excitement, he climbed down and asked the skipper to take him next to Shivering Sands.

The boat set off again and after a while Reg saw the eerie structure of Shivering Sands, like six cake tins on stilts rising out of the sea.

"There were seven towers last year," explained the skipper, pointing to a wreck jutting out of the water. "A ship collided with it in fog and the tower just collapsed into the sea but the ship was all right. The tower over there, on its own, is the Search Light Tower and has weather equipment on it. The Admiralty regularly send their boat out to check it."

Coming alongside the concrete base, the skipper steadied the boat as Reg made a leap to grasp the rusting iron ladder attached to the leg of the tower. He climbed up and up and through the open trapdoor. Standing inside the structure, he looked around in wonder. It was far better than he could have hoped, better even than Knock John. Hastily, he began to explore, his footsteps echoing in the void. The towers were made from steel with concrete floors and each tower had two storeys of airy, spacious rooms, with windows set high in the walls. On top, the flat roof was open to the sky with places for the army gun fixings. It had been a long day, but Reg was thrilled. Whistling happily, he retraced his steps, back down the ladder to where the fishing boat was waiting.

Early on Sunday morning, 24th May, Reg left Clifton Hall with Candy for company and drove to Butler's Wharf on the south side of the Thames, near London Bridge. Reg had hired a 60ft fishing ketch, the Cornucopia, from Colin Knapp in Southend-on-Sea. As they arrived, everyone was milling about in great expectation.

The ketch was prepared with a Jolly Roger and Radio Sutch banner strung between the masts while amplification equipment and loudspeakers were being loaded. David, his long hair covered by a triangular black headscarf, took on the role of pirate chief and brandished a cutlass. He had dressed to stand out in a crowd with bold black and white top, purple cloak and bright blue trousers. The press wanted to take photos so the Savages took off their warm clothing and braved the cold wearing only leopard skins. By contrast, Reg, Terry King and Brian Paull, were all soberly attired in smart suits.

The boat set off and cruised up and down the river to London Bridge and back, audaciously passing the Houses of Parliament and loudly playing Rock 'n' Roll music. The press, sceptical of the Cornucopia being suitable as a radio ship, began to ask questions.

"Can we look in the hold at the transmitting equipment?"

"Sorry, the hold is out of bounds. It'd be illegal to show you the equipment while we're in territorial waters," replied David, thinking quickly.

"What about the aerial?"

"We haven't fitted one yet but some wire attached to the top mast should be okay," replied David, as he flicked his head and looked upwards at the mast with a mischievous grin.

"We'll begin our trial broadcasts on Wednesday," added Reg. "You should tune into 197 metres."

"What sort of music will you play?"

"Records the BBC have banned and records of unknown groups. If they become famous, we hope they'll contribute to the cost of running the station," explained David, with a grin.

After the phony launch, Reg took to subterfuge so as not to annoy his wife. He bought some old radio equipment and tested it in the rehearsal room. Dorothy, who was used to him experimenting, was unconcerned. He had always dabbled in radio since she'd known him and knew he couldn't afford to buy a ship.

The Fortunes new record, *I like the Look of You,* was due for release on 29th May and Reg stayed longer in London on the pretext of promoting their record.

Plans were hastily made to launch the real Radio Sutch on Wednesday morning. The Savages, their girlfriends and a Daily Mirror reporter, were told to meet at Leigh on Sea and assumed they were to be taken to a radio ship, like Caroline and Atlanta. The fishing boat was loaded with provisions and radio equipment. When they were ready, the boat set off. Reg and David kept their destination a secret, smiling mysteriously as they avoided answering direct questions.

When they were on their way, the passengers were told where they were going. The sun shone and the wind blew and when the shape of the Shivering Sands Towers began to emerge on the horizon, Reg cheerfully pointed.

"That's it. That's where we're going. Shivering Sands Towers."

"Man, they look fantastic," grinned David.

"What are they?" asked one of the 'Savages'.

"Old wartime forts, abandoned by the army about eight years ago."

No one could quite believe what they were seeing. It was not what they had expected. When the boat came alongside one of the tower legs, each person took turn to make the perilous leap from the pitching boat to grab the ladder, taking with them what they could carry of provisions and equipment. When they reached the platform, they discovered that it had rusted away and to reach the next ladder, they had the terrifying 'tightrope' walk across a girder. When everything was stowed, they cheerfully waved goodbye to the fishing boat and began to explore the large empty rooms.

Reg and David were men on a mission, immediately setting to work, giving instructions to their crew of Savages. Today was the day they were going to become the third pirate radio station. Reg assembled the broadcasting equipment while David and the others set about erecting a makeshift aerial by hanging wire from the roof. When everything was complete and a Jolly Roger flying from the top of the tower, Reg made his first broadcast.

"This is Radio Sutch, Radio Sutch. The first teenage radio station broadcasting on 187 metres medium wave. Radio Sutch. Radio Sutch. This is our first broadcast. If you can hear this transmission, please telephone my wife, Mrs Reg, on Rugby 5460, and you can reverse the charge. Tell her you can hear Radio Sutch and let her know where you've picked up our transmission. This is Radio Sutch, Radio Sutch, now we'll play our first record, *Jack the Ripper*, from the man himself, Screaming Lord Sutch."

David gently let the needle in the arm of the record player engage with the first groove of the spinning disc and everyone cheered as they heard the eerie scream and sound effects of *Jack the Ripper*. The record had been produced by Joe Meek and never played on radio, as the BBC had banned it.

"We've done it man. We've made our first broadcast. This deserves a drink," laughed David, as he unscrewed the top of a lemonade bottle and took a swig, then passed it on.

Everyone joined in, cheered and laughed as they took turns to drink and began to eat their supplies and jammy dodgers. As they listened, the song became distorted.

"Ah, a technical hitch. We've run out of power," chuckled Reg, as the disc revolved slower and slower.

"What time are we going home?" asked one of the girls.

"Later," replied David, absentmindedly.

"Did you ask Fred Downs to come back?"

"No man, did you?" replied David, with a look of concern. "Did anyone think to ask the boat to pick us up?"

Everyone looked blank. The outing had been kept a secret and only the skipper of the boat knew where they were. One of the girls began to cry and the party atmosphere evaporated as they realised the seriousness of their situation. They were isolated on a tower at sea with no hope of returning to land, unless they could attract attention.

"We have a problem," sighed Reg, chewing his bottom lip. "Leave it with me. Let's see if I can get this generator to work again."

A little later, Reg took the microphone and made another announcement over the airwaves.

"SOS. Can anyone hear me? SOS. We are on the Shivering Sands towers in the Thames Estuary and our boat has gone adrift. SOS. Please can someone pick us up from Shivering Sands in the Thames Estuary. Our boat has gone adrift and we are stranded."

The SOS was heard by Tony Pine and Eric Martin who lived in Whitstable. A few hours later, they arrived on a fishing boat, rescued Reg and several girls but David and the others decided to remain on the towers and make more broadcasts. Once the lemonade was finished, they realised they needed fresh water and put out another appeal for drinking water and supplies.

The broadcasts had not gone unnoticed. Early next morning, a launch arrived with police and an army land agent who bellowed through a loud hailer.

"Come out with your hands up. You're trespassing on Government property and we're about to come aboard."

Startled, David jumped out of bed and looked through the window.

"It's the bloody Navy. Come on guys, let's see them off."

The previous night they had stayed up late, making intermittent broadcasts and partying.

"Piss off," replied Brian Paull, sleepily.

Geoff Mews and Colin Dale, also in no mood to cooperate, turned over and tried to go back to sleep. Dressing quickly, David climbed to the roof of the tower and looked over at the boat.

"Come out with your hands up," repeated the army man. "You're trespassing on Government property and we're about to come aboard."

Indignantly, David shouted back.

"We're not leaving. We've squatter's rights and we've a Daily Mirror reporter with us."

David's reply was relayed back to the army superior in his land-based office. Everyone waited anxiously while there was a pause in 'hostilities'. After a short while, a message was relayed to leave the intruders on the towers as they hadn't done any damage. Relieved there was to be no confrontation, David and the army man continued their conversation more amicably. As a parting gift, the boat crew left some fresh fruit and drinking water at the base of the tower.

The newspapers reported how Screaming Lord Sutch had turned the navy away. Questions were asked in Parliament and the Minister of Defence stated that although the fort was Crown property, it was not worth the time and effort involved in trying to remove boarders, especially as no damage had been done to the structure.

Tony Pine and his wife, Susanne, ran a small grocery store close to Whitstable harbour, in Island Wall. Tony arranged for the Harvester to take him out to Shivering Sands with supplies of fresh water and provisions. The boarders were pleased to see him and David agreed, that from then on, Tony could organise supplies for the station.

Reg returned to Clifton Hall triumphant. Finding Dorothy in the garden, he gave her a bear hug. William leapt from Dorothy's shoulder to the ground and standing on his hind legs, shrieked at Reg.

"What's put you in such a good mood?"

"Did you receive any phone calls asking to speak to Mrs Reg?"

Dorothy shook her head in reply.

"We've done it Doe Doe. We've actually started a radio station. It's not on a ship. I found some abandoned wartime forts in the Thames Estuary."

Dorothy raised her eyebrows in astonishment. She had hoped the Thames Rock 'n' Roll party would be enough but now she was under no illusion - it was not. Frowning, she looked sternly at her husband.

"We can't afford it Reg. We don't have enough money to start a radio station."

"It won't cost much. I've already bought most of the stuff second-hand from the Army & Navy Store."

"That's your answer to most things. It won't cost much. Listen to me. Give up this idea and think about making the nightclub at Loughborough work."

"It's a bit of fun, an adventure."

"You're like Peter Pan, you'll never grow up."

"It'll be good publicity for David and I've already played *I Like the Look of You* several times."

"Oh yes, and do seagulls buy records?"

Screaming Lord Sutch, Reg Calvert and Brian Paull (AL)

Radio Sutch: everyone (volunteers) took a turn at being a disc jockey but broadcasts were intermittent as the generator needed refuelling every two hours

3. SHIVERING SANDS

Shivering Sands towers - Reg Calvert, David Sutch, Brian Paull (AL)

It was a mystery to Terry King why Reg did so much for Sutch when he received nothing in return. Terry was money-minded and wouldn't consider promoting anyone without a proper contract and commission. His astuteness meant the office was running well and he had recently employed a new member of staff, Kenny Bell. When Reg made his visit to the office, Terry was keen to know how Reg had managed to start Radio Sutch.

"Why don't you and Kenny come out for a trip?" suggested Reg, spontaneously. "I've a Daily Mirror reporter who wants to go and he'll be here in a minute or two."

"Okay," agreed Terry.

Reg drove to Southend-on-Sea and after parking the car, went to find a fishing boat. He returned a little later having booked an open-top boat that did visitor trips around the pier. The skipper and his young son helped them aboard but it was not a good day to go to sea. The weather was cold with a strong gusty wind that buffeted the boat as waves flew over the sides. Quite soon, the passengers were drenched and feeling ill. The boat began to take in water and the skipper's son, picking up a bucket, began to bail out the bilge.

Reg was prepared for the weather and wearing a warm coat. He stood by the helm chatting to the skipper, oblivious to the plight of his passengers. Kenny Bell turned a green colour and was very sick.

"Will we make it back to land? Are we all going to die?" asked Kenny, plaintively.

"Don't worry," assured Reg, pointing out some towers in the distance. "Look, you can see Shivering Sands."

The passengers cheered up in anticipation of reaching the towers but as they drew closer, Reg became tight-lipped and his mood changed. The skipper had inadvertently taken them to Red Sands Forts. They were similar in design having all seven towers but closer to shore. Reluctantly, Reg accepted the weather was too bad for them to continue further out to sea and the boat turned back.

After four hours in an open boat, the passengers were cold and soaked through to the skin. They disconsolately made their way to a local pub for warmth and refreshments. The landlord, after hearing their story, kindly let them borrow some of his clothes for their return journey to London.

Southend-on-Sea was closer to London by car but after this aborted trip, Reg decided to make the longer journey to Whitstable and ask Fred Downs to provide a regular tendering service to Shivering Sands.

Terry King was still keen to visit Radio Sutch and Reg had assured him he was using a reliable fishing boat for the trip from Whitstable. Dressed in a Saville Row suit, brogue shoes and wearing a hat, Terry looked exceptionally smart compared to everyone else who was casually dressed in old jumpers and trousers. When they reached the tower leg, Terry made the leap from the Harvester but got his timing wrong and missed the ladder. Everyone watched in horror as he slipped down into the choppy sea and sunk below the water. All that was left was his hat as it floated away.

Like a cork, Terry bobbed up to the surface and gulped. Raising his hand, the passengers leaned over the side and tried to catch hold of it but he was too far away. Next, the boat lurched on a wave and tilted toward Terry, trapping him between the side of the boat and the tower leg. Gasping desperately for air as he was being squashed, he frantically paddled his arms to stay afloat with his clothes weighing him down.

"Get the boat hook," shouted Fred, urgently, pointing to a pole clipped onto his cabin.

A minute later, Terry was within reach and caught hold of the pole. He was heaved out of the water and landing in the boat, he flopped onto the floor and sat nonplussed, with water draining from his suit.

"Are you going to try again?" asked Fred, relieved. "I'll call to you when to jump. You'll be able to dry off and get a cup of tea."

"No thanks," replied Terry, shivering. "Never again."

Shivering Sands Towers (RC)

Reg was enjoying life, it was exhilarating and he ignored Dorothy's complaints that he was spending too much time away from her and Clifton Hall.

"You should hear the deejays on Radio Caroline when the weather's rough. They're being sick all over the place."

"That's what happens at sea. You get storms," muttered Dorothy.

"No seasickness on Shivering Sands," smiled Reg, proudly. "You can't imagine what these forts are like. Great big structures on tall legs standing out in the middle of the sea. It's much better than being on a ship that's rocking and rolling."

Dorothy, curious to see what her husband was up to, reluctantly agreed to join him on a day trip to the towers. Overcoming her fear of boats, Dorothy nervously stepped into the Harvester with William wrapped in a warm blanket.

"Come and stand in the cockpit with me," suggested Fred. "You'll be out of the breeze."

"It's a good day to be on the water, it feels quite calm," laughed Reg.

"It doesn't feel calm to me," replied Dorothy, nervously.

When they reached Shivering Sands, Dorothy's face flickered with fear when she realised she would have to leap from the boat to the ladder. Petrified, she glared at her husband.

"I can't swim Reg. What will I do if I fall in?"

"You won't fall in and if you do, I'll rescue you. You go first and I'll be behind you."

Dorothy made the leap and clung tightly to the ladder too frightened to move.

"You've got to climb, keep climbing," encouraged Reg.

"You didn't tell me I'd have to do this," protested Dorothy. "Never again. I don't know why I listen to you."

"We'll soon be at the top and then you can have a cup of tea," chuckled Reg.

Shaking all over, Dorothy reached the trapdoor and climbed through.

"Come on, I'll show you around." Taking his wife's arm, he took her to the different rooms. "This is our studio. Do you want to have a go at being a disc jockey?"

"No thanks. But I'd like a cup of tea," reminded Dorothy, in a flat tone, so her husband would realise she was not impressed with his radio station.

"Don't you think it's fantastic Doe Doe? Better than a ship?"

"It'll be freezing in winter."

"It used to have oil central heating, there's still radiators in all the rooms. Do you want to come up to the roof and look out?"

"No thanks. I've seen enough. I'd like a cup of tea."

"Okay, follow me to the galley. I managed to find a Belling gas cooker so we can have hot drinks and meals. A chap in Whitstable and his wife have a little store and they send out tinned food and water for us."

"Great."

"I'll leave you with the kettle while I go and see if the transmitter's working okay."

"Thanks. Is this all the milk you have? Fussell's?"

"Yep. Fresh milk goes off within a day. See you in a few minutes."

Dorothy made the drinks and stood on the balcony of the tower, staring out to sea. Far below was the Harvester bobbing on the water as Fred waited for their return. She could understand why her husband was so animated about Shivering Sands and admired his ingenuity and resourcefulness. Stroking William, she calmed her nerves while she considered how she could discourage Reg from wasting more time on the towers when he should be concentrating on the nightclub and the Fortunes.

"I'm back," said Reg, coming up behind her with his mug of tea. "Do you want a biscuit? I've got some cream custards."

"Thanks."

"I've a few more things to do. You can explore if you like but don't walk on that catwalk, it's not safe," pointed Reg.

"You're joking. There's no way I'm stepping on any catwalk," replied Dorothy, stiffly.

"See you soon," grinned Reg, giving her a kiss on the cheek and strolling off. He was pleased his wife had come and hoped she'd begin to take an interest.

When it was time to leave, Dorothy stood terrified by the trapdoor looking at the ladder and the sea way below.

"I can't Reg. I can't go down."

"You can stay on the towers if you like? We'll pick you up next week." Reg enjoyed teasing his wife and laughed at her. "I'll go first. Turn backwards. I'll be right behind you."

To maintain possession of the towers, volunteers constantly manned them and Tony Pine helped with his practical knowledge of engineering. Brian Paull, Colin Dale and Geoff (Pussy) Mew, all associates of David, spent weeks at a time on the towers.

Improving Radio Sutch was a challenge. The station was very amateur compared to Radio Caroline and Radio Atlanta, but it had a keen band of listeners and many volunteers who came out to help and have a go at being a deejay. What Reg needed was a manual called, 'How to set up a radio station on a shoestring!' As no one had written such a book, he had to guess and experiment. Life on the towers was fun, a summer camp at sea made more comfortable each week as camp beds and old easy chairs were ferried over.

In the US, it was relatively easy to purchase broadcasting equipment as there were many local radio stations. It was much more difficult in England. Reg mainly rummaged around Army & Navy Stores, searching for items he needed, then tested them at home in the rehearsal room. He soon realised the GPO, who were responsible for licencing radio transmissions, didn't work weekends, so he set up equipment to make regular weekend broadcasts from Clifton Hall, saying it was Radio Sutch on Shivering Sands. After several broadcasts, he was chuffed to receive reports saying Radio Sutch could be heard as far away as Germany.

Not only was radio and television tightly regulated in the UK, but other media was heavily censored. The publication of Lady Chatterley's Lover, written by D.H. Lawrence in the 1920s, had been prohibited in the UK. In 1960, Penguin Books caused a huge amount of controversy by publishing it. They were taken to court and the case went to the Old Bailey. Penguin Books won their right to publish. Reg and David, in keeping with their desire to break censorship, broadcast the book by reading it in instalments as a late-night story.

Brian Paull and Colin Dale were left on their own to man the towers and Reg gave strict instructions to broadcast for a maximum of two hours, then have an intermission while they recharged the batteries and fill the generators with petrol. They forgot the time and Colin, who was broadcasting, heard Brian shouting in panic.

"Fire. Fire. There's a fire."

The electrical wiring was ablaze like a Catherine wheel. Colin picked up a fire extinguisher and not knowing how to use one, accidentally sprayed Brian all over with foam before he managed to extinguish the flames. They thought it hilarious and laughed about it for several days, until Reg returned. They could see immediately by the expression on his face that he was furious and very quietly, he reprimanded them like naughty schoolboys.

"I thought I told you to turn everything off after two hours."

"Why don't you spend some money and buy decent equipment?" retorted Colin.

Reg said nothing in reply. For the remainder of the day, he ignored them while he concentrated on repairing the damage. The next day, there was no sign of his anger and he returned to his normal jocular self as if nothing had happened.

Concrete footings at the base of the tower legs were exposed with each low tide. The sea around the footings eddied and swirled with strong currents, even when the sea appeared calm. Brian Paull enjoyed swimming and one sunny day, he swam out and got caught in a current. Bobbing up and down in the water as he tried to stay afloat, he waved and indicated he couldn't swim back. A new crew member, Jon Walker, recognised he was in difficulty and immediately rushed down the ladders to untie a little dinghy from the tower leg. He rowed frantically. Brian was drowning. Jon reached him just in time and hauled him out. A moment longer, he would have been too late. From then on, anyone who wanted to swim from the towers had a rope tied around their waist so they could be pulled back to safety.

The crew cooked simple meals by heating up tins of food. Fussell's sweetened condensed milk was used instead of fresh milk. The longer the Fussell's was kept, the thicker and stickier it became and after a few days, could be spread on bread instead of jam or honey. On one occasion, a tin of salmon was opened and left for several days. Colin decided to make some sandwiches and within a short time, he was suffering from stomach cramps.

"Are you all right?" asked Brian, concerned.

"I shouldn't have eaten that bloody salmon," replied Colin, grimly, as he held onto his stomach.

The stomach pains became worse and the next time Brian saw Colin, he was rolling on the floor in agony. Realising the seriousness of the situation, Brian broadcast an SOS, hoping someone would hear his message. A little later, an RAF helicopter hovered above the towers and they quickly winched Colin aboard and flew him to Margate hospital.

Brian Paull knew what to do and was unperturbed about being left on his own. He told his listeners about the helicopter lift with Colin being rushed to hospital. When he concluded the broadcast, he turned the equipment off and went to bed.

When the sun went down, the towers were in pitch black with no moon or stars breaking through the thick cloud cover. It was a cold, stormy night and Brian wrapped himself in several army blankets to keep warm. Lying snug on his camp bed, he turned on his side to go to sleep but sleep would not come. The darkness of the night began to terrify him. He sat up to listen, shivering, then lay back down again. It was the wind. It was howling. The towers were starting to move, shuddering, shaking. Doors creaked on hinges. Outside, was a loud rattling, clanging, banging. The empty rooms took on a new supernatural form. Brian was sure they were haunted. In his solitude, his imagination began to do terrible things and there was no escape. Each strange, sinister sound seemed to amplify as the blackness became more intense.

In the cold dawn, light spread across the horizon, Brian apprehensively ventured out to see what was making the unnatural sounds. The loud clanging, he realised, was from the catwalks swinging. The eerie sounds, nothing more than the wind whistling through the towers. There were no ghosts. Relieved, he went back to bed and promptly fell asleep.

Shivering Sands Towers - catwalk (RC)

4. LIGHTING UP THE NIGHT SKY

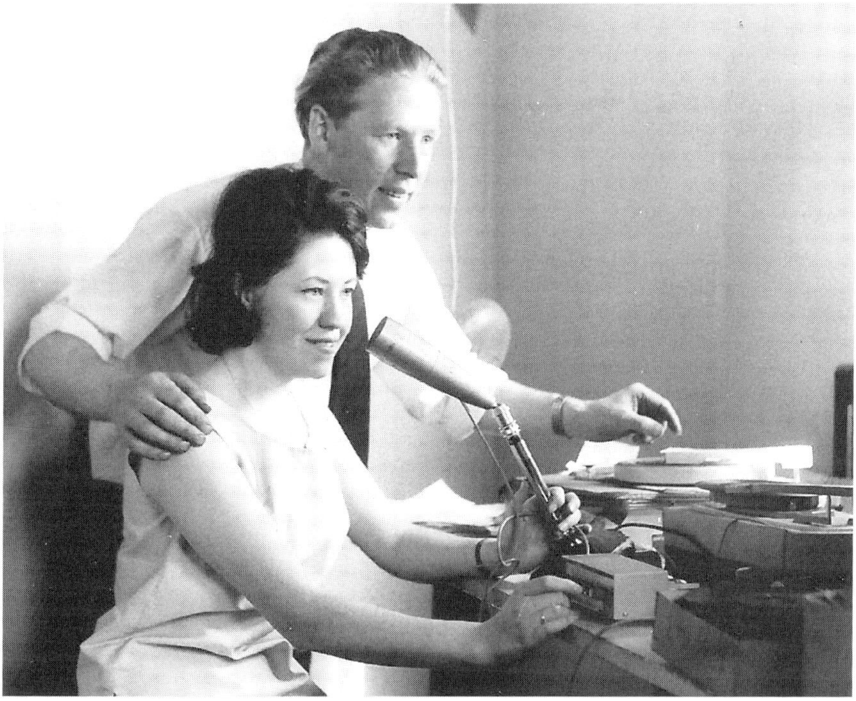

June 1964: Tamara Harrison, Reg's sister, the first female disc jockey (RC)

The boys who lived at Clifton Hall were curious about Radio Sutch. They were keen to have a go at being a pirate and Reg enjoyed the company of having someone with him on the journey. On Danny Storm's first visit, there was a gale blowing and the crossing took several hours. He had not been to sea before and was soon feeling ill.

"I think I'm going to die," said Danny, as he vomited into a bucket.

"You'll be okay in a minute," said Reg, sympathetically.

When the Harvester reached Shivering Sands, Fred called for each passenger to "Jump" from the boat to the ladder. When it was Danny's turn, he couldn't move. His legs felt like jelly as he stared terrified at the pounding sea and the rusting ladder. With some encouragement from Reg, he made the leap and clung onto the rungs. Taking a few deep breaths to calm his nerves, he slowly climbed up and up until he reached the belly of the tower. As he emerged through the hatch, Reg smiled and helped him in.

"Well done. Come and have a cup of tea."

When Danny had recovered, Reg showed him the studio and after demonstrating what to do, he left him to carry on while he worked on the equipment.

On another trip, Reg took the Strollers' drummer, Andy Brown with him. The weather was perfect and the sea crossing, smooth. When they arrived, Reg gave him the job of being their chef and disc jockey. Andy had never done much cooking but managed to heat up a few tins of food.

After their meal, Reg suggested they should have some fun.

"I've brought my firework powders from Clifton Hall and some scaffolding poles. Let's see if we can make the loudest bang ever," grinned Reg.

Andy watched as Reg explained what he was doing.

"Hold onto the scaffolding pole. Keep it still," instructed Reg. "First, I'm going to insert a long fuse and then you can help me pack it with the powders."

It was a warm summer's evening and once the sun had set, they climbed to the top of the towers. Reg took a few minutes to scan the horizon in all directions.

"Can you see any lights from shipping or boats nearby?"

"No, nothing," confirmed Andy.

When Reg was sure it was safe, he lit the fuse and threw the pole with all his might, away from the tower as far as it would go. It made a big splash and a few seconds later, there was a huge thunderous explosion as a blindingly bright white light lit up the dark sky and silhouetted the other towers.

"That was brilliant," exclaimed Reg, laughing, as the boom resounded, bouncing across the water. "The loudest bang ever!"

Returning to Clifton Hall, Dorothy was pleased to see Reg.

"You mother phoned while you were away."

"Did she?"

"She asked if she can come and stay for a holiday and bring Tamara with her. I said it would be okay. You can stay at home for a couple of weeks, take them out on day trips to Warwick and Stratford."

"Mm. How about we all go down to Whitstable and visit Shivering Sands?"

"You must be joking. It's a long way for me to drive there and back in a day. Not only that, I can't see your mother leaping off the boat and climbing the ladder."

"Would be funny," chuckled Reg, pausing. "You could have a little holiday, stay over in London in a nice hotel, see the sights and do a show. What about The Sound of Music? Then we can take a trip to Whitstable and you and Ada can stay somewhere while I take Tamara out to the station."

Dorothy considered the option. "Maybe we could but we'd have to leave the girls at home on their own."

"They'll be fine," said Reg. "Susan will look after things."

"Okay, I'll book a hotel and the theatre," smiled Dorothy.

The trip to London went well. Dorothy entertained Reg's mother and sister by taking them shopping while he worked in the office. The following day, they made their way to Whitstable. Ada and Dorothy stood by the harbour wall in the breeze, watching the Harvester being loaded with provisions. As the boat was ready to set off, several volunteers climbed aboard and Reg and Tamara waved goodbye. Brother and sister were pleased to have some time on their own and when they reached Shivering Sands, Reg proudly showed Tamara the large empty rooms.

"I'll make a cup of tea and then you can be a deejay."

"You're joking!" exclaimed Tamara.

"No, everyone has a turn. It's easy peasy."

Carrying their mugs of tea into the studio, Reg sat down and began to demonstrate what to do.

"Place a record on the turntable and simply announce the title of the record and who it's by. You can say anything else you like. Whether it's your favourite record or singer and don't forget to say this is Radio Sutch."

"No Reg, I can't," replied Tamara, backing away.

"There's no such word as can't. Of course, you can," assured Reg, as he began to prepare the next record. "Good afternoon listeners. It's Uncle Reg here and it's good to be back on Shivering Sands. This is Radio Sutch, and today we have our first lady disc jockey. Her name is Tamara and she's come all the way from Lancashire. Say hello Tamara."

"Hello."

"I'm now going to play the fabulous Fortunes, *I Like the Look of you.*"

Smiling, Reg stood up and offered the seat to Tamara. Apprehensively, she sat down and picked up a disc and nervously waited for the Fortunes record to stop spinning and spoke into the microphone while she replaced it on the turntable.

"See, there's nothing to it. I'll be back in a couple of hours. Have fun."

Late afternoon on the following day, the Harvester moored up alongside the harbour wall. Dorothy and Ada were waiting.

"What did you think of Radio Sutch?" asked Reg, as he kissed his wife and mother.

"Not a lot, we could hardly hear it," replied Dorothy, dryly.

"Did you hear Tamara having a turn at being a disc jockey?"

"There's a lot of crackle and interference," responded Ada, smiling proudly at her son.

"It'll get better," beamed Reg.

Back at Clifton Hall, life carried on as normal with the groups practicing in the rehearsal room, Dorothy organising the dances and Reg occasionally going to Loughborough to sort out his new nightclub.

Hearing Danny and the Strollers practicing, Reg decided it was time for them to change. He liked his groups to be versatile and as he entered the rehearsal room, he grinned mischievously.

"What are these for?" asked John, puzzled, as Reg handed him a pair of heavy, black-rimmed glasses with no glass.

"Put your head down, I'm going to put a centre parting in your hair."

"I look really silly," exclaimed John.

"That's the idea, now put the glasses on," chuckled Reg, as the other boys began to sing, "*Hey, Hey, Good lookin', whatcha got cookin'. How's about cookin' something up with me. Hey sweet baby, don't think maybe, We could find a brand new recipe.*"

"I've been thinking. How about doing a comedy act?"

"What sort of comedy?" asked John.

The boys knew when Reg suggested something, he meant for them to do it, but his smile was contagious and they all began to laugh as Reg brought out woolly hats.

"Here, put these on and I'll take some photographs. I'll leave you to work out a comedy routine. It'll be easier for Terry King to get more bookings if we can bill you as a double act. Danny Storm and the Strollers and Freddy Foureyes and the Niker Flikers."

"Freddy Foureyes and the Niker Flikers," they repeated, laughing even more.

"John will be Freddy Foureyes. Can you squint?"

"I'll try," replied John.

"Brilliant. That's it, you look really silly. Hold that expression while I fetch my camera."

A week later, Reg had large red posters printed with Freddy Foureyes and the Niker Flikers, all looking silly. The group rehearsed various comedy numbers and did their best to be comical but after a few gigs, by their own admission, they were not amusing and didn't go down well with the audiences. Reg did his best to encourage them but after seeing their act several times, he had to agree and Freddy Foureyes and the Niker Flikers were no more.

At the dances, Reg kept a fatherly eye on his performers and would step into the centre of skirmishes and sort out trouble makers. Although only 5 feet 8 inches tall, he was physically strong and would carry two lads at a time and take them outside to cool down, sometimes banging their heads together. He also employed stewards, ex-boxers and wrestlers to be a presence and prevent gang fights. At independent gigs, his musicians were afforded no such protection.

Freddy Foureyes and the Niker Flickers
Strollers: John Wileman, Dave Spence and Andy Brown (RC)

Danny Storm and the Strollers were booked to perform at the annual Rugby Club dance at the Benn Hall in Rugby. Wearing a white suit, Danny looked sexy and as he sang, he gyrated his hips and made eyes at the girls who stood by the foot of the stage. The Rugby football players were big, strong, sturdy lads. Fuelled by alcohol, they became rowdy and began to cause a disturbance as a way of objecting to Danny's performance. Finding it difficult to continue, Danny beckoned he would see them outside in the break.

In the interval, with some bravado, Danny went outside with the Strollers and saw the Rugby players waiting. It was obvious they were ready for a fight and he and the Strollers were going to get a hiding. Stepping forward, Danny insisted his band were not involved and the fight should be with him and one other.

Bravely, Danny stood his ground. The gang agreed and after receiving a good beating, Danny admitted defeat and returned to the dressing room to nurse his wounds. Andy Brown remained outside and without warning, the gang turned on him. As he fell to the ground, one of the lads took pleasure in putting his boot in his face until Chris Capaldi came out and stopped the fight. Cleaning himself up, Andy went back on stage. The show had to go on, and it did.

1940s photograph of the Maunsell Forts
Architect, Guy Maunsell designed two different types of armed forts to protect the Mersey and the Thames Estuary during World War II. The Shivering Sands style of towers were for the army. The other design with two enormous round legs connected by a platform on top were for the Navy and could house up to 100 men.

Shivering Sands originally had seven towers but in 1963, a ship collided with one of them in thick fog and the tower collapsed. The Search Light tower was left stranded and used by the Port of London Authority to measure wind and tides. The other five towers were abandoned by the Government in the mid 1950's and unused, until Reg discovered them and started Radio Sutch.

5.SUMMER OF FUN

1964 Shivering Sands Towers Radio Sutch (RC)

Staying away most of the week was putting a strain on Reg and Dorothy's marriage. Reg did his best to be cheerful when he returned to run the weekend dances but the more he was away, the more irritable Dorothy became. Not only that, Radio Sutch had become expensive to run and he was using money from the dancehall takings to finance it. The high rent on the nightclub at Loughborough had to be paid and Reg seemed nonchalant about ever making it profitable.

"It's about time you gave up Radio Sutch," snapped Dorothy.

"I'm just having a bit of fun and I'm gradually improving the signal."

"What's the point? I seem to remember you saying Radio Sutch would be a one-day publicity stunt. We'll soon run out of money if you don't stop playing about at being a radio pirate. It's great for David and he's doing well from the publicity but what do you get out of it?"

"He's signed up with King's Agency and he's due to tour Australia soon."

"You don't get your ten per cent manager's commission for making him famous. And I don't suppose he puts his hand in his pocket to pay for the radio equipment or anything else you keep buying."

Reg ignored his wife's criticism.

"A cup of tea would be good," suggested Reg, cheekily.

"It would. You can make it yourself and bring me one out to the garden," Dorothy replied huffily.

A little later, Reg found Dorothy kneeling next to a small pile of shepherd's purse and dandelions she had pulled out of the ground.

"Tea madam."

"Thanks. Weeds, they never stop growing. I wish my vegetables were half so good."

Reg stooped to kiss her. "I do love you, even when you're angry."

"I know you do. The trouble is, you seem to be neglecting everything while you're having your fun. Take the Fortunes new record, you've done hardly anything to promote it."

"I play it on the station and I've arranged for another recording session at the end of July with the American producer, Shel Talmy."

"Is he any good?"

"I think so. We've decided the A-side will be *Look Homeward Angel,* an old Johnnie Ray number but we've updated the lyrics and it's going to have full orchestral backing. On the B-side, they'll have a song the Fortunes have written so they'll earn royalties on sales."

"I've heard them working out their harmonies in the kitchen, sounds good," agreed Dorothy. "By the way, did you realise our daughter is going to be sixteen next week?"

"Yep, sweet sixteen. I see the boys' eyes follow her around when she walks in a room."

"That's not our only problem. Susan's mentioned she wants to buy a scooter with the money she's saved."

"Not good," replied Reg. "I'll speak to her about it and see if I can persuade her to change her mind."

In the evening, Dorothy was singing to herself as she served dinner. Her family watched with some curiosity as to what was being ladled onto their plates.

"What's this Mum?" asked Susan, puzzled, as she put her fork through long pieces of gooey string.

"You don't need to turn your nose up before you've tried it," replied Dorothy, as she spooned out the sauce on top.

"Very strange," commented Candy.

"It's Italian, spaghetti Bolognese," laughed Dorothy, as she gave William a long string of spaghetti which he took to the air dryer and then pulled into pieces and dropped.

"William doesn't think much to it," observed Reg, as he tried to fork in a mouthful of spaghetti. "How are we supposed to eat this?"

"Watch," replied Dorothy, smugly, as she demonstrated by twisting her fork around, making a clump on the end. Just as she opened her mouth, the spaghetti untwisted and fell back onto her plate.

“I thought spaghetti came in tins with tomato sauce,” laughed Susan, as she began to cut hers up into small pieces.

“You should do it like an Italian,” demonstrated Reg as he concentrated on twisting the spaghetti onto his fork before sucking it off.

“Think I should’ve given you a bib, you’ve got most of it down your chin,” smiled Dorothy.

“Taste’s good.” Reg wiped his face on his handkerchief before twirling more onto his fork. Turning to Susan, he smiled. “That’s cheating, cutting it into little bits.”

“Tastes the same.”

“Your Mum mentioned you’re thinking of buying a scooter.”

“I’ve saved up enough to buy one secondhand.”

“Scooters aren’t safe. They’ve small wheels and are unstable. If you go over a pothole you could fall off in front of a car or a lorry.”

“I agree. Scooters are really not safe,” added Dorothy.

“Dad had a motorbike when he was sixteen.”

“True,” agreed Reg. “Motorbikes are better. They have much larger wheels.”

“Motorbikes aren’t that safe either,” commented Dorothy, flashing a look at her husband to discourage him from persuading their daughter to buy a motorbike.

“I don’t want a motorbike,” replied Susan, interrupting her mother’s thoughts.

“Good,” murmured Dorothy.

“I’d rather have a scooter so I can put my feet in front of me when I’m wearing a dress.”

“Why don’t you save up to buy a car?” suggested Reg.

“I’d have to wait another year,” protested Susan. “Another year of cycling to work and college in the rain and snow.”

“How much have you saved?”

“Nearly one hundred pounds.”

“Fantastic. How about a bubble car?”

“I don’t think I’ve enough money.”

“Three wheels are safer than two and you’d be warm and dry inside a bubble. If you like, I’ll take you to Coventry to put a deposit down on a new one and you can pay the rest on hire purchase.”

Dorothy flashed her husband another look to tell him he was being even more ridiculous.

“Could do,” replied Susan, smiling at her father in response.

“Sweet sixteen. You’ll be able to leave home and get married,” joked Reg.

“One less thing to worry about when we’ve married you off,” laughed Dorothy.

"I wish you'd stop saying that," retorted Susan, angrily. "You know I don't want to get married."

"You're such a worry with having so many boyfriends," said Dorothy.

"Poor Eddie," commented Candy.

"Who asked for your opinion?" snapped Susan.

"You go out with other boys as well as Eddie," accused Candy.

"So," replied Susan. "We have an agreement. When he's away in High Wycombe he can go out with who he likes and I can go out with who I like."

"He's too nice for you," sneered Candy.

"That'll do you two. I wish we could eat our meal without you bickering," complained Dorothy.

"How about you try an Indian curry next?" suggested Reg.

"No way. And I wish you wouldn't eat them. You smell of curry when you come back from London."

Susan was looking forward to her sixteenth birthday. Sixteen was a special age, a rite of passage. No longer would she be treated as a child. On Sunday morning, the two sisters made breakfast together, without arguing, and carried a tray each to their parents' bedroom.

"Happy Birthday," murmured Dorothy, sleepily. "What time is it?"

"Ten thirty," replied Susan, smiling happily.

Laying the trays down, the two girls sat on the edge of the bed while Dorothy nudged her husband. He turned and seeing his daughters, stretched and wiped sleep from his eyes.

Laughing and chattering, the family ate toast and marmalade. When they had finished, Dorothy nudged Reg to pass their daughter's present which was next to his side of the bed in a large brown cardboard box. He lifted it up and Susan looked at it in excited anticipation as her family burst into song.

"*Happy birthday to you, Happy birthday to you, Happy birthday dear Susan, Happy birthday to you.*"

"Gosh, this is big," giggled Susan, as she tore away the parcel tape and prised open the flaps. Inside, she could see layers of tissue and white lace. Slowly, she pulled the contents out and then dropped it immediately.

"We thought we'd buy it ready for your wedding day," laughed Reg, gleefully. "Sweet sixteen."

"We can marry you off. One less thing for me to worry about," laughed Dorothy.

Susan sat in stunned silence, disappointed and humiliated. Bursting into tears, she ran to her bedroom, collected her coat and handbag and fled the house. Her parents and Candy were laughing so much, tears ran down their faces. It was hugely funny to see Susan's shocked expression but after she had gone, their laughter sounded hollow. Reg and Dorothy realised their mistake. What had begun as a joke had turned sour.

"I'd better go and talk to her."

Dorothy stepped out of bed and wrapped her dressing gown over her transparent nylon nightdress. After looking in her daughter's bedroom, she returned and hastily dressed. After searching the house, she returned to the kitchen and shrugged her shoulders.

"She's probably in the hayloft," suggested Candy.

"I hadn't thought of that," replied Dorothy. "I'll go and look."

Dorothy wandered over to the barns and climbed the ladder but the hatch was down and however hard she pushed, it would not budge. Standing at the bottom of the ladder she called up.

"Come down Susan. It was a joke. Your Dad and I saw the dress in a shop window in Coventry for £3 in a sale. It was a joke. Come on down. You can't stay up there all day."

Susan sat on the hayloft trapdoor and remained obstinately silent. After a few minutes, Dorothy gave up and returned to the kitchen to make herself a cup of coffee. Reg was sitting despondently at the table staring blankly into space while Candy was making more toast.

"She can't stay in the hayloft forever. She'll have to come down eventually," muttered Dorothy.

"Eddie's coming to take her out," said Candy.

"Oh, that's okay," nodded Dorothy, relieved.

Susan told no one of her humiliation, not even her best friends and refused to speak to her parents for three weeks. When they did make their peace, Dorothy took her to Rugby to choose a gold wristwatch and Reg to Coventry where he ordered a blue Trojan bubble car with a 198cc motorbike engine.

By the end of August, it became apparent that David Sutch was going to give up being a pirate and Reg contemplated whether he should continue or not. It was a hard decision. When he returned home for the weekend, he greeted Dorothy with a hug and kiss.

"Did you know that David's on tour in Australia."

"Yes, you told me."

"He's decided to give up Radio Sutch."

"Good. I've made some scones; would you like one?"

"Two please," replied Reg, grinning at her and William, who was hanging by his tail from a lath of the clothes airer.

"What's David going to do now?"

"Concentrate on performing."

"Sensible," agreed Dorothy, as she handed a plate to Reg with two buttered scones and gave William some raisins. "You've had your summer of fun, now you can return to running the business"

"I'm not giving up," said Reg, quietly. "I've agreed to pay David for the stuff he's bought."

"I don't suppose that'll be much. And what'll happen when the government close you down? They're bound to remove you off the towers."

"I've asked a solicitor called Timothy Hardacre to check my legal rights and give me his opinion. I want to know whether we've squatters' rights, especially as the towers are outside British waters. With a general election in October, the Conservatives won't do anything as it would cause a riot, so I imagine we've got at least another two months to run."

"And after the election, whoever wins, they'll close you down. They'll be nothing to stop them."

"Not if we're outside legal jurisdiction."

Dorothy took a deep breath. "One. Two. Three. Four. Five. Six …"

"Why are you counting?" asked Reg, innocently.

"To stop me exploding. You're like a man possessed. Since Radio Caroline started, all you've thought about is owning a radio station. You've had your fun. You should be sensible like David and realise it's time to move on."

"Why don't you come down next week and we can work out how to turn it into a professional station?"

"You must be joking," responded Dorothy, exasperated. "You're not listening to me. We can't afford to run a radio station while Loughborough is costing so much in rent. You need to spend your time in the nightclub instead of Shivering Sands."

"I know," admitted Reg. "But you know I've always dreamed of having my own radio station."

"You also dreamed of having your own nightclub. You haven't thought this through properly? You told me that Radio Atlanta had amalgamated with Radio Caroline as they'd run out of money. If they can't make a profit, how can you?" asked Dorothy, angrily.

"They've got the cost of two ships and two crews to maintain. I haven't and I'll soon get some local advertising."

"Where're we going to find the extra money before you make it profitable?" shouted Dorothy.

"We only need an engineer and a couple of volunteer disc jockeys," smiled Reg, blithely. He was prepared for his wife shouting at him when she didn't agree with his actions. "There's young lads waiting on the quayside every week to have a go at being a deejay."

"The other stations are companies with shareholders. To turn Radio Sutch into a professional station, you'd need investors and more money than we've got."

Reg glazed over. He wasn't listening. Dorothy realised then, there was nothing she could do or say to change his mind.

"I think I'll pop up to Huddersfield on Sunday and see my Dad. Do you want to come?"

Dorothy gave her husband a quizzical look. It was unlike him to want to visit his relatives and she realised there must be an ulterior motive.

Arriving in Huddersfield, they made a brief tour of their relatives, finally stopping at one of Reg's childhood friends, Arthur Addy. His wife, Margaret, gave them tea and homemade cakes while Arthur and Reg reminisced about their childhood, laughing at the mischief they'd got up to as young boys.

"Do you remember the time when you set up radio telephones between our houses?" laughed Arthur.

"It was funny. No one guessed what we'd done until their radios didn't work," chuckled Reg. "Have you heard, I've started a pirate radio station."

"Yes, I did see it in the paper."

"I'd like you to come and work with me? We'd make a good team. It's not on a ship like other stations but on an old wartime fort some seven miles out at sea. With your training in electronics and power generating, we could make it a really good station."

Arthur shook his head dismissively.

"Come take a look, then decide. Have a bit of a holiday with Margaret?"

"I've a good job and we're buying this house."

"If we can make it successful, we could earn a lot of money."

"It sounds exciting but I can't afford to give everything up."

Despondently, Reg put his head in his hands. "I don't know what to do. I was relying on you helping me."

"You'll find a way. You always do," replied Arthur, encouragingly.

The next time Reg was on Shivering Sands, he announced over the air, a vacancy for an electrical engineer with some experience in power generation. Paul Elvey, a young man in his mid-twenties who happened to be tuned into Radio Sutch, heard the request and contacted Reg. After a friendly interview, Paul was invited to visit Shivering Sands to examine the equipment and electrical wiring.

After a choppy sea crossing and making the hazardous leap to the ladder, Paul was shocked when he saw the equipment.

"If you want a strong radio frequency to pump out of an aerial system using medium wave, you'll need plenty of electrical power. These ex-army lorry batteries are just not good enough. You need a decent mains voltage generator to power a proper transmitter."

The two men talked for some time about pirate radio and installing a new generator. As Paul was confident and seemed to know what he was talking about, Reg offered him the job, paying £25 per week, with one week on and one week off. It was good money and Paul, excited about the prospect of working on a pirate station, was happy to accept.

In the middle of August, Susan had her annual holiday from work. With nothing else to do, Reg invited her to go with him to Shivering Sands, persuading Dorothy to come with them and stay in Whitstable with Candy.

Parking her car by the harbour, Dorothy stood with her daughters and waited while Reg wandered off to talk to a group of young men. When the Harvester had been loaded, Reg returned smiling cheerfully, his hair blowing freely in the wind as he kissed Dorothy on the cheek.

"Who's that man over there?" Dorothy asked, pointing with her head.

"Paul Elvey. I've just taken him on. He's a good engineer."

"Get rid of him."

"Why?"

"My sixth sense. I don't trust him. Get rid of him, he's no good."

Reg shook his head in surprise. He was used to his wife taking an immediate dislike to people, disregarding the fact she was usually right, he smiled and waved goodbye, ushering Susan onto the boat. It was a good day to go out to sea with a gentle breeze and waves sparkling in the sunshine. After a short time, they could see the forts emerging out of a heat haze, black silhouettes against a blue sky. Fred steadied the Harvester next to the tower leg for everyone to make the leap. Susan was fearless in jumping onto the ladder and climbing up to the base of the tower. Reg was waiting for her at the top and quickly showed her around.

"You can be head cook and bottle washer."

Susan smiled in response. She liked cooking and was happy to help.

"This is our bedroom," said Reg, pushing open a heavy door which creaked on its hinge. The tower was not furnished for comfort and inside was a large, airy room with two camp beds, pillows and brown army blankets. Susan loved her father's makeshift way of doing things and the way he made everything fun. This was luxury compared to her childhood memories of camping in the New Forest and sleeping in a cardboard box.

Outside on the walk-way, Reg pointed to a rickety catwalk strung between two of the towers.

"On no account are you to walk across there as it could collapse. And don't go in for a swim. It might look calm but there are very strong currents around the legs. Even a strong swimmer could easily drown."

After their tour, Reg took his daughter into the studio and asked her if she'd like to be a disc jockey. Susan was happy to have a go.

"I'll show you what to do," said Reg as he sat down on the office chair and casually chatted into the microphone while he placed a record on the turntable.

"As you take one record off, you put another on, say what the song is and don't forget to announce that this is Radio Sutch, the teenage station."

Reg watched his daughter as she settled into the routine and then went to find Paul to work with him on the equipment. Later in the day, Reg took his turn at being a disc jockey. He had brought with him a children's musical toy.

"Our first jingle on Radio Sutch. I hope you like it," chuckled Reg, as he rolled the toy backwards and forwards to make a tinkling, jingling sound. "My wife, Mrs Reg, is staying in Whitstable for a holiday. She is driving a lime green Ford Zephyr car and you'll know it's her because she has a pet monkey called William. I'm not joking. She really does have a pet monkey. He sits on her shoulder most of the time so if you see a lady with a monkey, say hello to Mrs Reg from me."

Shivering Sands jungle catwalk (EM)

Shivering Sands Searchlight Tower, stranded from the other towers and used by the Port of London Authority to monitor wind and tides (RC)

6. DISCORD

Danny Storm with the Strollers, Dave Spence, Andy Brown, John Wileman (RC)

Danny Storm and the Strollers had left England in August to work at the Storeyville Club in Cologne for a month, taking with them, Roger Chapman, the former lead singer from the Leicester group, Jimmy Stevens and the Jackpots. German nightclub owners paid British groups well, but in return, they expected them to perform unreasonable lengths of time which not only affected their performance but caused amplifiers to overheat and blow up. Danny borrowed one set and when these overheated, in desperation, he phoned Reg from Germany and asked him to send out two new amplifiers.

Since the arrival of the Beatles, singers like Danny were out of fashion. On their previous stay in Hanover, the group had gone down well but in Cologne, the audience didn't appreciate Danny's style of Rock 'n' Roll or Roger Chapman's rock and bluesy music. Returning to England, Danny felt disappointed and began to reflect on his career. Roger Chapman left and went his own way, forming a new group, the Family.

The Fortunes new record, *Look Homeward Angel,* was released on 18th September 1964. Reg did his best to promote it and arranged several 'live' television broadcasts. The record was, of course, played often on Radio

Sutch. It was a beautiful song and worthy to make the top 20 and Reg felt very disappointed when it didn't reach the charts. Even without a hit record, he was proud of the Fortunes reputation. They were in demand and acknowledged as one of the best and most versatile vocal groups in the country. Rod and Barry, with their increasing success, became more nonchalant towards Dorothy and did nothing to charm or mollify her. Coincidentally, Rod shared the same birthday as Dorothy and Barry's was a week later. Born under the birth sign of Aries, they all had strong personalities, had passed their eleven plus, gone to grammar schools and gave an aura of belonging to a superior class.

Dorothy was used to her word being law and regularly complained to Reg about their attitude.

"They won't listen to me. They're lazy and do nothing to help and it's a job to get them to rehearse when you're not here. I don't want them living at Clifton Hall anymore."

To appease his wife, Reg agreed to find somewhere else for them to stay, however, he did nothing. Dorothy continued her complaints and for a quiet life, he reluctantly contacted local estate agents and found a pretty cottage to rent at Crick, about seven miles from Clifton Hall. It was ideal, close enough for them to return and use the rehearsal room and near to motorway networks.

When the Rugby Advertiser did a feature on the Fortunes and their new accommodation, the owner was outraged and gave them immediate notice to leave. He had not appreciated that a pop group was living in his property as it was rented in Reg's name. Dorothy refused to have them back, so the group dispersed, finding their own accommodation, only coming together for rehearsals and performances.

Reg purchased a large transistor radio, carrying it around like a handbag so he could listen to Radio Sutch wherever he went. It soon became apparent that the station could be picked up in various pockets of the country and abroad as listeners were asked to write in with record requests and say where they had heard it. Two weeks after Susan's broadcast, Reg handed his daughter a postcard from a listener in Guernsey.

"It's amazing where we can be heard, even as far away as Holland and Germany."

"Fantastic," responded Dorothy, sarcastically. "I wish you'd turn that radio off. All I can hear is crackle."

Reg ignored her and winked at Candy. "How would you like to become a deejay?"

"No way," replied Dorothy, sharply.

"I'd love to. Please," appealed Candy, to her mother.

"I've said no and I mean no. The summer holidays are over and you're still at school and you can't take time off to be a deejay"

"Candy would be the youngest female disc jockey. It would be good publicity for the station." smiled Reg.

"You've heard me. I've said no. She has school work to do."

"I thought we'd call her programme Candy's Pop Shop," persisted Reg, with a mischievous glint in his eyes as he teased his wife. "How about we record the programmes at Clifton Hall on a Sunday afternoon? I can take the tapes with me each week."

Dorothy raised her eyebrows at her husband, acknowledging defeat as Reg winked at Candy.

Susan tried not to show the disappointment she felt. Reg observed her fleeting expression and later in the evening, finding her alone in the lounge, sat down and explained confidentially his reason for not asking her.

"I thought I'd ask Candy to be a deejay to give her more confidence. Your Mum wants to keep her ordinary."

Susan said nothing but nodded her head in understanding.

Father and daughter had a close bond and few words were needed. Candy was her mother's child and Susan was his. Reg could see Candy growing-up with no ambitions, her head full of nothing but cotton wool and pop music. He wanted to reduce his wife's influence and give Candy wings to fly, whereas Dorothy wanted to anchor her daughters to the ground and reality.

The summer of fun was over. Autumn brought cold damp days, gales and storms but the weather did nothing to diminish Reg's enthusiasm.

"I'm going to change the name to Radio City and put the station on a more professional footing."

"That's all very well Reg. But how are you going to pay for it? You can't keep taking the dancehall money."

Dorothy stared at her husband angrily as she tried not to raise her voice but she was near breaking point. Since he had discovered Shivering Sands he had become like a man possessed and nothing she said dented his determination to make the station a success.

"I need better equipment to improve our transmissions. We'll soon attract local advertising once the station has more power and then we'll be profitable."

"Pie in the sky. We can't go on as we are. I need money to pay the bills and Radio City may never make a profit. You need to earn more before you can take more."

Life with Reg was like being on a rollercoaster, exciting when you are at the top but terrifying as you drop with twists and turns to the bottom. Dorothy dreamed of a quiet family life without worry and the more stressed she became, the more she raised her voice. She shouted at her husband, shouted at her daughters, and when Reg was away, complained unremittingly about him. Candy, being closer to her mother said nothing but Susan, disliking the criticism, would defend her father. This made Dorothy even more angry and she always came back with the same retort.

"I don't know why you stick up for him. It was me who brought you up, not your father."

Susan's life had become complicated. In the evenings, she went to college to study art and further her education. Lunchtimes, she secretly met Mike, the photographer from the Rugby Advertiser who she knew, her parents didn't approve of. At the weekends, she saw Eddie; he had become part of the family, often joining them for meals. To free herself she decided to break with both boyfriends, though Mike would not agree. When Eddie stopped visiting Clifton Hall, Reg and Dorothy made no mention of it but Candy became upset. She liked Eddie and after accusing her sister of being cruel, she burst into tears.

Living in a large house meant the family stayed apart much of the time, only coming together for meals. As Reg and Dorothy struggled to manage their own problems, they seemed to barely notice either of their daughter's growing-pains.

Candy's role as the youngest deejay had created a small amount of press interest but when Reg was introduced to Lyn Bass, an exceptionally pretty girl who was Romford Carnival Queen, he realised Lyn would attract even more media attention.

"I like your voice," said Reg, warmly. "Would you like to come to my office in Denmark Street and do a voice check?"

It was an unusual chat-up line but Lyn was happy to agree. The role of a disc jockey was considered to be a male preserve but Reg liked to break with tradition. He had already had three female members of his family breaking the mould. Lyn came several times to the office and made a day trip to Shivering Sands, adopting her mother's maiden name, Peggy Knight, as her pseudonym. There were no other female disc jockeys and Radio City received good publicity with Lyn's photograph appearing in many newspapers.

The General Election was planned for 15th October,1964 and the offshore radio pirates hoped that a change of government might improve their chances of being granted a licence and moving to land-based stations.

"They say Harold Wilson will be the next Prime Minister," mentioned Reg, casually, while drinking his morning cup of coffee.

"I hope not," retorted Dorothy.

"Don't you like him? He was born in Huddersfield."

"Not much. He went to the same school as me, but for boys. Pretends to smoke a pipe to make him look working class when he's not."

"I'm pretty sure the Conservatives will lose, especially after the scandal of the Profumo affair. Sir Alec Douglas-Home is a very unpopular Prime Minister. David Sutch has decided to stand against Wilson at Huyton and has asked me to represent him as Campaign Manager."

"I hope you've said no."

Reg shrugged his shoulders nonchalantly and smiled. "The Stratford by-election was fun so I thought I might do it again. We've got some good ideas for the manifesto."

"And what do you get out of it? No Reg. Let David organise his own election and pay his own expenses. You've done enough to promote him. I even read in the newspaper that he sold Radio Sutch to you for £5,000."

"You shouldn't believe everything you read in the newspapers," chuckled Reg. "For the election, we're going to campaign for local and commercial radio stations and end the BBC monopoly. And for teenagers to get the vote at 18."

"Oh yes, and what bright ideas has David come up with?"

"He wants to fight discrimination against men wearing long hair."

"Ha, ha," frowned Dorothy. "I hate his long greasy black hair. If he washed it more often it might be a good idea."

"And that the Beatles should all get Knighthoods," added Reg.

"Another silly idea."

During election week, the press were out in force and delighted to interview Screaming Lord Sutch as a form of light relief from the heavier politics. David had his speech rehearsed and knew exactly what he wanted to say to make his point.

"It's a way to rebel against the old fogies. There are over 600 MPs but not one youngster can speak. They're all old men. My main platform will be votes at 18. You can get married at 16 and a lot of people have families and yet are still classed as children themselves. You can fight for your country at 18 and you can be hung for murder. But when it comes to voting, you're a child. And I'd like to have localised commercial radio stations, like local papers. We could have radio stations across the country so people have a free choice about what they listen to."

Reg and David stayed up all night while the votes were counted and afterwards, Reg returned to Clifton Hall, tired but in jubilant mood. David had received 518 votes, more than double what he had at the Stratford by-election.

"Is Harold Wilson Prime Minister?" enquired Dorothy.

"Don't know yet. The voting's tight, could go either way."

The next day, the Labour Party were triumphant after receiving confirmation they had gained a small majority of five seats. Anthony

Wedgwood Benn was appointed as Postmaster General and almost immediately announced in his upper crust manner, he would close all illegal pirate radio stations. A change of government had made no difference and it was a big disappointment to the thousands of supporters of free radio.

The Convention of the Council of Europe were trying to bring in legislation to ban all European offshore radio stations. Wedgwood Benn paid lip service to this but he had to walk a fine line, knowing he could risk the Labour government losing the next general election if he tried to close the increasingly popular 'pirates'.

Shivering Sands Towers (RC)

7. CRASH

Radio City studio, Shivering Sands Towers (EJ)

Dorothy hid the dancehall earnings in her dressing room and Reg took what he needed each week, leaving only a small amount for Dorothy to bank.

"You said it wouldn't cost much," shouted Dorothy.

"It won't be long before it's profitable," answered Reg, quietly, as he stuffed money into his inside pocket.

"And pigs can fly."

"I'm going to employ freelance sales reps to bring in advertising and I'm planning to run some local Radio City discos."

"If you keep taking the money, we'll soon be bankrupt. We could lose everything. What's the point of me working my socks off if you throw it away on a dream? You can't keep spending more without earning more," barked Dorothy.

Reg shrugged her wise words away like a dog shaking off muddy water. He wasn't ready to give it all up and wouldn't change direction. He liked excitement and new challenges. At the same time, he recognised that he needed his wife's support, with her sharp instinct and logical mind. They were bonded closely together, two sides of the same coin, heads and tails, but being on differing sides, rarely saw eye to eye.

"Why don't you come to London and help with Radio City? You don't need to go out on the boat, you can run things from the office. You could do the programming, organise the deejays."

"Don't be ridiculous," snapped Dorothy. "I'm not like you. I can't just drop everything and go to London. What about the house and our daughters? Our lives are here, at Clifton Hall. It's about time you realised it and moved back to reality. You've had your fun. You should be running more dances and making Loughborough profitable."

"You're right," agreed Reg. "I've been thinking about booking the Matrix Ballroom in Coventry on Saturday nights."

"I thought you said it was too big."

"It's a bit of a barn of a place with no atmosphere but I thought I'd give it a try." Reg picked up his small suitcase and large portable radio. Kissing his wife on the cheek, he turned away. "I'll be back Thursday."

Tight lipped and angry, Dorothy stood motionless as she heard Reg's quick footsteps on the stairs. Her heart sunk. Each week as he left, she became depressed as a feeling of utter loneliness overwhelmed her. William, seeming to understand her mood, chuntered quietly from the curtain rail, reminding her he wanted to return to his place on her shoulder.

Teenage dances were becoming less popular as discos replaced them. All the midweek dances had to be closed except for Tuesdays at the Camp Hill Club, near Nuneaton. Only three years ago, Reg had Dorothy had organised over 20 dances a week. Now there were five.

Friday nights, a few Rugby teenagers caught a bus to Nuneaton to go to the dance at the Co-op Hall. After the show, Reg filled his car with anyone who wanted a lift back. When Reg did not return as usual one night, Dorothy began to worry. Her sixth sense told her something was wrong.

The journey from Nuneaton to Rugby was one Reg was familiar with, driving through Bulkington and then winding country lanes until he passed through the pretty village of Withybrook. At the Fosse Way crossroads, he stopped and looked to his left, to his right, and to his left again.

First, he heard the crash and instantaneously, felt the impact as it jolted his whole body. It was a shock. His passengers were screaming. He hadn't seen the car coming full speed toward him with its headlights dazzlingly bright. Grasping the steering wheel tightly, he tried to right his car as it twisted, turned and spun into the hedge.

Dorothy had been unable to sleep so stayed in the warmth of the kitchen, waiting. Reg was normally home by midnight. By one o'clock, she was really worried. Clifton Hall was unusually quiet and Dorothy became aware of the loud tick of the wall clock above the Aga. Gazing at it, she became mesmerised by watching the hands slowly moving. The dark of the night seemed endless. Restlessly, she alternated between staring at the clock, looking out of the kitchen window and aimlessly flicking over pages of her latest House & Gardens magazine.

The telephone rang and with dread, Dorothy picked up the receiver.

"It's me," breathed Reg, tremulously.

"Where are you?"

"At Warwick hospital. Can you pick me up?"

"What happened?"

"There's been an accident at the Fosse Road crossroads. I didn't see the other car. I'm all right Doe Doe but some people have been injured."

"Anyone seriously?"

"Quite, but no one has been killed."

"Thank God for that."

At the hospital, Reg was waiting for her huddled in a chair. He looked shrunken, his face ashen grey and expressionless. Gently, she took his arm and led him outside to her car. When they reached Clifton Hall, Reg sat on their bed, motionless and silent.

"What happened?"

"I didn't see the headlights," answered Reg, in a quiet, matter of fact voice.

"Which side was the car coming from?"

"The right."

"Can you see anything out of your right eye?"

Reg shook his head.

"You ought to see a specialist."

"No point, they can't do anything."

Dorothy observed an expression of desolation she had never seen in her husband before. He was lethargic and moped around the house all weekend, uncommunicative, not wanting to talk about his problem. The accident had been a sharp reminder. He was losing his sight and it was only a matter of time before he went blind.

The following weekend, Reg was seemingly back to his normal self. It was not in his nature to dwell on problems or soak in self-pity. What he couldn't resolve he ignored.

The larder by the back door was a small walk-in room with floor-to-ceiling shelves that was never used to store food and collected dust and cobwebs. On one of the shelves were a few glass jars that contained various powders that Reg mixed together to make 'bangers'. Every autumn, he enjoyed planning the bonfire night battle and experimented in making the 'loudest bang ever'.

Dorothy was outside deadheading the last of her roses and Reg waved to her as he wandered outside. He made his way to the brick walled area he had specially built as a 'safe' place on the vegetable plot to test fireworks.

"Take cover," yelled Reg, as he ducked behind the wall with his hands over his ears. Dorothy moved away to stand behind the billiard room, but after a few minutes when there was no explosion, she carried on with her gardening.

Reg remained behind the wall, waiting for the firework to ignite. He had heard the fuse fizzle and was sure he'd done everything correctly. After half an hour, he went to examine it. As he bent down there was a terrific white flash. It was the biggest bang he'd ever made but Reg heard nothing. With a power and force he had not expected, he was thrown backwards and fell a few feet away.

Dorothy heard the explosion and almost instantaneously, the scream. Looking up, she saw her husband running towards the house holding his face. Chasing after him, she took his arm and led him into the kitchen, sitting him on a chair. Moaning and rocking backwards and forwards in agony, he held onto his face. Dorothy kept a tube of Acriflex burn cream in the fridge and as calmly as she could, squeezed the cold cream all over his face. Reg moaned even more. The pain of icy cold against his burning skin was excruciating.

"I'll take you to hospital."

"No. I don't want to go."

"You've got to. This is serious."

"I'm going to burn the burn out."

"What do you mean?"

"I'm going to burn the burn out," repeated Reg, as he rocked backwards and forwards.

"You're in shock Reg. I'll make you a sweet tea and then we'll go to the hospital."

"I've told you, I'm not going."

"You're being pig-headed. You need to go. You should look at yourself in a mirror and see how badly you're burnt."

Reg made no reply. He stood up and went to the lounge, turned on one bar of the electric fire and lay across the floor with the right side of his face close to the red heat. Dorothy followed and protested to no avail. In frustration, she walked out, leaving him on the floor in obvious agony.

The next day, Reg's face was maroon red but he ignored the pain and went to Newcastle to look at some new groups. On Tuesday, he asked Candy, who was on half term holiday, if she would like to go with him for the day to Shivering Sands. That evening when he returned home, he asked Dorothy, sheepishly, if she could take him to the hospital. The pain in his face had become more intense, made worse by the wind and sea air on the boat crossing.

The doctor, after examining Reg's burn, sprayed it with an antiseptic which formed a protective layer over his skin. The next day his face began to bubble up and by Thursday, he had a patchwork of ugly coloured scabs which made him look like the Phantom of the Opera. Reg made fun of the situation. At every opportunity, he stood behind unwary people he knew, especially teenage girls at the dances, tapped them on the shoulder and thought it hilarious when they turned and screamed in horror.

A week after the explosion, the scabs became itchy and began to curl around the edges. William, who disliked Reg intently, came and sat on his shoulder and chuntered contentedly, gently picking away at Reg's scabs with his little fingers to reveal the pink skin underneath. A few weeks later, Reg's face healed as though it had never been burnt.

The groups who worked for Reg looked forward to 5th November and the annual firework battle and formed themselves into two teams. This year it would be the Fortunes against the Strollers, although inevitably, on the night of the battle, they joined forces to fire at Reg.

A large bonfire was built on the vegetable garden and the party took place as planned but no one, especially Reg, had the same enthusiasm as they had in previous years. It became more a firework display than a battle and was soon over.

Chris Cross in the galley opening a tin of Fussell's Condensed Milk (EJ)

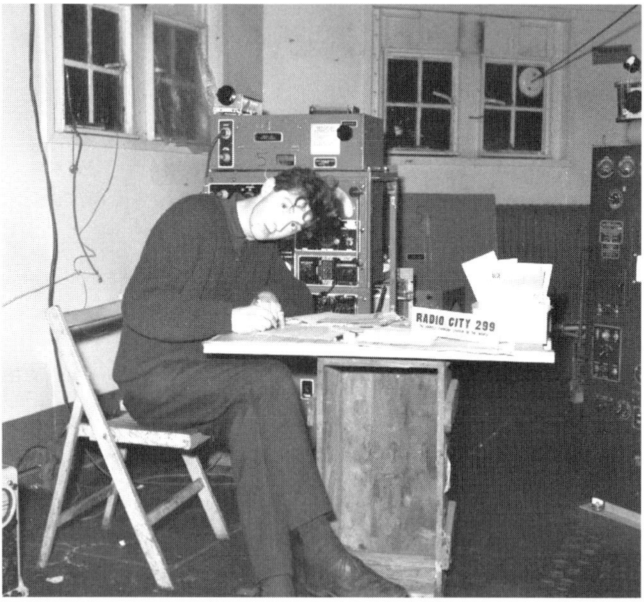

Top: Disc jockey Chris Cross replying to fan mail in the transmitter room (EJ)
Engineer Paul Elvey who doubled up as a disc jockey (EJ)

8. RELIGION A SAVIOUR

While in London, Reg worked relentlessly, dipping in and out of his various enterprises, helping to establish King's Agency and promoting the Fortunes. He became a familiar figure in television and recording studios, respected as a manager by other groups who wished Reg would take them on.

To make Radio City a success, Reg needed to bring in advertising revenue but this was proving difficult due to the station's small transmitter and low output. To increase the power meant installing a better aerial and buying a larger generator and transmitter. It was a catch-22 situation. If he didn't invest, he wouldn't be able to make the station more powerful and attract advertising.

Reg began to employ freelance sales reps on a 50 per cent commission basis. With Paul Elvey working a rota of one week on and one week off, Reg needed a second engineer and recruited Don Witts, a television engineer who had worked from Eric Martin's Record Centre in Whitstable. The escalating cost of running the station included paying for provisions, oil for the generator, boat tendering service and wages. His salvation came in the post from the Pan American Broadcasting Company, dated 6th November, 1964.

PAN AMERICAN BROADCASTING COMPANY

Dear Mr Calvert:

I was in London over a month ago talking to Mr Allan Crawford, the Manager of Radio Atlanta. He expressed the hope that you might be able to do business with us and promised to write to me soon about this. However, I have not heard from him until yesterday when he phoned giving me a free hand in dealing with you directly.

I understand that Radio City is broadcasting on Medium Wave with 1 kW (effective 2 kW) power on the 299-metre band. I further understand that you have some listeners in the area south of London populated by 3,000,000 people. It is our understanding that as of a month ago this was not yet a commercial operation – in other words, that you don't have any sponsors. I would therefore, like to present the following proposal to you, which I hope you will find of interest.

We have clients who are interested in reaching England. They are religious broadcasters – have been using our facilities for many years – and we are prepared to refer them to Radio City provided, of course, that you can assure us of a certain amount of good coverage in England. In short – and putting it bluntly – you have the station and we have the business.

We would be interested in joining forces with you and sharing our profits on a 50/50 basis. We could book 1.5 – 2 hours daily on Radio City, establish the proper rate and go into operation immediately.

I would imagine that our gross rate for this type of coverage could be between $50-$60 per 15 minute session. From this, we would naturally have to pay 15 per cent commission to the advertising agencies involved. The remainder will then be shared equally between us.

I am looking forward to your reaction to all this. If it is positive, I will have our lawyer draw up an agreement and we shall go to work right away. Actually, if you prefer you can have your lawyer do it – this makes no difference to us as long as we are assured of two points in our agreement:

a) that the income from this operation will be shared equally, and

b) should you decide to terminate our agreement one day, we will still be entitled to our share of the profits as long as the clients we have placed with Radio City remain on the air.

Sincerely yours,

PAN AMERICAN BROADCASTING COMPANY

Leo Shore,

Vice President

Reg was delighted. Smiling broadly, he immediately telephoned Dorothy to tell her his good news.

"What do you think Doe Doe?"

"I'm not sure," cautioned Dorothy. "Having religious programmes on a pop station isn't a good idea."

"Even the Church is fed up with the BBC's monopoly," smiled Reg. "It means I can improve the station and have a regular income coming in."

"You might lose listeners."

"With a regular income, I can make Radio City the most powerful offshore station in the country and end our problems."

"Pie in the sky," quipped Dorothy, more cheerfully.

With new confidence, Reg began to spend money buying better equipment and bought a MOD Air Force Cossor transmitter. The engineers tuned the transmitter to 188 metres, the lower end of the medium wave which proved a bad choice as they soon received complaints from the Coastguard Service about interference.

At the beginning of December 1964, daily religious and evangelist transmissions began to be broadcast.

To say Dorothy was worried about what she saw as her husband's irresponsible expenditure would be an understatement. She was quick to lose her temper and Reg dismissed all her arguments as trivial. When he tried to console her with love and affection, she pushed him away.

"You have to invest to get a return," explained Reg.

"You're living in cloud cuckoo land," shouted Dorothy. "Even if you do make it successful the government will close you down. Don't you listen to the news?"

Reg shrugged his shoulders. Of course, he heard the news but he knew the pirates were too popular for the government to close.

"You have to stop now. We can't afford for you to go on any longer with the station. Money doesn't grow on trees. You've had your fun now move on."

Provocatively, Reg reached out and picked up a Superman comic from the kitchen counter. Flicking over the pages he ignored her and began to read.

"For heaven's sake," Dorothy shouted, infuriated by his indifference. "I told you I wouldn't pick up the pieces from the nightclub when you got bored with it. You need to make the nightclub work and then you'll have money to spend on the station."

Reg put the comic back and stood up to go.

"That's it. Walk out," ranted Dorothy. "You never want to face your problems. Just walk away and leave me to manage everything while you're not here."

Reg glanced angrily at his wife with steely grey eyes as he left the kitchen. He was angry by her outburst. Angry she refused to help. Angry she no longer showed him any signs of affection.

Over the next few weeks, a grey depression enveloped Dorothy like a heavy cloak she couldn't shake off. Dorothy knew Reg always followed his dreams, but what about her dreams? She had dreams too. Dorothy felt helpless in trying to make Reg change his reckless course and knew she had to be strong to survive the storm that was surely brewing.

Shivering Sands - from Harvester (E J)

9. SCHOOL'S OVER

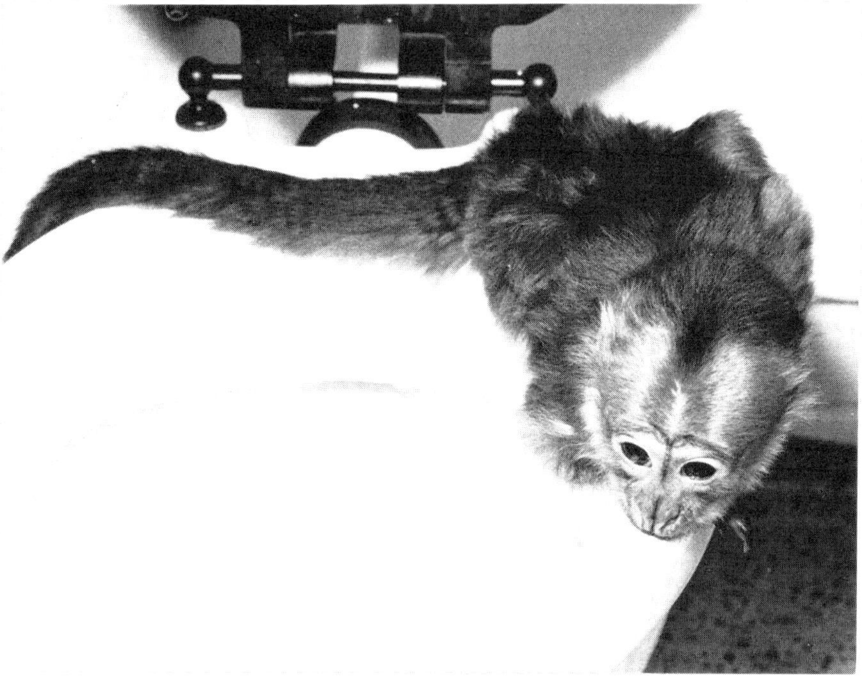

William, toilet trained (RC)

In December, arctic air blew across England and Dorothy began the routine of preparing for Christmas, even though she was in no mood to celebrate. 1964 had been a stressful year with so many arguments about money and the way Reg was spending it. Living with him was hard. They were now at their lowest point and Dorothy was at her wit's end.

Danny Storm was accepted as part of the Clifton Hall family. He had started to work for Reg when he was only 16 and now at the age of 21, he was maturing into a young man who wanted more out of life. He was a superb performer but aware that onstage charisma and boyish good looks were not enough to sustain him for a life in the entertainment business. Five years of touring in uncomfortable vans and performing to screaming girls had lost some of its thrill. When he told Reg he wanted to leave, Reg was shocked and tried to persuade him to stay.

"I'll be okay," explained Danny. "I've enough money to last about a year from the *Honest I Do* royalties you had put in the bank for me."

"That's good, but it seems a shame to give it all up and go back to a nine to five job while you're doing well."

Danny shook his head, he had made up his mind and asked Reg not to tell the Strollers. Reg agreed. He was sad to see Danny go but accepted it. He didn't believe in contracts to tie people down and even his best performers were free to stay, and free to go. Danny agreed to work to the end of the year and Reg opened the large desk diary and looked through it.

"You've got bookings at the Majestic Ballroom, Barnoldswick, on Christmas Eve. The Royal Links Pavilion, Cromer, Boxing Day and the Scala Ballroom, Dartford, on New Year's Eve. You've got another booking at the Dreamland in Margate for 2nd January 1965."

"I'd rather start the New Year afresh, with no bookings."

"Okay, we'll try and cancel that one for you."

Reg found Dorothy in the lounge on her knees, decorating the imitation Christmas tree with brightly coloured glass baubles. William was up to mischief, taking baubles out of the box and running away with them.

"Come back here you scamp," called Dorothy.

"William causing you problems?"

"No more than usual."

Reg related the news of Danny's leaving. "That's life. Boys come and go."

"We'll miss him. It's like the end of an era. What will you do with the Strollers?" asked Dorothy.

"Not sure. I've been pondering whether I should ask John Wileman to work for me. He's steady and reliable, good at sorting out problems with the PA systems and things like that. And I do need a driver."

Dorothy nodded in agreement and continued to dress the Christmas tree.

"By the way. I've invited Fred Downs and Tony Pine to spend Christmas with us."

"You've done what? I wish you'd ask me first," shouted Dorothy, her mood abruptly changing.

"And their wives and children," added Reg, nonchalantly.

"It's all right you inviting people I don't know but I'm the one who has to do the work. Not only that, we've dances to run on Christmas Eve and again on Boxing Day."

"You'll soon get to know them and it'll be good to have people in the house over Christmas."

"You might think so. How about you take a turn at cooking the Christmas dinner instead of me?"

"Give's a kiss," replied Reg, as he lovingly put his arms around his wife.

"You think you can get round me Reg Calvert," responded Dorothy, pushing her husband away with just a hint of a smile. For all that they argued, she couldn't help loving him.

"Me, never," laughed Reg. "What d'you think we should have for prizes this year?"

"No idea."
"I'm trying to think of something different."
"I don't mind so long as it's not snakes or spiders."
"How about a donkey?"
"Mad idea," Dorothy replied, suppressing a smile.
"You like donkeys," grinned Reg.
"Not enough to want one as a pet. How are you going to get a donkey to the dances? They're too big to fit into the back of a car?"
"I'll find a way and I'll only need one as no one will want to take a donkey home with them."

The next time Reg saw Tony Newman, he casually asked if he would help transport the Christmas Eve prize in their van and take it to the Matrix Ballroom in Coventry.
"I'll pay you an extra £5."
"Okay," agreed Tony, without thinking to ask what the prize was.
The Liberators had worked hard and improved since their first audition in March and Dorothy liked the boys. She gave them regular bookings and with other gigs they got, they had given up their day jobs and turned professional. They arrived early at Clifton Hall and Reg went to greet them.
"Wait there, boys, I'll just go and fetch it."
Reg, grinning widely, walked off to the stables. It was a freezing cold evening with an icy wind and the boys shivered while they waited. A few minutes later, they began to laugh nervously as they saw him leading a donkey towards them.
"No Reg," laughed Tony, incredulously. "You're joking. We can't get a donkey in the van."
"Let's have a look," said Reg, opening the rear van doors. "Lots of room boys. Heave ho."
The donkey was obstinate and determined not to step into the van.
"I think we need a ramp. I'll go and find some planks."
Reg headed back to the barns and returned a little later carrying several planks of wood.
"Heave-ho, you push while I pull," instructed Reg. "All together boys, one, two, three. Push."
Everyone began to laugh hysterically at the absurdity of it. The donkey was not going to budge. Reg began to talk to the donkey and one of the boys suggested he find a carrot.
"Come on boys, all together. I'll pull and you push."
Eventually, the donkey succumbed, braying loudly as he walked up the planks. The two boys who's turn it was to sit in the rear of the van, wedged themselves in between equipment and donkey. As soon as the van started to move, the donkey stepped forward, pushing his head between the front seat

passengers so he could see where he was going. The journey proceeded well until the donkey did what donkey's do. He lifted his tail and deposited a large heap on the floor. The smell was too much, even for the front seat passengers, so they had to stop and shovel the mess off the floor.

Needing fuel, they pulled into the forecourt of a petrol station. The attendant, intoxicated and very merry with Christmas cheer, came over to serve them and put the nozzle into the tank. As he did so, he happened to glance through the window of the van. Seeing the donkey's head jutting out over the steering wheel, he abruptly stopped what he was doing. Horror stricken, he ran off down the road and away from the petrol station.

Liberators:
Left to right:
Tony Newman
David Holland
John Wallbank
Sam Kemp
Tom Long

In due course, the Liberators arrived safely at the Matrix Ballroom and Reg went out to greet them and led the donkey backstage. The boys in the other two groups, the Impacts and Tuxedoes, came out to pet the donkey and everyone made a fuss of him.

The dancefloor soon filled with a lively crowd in a happy mood and when it came to competition time, Reg's enigmatic personality had them guessing what the prize could be. The competition winner was a girl and when she came onstage to collect her reward, she was told to wait with her eyes closed.

"You have to guess what it is, no peeping," said Reg, mysteriously. "I'll be back in a moment."

The crowd roared with laughter when they saw Reg leading the donkey and some of the boys in the audience started to chant eeyore, eeyore.

"No peeping," repeated Reg. "Give me your hand. Now feel here. Can you guess what it is?"

Taking the girl's hand, Reg let her feel the long hairs of the mane, then down to his nostril.

"It's warm and hairy. And it smells," laughed the girl, nervously.

"Can you guess?"

"No," replied the girl, shaking her head.

"Open your eyes. What d'you think?"

"Oh, he's lovely."

"Should she keep the donkey or take the money?" called Reg to the audience.

"Keep him, keep him," chanted the excited crowd.

"I'll keep him," smiled the girl as she stroked the donkey.

Reg beckoned the group to start playing and led the girl and donkey offstage. Taking a £5 note out of his wallet, he offered it to the girl. It was as much as her weekly wage but she did not want the money. She wanted the donkey.

"I don't think you should. What will your parents say?"

"They won't mind," giggled the girl.

"I'm sure they will if you take a donkey home with you. How about I give you £10?"

"No, I want to keep him. We've got a big garden."

Reg, thinking the girl was inebriated, did his best to persuade her to take the money and kept increasing the amount. In the end, he conceded with good grace. The girl had won the donkey and she should have it.

The evening ended on a high with Reg putting on his tartan slippers and rolling up his trousers. He ran on stage and began to do a silly dance, singing the *Hully Gully*. The audience followed his moves and the fun continued as he sang *Knees up Mother Brown* and finished with the *Hokey Cokey*. It had been a good night and in the early hours of Christmas morning, the Liberators delivered the donkey to the prize winner's home, near Bedworth.

Returning home to Clifton Hall, Reg was in a good mood but when Dorothy arrived back from Kettering with Candy, she was tired and irritable.

"It's not much of a Christmas for me, having to get up in the morning to cook a big lunch."

"You'll be fine," smiled Reg. "It's Christmas."

Reg ignored Dorothy's black looks on Christmas morning, whistling and busying himself by turning the rehearsal room into a festive dining room. His guests arrived after their long journey, just before lunch and Reg acted as the jovial host, pouring drinks and entertaining everyone.

"Shall I cut the meat?" asked Reg, politely, as Dorothy lifted steaming joints of roast pork and beef from the Aga.

"The Yorkshire puddings have gone flat. Don't you ever invite people again without asking me," complained Dorothy, as she served into dishes the roast potatoes and vegetables.

"You'll like Fred and his family."

"Liking someone doesn't mean I want to spend my Christmas slaving over a hot cooker."

Dorothy put on an air of politeness and did her best to be pleasant. On Boxing Day, after a late lunch, she was relieved when they returned to Whitstable. That evening, there were more dances to run and Reg went to Coventry, Dorothy and Candy to Banbury, Susan to Nuneaton.

By New Year's Eve, the weather became colder as more arctic winds blew across the country. Dorothy planned a day in the office to sort out the accounts and had put the electric fire on so the room was warm enough for them to work together. On Reg's desk was a neatly stacked pile of unopened bills. Reg had seen the pile of envelopes and knowing what they were, had ignored them.

"We need to discuss how we're going to pay the overdue accounts," said Dorothy, quietly. "There are some we need to pay immediately, like the electricity, or we may be cut off."

Reg nodded his head, acknowledging the seriousness of the situation.

"The newspapers have said they won't accept our advertising for the dances until their accounts are cleared and the printer has refused to print more posters. Every day, the telephone rings with companies asking me for money. I can't stand it any longer." Dorothy sucked her lips tight together as she tried to control her anger and not raise her voice. "We have to clear our debts and start the New Year afresh."

"It'll be all right. Things are improving and it won't be long before we're in the black again."

"You're not listening to me Reg. Things will not be all right. We can pay our debts if you don't take the money from the dancehall takings this week."

Reg didn't reply as he gazed ahead. He was in a quandary. If he paid the bills there would be no money to pay the wages and overheads of running Radio City.

Dorothy stared bleakly at Reg with her large blue eyes, hoping he would see reason but instinctively knowing, he would not. The telephone rang and broke the tension. Reg picked up the receiver and after a few minutes of chatting about horses and donkeys, he smiled at Dorothy.

"I've found another donkey and arranged for it to be taken to Nuneaton tonight."

"I guessed that's what you were talking about. But have you thought it through? I'll go to Kettering again, but who's going to run the Matrix?"

"It'll have to be Susan, there's no one else."

"Do you think she can do it? She's not been there before. It's not like running Nuneaton where the amplifier and speakers are permanently set up."

"I'll go through it with her this afternoon."

Dorothy picked up the diary and looked at the entries for Thursday 31st December, 1964. "I've booked the Shades of Blue, the Brewers and the Demons for the Matrix."

"She'll be fine, it should be a good show." smiled Reg, confidently.

Crowds of young people made their way to the various venues. The New Year's Eve party night dances were the most popular in the year when everyone wanted to celebrate. In Nuneaton, Reg organised party games and the competition winner took the money and not the donkey. Snow came late and by midnight, when everyone was leaving the dances, the snow had settled and was several inches deep. Reg arrived back at Clifton Hall first and set about making his own supper of Gorgonzola and pickled onions while he waited for his family. It was after one in the morning when Dorothy and Candy returned.

"Is Susan not back yet?" asked Dorothy.

Reg shook his head. "She shouldn't be long."

"Have you noticed the snow? We had a horrid journey back from Kettering; the roads are really slippery. Susan'll find it impossible to drive in her bubble."

Reg nodded and took a deep breath. "You're right. The kettle's just boiled so have a quick drink and then we'll go and search for her. She's sensible enough to drive very slowly so she may be back soon."

The telephone rang and Dorothy picked up the receiver. Within a second, her face relaxed and Reg, who was watching her, realised their daughter was safe.

"The hall manager has taken her home and is putting her up for the night," explained Dorothy, relieved.

By lunchtime the following day, the snow had melted to slush and Susan returned safely. The house seemed deserted and unusually quiet with no music coming from the rehearsal room. Susan found her mother alone in the office and handed her the brown leather bag, heavy with money.

"Thanks. You can help me count it."

Dorothy handed her daughter three one pound notes as payment for her night's work. It was a good wage, nearly as much as Susan earned working a whole week at the Rugby Advertiser. Mother and daughter sorted coins from notes and made piles of sixpences, shillings, two shillings and half crowns, pushing the pennies out of the way. The silver coins were packed into small, thick paper bags to a value of £5 each. Ten shilling and one pound notes were counted and placed Queen's head uppermost in ten and twenty pound batches.

Dorothy looked at the ticket roll and could see that more than 800 tickets had been sold which meant that after paying the groups, the hall, stewards, and advertising, they had made a profit of over £100. When they finished the count, Dorothy took the bag to her dressing room and left it where she knew Reg would find it, but first, she removed some money and placed it in another hiding place

For Danny Storm and the Strollers, it was their final New Year's Eve performance at the Scala Ballroom in Dartford. Their show had gone down well and the crowds had loved them. Afterwards, they packed their equipment away and when they were ready to leave, John Wileman, instead of getting into the driving seat, sat in the back and quietly explained it was his last gig as he was going to work for Reg as his driver.

Neither Dave Spence or Andy Brown could drive and they needed John, not only as their bass player, but to get them to the various gigs. Danny, then revealed that he too was leaving the business and returning to normal life. He had not wanted a fuss or big farewell, so had not announced it in advance. Dave and Andy were shocked. It was the last thing they could have expected. They'd worked together for two happy years and were a successful group earning good money. Outside, the night was freezing cold and the four of them sat disconsolately, huddled in the rear of the van, talking for several hours, as Dave and Andy tried to convince their companions to continue.

Neither Danny or John had wanted to cause an upset but the die was cast. When there was nothing else to say, John began the slow drive back in the early hours of the morning with snowflakes dazzling and dancing in the van's headlights. As they reached London, Danny suggested that John could drop him off at any underground station.

After saying their sad farewells, knowing they may not meet again, Danny picked up his belongings and the boys watched him walk through a swirling snow storm and disappear into the dark cavern of the underground. Within an instance, the bottom had fallen out of their world and for Dave and Andy, the future looked bleak. It was not a good way to start 1965.

Within a few days, Dave Spence was asked to join another group but Andy had no offers and in desperation, he considered looking for a 'normal' job.

The Fortunes were on the cusp of success but their sax player, Tony Britnell, wanted to move on and persuaded Gary Fletcher to leave the group and work in Switzerland with him. Rod, knowing that Andy was out of work, asked if he would like to become their new drummer. The next time Reg saw the Fortunes, his displeasure was obvious.

"When are you going to get another drummer?" asked Reg.

"Andy's Okay," replied Rod, shrugging his shoulders.

"He's not the right sort of drummer for the Fortunes. You need to look for someone with cabaret experience."

Andy was young and had been good in the Strollers playing Rock 'n' Roll, but he lacked the subtlety required for the Fortunes' complex repertoire. Each time Reg saw the Fortunes perform, he made it clear he was unhappy and they should look for a new drummer. Andy knew Reg was right and began to spend hours and hours practicing. Unlike the Strollers, the Fortunes were not a happy group and often squabbled between themselves, nevertheless, Andy decided to stay with them. After a few months, Reg surprised him after a show by coming up and companionably putting his arm around his shoulder and saying, "Well done."

"Thank you," replied Andy, acknowledging the compliment.

After that, there was no more comment about the Fortunes needing a new drummer.

The era of Clifton Hall, the School of Rock 'n' Roll, was no more. It was a time Dorothy had dreamed of, when she and Reg could enjoy living like a normal family in their beautiful home. She hoped Reg would mature and settle down but Realised now, he had not grown-up. He was still like Peter Pan, looking for excitement and following his dreams.

Car window sticker

Singers and groups
Booked into the dances during 1964 included

Atlantics, Astonaires, Astranoughts, Baby Bubbles, Brian Bass and the Brewers, Beachcombers, Beatmen, Beat Preachers, Berkeley Squares, Dave Berry and the Cruisers, Black Hawks, Blackwells, Steve Brett and the Mavericks, Caroliners, Carpet Baggers, Cascades, Cheetahs, Chickanes, Christie and the Group, Clansmen, Country Gentlemen, Creators, Crusaders, Defenders, Dakotas, Delmonts, Demons, Denny Laine and the Diplomats, Dukes, Dwellers, Alan Dean and the Problems, Bern Elliott, Establishment, Earl Royce and the Emperors/Olympics, Mike Everest and the Alpines, Exciters, Wayne Fontana and the Mindbenders, Fortunes, Wayne Gibson and the Dynamic Sounds, Gravediggers, Guitars Incorporated, Brian Gulliver and the Travellers, Gary and the Hornets, Hunters, Impacts, Interns, James Boys, Johnny Keen and the Freemen, Nicky James and the Daltons, Jumping Jacks, Jangles, Sonny Kaye and the Reds, Johnathon Kane, Kontikies, Dave Kaye and the Dykons, Sonny Kay, Liberators, Little Darlings, Little People, Gerry Levene and the Avengers, Jackie Lynton, Rockin' Mantells, Megatones (audition), Midnighters, Moody Blues 5, Mysterians, New Cyclones, Barry Noble, Nocturnes, No Names, Pack, Panthers, Peter and Gordon, Pickwicks, Pips, Keith Powell and the Valets, Puppets, German Beatles – Rattlers, Phil Ryan and the Crescents, Rayvons, Reds, Rocking Renowns, Rockin' Berries, Lee Rogers, Ronettes, Screaming Lord Sutch, Searchers, Shades 5, Shades of Blue, Size 7, Solitaires, Sombreros, Sorcerers, Jimmy Stevens and the Jackpots, Stormbirds, Stormriders, Danny Storm and the Strollers, Sunspots, Swing Beats (audition), Teddy Bears, Thrills, Transatlantics, Tuxedos, Undertakers, Unit Four, Unones, Steve & the Veldons, Venom 4, Victors, Marty Wilde and the Wildcats, Johnny Washington.

10. PIRATE RADIO 1960'S

A Brief History

With the generation of post-war baby boomers came the Beatles, the Rolling Stones and libertarian attitudes. The UK purported to embrace freedom of speech and not to be an authoritarian state like Russia or China, but, anyone who wanted to start a land-based radio station had to apply for a licence from the GPO and all applications were refused. The BBC reigned supreme, providing an inadequate service funded by licence payers. The broadcasting laws were unreasonable and radio pioneers made history by broadcasting three miles off the coast, outside British territorial waters.

The British government was in uproar about the proliferation of offshore radio stations and threatened to close them down, accusing them of being pirates, illegal, affecting shipping and not paying performing rights on the records they played. The facts, however, were distorted. They were not illegal and nor were they pirates. It was perfectly legal for anyone to broadcast outside British waters and already being done by Radio Luxemburg where the four big record companies paid to have their records promoted. Not surprisingly, most record companies began to send samples of new releases to the offshore stations in the hope they would play them for free.

Most European countries also maintained control of the airwaves but in America, commercial radio stations flourished. In Europe, entrepreneurs realising there was a need for commercial radio, began to fit ships with radio equipment and start broadcasting off the coast, outside of legal jurisdiction. Some stations were proving very popular with tolerant governments who ignored their broadcasts. Other governments were not so amenable.

Experiments with radio had begun in the 19th century. By the turn of the 20th century, the government felt it needed to have some control over this fantastic invention and introduced the Wireless Telegraphy Act, enabling the General Post Office (GPO) to issue licences for the experimental receipt of radio transmissions. In 1912, Marconi opened the first wireless factory in England, but there was little incentive for people to buy his radios, unless there was something to listen to.

The British Broadcasting Company was set up in 1922 by a group of radio manufacturers to create programmes to help them sell their products. It was structured by John Reith and his ambition was to make the station, 'independent, to educate, inform and entertain the whole nation, free from political interference and commercial pressure.' The radio licence fee was ten shillings and by 1927, the GPO dedicated most of this money to fund the

BBC. The company was renamed the British Broadcasting Corporation and from then on, the government retained a tight control of radio broadcasting.

Radio Atlanta and Radio Caroline

Allan Crawford, an Australian living in London, had formed his own record and publishing company but soon discovered that, unlike Australia, there was no commercial radio in England and he was unable to promote his records on either the BBC or Radio Luxembourg. He had heard about the European offshore stations and began to look at the possibility of starting his own. Collaborating with Kitty Black, a theatrical impresario, they formed a shell company, CBC (Plays) Ltd, as commercial radio agents. The two of them had insufficient funds to launch a radio station so teamed up with chartered accountant Major Oliver Smedley, who had an office in east London. They formed a new company, Project Atlanta, with Major Smedley as Chairman, issuing shares at £1 each.

Radio Nord had been broadcasting off the Swedish coast for more than a year but closed in June, 1962 when the Swedish government brought in new legislation to outlaw them. Crawford contacted Radio Nord's Texan owners, expressing his interest in renting the Radio Nord ship but they wanted to sell it. Impatient with Crawford's effort to raise funds they sailed it to Texas, changed the name to the Mi Amigo and began decommissioning the radio equipment.

It wasn't easy to persuade people to purchase shares in Project Atlanta as their plans were kept secret. By late 1963, Project Atlanta managed to raise the capital they needed with just over 100 shareholders. A Thames Pilot, Major Horsley, was so keen about the concept of offshore radio, he used his aunt's pension money to invest in the company and encouraged other Thames Pilots to do the same. He also advised Crawford on the best location to moor the Mi Amigo, three miles off the coast at Frinton on Sea.

A young Irishman, Ronan O'Rahilly, was working in the music industry and heard about Project Atlanta. He persuaded Crawford to provide him with a copy of the business plan so he could show it to his wealthy father. His father declined to invest, but offered the use of his deep-water port at Greenore, Southern Ireland, to refit the Mi Amigo again as a radio ship.

O'Rahilly was charming and wily, and using Crawford's business plan, quickly found his own wealthy investors. He purchased a large ferry, the Fredericia, and renamed it Caroline. When the Mi Amigo sailed into Greenore, Crawford was shocked to see O'Rahilly had bought his own, larger boat and became angry when he realised he had to tie his smaller boat alongside, climbing over the decks of the Caroline boat to get to shore and back. It was inevitable that a war of sabotage would break out as it was a race against time to see which boat could be fitted-out and first on-air.

The Mi Amigo left Greenore first but Crawford did not have the luck of the Irish. As the ship sailed round Cornwall it got caught in a storm and had to go into Falmouth to have repair work. O'Rahilly won the race and began broadcasting at the end of March, Easter 1964. Radio Caroline caused a sensation. Within a few weeks, listenership was estimated at about 6 million.

The Mi Amigo broadcast in 1964 as Radio Atlanta and then as Radio Caroline South when Project Atlanta ran out of finance (SH)

Radio Atlanta began to broadcast six weeks after Caroline on 12th May, 1964. Most programmes were prerecorded in Crawford's studio. The principle disc jockey was Major Smedley's cousin, Churton Fairman, alias Mike Raven. Crawford's concept was to use the station as a means of promoting his own records and these were mainly cover versions of other songs. The recordings lacked spontaneity and most listeners preferred tuning into 'live' broadcasts coming from Radio Caroline.

Radio Sutch was the third station to begin broadcasting at the end of May, 1964 from the Shivering Sands towers in the Thames Estuary. Reg Calvert and David Sutch (Screaming Lord Sutch) started it together for fun and as a publicity stunt. In October, 1964 David Sutch returned to performing and Reg continued to run the station, changing the name to Radio City and turning it into a professional station.

Neither Radio Caroline or Atlanta had anticipated the government's propaganda machine which made it difficult for national UK companies to be seen to support them and flout the law. Both stations had taken a gamble and did not have a large reservoir of funds. Their survival depended on attracting advertisers, for without them, they would surely sink.

After only six weeks, Radio Atlanta ran out of money. Allan Crawford was bitterly disappointed. He had made a serious error of judgement when he turned away lucrative religious advertising, suggesting that Reg Calvert might accept it.

In an effort to survive, Crawford agreed to merge with Radio Caroline but continued to operate the business separately. The Mi Amigo boat, (Radio Atlanta), became Radio Caroline South and remained moored off Frinton on Sea. The larger, Caroline boat, became Radio Caroline North and moved to broadcast off the Isle of Man. O'Rahilly and Crawford were joint managing directors but it was not a satisfactory business arrangement with an unequal split of the profits, 55 per cent going to Radio Caroline North and 45 per cent to (Atlanta) Radio Caroline South.

Radio Caroline, annoyed with the Postmaster General, Wedgwood Benn, and his pronouncements to close them, mounted a pressure group with the slogan, 'DON'T VOTE LABOUR. THEY ARE TRYING TO KILL CAROLINE.' In January, 1965 there was a by-election at Leyton, East London. What should have been a safe win for Labour resulted in a dramatic swing to the Conservative candidate, reducing the Labour Party's majority to only four seats. Prime Minister, Harold Wilson, knew he would struggle to govern the country with such a small majority and planned another general election for March 1965. This put Wedgwood Benn in a quandary. How could he bring in new legislation to end the scourge of pirate radio without the Labour Party losing the next election?

Voice of Slough

John Thompson was another man who wanted to have his own offshore radio station. He planned to start the Voice of Slough, as early as 1961 and fund it with broadcasts from the World Tomorrow by American evangelist, Herbert W. Armstrong. The enterprise was doomed to failure. Thompson didn't have enough money to pay for a seaworthy boat and the transmitter wasn't powerful enough. Next, Thompson teamed up with a Canadian millionaire, Arnold Swanson, to start another pirate station, GB-OK, but this came to a halt when Swanson pulled out of the project.

Radio Invicta

When Radio Sutch was not evicted from the Shivering Sands towers, it spurred Thompson to team up with Charles Evans and fisherman, Harry Featherbee, alias Tom Pepper. They started a new station, Radio Invicta from the Red Sands towers in July 1964. These were in better condition than Shivering Sands with all seven towers still interconnecting, but as they were closer to land they were probably within the three-mile limit.

Radio Invicta did not prosper and after a short time, Tom Pepper gave John Thompson and Charles Evans notice to quit so he could run the station on his own. Pepper recruited several good disc jockeys, including Ed Moreno and a young electrical engineer, Phil Perkins who was a radio ham. Phil had tuned into Radio Invicta while on holiday in Whitstable and realised how transmissions could be improved and after meeting Tom Pepper, he was offered a job.

Living conditions on Red Sands were poor and Phil Perkins slept in a large chest of drawers until the station received complimentary mattresses from a bed company they had done some advertising for. Phil relished the challenge and tried to improve the station and reinstate the old wartime equipment to make life on the tower more comfortable.

Financing Radio Invicta was a struggle and with little revenue coming in, Pepper couldn't afford to hire a regular boat so hitched a lift with fishing boats. When he wanted to return to shore, he attracted the attention of local fishermen by flashing mirrors at them. On occasions, when the weather was rough, the crew were left on the towers with little food or drinking water. To survive, they ate strange concoctions of tinned food and improvised by collecting rain water from the roof and boiling it to make tea, sifting out bits of dead bird.

Tom Pepper realised he needed his own boat and purchased a 36-foot former lifeboat that had been on the side of a ship. It was a poor design, with a wheelhouse quite high out of the water and planked-in deck almost level with the top of the boat. He named it the David, after his son. With no partners to share the burden of running the station and few advertisers, he went to the News of the World and persuaded them to give his station a trial run and advertise over the Christmas period. Pepper needed his best disc jockey to make the broadcasts and persuaded Ed Moreno, who was off-duty, to return to the towers so he could read the advertisements.

Early on 16th December, Ed Moreno and Pepper arranged to meet at Faversham Creek. It was a freezing cold morning and after they had loaded the David with provisions they had to sit and wait for the tide to come in and float the boat off the mud. Pepper felt very unwell as he was going down with flu and with no proper cabin to shelter in, they both became bitterly cold. When afloat, Pepper tried to start the engine but it would not fire. Swearing loudly, he tried different ways to swing the engine into action and eventually succeeded.

The weather changed for the worse with a gale howling but Pepper doggedly continued out to sea. The success of the station depended on them reaching the towers and broadcasting the News of the World advertisements.

The David was unsafe to sail in rough weather and struggled to make way. Waves crashed against the sides and Ed and Pepper became drenched. Tom Pepper, feeling too ill to helm, let Ed take the tiller until he too became sick.

When they reached the towers, Ed managed to jump off the boat and climb the ladder. At the top, he told the crew of the changeover and as he needed his best engineer, Phil Perkins was asked to remain on the station and the young engineer, Martin Shaw, and disc jockey, Barry Hoy, alias Simon Ashley, had to return to land.

They waved goodbye, wishing each other a merry Christmas. As the boat was leaving, Phil picked up a telescope and watched the David go through the waves and saw Tom Pepper waving at him with his arms crossed above his head.

"Tom's waving at us," observed Phil, as he and the crew, merrily waved back as they went to find warmth inside from the freezing gale.

The following day, Tom Pepper was found dead. He had drowned in the icy waters tied to a board. The David's engine had broken down and no one had realised he was waving an international distress signal. The bodies of Simon Ashley and Martin Shaw were missing. Phil Perkin's mother was distraught, believing her son had drowned as he was due to come off duty and be home for Christmas. A few months later, a body was washed up on the Spanish Coast that could only be identified by the discovery of a Radio Invicta tape recording in a pocket.

Tom Pepper's wife and ex-partners asked the crew to keep Radio Invicta running. Roy Bates, another indomitable character, wanted to take advantage of Pepper's demise and sailed to Red Sands. He offered the crew £100 each to leave the towers but they refused in loyalty to Pepper's wife. The weather deteriorated and the supply boat did not arrive. The station limped on until February, 1965 when the crew became desperate, stranded at sea with no fuel, food, or fresh water. They made an appeal on-air for help and the Southend-on-Sea lifeboat came out with provisions and water.

King Radio

Radio Invicta was renamed King Radio and reformatted to play 'sweet' music of older listeners. It was organised by Tom Pepper's former partners and Mike Raven, who was an actor with experience of working on Radio Atlanta. Fearing Roy Bates might come again and forcibly take possession of the fort, they left three men on board. The men were seemingly 'forgotten' and when Mike Raven returned a month later, he found them freezing and starving. They had run out of provisions and survived for ten days by eating dried peas.

King Radio, when it did begin to broadcast, fared little better than Radio Invicta. Without a powerful transmitter, its broadcasts were weak and attracted few advertisers.

Radio London

Don Pierson, a successful Texas businessman, flew to England in the summer of 1964 to investigate the possibility of starting a radio station. He had read an article about the new British pirate stations and their lucrative profits. After listening to the dull BBC programmes, he appreciated why there was so much enthusiasm in England for the pirates. To see for himself where Radio Caroline was anchored, he hired a light aircraft to fly over the boat. What he did not appreciate, was that O'Rahilly was prone to wild exaggeration about his profits, and Radio Atlanta had only publicised 'projected' earnings, not their actual loss.

In America, where there were many vibrant local stations, it was easy to purchase new and second-hand broadcasting equipment. Pierson decided he would bring the Americanised style of programming to England, but first he needed a suitable ship and investors. He agreed to purchase a US ex-Navy minesweeper from a Greek syndicate, and renamed it the Galaxy. To convert it into a radio ship, work was undertaken in Miami, and anyone who enquired was told it was for oceanographic surveys. The ship took longer to convert and cost more than anticipated. When Captain Tsirbis pressurised Pierson to pay for the ship, he responded by saying, "The money's in the bank." In frustration, Captain Tsirbis foolishly took the boat out at night and sailed it in a storm. The ship ended up on some rocks and was brought back to dry docks for repair and repainting, which delayed the project even more.

By the end of October, 1964 the Galaxy was still in the dock. Investors, who wanted a quick return on their money were becoming impatient with the delays. The first sea trial with a full crew of 27 was prepared. With less than one hour's notice, Pierson gave reckless instructions to the captain to sail for England. The crew who were not informed, became very angry when they realised the first port of call would be San Juan, Puerto Rico, for refuelling and provisions. The captain decided to sail south to Madeira to avoid the stormy Atlantic weather. It was a dangerous journey as the engines were in poor condition, breaking down five times during the crossing and essential equipment, including the ship's radio, was out of order.

After months of wrangling, disputes and disagreements, the Galaxy arrived and moored off Frinton on Sea, not far from Radio Caroline and began broadcasts Christmas 1964. Radio London was an immediate success and compared to the other stations, slick and professional. More importantly, it had sufficient advertising to pay its running costs. Despite teething problems, Radio London was larger, better equipped with a powerful transmitter and tall aerial. It could be heard by 1000's more listeners who enjoyed the Americanised programming, jingles and good disc jockeys.

To finance the Radio London project, the Marine Investment Company Inc was set up in the Bahamas with a zero rate of tax. Philip Birch was recruited to plan and manage the London side of the operation. Advertising revenue was essential and the first advertisement they aired was for the News of the World. They also accepted religious programmes.

The crew were upset when the disc jockeys arrived as they were given the best cabins. Behind the professionalism, gaiety and jolly jingles, there was trouble on board as different nationalities clashed. They were permitted to drink alcohol and on New Year's Eve, the cook, a very large Scottish man in a drunken state, tried to kill a member of the crew with a knife. After being forcibly restrained and pinned to the floor, he was removed and taken back to shore. After this, alcohol was limited to two pints of beer a day.

During the process of developing Radio London, Pierson was involved in many disagreements with his board of directors, lost managerial control but still retained a financial interest. Radio London proved pirate radio could be successful and highly profitable. With the experience he'd gained, Pierson began to plan two more offshore radio stations, **Swinging Radio England and Britain Radio**, to be broadcast from the same ship. It was an ambitious plan and would take time in the making.

Radio City Poster

11. A LIFE OF ITS OWN

Reg Calvert being hoisted up Shivering Sands tower. Behind: Paul Elvey

Radio City had taken on a life of its own as enthusiasts worked together to improve the station and living conditions. Numerous fishing boats sailed close to the towers and sometimes dropped off a few fish. In return, disc jockeys played them a record, wishing them a safe return to land. The

Admiralty Trinity House Ship, the Patricia, made regular trips to check the equipment on the Search Tower and service the nearby buoys. They were always greeted with a friendly wave and played a request.

Eric Martin was a jovial character who took on the role of Station Manager. He was middle-aged with a good moustache, smartly dressed in check tooth jackets and always wore a tie. Eric owned the Record Centre in Whitstable's High Street and his office above the shop became a regular meeting place for crew and doubled up as off-duty accommodation. He did numerous small jobs to help Reg, sometimes going out to the station where he broadcast as Rick Martin. He bought provisions and organised the shift rota so at any one time, a skeleton crew of one engineer and two volunteer disc jockeys were on the towers. A back room in the Wall Tavern became the regular meeting place where crew were paid in a little back room. Eric listened to broadcasts and if he thought there was a problem, he drove his Jaguar to a cliff top near Whitstable and made 'illegal' contact with his ship to shore radio set. Tony and Sue Pine also made radio contact with the towers to check what food and other items they needed sending out each week.

To carry heavy equipment onto the towers was proving difficult so engineers with volunteers, installed a crane jib. To test it, Reg gleefully sat in the hoist and laughed all the way to the top as he swung from side to side above the water.

The old Halifax Aircraft transmitter needed replacing for a more powerful one. After some research, Reg managed to locate a former US Naval General Electric TCJ-7 transmitter which had come off an aircraft carrier. He asked the Liberators if they could transport it to Gravesend for him in the rear of their van and from there, he booked a charter boat to carry it out to Shivering Sands.

In the evening, the Liberators waited in a guesthouse for Reg to return so they could go for a meal together. Reg was late and when he arrived, he flopped onto the bed to relax.

"Do you know who Uncle is? He's supposed to be arriving soon," asked Tony Newman.

"Why?" asked Reg, his face breaking into a smile as he began to chuckle.

"The landlady gave us a message from Uncle. She said he'd phoned and would be arriving shortly. We wondered whether it's to do with the TV programme, the Man from U.N.C.L.E.?"

Reg chuckled even more. "I'm the man from uncle. Lots of people around here call me Uncle. They know me as Uncle Reg on the radio."

The new transmitter was nicknamed 'Big Bertha'. To help Don Witts rebuild it, Dick Dickson was recruited to double up as a disc jockey and engineer. When they managed to get it to work, it was a marked improvement on the original Halifax transmitter and Reg was thrilled when he picked up a signal in London, and even as far away as Clifton Hall. The station began to broadcast on 299 metres but there were still many technical problems to overcome as they needed more power and the transmitter was unreliable.

The next project was to improve the studio and Reg ordered two Garrard turntables, Decca Deram Cartridges, a Brenell Tape Deck to play advertisements and jingles, plus a Ferrograph tape recorder to play tapes and prerecord shows. There were no slipmats on the record players and disc jockeys had to keep talking and judge when the record would start to play. They also had to keep an eye on the glow of the valves and modulation of the transmitter to ensure it didn't overload.

Volunteers, either went to see Eric in the Record Centre, or waited on the quayside for an opportunity to go out to Shivering Sands. They were mostly young boys keen to have a go at becoming a pirate disc jockey. If they saw Reg, he often put his hand in his pocket to pay them £5 for their holiday. The leap from the bobbing boat to the rusting ladder could be terrifying if the weather was rough. If that wasn't bad enough, before they reached the safety of the single-man access hatch under the tower, they had to go through a thick fog of black, smelly, diesel smoke, which belched out from the generator. The regular crew tended to ignore volunteers when they first arrived as they concentrated on winching up supplies of diesel, water and basic foodstuffs. It was an anxious time to get provisions aboard and everyone had to help, including disc jockeys.

When the winch was in use, the record player slowed. To continue broadcasting without a deejay, they played home-produced tape recordings that listeners sent in. These were called 'tender tapes' and some were very good. Regular contributors included Phil Jay with Discomania, and John Martin, who sometimes worked on the station. He recorded the Anti-City show and listeners were asked to send in comments, saying whether the station was good or bad. It was fun and Chris Cross continued the programme, compiling and presenting listener's complaints, which ended up being about anything and everything they wanted to grumble about.

The financial cost of paying wages and buying new equipment was beginning to take its toll on Reg's marriage. Returning home each weekend, Reg continued to help himself to the dancehall takings while Dorothy looked on in despair.

"You can't keep doing this. We'll soon be bankrupt. You need to close Radio City and call it a day."

Reg gave her a half-smile and shook his head. "I can't close Radio City. So many people depend on me."

“But I depend on you. Don’t I count?” snapped Dorothy.

“It won’t be long before we’re making a profit. I’ve got salesmen and I’m running several Radio City discos.”

“And it won’t be long before the government closes you down.”

“Wedgy Benn won’t close us. We’re too popular,” replied Reg, flippantly.

Dorothy was stressed about the increasing amount of bad debts and decided to hide the takings one week so she could pay some off. When Reg went to take the money, he realised what she had done and went to confront her.

“Where is it?” demanded Reg, very quietly with steely determination.

“Where is what?” asked Dorothy, innocently.

“The money. What have you done with the money?”

“Nothing,” answered Dorothy, defiantly.

“Where’ve you put the money?”

“Go away Reg and leave me alone.”

“I need that money to pay the wages and overheads.”

“You need to close Radio City and go back to making the nightclub work. We can’t go on as we are,” replied Dorothy, raising her voice.

You will tell me,” persisted Reg, his voice almost a whisper. Grasping his wife’s arm, he squeezed so tightly, she screamed. “Where is it?” he demanded, squeezing tighter.

“You’re hurting,” shrieked Dorothy, as she struggled helplessly to get free. Knowing there was no escape, she spat out the answer. “It’s in the cellar.”

Reg let go and they momentarily stared at each other with contempt. Turning on his heels he went down to the cellar. It had come to breaking point and Reg felt demoralised. The money was his to take but he felt like a thief and realised he needed to find another way to resolve his current financial difficulties.

The following week, much to Dorothy’s surprise, there were no more arguments and Reg took very little cash. She was pleased and after banking the money, began to organise their accounts and deal with some of the bad debts.

When Reg returned on Thursday evening, he kept himself busy and tried to avoid his wife’s attention. He could see by her face that she was furious and was surprised when she said nothing. Dorothy, however, was biding her time and waited until after lunch on Sunday when she suggested they go to their bedroom to talk. With quiet determination, Dorothy led the way. She’d been rehearsing what to say, over and over in her mind, aware she must be strong and not lose her temper.

“I need to get ready to go,” complained Reg, as he followed her.

“And we need to talk.”

In the bedroom, she seated herself in an easy chair in front of the large window. Reluctantly, Reg took his place on the chair next to hers. He knew he was going to receive a verbal battering and accepted he must take his punishment. William settled on Dorothy’s lap and she calmed her nerves by stroking him rhythmically while she gazed out at a clouded sky.

“On Wednesday, I received a letter from the bank, asking me to make an appointment to see the manager. A few months ago, I told you we’d paid the mortgage. When times were good, the extra money we earned from the dances, I put in the bank and paid off the mortgage. Not in twenty-five years, but four years.”

“I know.”

“We’ve both worked long and hard to do it. Clifton Hall was ours. Yours and mine to enjoy for the rest of our lives.” Dorothy paused for a moment while she swallowed the lump that was forming in the back of her throat. “And you know why I went to the bank? Why the manager asked me to call?”

Reg was silent and averted his eyes as he began to feel humiliated.

“He told me, I’d have to start paying the mortgage again.”

“I’m sorry,” said Reg, almost inaudibly. “I was going to tell you.”

“When Reg? When were you going to tell me? You’ve remortgaged the house, our home, and taken all that money without telling me. I couldn’t believe it. What have you done?” accused Dorothy, as she tugged a lace handkerchief from her cardigan sleeve and mopped tears that stung in her eyes.

Gently, Reg put his hand out to hold hers but she rebuffed him, pulling her hand away.

“I needed the money for the station. A transmitter, generators and equipment. Wages to pay.”

“I thought you said the revenue from the religious programmes would pay the wages,” retorted Dorothy.

“It does,” agreed Reg. “But things are tight. I couldn’t go on without more money. I had no choice. I didn’t want to close the station and give everyone the sack. Lose everything. We’re so close to making it successful. I’m sure it’ll soon be profitable and then I can pay it all back. It’s just a matter of time. Radio City could be the most powerful of all the pirate stations.”

“That’s fine. You can have your pirate radio station and all the equipment you need, until Wedgwood Benn finds a way to close you down.”

“The Government can’t close us, we’re too popular.”

“So you keep saying. But they will. They’ll find a way and then what? You’ll have lost everything.”

“It’s not that bad. We can pay the mortgage again.”

Dorothy stared out of the window and her attention was drawn to a squirrel running along a branch of the oak tree. She remembered the boys, the music, and the tree swing. The laughter and fun. They were happy memories but it was over. Quietly, with composure, she explained to her husband that she was leaving.

“I’ve had enough Reg. You can pay the mortgage and keep Clifton Hall. I’m leaving.”

“You can’t Doe Doe. I know it’s been a difficult year but it will get better. You could help and spend time in London. I’m lonely during the week without you.”

“No Reg. I can’t cope any more. You need a secretary, not me. I’m tired of your dreams, your ideas and your new adventures. I can’t keep track of you. You’re either in London or on Shivering Sands, and when you’re home, you’re not interested in me. You even take the radio to bed with you.”

Tenderly, Reg put his hand out in a vain attempt to hold hers. “I love you. You know I love you.”

“I know you do, in your own way.”

“You’re just upset since your mother died.”

“You’re not listening to me. I feel empty inside. Like all the stuffing’s been pulled out, piece by piece. I’ve made the decision to start a new life, on my own. You can keep Clifton Hall or put it up for sale.”

“But you love it here.”

“Are you going to pay the mortgage? Where’s the money coming from after we pay the rent at Loughborough and the running costs of Radio City? The affair you had with Carol was bad enough but this is worse. Far worse. I can’t compete with a radio station. It’s all you think about. It’ll break my heart to leave Clifton Hall but you’ve left me with no choice.”

“You do have a choice,” replied Reg. “You just have to be patient until I make things work.”

“You’re good at making things work, then you lose interest and I have to pick up the pieces. I haven’t picked up the pieces from the nightclub which is costing thousands, and, I’ve no intention of picking up the pieces of the radio station when you get bored with that.”

“I won’t lose interest in Radio City, I promise you,” replied Reg, fervently. He could see his words were having no effect. Glancing at Dorothy’s calm exterior, he realised she was not making an idle threat, but a promise. As the full implication of what she said permeated his being, he suddenly felt wretched. He had a choice. To give up Radio City or lose his wife.

There was a brief knock at the bedroom door and Susan burst in, smiling at her parents. “Have you seen my bubble keys?”

Reg, in that instant, flipped and lost self-control. He jumped up from the chair, his face ashen with anger and strode toward his daughter.

"You little madam."

"Go, Susan go," shouted Dorothy at her daughter, as she grabbed hold of Reg's arm and held him back to give Susan time to run from the bedroom.

"She's laughing at me. She knows, doesn't she? You told her? She's been listening outside the door and she wants you to leave?"

"No Reg. No. Susan doesn't know. The girls have no idea."

Dorothy let go of his arm. She could see his anger was spent, like air deflating from a balloon and he sunk back into the chair, ashamed of himself. If Dorothy hadn't held him back, he knew he would have hit his daughter, smacked her across the face and sent her flying for her seeming impertinence.

"You can't blame Susan. It's nothing to do with her."

For a time, the two of them remained silent, side by side as they stared out of the window. Reg had gambled and lost.

"What do you plan to do?" Reg asked, politely.

Dorothy, strong in the knowledge she had not shown anger or weakness, explained she would buy a smaller house and make a new life for herself and their daughters.

"We can both start again. You can follow your dreams and do whatever you want. You can find someone who'll make you happy and doesn't argue with you," said Dorothy, gently, with just a hint of her enigmatic Mona Lisa smile. It was done. Their marriage was almost over.

When Susan returned home later, she noticed her father's car had gone and her mother was sitting alone in the kitchen.

"Why was Dad angry with me?"

"You came in at the wrong time."

"Why did I?"

Dorothy sighed, not sure how to break the news, knowing her daughter would take it badly.

"I'd just told him that I was going to leave. He thought you knew and were laughing at him"

Susan blinked and shook her head as she comprehended the seriousness of what her mother had said.

"You can't Mum."

Tears began to stream down Dorothy's face and her body trembled. Susan put her arm around her mother's shoulder and stood silently, waiting for her to explain.

"This time he's gone too far and I've had enough. He's remortgaged the house without telling me. He expects me to pay the mortgage again. I told him I'm not going to do it. He'll have to put Clifton Hall up for sale or pay the mortgage himself."

"No Mum, you can't."

"Why can't I?" snapped Dorothy. "What sort of life do you think I'm leading?"

"I think you lead a much more interesting life than all my friend's mothers."

"You never see any bad in your father. You always stick up for him."

"I wouldn't leave Clifton Hall. I'd fight to stay. I don't understand why you can't pay the mortgage," asked Susan.

"It's like treading water and going backwards. I've done that once and I'm not doing it again. Marriage is about working as a team and trusting each other. How can I trust your dad when he went behind my back? When you get married, you'll understand."

"If this house was mine, I'd want to keep it."

"You might do, but I'm the one left to run everything while your father goes off enjoying himself with no thought or care about what he's doing to me or us as a family. I've told him I'm leaving him and he knows I mean it."

Reg was subdued when he returned to London. He didn't want to lose Dorothy but he wouldn't have her telling him what he could, and could not, do. He'd tried so hard to get her to join in with the adventure and wanted her by his side. She was good at managing things but this time, her flat refusal had made life difficult for them both. The dancehall business was dying and she wouldn't accept it was time to change. Remortgaging Clifton Hall had been the sensible thing to do while the station was in its infancy but he realised now that for Dorothy, it had been the final straw.

12. SPIRIT OF ADVENTURE

Platform hoist for lifting crew onto Shivering Sands (SC)

With the demise of Radio Invicta, Ed Moreno and Phil Perkins were out of work and seeking employment and Reg offered them both a job.

Ed had decided not to go to sea again as he felt a sense of guilt for being the person to instruct Martin Shaw and Simon Ashley to return to shore with Tom Pepper. He was also diabetic and not in the best of health. He offered to work for Radio City by sending in prerecorded tapes and Reg agreed.

When Phil Perkins joined Radio City in April 1965, there was a conflict of personalities as he and Don Witts disagreed how the station could be improved. Phil was a radio ham and dismissive about Don's expertise as a television engineer. Don had built Big Bertha and Reg put his trust in him. On Don's recommendation, expensive equipment was purchased which proved useless. This frustrated Phil as he could see it was a waste of money Reg could ill afford to lose.

Phil wanted a new crystal to stop the frequency drifting which worsened at night with interference from foreign stations. On his first shore leave, he went home and spent hours grinding a standard 1 Mhz crystal to 1034 kHz. When he returned to Radio City, the new crystal kept the transmitter on frequency. Reg was delighted. For the first time, the station could broadcast later in the evening with only a slight burbling interference instead of an unpleasant whistling. This improvement did not endear Phil to Don and they continued to disagree.

Reg recruited a steady flow of enthusiastic, temporary disc jockeys to keep his overheads down and paid most of them £5 per week. Some of them had such a miserable time on the towers, they never wanted to return.

Howard Michaels, aged 19, fancied himself as a pirate deejay. He sent in tapes and Reg agreed he could have a trial. Excited, he met the change-over crew in Whitstable and went with them to Shivering Sands. He soon fitted in and was pleased to be given two shows a day. When the weather turned stormy, Fred Downs was unable to reach the forts and the crew went into survival mode. They ran out of clean drinking water and food supplies were short. Water was collected from the roof and for a few days, they lived on porridge and black coffee. Howard, in a strop, told listeners how bad conditions were on Radio City and closed the transmitter down. Shortly after his announcement, the Harvester arrived and he was given immediate notice to quit.

A young Australian, Norman St John, had just completed working on board a cruise ship in relative luxury and was fortunate to meet Reg. He told him about the experience he'd gained as a deejay in Australia and Reg agreed to give him a trial but explained the accommodation was basic and about to be refitted.

A week later, Norman set off from Whitstable with Reg and the relief crew. It was a bad day to go to sea with a gale blowing and when Fred told Norman to "jump", he took a leap of faith and grasped the rusty ladder. Fred circled the boat into position for Reg's turn to jump but the waves were too high. Waving goodbye, Reg shouted to Norman so he could be heard above the engine noise and pounding waves.

"I'm going back. Make yourself known to the other crew."

At the top of the ladders, Norman St John introduced himself and was given the mid-morning programme slot between 9-12p.m. Five days later, the storm had subsided and the Harvester returned with provisions and change of crew.

"How did it go?" enquired Reg, who could see from Norman's expression that he was unhappy.

"Not good. The station's a shambles. The accommodation's disgusting and the food awful."

"You should take it with a spirit of adventure." Reg smiled, not at all bothered by the criticism. "I'm gradually making improvements. You should give it another try."

Norman had no other employment so agreed to return. After a further eight days on the towers, he left, vowing never to return. Next, he applied to Radio Caroline South where he was happy to work in more luxurious surroundings.

Bob Le-Roi, aged 15 with dyed blond hair and wearing Buddy Holly style glasses, often listened to Radio City and sent in a few tender tapes. During the school holidays, he managed to convince Eric Martin at the Record Centre to let him go to the fort. When he arrived at Shivering Sands, Alexander Dee and Dick Dickson came off and he went on as crew with Paul Elvey and Chris Cross.

With only three of them manning the towers, Bob took his turn at being a deejay. Paul Elvey took him under his wing and Bob helped him with the engineering, filling generators with fuel, hauling up sea water, cooking and cleaning. When it was quiet, he replied to fan mail. Everyone who wrote in was replied to and whenever possible, their record requests played. Bob loved his time on the station and tried to go out whenever he could. To have the opportunity to be a pirate deejay was a school boy's dream. It made Bob appreciate just how important speech is and he began to listen to BBC presenters to try and improve his pronunciation.

The cost of running Radio City continued to increase. With money in the bank from the remortgage, Reg improved equipment and took on more staff. Paul had asked for a larger generator to give more power to Big Bertha and Reg had managed to find one. It was too large to go in the Harvester so Reg booked a charter boat from Gravesend. Everyone waited and looked out for the boat. When Tony Pine saw the generator, he shook his head in dismay as he called down to Reg.

"I think it's too heavy. The hoist will only take one ton and the generator looks as though it weighs about three."

"You never know till you try," replied Reg, as he helped put straps around the generator and attach it to the hoist.

Bob Le-Roi, on holiday from school, was asked to operate the crane hoist and watched the proceedings from above. It soon became obvious that Tony was right. The hoist groaned with the weight and the cable runs contorted under the jib arm. The lift was halted while a lump of timber was hammered in to prevent the jib from contorting further. The electric hoist was restarted and they tried again.

A disc jockey came running from the studio and shouted down to the boat to stop as the record decks were slowing and the transmitter cutting out. At the same time, the timber sprang out from its wedge and falling from height, hit Reg on his back and knocked him to the deck of the boat. Everyone looked on in shock as Reg lay sprawled out. Slowly, he picked himself up. In pain, he looked at the generator and the hoist, biting his bottom lip while he considered the situation.

"What do you want to do?" asked Tony. "Do you want to try again?"

"It's not going to work," agreed Reg. "We'll have to think of another way of getting it up."

Disappointed, Reg sailed back to Gravesend with the generator. It was a wasted day and the boat hire had been expensive. The problem was resolved by the engineers who set about disassembling the generator on land, then ferried it out on the Harvester in smaller pieces.

The terrifying leap from the boat to the ladder was something everyone dreaded. Fred Downs came up with a solution. He made a wooden platform, like an open crate, with a rope secured to each corner so it could be lowered directly onto the boat. Instead of making the 'jump', the crew were given the choice of being hoisted up on the platform. It was still a scary experience, especially when there was a strong wind as the platform seemed to swing precariously about.

One afternoon, Reg began to receive numerous telephone calls from listeners who informed him of an enormous explosion and fire on Shivering Sands. Worried, Reg immediately contacted Fred Downs and Eric Martin from the Record Centre, to see if they could find out what had happened. Later, they reported back it was all safe on the towers. Phil Perkins had been experimenting.

When Reg made his weekly trip to the station, he was furious and brought the crew together so he could speak to them.

"Exactly what were you doing?" asked Reg, very quietly.

"It was a bit of fun Reg," replied Phil, guiltily.

"What was a bit of fun?"

"I took an empty dustbin up to the roof and filled it with some calor gas."

"And."

"I lit it with a central heating lighter and it exploded."

"Why?"

"I was trying to make a loud bang."

"And you could have blown yourself up and damaged the tower. It's what I call crass stupidity and I would have expected more from you. The explosion was heard nine miles away in Whitstable and I've had to pay for Fred Downs to come out to check you were all okay. Not only that, you had a helicopter flying over to investigate. The last thing we want is for the government to tell us we're damaging the towers and have to quit."

Reg managed to keep a serious face while reprimanding Phil and the crew. He understood Phil's sense of adventure and the fun he got in making loud explosions. It was a case of do as I say and not as I do. Reg was responsible for their safety and since a firework had exploded in his face, he appreciated the danger and agonising pain of playing with explosives.

Phil's next project was one Reg agreed with. He set about improving the bathroom by throwing empty diesel drums into the sea and installing a pump. After a few attempts, Phil was jubilant when he managed to get the seawater pumped up to the bathroom so the crew could enjoy the luxury of hot seawater baths. To get a lather, they had to use washing-up liquid or special soap. One of the crew who preferred showers, improvised by suspending a large aluminium watering can to the top of the bathroom door and filled it with water.

No one liked to use the rickety interconnecting suspension bridges so everything was done on the central tower. One bridge was far too dangerous and past repair but two of the bridges were usable but there were wide spaces between the planks. Reg agreed to pay for more timber and Paul Elvey and Tony Pine collaborated to rebuild the bridges by spacing out planks of wood across them. Walking across was still a scary experience as the sea below could be seen through the gaps. With safer access, the central tower became living accommodation, with lounge-dining room, bedrooms and kitchen. The south tower was refitted with a much larger studio and recording area. The other tower was used for storage.

Clandestine two-way radio contact was frequently made between land and Shivering Sands. The GPO had refused to provide a licence and instead, did their best to catch the 'pirates' out. Eric Martin was never caught as he put his radio equipment in his car and drove it to a cliff top to make contact. Sue and Tony Pine had their radio equipment in their shop where it was discovered. The call sign, Pidgeon, with Reg speaking and with his Yorkshire accent, the GPO thought it was Pagan. They were prosecuted for operating an illegal radio set, fined and their equipment confiscated. Reg, of course, reimbursed them the costs.

By the spring of 1965, Reg was ready to promote the station on a professional basis and to bring in more advertising revenue, he formed a new company, RaCity Sales. Peter Jameson was recruited as Sales Director with the incentive of 50 per cent commission. Peter was well dressed, in his 30s and with good sales experience. He soon succeeded in attracting regular advertisers and where the reception was good, such as Basildon and

Southend-on-Sea, he arranged local request programmes. Listeners were asked to send in their record requests and local businesses were invited to participate. Peter produced the programmes and sent tapes out to the station each week. He also obtained some large company advertisers including Green Shield Stamps sponsored programmes.

To compete with Radio London jingles, Reg asked the Liberators if they would come to London and record some catchy Radio City and Green Shield Stamp jingles in the Central Sound Studios, two doors up from his office in Denmark Street. Reg wrote down a few key words and catch phrases and they spent several hours having fun as they improvised, making up tunes and harmonies, with Reg saying the words.

Realising that the Labour Government were planning new legislation from August, 1965 to prohibit tobacco companies from advertising on television, Reg and Peter began to think of ways they could attract the companies to advertise with them. Reg researched the possibility of purchasing an ex Royal Navy supply boat and moor it off Lundy Island. Peter then approached the tobacco companies with the plan to see if they would advertise on a pirate television station. It was an exciting project that came to nothing. The companies, although interested, were unwilling to commit themselves in advance.

Reg was constantly looking for different ways he could improve the station and a surprising contact was made with Bill Crozier. He was famous as a BBC radio presenter on the record request programme, Two-Way Family Favourites which broadcast on Sunday lunchtimes. It had millions of listeners and was one of the few BBC programmes that played records. Bill was based in Cologne and Reg suggested he might like to work with him on Radio City as Assistant Controller.

1st April 1965 (extract) To: Bill Crozier, BFN., BFPO 19, Germany.

Dear Bill,

I was delighted to be able to talk with you the other evening.

I would like to offer you the job of Assistant Station Controller, with a view to becoming Station Controller. Either a fixed salary, or a lower salary, say £1,500 - £1,600 pa plus commission on total advertising revenue.

Radio City is in its infancy, but during the next few weeks our power is to be increased some twenty times our present output. The biggest difficulties we have had in the past have been in lifting heavy diesel generating equipment on to the towers, but now the power installation is completed, it is only left to our engineers to complete the transmitting unit.

I cannot paint a bright picture for the future because of some level of uncertainty as to our continued existence, but with our revenue increasing, I am negotiating to buy a boat as an alternative. Our present site is on the towers at Shivering Sands, situated nine miles from Whitstable.

If you will help me to build this station into one of high repute, I will further assure you of better and better payment for your services, and as we are balanced on the point of extremely rapid expansion, I feel that I can offer you this position to your advantage.

On Bill Crozier's return to Germany, he sent Reg a pleasant reply, declining his offer.

Radio City was still not so professional or powerful as Radio London or Caroline, but it had a growing number of fervent listeners who tuned in every day. Reg was cautious about spending too much on better equipment while the government prevaricated about closing the pirates. Instead, he began to think about the quality of his programmes. Instead of relying on volunteers and one-week trial disc jockeys he started to recruit permanent staff.

Tony Carroll had gained experience as a radio presenter working with the RAF in Aden and was eager to go out to the forts. For the first few days, he enjoyed life on Shivering Sands until he began to suffer from severe stomach pains. He tried to ignore them, thinking they would go away but when he collapsed, the crew realised he probably had appendicitis. Making several urgent radio appeals for assistance they had to wait and hope someone had heard them. Getting Tony off the station and onto a boat was going to be a problem and if no help came, they knew he would probably die.

Time seemed to pass slowly as they watched over the sick man but fortunately, help came quickly. The crew had never been so relieved to hear the noisy sound of whirring rotor blades and rushed up to the roof, waving furiously to let the helicopter pilot know which tower they were on. Within minutes Tony was taken out on a stretcher and airlifted to Margate hospital.

Reg was relieved to hear Tony had been rescued and was making a good recovery but it left him short of crew. Looking through the many applications he'd received he decided to interview a young American who was studying at the London School of Economics.

Ricky Michaels had sent letters and tapes to all the pirate stations but received no response and was delighted when Reg offered him work on Radio City. Dark haired and good looking, with an attractive mid-Atlantic accent, he was everything a disc jockey should be. With Ricky's interest in economics and business studies, he paid attention to the management of the station and helped Reg with promotions and selling airtime.

Tom Edwards lived in Norwich and was intrigued by pirate radio. During the summer of 1964, he worked as a Bluecoat at a Pontins Holiday Camp and gained experience making announcements over the Tannoy system. He put together a tape and posted it to Radio City. After listening, Reg offered Tom a week's trial on the station. Tom soon learnt that all disc jockeys were offered a week's trial and paid £5. However, at the end of the week, Reg surprised Tom by offering him a permanent position.

Alan Clark had just left school and with school boy optimism, sent a letter with a tape to Radio City. What he lacked in broadcasting experience he made up for in enthusiasm. Reg offered him a week's trial with instructions to go to the Record Centre in Whitstable where he should meet Eric Martin, the station manager. Alan was shown to the office above the shop and introduced to Ricky Michaels. Together, they made the short walk to the harbour and were soon aboard the Harvester and heading out to Shivering Sands. When Alan arrived at the forts, he had no idea what to do. Ricky and Denis (the Menace), gave him a few tips and then left him to it. After the trial week, Reg drove Alan back to London and paid him £5 but made no offer of further employment. Although disappointed, he was determined to become a deejay, and week after week he made himself available for temporary work in the hope he could gain the experience he needed.

Reg Calvert – holding his camera in his hand on the sea crossing to Shivering Sands. He loved to take photographs and was more comfortable behind the lens rather than in front. He had a darkroom under the stairs at Clifton Hall and many of the photographs in this book were taken by him and acknowledged (RC)

13. YOU'VE GOT YOUR TROUBLES

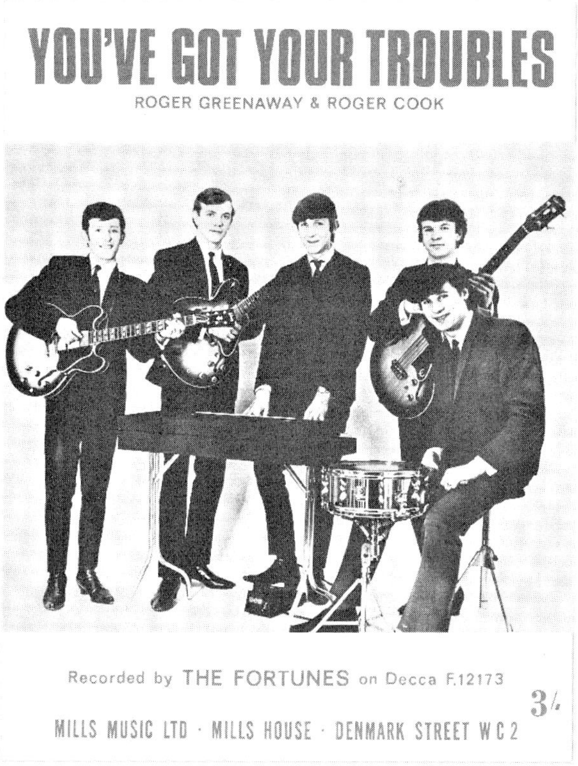

Sheet Music

Visitors to Clifton Hall would have been unaware that Reg and Dorothy's marriage was on the cusp of breaking up. They made no mention of it and at weekends, Dorothy was distant but polite. Reg greeted her with respect and they continued to share the same bed. It was a surreal arrangement, both knowing that these were their last days together.

Reg found a flat to live in London, located above the Phoenix Theatre on Charing Cross Road and just a short walk from Denmark Street. He bought the basics, cheap beds and bedding, a few cups, plates and cutlery, but it was more like camping. John stayed there with him and anyone who was in London, was welcome to stop for the night.

Clifton Hall was no longer a happy household. Reg was hardly there and Dorothy was in a state of permanent stress. Candy kept out of her Mother's way, seeing friends, playing records in her room and spending time with her pony. Susan went to evening classes and other times, she secretly met Mike or visited her former school friend, Elizabeth, who lived with her parents in a modest terraced house in Rugby. The Lamont's were a lively Scottish couple who came from wealthy backgrounds but had not fared so well. They were quick to argue and quick to make fun, and welcomed Susan's visits, treating her like a second daughter.

Since moving to Clifton Hall, Dorothy had managed the finances and not only paid off the mortgage, but secreted money into her own building society account. She justified this to herself as wages she would have earned if she had been paid for the work she was doing as a secretary and manager. It was her 'rainy day' fund and there was sufficient to resolve Reg's financial problems and retain Clifton Hall, but instead, she chose independence.

Dorothy scoured the area for a house she could afford to buy, taking her reluctant daughters to view numerous properties. She eventually decided on a semidetached house being built by Wimpey on the other side of Rugby.

Without Dorothy's support, Reg found the administration of running his business more than he could cope with. He had the Fortunes to manage, King's Agency to support, Radio City to organise and wages to pay, advertising, programming, promotions, dances and events to run. The nightclub at Loughborough was a forgotten dream and in May and June, he sent cheques amounting to more than £3,000 to pay the rent but ignored the demands from the bank to repay the mortgage, explaining the house had been put up for sale.

Following his dream had brought consequences. Living in the fast lane with the stress of managing everything on his own, Reg was not so ebullient and had seemingly lost his boyish zest for life as he rapidly matured into a businessman with grey hair. John Wileman was his right-hand man, driving him to the dances, to London, to Whitstable and anywhere else he needed to go. John was neatly dressed, pleasant to be with, quietly spoken, thoughtful and practical. He would do almost any job, only protesting when Reg asked him to do some decorating and paint the front door and stairway to 7 Denmark Street, as he had someone 'important' coming to see him.

Reg advertised for a secretary and interviewed a series of young women until he found the right person. Jill Farr was perfect, in her mid-twenties, quick to learn, intelligent and capable of doing much more than an ordinary secretary. Petite and neatly dressed, she wore high heeled stilettos and twisted her long, light brown hair into a French roll. Reg acknowledged she was as good as any man and accordingly, paid her a man's wage, £20 per week, the same as he paid John.

At the beginning of June, 1965 Reg received a letter in the post from David Watchman of West Advertising and he could have jumped with joy. An American Evangelistic Mission wanted to prepare a campaign using radio stations from September. It had come just in time. When he returned home at the weekend he told Dorothy his good news.

"We've made it Doe Doe. It's all going to work out okay. We've got another religious advertiser starting in September. Radio City's paying its way and it won't be long before we're making a profit."

Dorothy remained cool and detached, realising her husband had proved her wrong. "That's good. What about the nightclub?"

Reg ignored her comment about the nightclub and smiled. "I'll be charging them $320 per hour and they're happy to pay. If we can improve our transmissions with a larger transmitter and better aerial, we could earn even more. You can stay at Clifton Hall. I'll pay the mortgage."

Dorothy raised her eyebrows and shook her head in response.

"I'll play you the Fortunes new demo? It's written by Roger Cook and Roger Greenaway. They're in a group called the Kestrels. The song's called, *You've Got Your Troubles.*"

"It's a good title. It could have been written about us," commented Dorothy, wryly, as she followed Reg in the rehearsal room and sat on the windowsill. When the record stopped playing, Dorothy nodded.

"Very good. The best so far. Have you heard how the sale of Clifton Hall is going?"

Reg shook his head in response and changed the subject.

"Decca are doing a full orchestral backing and Les Reed is musical director with Noel Walker as the producer. Why don't you come down to the recording session? You could stay over in London for a few days and meet Jill, my new secretary?"

"No Reg. What you do in London is up to you. I'm not interested. Why don't you manage the Liberators? They've got potential and they're a nice group of boys."

"I might do later but at the moment, I'm too busy to take on another group."

Dorothy's new home was due to be completed in July and to involve her daughters she took them shopping to choose new curtains and carpets for their rooms. As the date of the move came closer, a surreal atmosphere developed between Reg and Dorothy as neither mentioned it. Tea chests were placed in most rooms and Dorothy began to pack away her belongings. Reg made no claim to any of the household contents and seemed almost oblivious to what she was doing.

On the Monday morning, Reg kissed his wife goodbye for the last time. When he returned at the weekend, he found the house deserted. The kitchen was cold as the Aga had gone out with no one to tend it. He wandered aimlessly through the empty rooms realising what he had done. Life was about making choices and he had made his. To follow his dreams and not be told by his wife what he could, and could not do.

The move to Macbeth Close had gone smoothly and Dorothy was pleased that Reg had not been difficult. She had given notice to her cleaner, Mrs Podgson, and the gardener, 'Old Jack', sold Susan's chickens and Candy's pony. On Wednesday morning, she informed her daughters they were to go to Macbeth Close that evening. She felt an immense sense of achievement and relief at making the break. Dorothy had triumphed in an unequal society where men were paid two or three times more than a woman for doing the same work, and where banks and building societies refused to grant a mortgage without a male guarantor,

The weekly routine remained much the same with Dorothy booking the groups for the dances and keeping Reg's secretary informed. He had kept numbers up at the Friday night Nuneaton dance by booking star names throughout the year, including the Hollies, the Pretty Things, the Kinks and Gene Vincent. Saturday nights, Susan ran the dance in Nuneaton, Reg to Kettering, Dorothy with Candy to the Banbury Winter Gardens. The Banbury dance was in decline and when it was closed, Dorothy went to Kettering and Reg started a new dance at High Wycombe.

Candy and the Kinks at Nuneaton Co-op Hall, Nuneaton (RC)

Reg missed his home comforts and often passed time on Saturday afternoon by arriving early in High Wycombe to go to Phil Perkins' house, not to see Phil, but his mother. She was a homely woman who made him welcome and they had lively conversations while he enjoyed afternoon tea with freshly baked cakes and scones.

Dorothy's new house was warm and cosy with gas central heating, modern fitted kitchen and L-shaped lounge with dining area overlooking the garden. In the bathroom, Dorothy had selected the latest peach-coloured bathroom suite and for the ground floor cloakroom, a pink toilet and sink.

As new neighbours moved in, Dorothy began to make friends. She was content and life would have been perfect, except for her daughters. She now had to find a way to manage them as living in a small house meant they were in close quarters and quarrelsome. Both girls resented the move and were upset not to see their father. Candy started to take money from her purse and Susan was petulant.

"I don't like living here. It's too small and I feel claustrophobic."

"You can't return to Clifton Hall so you may as well get used to it. This is how normal people live."

"If this is how normal people live, it's not how I want to live," retorted Susan.

Dorothy, irritated by her daughter's attitude, snapped back, "It's about time you had your feet on the ground instead of living in cloud cuckoo land like your father."

"I'm going out."

With a flick of her head, Susan walked off, picked up her bubble keys and slammed the back door behind her.

Dorothy had discovered that Susan had been having a secret affair with the photographer from the Rugby Advertiser and knew she had to confront the issue. She didn't want to make the same mistake as her own mother who had been vociferous in her dislike of Reg, so, when the moment was right, she suggested to her daughter that she could invite Mike back for a meal.

"How did you hear?" asked Susan, surprised.

"The village hairdressers."

"Okay, I'll ask him."

Mike was delighted by the invitation and brought Dorothy a bouquet of flowers. Much against her instincts, she was won over by his easy charm and lively sense of humour. After dinner, she broached the subject of their marriage plans and Mike was elated when he realised he had Dorothy's permission.

"I'd be happy to marry in the autumn when my divorce comes through."

"That's fine," agreed Dorothy, smiling.

Susan was astonished. "I don't want to get married until I'm a lot older."

"It'd be best if you married sooner, you're seventeen now and old enough."

"I don't think so. I'm sorry, I have to go out."

Standing up, Susan walked out and drove to the Lamont's house in Rugby, leaving the two of them to discuss a wedding she had no intention of attending.

Mike had often broached the subject of their marriage and Susan had made it clear she would not marry until she was older. Her mother's consent had surprised her and she was taken aback by her callousness. Dorothy had an innate fear of her daughters bringing shame on the family by becoming pregnant before marriage, or even worse, bringing an illegitimate child into the world. There was a wall of silence when it came to sex. It was a word never spoken, only intimated and something she had educated her daughters not to do until they were married.

Mike began to call regularly at Macbeth Close and Dorothy welcomed his visits. She was surprised to find she enjoyed his company and they laughed and joked together. He made himself useful, offering to fit curtain rails and shelves and Dorothy often invited him to eat with them. Susan was disgruntled by their friendship. Instead of it being just the two of them, it was now a threesome. She changed jobs and no longer saw him at work. When his divorce settlement came through, he surprised her one evening by meeting her in the town.

"Would you like to come for a ride?" asked Mike, opening the door of a red sports car parked next to her bubble car.

"Is this yours?"

"Yes, I've just bought it with my settlement money. I've always wanted a MGB GT. What do you think?"

"It's lovely," smiled Susan, as she stooped to sit in the low, black leather, bucket seat.

It was a beautiful car and Susan understood why he had wanted to buy it but couldn't help feeling disgruntled. She had learnt many lessons from her parents and remembered her mother's mantra. 'Marriage is a partnership and you don't go spending money, or doing something big, without first discussing it.' Mike had broken that golden rule. How he spent his money was up to him but if he had been serious about getting married, he would have used it as a deposit on a house. Susan realised that however much she liked him, she would not marry him, not now, and not in the future. It was a painful separation and it took her several months to break free and end the friendship. When Mike stopped visiting Macbeth Close, Dorothy, although curious, never questioned her daughter to find out why.

14. CAT AND MOUSE GAMES

Knock John Fort (photo supplied by www.offshoreradio.co.uk)

Reg was surprised when he heard rumours that a new radio station was being planned on Red Sands Towers that was not going to play pop music. He waited with interest to see if it would fare better than its predecessors, Radio Invicta and King Radio, both of which had failed to attract enough advertising.

In September, 1965 Radio 390 took to the airwaves. It was quite different to the other stations, their format, to play 'sweet' music with on-air Eve magazine programmes for women listeners. It was to prove a recipe for success. Ted Allbeury was the brains behind the new station. He was an astute businessman who had been employed during the war in the Intelligence Corps, afterwards, working in advertising and public relations. He obtained investors, refitted the studio and installed a better transmitter. Wisely, he didn't try to compete with the pop music stations but targeted housewives.

Radio London was the most popular and powerful pirate radio station. Caroline South, (Atlanta) was finding it difficult to compete and losing money. Behind the scenes, there was a conflict of personalities with Atlanta's chairman, Major Oliver Smedley, frequently clashing with Ronan O'Rahilly about the way he ran the operation; while Allan Crawford, who was more evenly tempered, did not approve of the way O'Rahilly squandered Caroline North's resources by living an extravagant and flamboyant lifestyle at shareholders' expense.

Crawford and Smedley decided to investigate the possibility of transferring their broadcasting equipment from the Mi Amigo to the Knock John Fort, the last good remaining fort not already occupied, agreeing it would be less expensive to run than a ship. They arranged a boat trip to view, leaving a crew of two men on the tower while they organised the transition from ship to tower.

Another group of pioneers arrived at Knock John only to discover the Caroline crew had already taken possession. Instead, they sailed to Sunk Head Fort, 11 miles off Walton-on-the-Naze. Sunk Head was similar in design to Knock John but in very poor condition. The legs flooded with the rise and fall of the tide and getting aboard, especially in rough weather, was particularly hazardous. They had ambitious plans to broadcast both a radio and television station but not the necessary finance or equipment. Nevertheless, they had fun, managing to make low-powered radio broadcasts for a few months as Tower Radio. They were unsuccessful in their ambition to start Tower Television but it was enough to worry the government who announced they would not tolerate pirate television.

Roy Bates, a local fisherman and retired army major, also wanted Knock John. He had little money but what he lacked in finance he made up with force and iron determination. Previously, he had unsuccessfully tried to bribe the Radio Invicta crew on Red Sands Towers after the drowning of Tom Pepper. When he heard that Radio Caroline had put several men on Knock John, he organised a boat trip to the fort and ruthlessly removed them.

When Knock John was once again vacant, more men were sent from Caroline South (Atlanta) to occupy it and prepare for broadcasts. Shortly afterwards, Bates returned and forcibly removed them. Admitting defeat, Crawford and Smedley, turned their attention to Radio City.

In August 1965, Reg was surprised to receive an invitation to meet Allan Crawford at Caroline House. He was impressed by the very grand offices at 6 Chesterfield Gardens, Mayfair, and taken in by the outward appearance of wealth and seeming success of Radio Caroline. His own offices in Denmark Street by comparison were shabby and run-down.

Crawford, in his Australian drawl, was straight talking and forthright in his approach and Reg listened to his proposal with interest.

"If our three stations were to merge, we would have almost complete coverage of England and be able to compete with Radio London."

Reg had not considered selling or merging with another station but what Crawford said made sense. "It could be good," agreed Reg, thoughtfully.

"We thought Caroline North could remain off the Isle of Man; Caroline South could move further up the east coast."

"Or it could go off the West Coast near the Isle of Lundy," suggested Reg.

"It's possible," agreed Crawford. "Radio City could become the new Caroline South and broadcast to the London area. If you're happy to manage the programming and technical side of all three stations, we could offer you a salary of £1,500 per month, if all goes well. We would organise the administration, sales, and pay the expenses and wages. You would send us your accounts and we would receive all the income from Radio City, and in return, you'd receive 50 per cent of the profits.

"What happens when we need new equipment for Radio City?"

"I would be responsible for expenditure and before you buy new equipment, you would have to get clearance from me.

"I could do that," agreed Reg, who disliked administration and accounts. "I think it all sounds okay but Radio City won't be able to compete with Radio London if we don't have a larger transmitter. The trouble is, if we buy one, who knows how long it will be before this government closes us down."

"I think it'll be a while yet before they get their act together," replied Crawford, optimistically. "Anyhow, we thought of that. We've found a 10kW transmitter in Texas going cheap."

"How cheap?" asked Reg.

"£700 plus freight," smiled Crawford.

Reg was sceptical and shook his head. "For that amount, it'll be old and no good. You really need to buy a much more modern transmitter."

"To be honest, for the time being, we haven't sufficient funds for a newer transmitter, but they've assured me this one's working well."

"We'd need a much larger generator to power a 10kW transmitter. The generators we have on the station won't do."

"Okay, I'll look into that."

"What happens if the merger doesn't succeed for any reason?"

"If the Caroline Board fail in their obligations, the transmitter would become Radio City property. I'll get a legal agreement drawn up by our Solicitor, Michael Simkin."

"That's fine."

In agreement, the two men shook hands and numerous meetings were arranged to organise the merger. Reg was introduced to Major Oliver Smedley who took him out to view the Mi Amigo, moored off Frinton on Sea. It was smaller than Reg had thought and after discussing various options with the crew, it was decided it was unsuitable to moor off Lundy.

The merger was announced in the press on 22nd September, 1965 and in preparation, Reg submitted all his accounts and from 4th October, all money and cheques received, were forwarded to Crawford at the Caroline offices.

The merger surprised everyone on Radio City but life carried on much the same except that they now played Radio Caroline news reports. Advertisers were informed that Radio City was now part of the Radio Caroline Network and that the power of the station would, in the next month, be vastly improved.

Crawford arranged to purchase the transmitter from East-West Broadcasting Company KCUL Ft. Worth, Texas and made enquiries to hire a 100kW generator from George Cohen Machinery. Reg went to see the set-up on the Mi Amigo and Smedley visited the towers and was shown where the new transmitter would be housed and was introduced to the crew, including engineer Paul Elvey.

News Report: Ipswich Evening Star, 22nd September, 1965 (Extract)

RADIO CAROLINE POLICY SPLIT?

A split is believed to have arisen over the joint operating policy of the pirate radio ships, Caroline North and Caroline South. This follows an announcement late last night that Radio Caroline had made arrangements to take over Radio City, situated on an old wartime fort in the Thames Estuary off Southend.

Mr Ronan O'Rahilly of Caroline and Mr Allan Crawford, of Atlanta, became joint managing directors of the new company. Neither was available to comment this morning but it is understood that a series of meetings is taking place at Caroline House, London, during the day. A statement on the future constitution of Radio Caroline may be issued late tonight or tomorrow morning.

Reg submitted to Allan Crawford his expected revenue. Expenses and staff wages were about £400 per week. Income from advertising and religious broadcasts was about £800 per week. Radio City was making a profit of about £400 per week.

By the end of September, Reg became uneasy about the way the merger was progressing which up to now had been agreed on a handshake. The legal contract had not been prepared and there was no mention of payment for his work. Keeping his options open, Reg prepared a second station for religious broadcasts, Radio City 2, on the unoccupied Knock John Fort. He arranged a day trip to inspect the towers to see how he could organise it. The towers were filthy with bird droppings and 10 years of detritus so he asked deejay Alex Dee, and engineer Dick Dickson, to stay on the fort to clean and prepare it.

Alex and Dick spent two weeks cleaning the towers and were keeping a watch for the Harvester to come out and relieve them. When they saw a boat heading straight towards Knock John with a number of men on board, they realised it was a boarding party. Locking all the hatches, they hoped they would be safe. Roy Bates, however, was determined, unscrupulous and reckless. He climbed aboard using a derelict crane which was alongside, and crawled through, backed by nine, very large men. Alex and Dick were outnumbered and taken back to Shivering Sands, four miles away.

Reg was unaware of the previous cat and mouse games played between Bates and Caroline South (Atlanta). Indignant at having his own men removed, he evicted the two men that Bates had left behind. Dick Dickson was put in charge with a small crew to help him install the new radio station with equipment including the Cossor transmitter and a generator. Bates returned when Radio City 2 was almost ready to begin broadcasting. The Radio City crew were sailed back to Shivering Sands and on the journey, Bates offered Dick a job which he turned down.

Reg was dismayed when he heard the news. Not only had his men been removed after all the work they had done but his broadcasting equipment had been left behind.

"Why did you leave the transmitter on Knock John?"

Dick Dickson looked blank. "I didn't think about it. We were told to leave."

"And you didn't think about taking the transmitter and generator?"

Dick shook his head.

Reg continued to ask questions, his voice becoming quieter as his anger and frustration grew. He stared, steely eyed at Dick, trying to make up his mind whether Dick had been genuinely incompetent or less than honest. Chewing his lip while he thought for a moment, he shook his head in disbelief.

"I think Dick, you should have thought. You know how difficult it is to find good radio equipment and transmitters. I think you should pack your bags and leave immediately."

Without the Cossor transmitter, Reg was unable to start a second station and when he got back to the office, he looked at various ways he could retrieve his equipment. Realising it would be almost impossible to board Knock John as the hatches would be closed, Reg looked at alternative ways of getting aboard. He had no intention of risking life and limb but considered flying in by helicopter and landing on the roof. In the end, he decided against it.

A few days later, 27th October, 1965 Radio Essex began test transmissions from Knock John towers. Dick Dickson accepted the offer of work with Roy Bates and reports came back that Reg's equipment had been thrown overboard. Even with evidence of theft, the towers were outside British jurisdiction and unless Reg was prepared to use force, which he was not, there was nothing he could do about it. Bates had won and Reg would play no more cat and mouse games in his quest to possess Knock John.

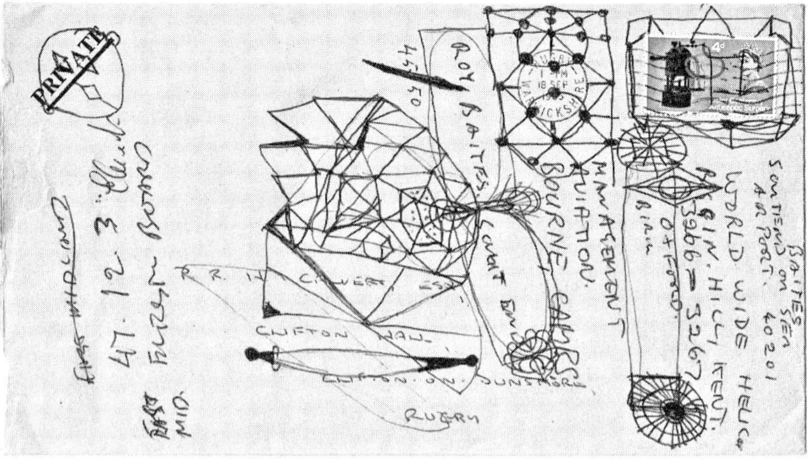

Manilla Envelope with Reg's scribblings and hiring a helicopter

Dick Dickson and Don Witts with the Cossor transmitter (EJ)

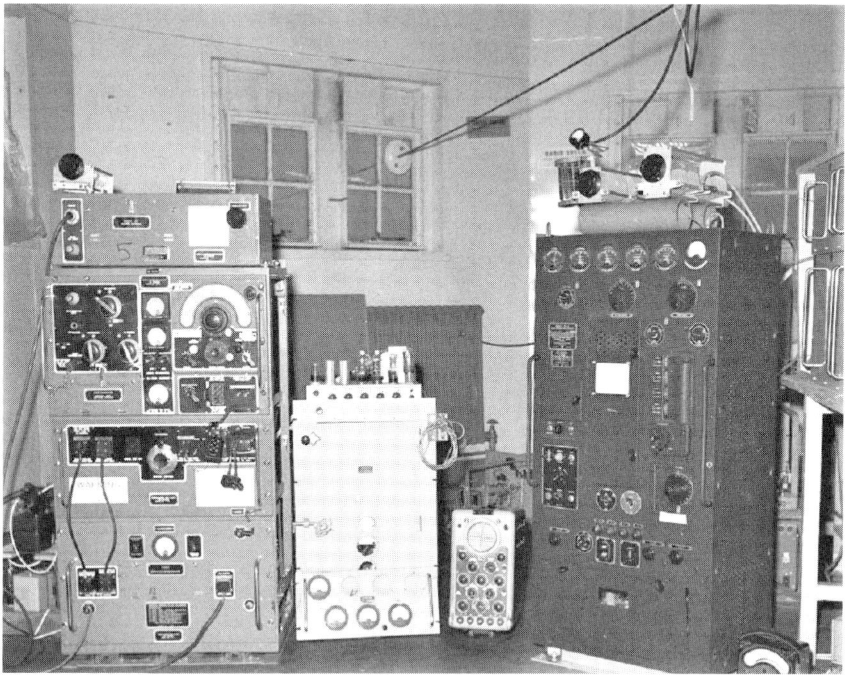

Radio City transmitter room: Left: Cossor which was left behind on Fort Knock John and was used to start Radio Essex, Right: Big Bertha. (E J)

Tony Pine and Don Witts with Cossor transmitter (EJ)

The date was set for Tuesday 12th October, 1965 for the 'new' transmitter to be delivered to Shivering Sands. It had been transported from Texas to Holland where the Caroline supply boat, Offshore One, was going to collect it. Radio City engineers had prepared for its arrival but when they saw the boat coming closer with three enormous wooden crates on deck, about 8ft tall by 6ft wide and 6ft deep, they shook their heads in dismay. From previous experience, they knew how difficult it was going to be to hoist up heavy crates the size of telephone kiosks.

Disc jockey, Alex Dee, was put in charge of working the crane handle. The first and largest crate was strapped up and slowly hoisted into mid-air. Everyone watched the lift apprehensively, the engineers joking, half seriously, that it was so heavy, it might pull the tower over. Alex stopped the crane when the crate reached the first level, about 70ft above the sea, expecting the automatic braking system to activate. Nervously, they watched as the crate hung for a second, dangling, and then began to descend, picking up speed towards the boat. The engineers yelled at Alex, "Brake, brake." Alex could do nothing. The brake would not work. Everyone watched in horror as the crate plummeted. The boat crew, seeing it was about to land on them, scattered, leaping out of the way as it crashed to the deck.

The next attempt to lift the crate went well until again, it reached the first stage but learning from the last episode, they did not stop the crane and pulled up as fast as they could. As the crate went higher, it began to swing from side to side, hit the fort, rolled over and fell towards the sea, stopping with a jolt as the ropes holding it got caught on the railings around the side of the fort. Everyone looked aghast at the crate hanging precariously. Quickly, the engineers set to work to untangle the ropes and pull in, but it was too heavy to hold and began to pick up speed as it plummeted downward. The skipper, anticipating an imminent disaster, manoeuvred his boat out of the way just in time and instead, the crate crashed into the sea making a monumental splash.

The engineers decided to try and lift the slightly smaller and lighter crate next. With great care, they successfully winched it up and in the same manner, they lifted the third crate.

When Reg heard that one of the crates was on the sea bed he arranged, at his own expense, to get divers out the next day from the Folkestone and East Kent Sub Aqua Club. The crate, imbedded in the sands by the tower leg was difficult to move. The divers managed to put straps around it and with a great deal of effort and skill, it was hoisted onto the tower.

The engineers immediately set to work on stripping down the relay and switching cabinet that had fallen into the sea. The components were washed in fresh water, dried and laboriously reassembled. Two Radio Caroline engineers, Carl Thomson and Ted Walters, were invited to help Ian West prepare the transmitter ready for use.

Phil Perkins watched their progress with interest but was sceptical.

"It's a load of junk and you're wasting your time. I reckon it's a homebrew hash-up of a commercial RCA point-to-point transmitter. It may have been used as an early ship-to-shore communication device but it'll never be any good."

The transmitter came with an engineering report describing the modification of KCUL's FCC approved 5,000 watt composite transmitter to increase power to 10,000 watts, but someone had penned over the 10,000 to make it 20,000 watts. The report included all the modifications of the original transmitter and performance specifications. "Except for the low voltage rectifier and the PA neutralization which is inductive, this transmitter is very similar to the RCA type BTA-10F."

Ian West who had joined Radio City at the end of August, ignored Phil as he continued to work on the transmitter. When the day came to test it, everyone who was involved with the station tuned in and waited for the power surge in anticipation of Radio City becoming the most powerful of all the 'pirates'. With everything connected, the new transmitter began to broadcast with a big burst of sound. Then nothing but silence. Within two minutes, the transmitter had broken down and the engineers quickly reverted to using Big Bertha.

To say Allan Crawford was disappointed would be to underestimate his feelings of frustration. Nothing had gone right since he had started Project Atlanta. To hear he'd been sold a 'dud' transmitter was the final straw. Radio Caroline South (Atlanta) was in serious financial difficulty with more bills coming in every day. He didn't want to reveal the truth to Reg that he, and the other directors, had optimistically pinned their hopes on the transmitter being good to turn their business around and save Caroline.

"It uses too much power," explained Reg. "I did say that I thought we'd need a larger generator."

"I've already spoken to George Cohen Machinery about hiring a 100kW Rolls Royce generator and I've got the specification here. Have a look, see what you think."

Reg quickly scanned the details.

"It says its 5 tons in weight and 12ft by 3ft by 5ft. It'll be very difficult to get onto the towers. Can you ask Cohen's to send me a copy of the specification and I'll speak to my engineers about where we can site it? Our hoist won't lift anything that heavy so we'll need a crane lift and we'll have to reinforce the floor."

"Okay," replied Crawford, slowly, realising that to hire a large generator and pay the cost of getting it to Shivering Sands would be expensive.

"I can't guarantee it'll work even with a more powerful generator. One of my whiz kid engineers is sure it's too old and the wrong sort of transmitter."

Crawford considered the situation and put on a brave face.

"It'll be worth a try," agreed Crawford. "I'll make arrangements for it to be delivered if you can check with your engineers about strengthening the floor."

Top: Offshore One, Radio Caroline tender boat (SH)
Bottom: Second-hand transmitter from Texas, purchased by Allan Crawford (RC)

15. HERE IT COMES AGAIN

Dorothy Calvert gardening at Macbeth Close (RC)
Cars: Trojan Bubble car, Triumph Herald and Ford Zodiac

Thursday afternoon, Reg opened the back door to Clifton Hall and made his way through the deserted house. Scattered on the hall floor lay a pile of letters. Scooping them up he browsed through, separating those addressed to him and those addressed to Dorothy. Taking them to the kitchen, he placed two piles on the grubby table and made himself a hot drink. It was the end of October and he shivered in the cold, aware of his own existence and loneliness as the stillness of the house shrouded him.

To warm his hands, Reg clasped the mug of tea while he meditated. There was no sugar bowl on the table in which to stir his spoon, round and round, only a crumpled, coffee stained Tate & Lyle bag. Reg smiled as he remembered the music and fun he'd had with his family and the boys who had lived with them at Clifton Hall. This time last year, he had nearly blown himself up with a firework and more cautiously, organised a firework battle. So much had happened since then. Now he had no place to call home and Clifton Hall was an empty shell.

Reg had married when he was 18, and by the time he was 22, had a wife and two children weighing him down. He recollected his boyish frustration and how he'd longed to be free. Now he was a man, he owned his freedom and knew he did not want it. On impulse, he picked up his coat and began to whistle, *I'm off to see the Wizard, The Wonderful Wizard of Oz.* Fifteen minutes later, he stopped his car outside 5 Macbeth Close.

Dorothy had bought a new, turquoise blue Triumph Herald and it was parked on the drive. It was the first time Reg had visited the house and he walked to the front door and rang the bell. After several minutes, he went to the side door and knocked. Getting no response, Reg wandered into the back garden. A cool, lemon-yellow sun hung in the sky above an old oak tree in the field beyond, momentarily sparkling as it broke through the layer of clouds. Reg squinted his eyes in the brightness and paused. Dorothy was digging a hole in the damp earth and his heart leapt as he watched her. She was casually dressed, wearing an old quilted jacket and baggy blue trousers, her hair tousled and windswept.

"Hello," called Reg, cheerfully. "I wondered where my grey socks were."

Dorothy looked down at her feet and frowned. "What are you doing here?"

"I rang the doorbell but no one was in."

"No, Candy's at School and Susan's started a job."

"I've brought your post."

"You needn't. Jill could have forwarded it."

Ignoring Reg's presence, Dorothy put her foot on the spade.

"What are you doing?"

"It's obvious isn't it."

"I'll do that. How deep do you want the hole?" asked Reg, taking the spade.

"I'm okay. I can dig," retorted Dorothy, as she took her spade back.

"As independent as ever," smiled Reg. "I've a copy of the Fortunes latest record. Have you heard it? It's good. *Here It Comes Again*."

"It's a bit like you. Here you come again."

Dorothy resigned herself to Reg watching her every move. She had hoped he would never come back but now he was here, she felt a tingle of joy which she tried to suppress. After digging the hole, Dorothy sprinkled grey bone meal into the hollow while carefully holding a rose bush in position.

"Shall I water it for you?" offered Reg, picking up the watering can.

"If you like," replied Dorothy as she covered the roots with a mixture of peat and soil before stamping on the loose earth to anchor the roots.

"Can I come in for a coffee?" asked Reg tentatively as he took the spade from her and leaned it against the side of the house.

Dorothy grudgingly agreed and the two cats who had kept Dorothy company in the garden, followed her into the kitchen, lithely twisting and curling between her legs in anticipation of their meal. William, who had been watching through the lounge window, scampered into the kitchen and screeched in displeasure at his enemy. Smiling, Dorothy scooped him up so he could settle on her shoulder with his tail curled around her neck.

"Did you see *You've Got Your Troubles,* went right up the charts?"

"Yes, I noticed. I was pleased for you," replied Dorothy.

"I couldn't believe it when it got to number three then number two. I was hoping it would make it to number one."

"Pipped by the Beatles."

Shall I play *Here It Comes Again*?"

"Can do. If you want."

"New radiogram I see," smiled Reg, as he lifted the arm and placed the record on the turntable. The refrain of *Here It Comes Again,* began to play. The lyrics were poignant and seemed to have been penned especially for them.

".....Here it comes again, that feeling, here it comes again. I find I'm cryin' over you. I know it's not the thing to do. Now I'm on my own, I walk alone, a heart without a home. Here it comes again, that feeling, here it comes again. ....."

When the song ended, Reg took the disc off the record player, put it back in its sleeve and handed it to Dorothy.

"It should go to the top of the charts and the B-side was written by the Fortunes so they will receive a good royalty," smiled Reg, proudly.

"I hope you get a good commission after all the work you've put in."

Reg said nothing in response as he stood and watched his wife.

"We're going to use *You've Got Your Troubles* as the distress signal on Radio City. The deejays will only play it if there's a serious problem, so if you hear it anytime, let me know."

"Oh yes, and how am I going to hear it in Rugby?"

"You might do, one of these days," grinned Reg, as he dunked a biscuit into his coffee. "Have you heard that I've merged with Radio Caroline?"

"What for?"

"The idea's to be part of the Caroline network and cover most of the country. Radio City will become Caroline South for the London area. The Mi Amigo will probably move up the East Coast to cover that side of England and Caroline North will remain where it is off the Isle of Man."

"Sounds okay in principle but what do you get out of it?"

"They pay the bills, organise sales admin and I get half the Radio City profits, plus a salary of £1,500 a month to run the technical side of all the Caroline operations."

Dorothy raised her eyebrows in disbelief. "That seems an awful lot of money. Too good to be true."

"We're already broadcasting Caroline advertising and news reports and they've supplied a huge transmitter from Texas but it uses too much power and keeps breaking down. Allan Crawford's arranging delivery of a larger generator to see if that might solve the problem. We also need a better aerial."

"I hope it goes well for you."
"Would you like to go for a meal at the Spanish Restaurant to celebrate?"
"No thanks."
"Or, we could see a film?"
"What, Peter Pan?" replied Dorothy, suppressing a smile.
"There's Mary Poppins or The Sound of Music."
"No Reg."
Dorothy stood up to indicate it was time for Reg to leave. Reluctantly, he made his way out of the back door and waved goodbye.
"I'll pop in again next weekend with the post."
"I'd rather you didn't. Please get Jill to post it," responded Dorothy as she shut the door behind him.

Reg ignored Dorothy's request about the post and began to make a habit of calling in to see her. It seemed that, no matter how rude she was, he persisted with friendly and polite conversation, telling her his news and bringing her gifts.
When the doorbell rang early one evening, Susan answered it, returning to the lounge with a large bouquet of flowers.
"Which boyfriend this time?" asked Dorothy, smiling at her daughter.
"Not for me, for you," grinned Susan, presenting the bouquet to her mother who immediately dropped them to the floor.
"Aren't you going to put them in water?"
"No. I don't want them."
"Really Mum! You can't let them die."
"I can."
"You know he loves you."
"I should have listened to my mother. When you get married Susie, make sure you marry an ordinary man who has a nine to five job with a regular wage, so you won't have to live a life of worry."
"You've told me that before. Boring, boring, boring. And live in a little house like this one? No thank you."
"There's nothing wrong with being ordinary or living in a house like this," retorted Dorothy.
Ignoring her mother's angry looks, Susan picked the bouquet off the floor, taking the flowers to the kitchen where she arranged them in a cut-glass vase. A few minutes later, she returned and placed the vase in the centre of the windowsill. Dorothy frowned as she glanced at the flowers, then at her daughter.
"I think it's funny," smiled Susan.
"You would," retorted Dorothy.

Susan sat down on the settee next to her mother and Katy jumped onto her lap and began to purr loudly. William was wrapped like a stole around Dorothy's shoulder and looked in alarm at the cat.

"Katy won't hurt you."

Dorothy spoke soothingly to her monkey while she stroked him. Blinking her eyes rapidly, she tried to stop the flow of tears that began to stream down her cheeks. Pulling a handkerchief from her cardigan sleeve, she dabbed her face.

"I was fine while he stayed away."

"But you love him. I can see you love him."

"But I don't want him anymore. I want a clean break and I don't want him to keep coming back. If he were dead it would be easier. I would know where I was."

"What an awful thing to say."

"You don't know what it's like. What sort of life will I lead if I go back? I can't control him and I never know what he'll do next. I'm constantly living on tenterhooks. I've tried to be reasonable, to let him have his head, but then he does stupid things like starting a nightclub and a radio station at the same time. We should make a clean break. But how can I be free when he keeps coming back? And he's promised to dig the garden. I could never get him to do jobs before but now he volunteers to do anything."

Susan listened quietly, stroking her cat, while her mother cried and poured out her emotions.

The following weekend, Reg rang the front doorbell and waited for Dorothy to open the door. Seeing Reg on the doorstep, she barred the entrance as he presented her with a large box of Black Magic chocolates.

"I don't want them. I'll get fat."

"More to cuddle," smiled Reg. "I came to tell you that the Estate Agent telephoned yesterday. He thinks they have a buyer."

"That's good. But you could have phoned to tell me that."

"I thought you'd like to go for a meal?"

"No thank you." replied Dorothy, abruptly.

"Can I come in for a coffee?"

Dorothy opened the door wider to let him enter and William screeched.

"Have you seen the charts? *Here it Comes Again* went straight in at number 18 and is now number 5, and *You've Got Your Troubles* is number 1 in Canada and number 7 in America. Can you believe it?"

"They don't deserve it, they're such an ungrateful group."

"It's only Rod and Barry who are sometimes difficult, the others are okay."

"I've heard that Rod is buying one of the new detached houses they're building on the estate," said Dorothy, with more than a little irony in her voice at the injustice of Rod being able to buy a larger house than she could afford.

"Yes. It's surprising. Since the boys left Clifton Hall, they seem to be settling down. They've been booked to tour Germany, Holland, Sweden and the USA. I was puzzling about their image. What do you think of dressing them as typical British gentlemen, bowler hats and the gear?"

"Could do. They're not exactly fashionable."

Reg relaxed back on the settee and put his feet up on a cream leather pouf. It was good to be with Dorothy again.

"We're having a problem finding the next good song. Barry keeps trying to write but nothing he's composed so far has been good enough. Now the Fortunes are successful, I might take on other groups as it'll be easier to get recording contracts."

"Why don't you think about managing the Liberators?

"Could do," replied Reg, thoughtfully. "And I've decided to start a publishing business. Having our office in Tin Pan Alley is exactly the right place to be. I've spoken to Terry and he'll organise the admin and we'll call it King Music."

"Sounds like a good idea," agreed Dorothy.

"Everything's going to be all right Doe Doe. I've a feeling that 1966 will be a really good year."

"Has Radio Caroline paid you for the work you've done or given you half of the profits?"

"Not yet," admitted Reg.

"Thought not, and what about the nightclub?"

"Don't let's go over that. I've still got it to do," replied Reg. "When the sale of Clifton Hall goes through, we'll be financially on our feet again. Will you come back? Live with me in London?"

"No Reg."

"It's not the same without you."

"It's no good. We're opposites. What I want and what you want are two different things. We need to start again. You on your own and me on my own."

"But you love me. We belong together. It's not right when we're apart," replied Reg, looking directly into her large blue eyes. "Please come back. I've been so lonely. Life seems pointless if you're not there. I'll try to be better. I know I'm not good, but I promise, I will try to improve."

"Promises, promises. I've heard them all before."

"I'll find somewhere nice to live in London," persisted Reg. "We can return to Rugby for the dances at the weekends."

"It's time for you to go."

Abruptly, Dorothy stood up and led the way to the back door. Her whole being yearned for his touch, to be kissed and held by him, but her head knew she must stay strong. Reg followed, and as she opened the door, a gust of icy air blew between them.

"Do you prefer being on your own?" asked Reg, as he stepped halfway across the threshold, one foot outside and one foot in the kitchen.

"I'm happy and at peace. My only problem is that you keep coming back," replied Dorothy, with just a hint of mockery as she firmly pushed the door to. "Goodnight Reg."

Not wishing to leave and with his foot in the way, Reg pushed the door open and stepped back into the warmth of the kitchen. Gently, he took Dorothy by her shoulders, circled her in his arms and kissed her.

Sheet music. The Fortunes were not 'trendsetters' so Reg dressed them as London city gents in bowler hats for their tour of the USA

Pinkerton's Assorted Colours on the fence at Clifton Hall.
Back: Tom Long, Samuel Pinkerton Kempe, David Holland.
Front: Barrie Bernard, Tony Newman (RC)

16. PINKERTON'S ASSORTED COLOURS

Pinkerton's Assorted Colours: Back: David Holland, Stuart Colman (replaced Barrie Bernard) Front: Tony Newman, Tom Long and Samuel Pinkerton Kemp (RC)

Reg returned to Macbeth Close the following weekend, lightly knocking at the back door before opening it to see his wife in the kitchen, preparing an evening meal. Putting his suitcase and radio down, he wrapped his arms around her waist and kissed the nape of her neck. William, displeased to see his enemy again, scampered from the kitchen and sat on the lounge windowsill, chuntering angrily.

"It looks like you're planning to stay tonight."

"I thought I might. I've got some good news for you. It was your idea," teased Reg, as he walked through to the lounge.

"What was my idea?"

"The Liberators. I've asked if they'd like me to manage them and they've agreed. They're doing well, organising their own gigs but I said we'd pay them £20 a week each as a retainer until they're established."

"That sounds fine," smiled Dorothy. "They can collect the money from me. Are you going to keep their name as the Liberators?"

"I've been thinking about that. To look different from other groups, they've dyed their jackets various colours. I thought I'd get new ones made and order black, tight-fitting trousers with no pockets so they can't stuff things in and spoil the shape."

"You could call them the Colours," suggested Dorothy.

"And I've suggested to Sam Kempe that he learns to play the autoharp."

"What about Kemp's Colours."

"Don't think so," mused Reg, as he began to suggest ideas for Dorothy to consider. "What about the Crazy Colours?"

Laughing together, they began the 'name' game as they both came up with ideas. Seeing a pack of pink rolls of toilet paper Dorothy had bought to match the downstairs cloakroom, she began to think of pink.

"What about Pink's Colours?"

"Nope, not right. How about Pink's Assorted Colours?" suggested Reg.

Eventually they agreed on Pinkerton's Assorted Colours.

"I'll suggest it to them and see what they say," said Reg, smiling. "Why don't you move to London in the New Year? You could stay with me during the week and come back to Macbeth Close at weekends."

"There's no way I'm moving to that grotty flat in Phoenix House."

"You could do it up, get curtains and carpets and things."

"No Reg. If you want me to move, you'll have to find somewhere decent."

Reg smiled. It was one step forward, a tentative agreement that Dorothy would live in London. Wrapping her in his arms, he kissed her tenderly.

"I'll ask Jill to get property details and I'll look for somewhere nice."

"I don't know what the girls will say about it."

"They'll love it in London, much more exciting than Rugby."

"Candy's just had her 15th birthday and she can leave school at Christmas. She has her first boyfriend now and he comes to the Kettering dance each week and they sit and hold hands."

"More trouble looming," laughed Reg.

"I don't think she'll be as much trouble as Susan. She's been seeing that photographer from the Rugby Advertiser?"

"He's much too old for her. He's nearer our age than hers."

"I've met him and actually, he's very nice. He hasn't called at the house for a while so I've no idea what's going on. She never tells me anything."

"I've an idea."

"No ideas. Don't interfere," warned Dorothy.

"I'll ask Ricky Michaels to take her out next time she's in London."

"Why?"

"I thought if a dishy looking American wined and dined her, she might think less about this photographer chap."

"You're mad," laughed Dorothy. "And I suppose you'll pay."

"Ricky's due to leave us soon and go back to America. The US draft board have written to say that if he doesn't resume his education he'll be eligible for military service in Vietnam."

"The fighting in Vietnam sounds terrible. I don't suppose he'll want to go."

"No, it's a pity he has to leave. He helps me with running gigs and organising sales. When he leaves, I'll need more help with the programming. That can be your job when you move to London."

Dorothy smiled, her eyes twinkling. "Oh yes. You know I said I wouldn't have anything to do with Radio City"

The Liberators had released a record in October called *It Hurts So Much*, composed by Tony Newman, but it had not made the charts and they were happy with Reg's decision to change their name to Pinkerton's Colours but were not keen on Assorted. Reg explained they could drop 'Assorted' when they were famous and people knew they wore different coloured jackets.

Finding a suitable song to record was Reg's next quest. He arranged for Pinkerton's to rehearse at Clifton Hall and showed them a song he'd composed but soon realised, none of Pinkerton's could read music. Instead, he set up the recording equipment with the intention of recording himself singing so they could play it back to learn it.

When Reg was ready, he began to sing *Heaven Knows* and the boys listened, joining in when they could, strumming their guitars. As the song progressed, they did their best to maintain straight faces. They considered the song very old fashioned and Reg didn't have a good voice. When he tried to reach the top notes, they all fell about laughing.

"If you don't like my song, try writing your own," spluttered Reg, bursting into laughter. "If you can write your own music, you'll make some money. It's the writers who become rich, not the singers."

The next time Tony Newman saw Reg, he tentatively played guitar and sang another song he had written.

> *'Mirror, Mirror, on the wall, Mirror, Mirror, on the wall,*
> *Who is the fairest of them all and in the mirror,*
> *I can see your pretty face.*
> *And now I'm sorry, what I have done to you.*
> *Those few harsh words that we are through. .....'*

"That's good. Very good," grinned Reg. "I like it. I'll arrange an audition at Decca and I know just the man to produce it for you."

Pinkerton's passed their audition and Reg made a request that Tony Clarke should produce *Mirror Mirror*. Tony had started his musical career performing with the Strollers, playing double bass, impressively but badly.

Roger James taught him to play bass guitar and Reg put them together to perform a double act, Rog and Ton. Clifton Hall had been a 'hothouse' for young musicians and Tony, with his eclectic taste in music, began to influence the others to listen to different genres. He had since changed musical careers and it was appropriate that Reg now gave him his first opportunity to produce a record in his own right.

The recording session went well and afterwards, Tony Clarke played the track back and asked Reg what he thought. In reply, Reg screwed his face up into a comical expression, making Tony laugh.

"Great, except for the backing singers. They sounded like three old cows. I seem to recognise them. Weren't they called the Vernon Girls?"

"They've changed their name to the Breakaways. They're usually okay, but I agree, they don't sound good on this. Would you like me to arrange another recording session with the girls from the Mike Sammes Singers?"

"That might be better," agreed Reg, still laughing.

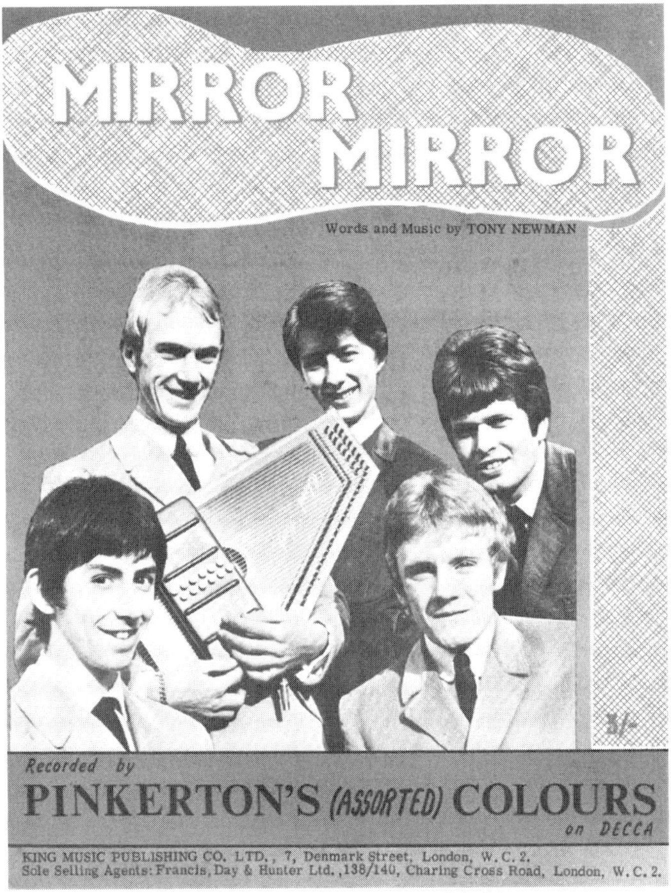

Sheet Music – King Music Publishing

17. DEMISE OF ATLANTA

As each week went by, Radio Atlanta/Caroline South, was getting deeper into debt. A wealthy sports promoter, Jarvis Astaire, indicated an interest in financing Caroline South and for a short time, Crawford was optimistic that everything would work out well. He arranged to hire the Rolls Royce generator and ship it from Burnham-on-Crouch in mid-November, however, his plans were scuppered when Harwich Customs barred the skipper, Ron Pipe, from delivering the cargo to Shivering Sands. Frustrated by the delay, Crawford made new arrangements to ship it with the London & Rochester Trading Company and have it delivered to Whitstable on 6th December.

When Jarvis Astaire pulled out of the negotiations, Crawford cancelled the generator. The financial situation of Atlanta/Caroline South had become so poor, O'Rahilly stepped in and arranged a meeting with the directors about the accumulation of long-term debts and complained they were giving Radio Caroline a bad name.

The planned merger with Radio City had failed to bring in sufficient revenue to keep the Mi Amigo afloat, forcing Crawford to resign his directorship of Radio Caroline. O'Rahilly took control of both stations, Caroline North and Caroline South, but his management skills were badly lacking and he was also in debt. Fortunately, one of the Caroline investors, Philip Solomon, stepped in and rescued the company.

Philip Solomon owned Major Minor Records and managed artists, including the Dubliners and the Bachelors. He paid off Radio Caroline debts but refused to pay debts incurred in the attempted merger with Radio City as he considered these were the responsibility of Crawford and Smedley.

Unaware of Atlanta/Caroline South's financial crisis or why the delivery of the generator had been cancelled, Reg was surprised when the wages cheque didn't arrive on 9th December and he spoke to Crawford who made excuses and eventually paid them.

The following week, money for the wages were again unpaid and two reel-to-reel tape machines that had been ordered from Brenell Engineering in Islington were cancelled as Crawford had not settled the account.

Guessing something was seriously amiss, Reg tried to contact Crawford at both the Caroline offices and his Dean Street office. No one knew where he was or when he would be back. Picking up a pen, he began to doodle on his desk's blotting pad, making honeycomb patterns in a corner while he considered what best to do.

"Jill. Can you make out cheques to the crew and ask John if he can take them to Whitstable? And keep trying Mr Crawford's office. If you get hold of him, tell him I've paid the wages and ask him when he's going to send a cheque."

The offshore radio pioneers had so many problems to overcome that few survived for long. The ones that did, hoped the government would eventually change its prohibition on free radio and allow them to have a land-based station. Pressure was put upon the government from large companies, including Radio Rentals, Pye Group and the Rank Organisation, who had joined with many small companies and individuals, to register their interest in obtaining a commercial radio licence.

Crawford had tried everything possible to make his station a success. Disheartened to have lost his dream, he took time out to recover his equilibrium before concentrating on his other business interests.

The promise of making large amounts of money had come to nothing. Smedley continued as Chairman of the defunct Radio Atlanta and began to buy up redundant shares from disenchanted shareholders for as little as a few pence each. He took over responsibility of the company and, in principle, agreed to pay the bad debts that had accrued from the merger. Both Smedley and the other director, Kitty Black, felt that Crawford had let them down by not negotiating a better deal with O'Rahilly. Disappointed but not defeated, Smedley still wanted a radio station and began instead to turn his attention towards Reg Calvert and Radio City.

Reg was so pleased to go home for the weekend and spend some time with Dorothy. He lightly tapped the back door and stepped into the warmth of the kitchen. "Something smells good."

"Mince pies, ready for Christmas. Do you want one?"

"Mm. I'd love two." Reg stood behind Dorothy and put his arms around her waist, shadowing her every move whilst nibbling her ear.

"Get off Reg Calvert, or you'll get flour on your suit," laughed Dorothy.

"It's good to be back. I've had an awful week."

"I've had a bad week too. Who'd have daughters?"

"I would," replied Reg, smiling.

"Candy doesn't mind but Susan's upset about moving. I told her she had to give her notice in and we had a big argument. She likes her job and said she'd stay here while we lived in London and I told her she had to move whether she liked it or not."

"That's a pity. Is Susan still seeing that photographer?"

"No idea. She's out most night going to evening classes."

"What for?"

"Studying for her A-Level art and O-Level in Biology and German. She wants to go to Art College. I've told her that Art College is for beatniks and drop outs and I won't allow her to go. But she never takes any notice of me."

Reg nodded his head in understanding and a little later, when they were both relaxing in the lounge, he began to tell her about the merger.

"When I eventually managed to speak to Mr Smedley to try and find out what was going on, he told me that Radio Atlanta was no longer connected with Radio Caroline."

"Nothing ever runs smoothly on Radio City. I suppose you didn't sign an agreement?"

"We shook hands on the deal and they were supposed to have had a contract drawn up but it was never completed."

"So, who's this Mr Smedley?"

"I never know whether to call him Major, Mr or Oliver," replied Reg, shrugging his shoulders. "He's in his fifties, ex-public schoolboy type, a chartered accountant and has been vice-chairman of the Liberal Party. He's into politics in a big way, believes in the free market and all that."

Dorothy raised her eyebrows. "Why does a retired Major want to be involved in pirate radio? My sixth sense. He doesn't ring true."

"From what I can gather, he has fingers in lots of pies. He knows people in high-up places and finds backers for small companies. He told me that he regards pirate radio as the last bastion of freedom if the country ever went Communist."

"Really! How much have they had off you?"

"About £8,000 and the company who transported the transmitter have sent me an invoice for £600 costs because they can't get payment out of Atlanta."

"You're a fool Reg Calvert to trust people. What are you going to do now?"

"Carry on as before and try to improve transmissions. We need a better aerial so I've just ordered some scaffolding poles and the engineers are going to construct a sort of tower. And Jill has details of a few apartments but I haven't had time to view. Why don't you come down with me on Monday and do some Christmas shopping and flat hunting at the same time?"

"I could, but talking about Christmas, I'd like to stay in a hotel this year so I don't have to do any cooking."

"Okay, I'll get Jill to book something," agreed Reg. "Do you have any ideas for unusual prizes?"

"Money and a big box of chocolates. No more piglets or donkeys."

"And no more monkeys," chuckled Reg. "By the way, could you buy me two pairs of very frilly lace knickers when you go to town?"

"Oh yes, and who are they for?"

"The competition, of course. You have a suspicious mind," laughed Reg.

Reg had a hectic weekend planned. Friday night, Pinkerton's Assorted Colours were to launch their new record at Nuneaton Co-op Hall. Saturday, Reg had to return to London to be with the Fortunes while they recorded their next song, *This Golden Ring,* and afterwards, to run the dance at High Wycombe with Pinkerton's on the show. Sunday morning, to the ABC television studios in Birmingham with the Fortunes who were being filmed for Thank Your Lucky Stars, to be shown on New Year's Day.

The following Friday was Christmas Eve which was a good night to run dances. Susan went to Nuneaton and appearing on the show were the Unit 4, Veldons and Caroliners. Dorothy and Candy went to Kettering with the Tea Set, My Generation and Cardinal Sins. Reg went to High Wycombe with Pinkerton's and the Flamingos. Mistletoe was hung above doorways, party hats, balloons and streamers were handed out and the season of goodwill spread like a golden glow as teenagers in party mode, sang and danced all evening until they had to go home at the witching hour.

Christmas morning, the Calvert family awoke early and ate breakfast of chocolates and toasted teacakes as they merrily opened their Christmas gifts.

"Come on you lot," laughed Dorothy. "You need to get dressed and be ready to leave by 10.30 or we won't get our Christmas lunch."

"I'm not hungry now I've eaten all those chocolates," grinned Reg, putting his arm around his wife and kissing her.

The Royal Garden's Hotel overlooking Kensington Gardens was palatial compared to anywhere else they had stayed. The girls were excited when they discovered, luxury of luxuries, all the bedrooms had a black and white television set and en-suite bathroom. After gorging themselves on Christmas lunch, they lazed on their beds watching television. By mid-afternoon, the family became bored and ventured out to walk in Kensington Gardens but the weather had turned cold and damp. After aimlessly walking around, they returned to the warmth of the hotel to wait for dinner.

Dorothy's dream of enjoying a lazy Christmas was proving a big disappointment and they soon became tired of watching television. All of London seemed to be closed and Boxing Day was the same. After breakfast on Monday the family were pleased to return to Rugby.

"I shan't do that again. I wanted to go to a country hotel, not a London hotel," complained Dorothy.

"Ah well, you didn't say and Jill wasn't to know. What's for lunch?"

"Bread and cheese," smiled Dorothy.

The telephone rang and Dorothy picked up the receiver. A moment later, raising her eyebrows inquisitively, she passed the phone to her husband. "Mr Smedley for you."

After a long conversation, Reg replaced the receiver and shook his head.

"He wants me to invest my money in a tax saving scheme he's organising in the Isle of Man. He believes we pay too much tax in this country and I can save money by investing abroad."

"Is the Isle of Man abroad?"

"Not really. I think you can do the same in Jersey."

"Did you tell him you've no money especially after your fiasco with him and Allan Crawford? I told you this Major chap doesn't ring true."

"He seems respectable enough."

"What, doing tax fiddles?"

"Don't all accountants fiddle tax?" replied Reg, thoughtfully. "I think I'll open an account in Switzerland so that money from overseas advertising and religious broadcasts can be paid in there. Save for a rainy day, like you do."

Dorothy and Reg Calvert (SC)

CALVERT FAMILY SNAPSHOTS

Above: Candy and Dorothy (RC)
Centre Left: Dave Davies, Kinks, with Candy (RC)
Centre Right: Reg laughing (SC)
Below left: Candy with William (RC)
Right: Susan (Mike Burnett)

18. TRAGEDY

During the winter months, living out at sea on Shivering Sands was only for the hardy. While gales howled, the towers creaked and juddered, but still the crew preferred being on them to a radio ship rocking and rolling in the waves. Listeners, sympathetic to their plight, knitted jumpers, thick socks and hats, to keep them warm. The engineers decided to collaborate on reinstating the fort's original central heating system. It was a challenge and as the boiler had been out of use for ten years, there was a serious concern it could explode. They told Reg they were going to try to get it running and after checking it out, Phil Perkins decided to do an 'outside' test.

"This is it," said Phil, nervously, as he fired it up. "Stand back everyone."

The next moment, there was an enormous sooty bang that resonated through the tower and far beyond. Large flames flickered up to the sky and everyone cheered as the boiler chugged into action. Within minutes, Reg received numerous phone calls from people in the Whitstable area who heard the explosion and thought the forts were on fire.

For a Christmas treat, Reg relaxed his no alcohol rule, allowing the crew to have a couple of bottles of beer each. On 30th December, Tom Edwards, broadcasting the late afternoon Beatles and Rolling Stones programme, happened to look through the window and saw a yacht heading straight for the towers. In alarm, he announced, "A ship is heading straight for us." Quickly, looking up information, he broadcast an appeal. "Please contact the GPO radio station at North Foreland to warn shipping that a yacht is out of control and needs help."

The engineers closed the transmitter and broadcasts stopped.

Everyone rushed from the studio and across the catwalk to the relative safety of the central tower, fearful that if the yacht collided with the structure, it could buckle and collapse into the sea. One of the towers had been hit before and the collapsed wreckage jutting out of the water was a constant reminder of just how unstable they could be.

The yacht was being pounded mercilessly by relentless waves and as it came closer, the Radio City crew saw the terrified faces of the passengers. There was nothing anyone could do to prevent the impending tragedy as treacherous white waters eddied in swirling whirlpools around the legs of the tower. The crew held their breath, waiting for the crash, knowing that if the yacht sunk, none of the passengers would survive for more than a few minutes in the icy water.

At the second of the expected collision, a strong underwater current thrust the yacht away, miraculously missing the tower leg as it headed off on another course out to sea and away from danger. Broadcasts resumed and news came through later that the yacht, the Scarab, and passengers, had been safely rescued and towed back to land.

New Year's Eve, Mrs Thomas sat in the ground-floor kiosk at Nuneaton Co-op Hall in readiness for the front doors to be opened promptly at 8p.m. Outside, a crowd were eagerly waiting to enter the hall. After paying their money, they made their way up the well-lit, wide dogleg stairway which opened to a broad passageway leading to the cloakrooms, ballroom, and at the far end, the stage door.

Jim, a small stocky man in his mid-70s, leaned on the balustrade at the bend in the stairs between the first and second floors, nodding at the young people as he took their admission tickets. By 10.30p.m. the hall was full and the entrance doors closed.

On the show were the Flamingos, Tea Set and Pinkerton's Assorted Colours. Susan had set the crystal ball to sparkle in the darkness of the dancefloor and girls jived and twisted together as they waited for boys to arrive after the bars closed.

Reg could see the dance was going well and prepared to start the first party game.

"Don't go into the hall while I organise this competition," grinned Reg.

"Why not?" asked Susan, curiously.

"Wait and see."

Reg put on his tartan slippers and rolled up his trousers. Walking onto the stage with a skip and a jump, he took the microphone and began to sing and dance the Wooly Bully by Sam the Sham and the Pharaohs.

"Uno, dos, one, two, tres, quatro,
Marty told Hatty about a thing she saw,
Had two big horns and a wooly jaw,
Wooly bully, Wooly bully.
Wooly bully, wooly bully, wooly bully... "

Flushed in the face and smiling broadly, Reg held up a pair of lace frilly knickers, waving them about as if they were a flag.

"Ladies and Gentlemen, girls and boys, are you having a good time?"

Reg waited for the response and repeated his question.

"Let's hear it again. Are you having a good time?"

When the loud cheering subdued, he held the knickers in front of his crotch and slid them sexily from side to side.

"Tonight, we have a fantastic crazy striptease competition. All you have to do is find the girl who's wearing a pair of these identical frilly knickers and bring them to me."

Laughing with glee, Reg called out, "One two three. Go boys go and all you girls, hang on to your skirts."

The music resumed and the girls continued to dance, laughing and giggling, as they held their skirts down. Within seconds, there were screams of laughter as boys ran amok in a hunt for the knickers.

Reg watched the proceedings but his sixth sense was prickling. Something was amiss and he immediately walked off stage to investigate.

The doorman let in a few latecomers, as he often did with people he recognised, sometimes in exchange for a tip. Jim, at the bend of the stairs, nodded at two young men, Lyndon and Peter, as they made their way up to the second floor to buy a drink. When they reached the bar, it was closed and they joined the crowd who had decided to go down to the dancefloor. In front of them in the bend on the stairs, a young girl, Pauline Swingler, tripped and fell. They paused to let her stand up but the people coming from behind and in front couldn't see what had happened and impatiently, began to push their way through.

"Wait here," Reg instructed his daughter, as he dashed out of the stage door and into the wide corridor. Immediately, he could see the problem. A large crowd of teenagers, singing and chanting, had congregated at the bottom of the stairway and were trying to make their way up. Reg began to pull teenagers back and tried to direct them into the ballroom. They laughed and ignored him. Returning backstage, he saw his daughter.

"Susan, quickly go up the back stairway and find the steward at the top and tell him there's a crush on the stairs. Get him to lead the kids down the backstairs. We have to get the pressure off the main stairs."

On stage, the group were playing as a young man jumped onto the stage holding up a pair of frilly knickers.

"Well done," congratulated Reg, as he patted the winner on the back and flamboyantly flashed a £5 note and waved him goodbye. Standing in front of the microphone, he announced solemnly, "Will the people by the stairs please come back into the dancefloor and stop pushing."

Reg repeated the announcement several times, to no effect. The crowd by the stairs could not hear him above the noise and had started to chant, "Push, push, push."

Susan ran to the end of the bar and seeing no steward, immediately took control, pulling teenagers away who were at the top of the stairs and leading them through the bar into the kitchen and down the back staircase. A stream of teenagers followed, much to the surprise of the tearoom ladies who were aghast at their kitchen being invaded.

"There's a crush on the stairs," called Susan, as she went to find the steward. He was standing at the back of the balcony, blissfully unaware of what was happening. Bemused by her urgency, the steward followed her to the top of the stairs and immediately realising the situation, began leading the teenagers away.

Susan ran down the back stairway and out of the stage door into the wide corridor. Her father was again on the stage asking teenagers to stop pushing and come into the hall. The crowd had now built up and was halfway back to the ladies' cloakroom. Hopelessly, she pulled first one teenager and then another, shouting at them above the din to go into the hall. Laughing and cheering, they ignored her and continued chanting, "Push, push, push". Realising the hopelessness of the situation, she returned backstage.

Reg came off stage and looked bleak as he quickly gave his daughter instructions.

"Susan, phone 999 for an ambulance. Tell it to go to the rear entrance as they won't be able to get in through the front door. Put your coat on and wait outside and show them where to come. I'm going to stop the dance."

The young people trapped in the centre of the crush were hanging onto life. People from above and behind had formed two walls and pushed against each other. Some lost consciousness and were trampled on.

The man standing next to Lyndon, realising he needed air, spread out his arms and gave a big push to make space. Air rushed into his lungs and he gulped a breath. Everything went black and when he awoke, he had no sense of time or even that he had been unconscious. Smelling the stench of sick, he realised someone had vomited down the back of his jacket. Unsteadily, he went down the stairs and seeing Jim, called out, "I'm going home to get changed. I'll be back shortly."

"I don't think you will, lad," replied Jim, solemnly.

Pinkerton's Assorted Colours were watching the show from the balcony and completely unaware of the drama unfolding on the stairs. They were due to be the last group on and as it was near the time for them to perform, they made their way down the backstairs, passing through the almost deserted bar. As they reached the stage they heard Reg announcing that the dance was closing. The main ballroom lights were switched on though many teenagers, unaware of the crush, stood waiting for the music to resume.

Susan stood by the back entrance and led the ambulance men up the stairs to the main hallway. Quickly, they went backwards and forwards, lifting people and carrying them on stretchers to the office floor. Some recovered quickly and made their way home. Others did not and were taken to hospital.

It took a time for the disappointed crowds to leave the hall and when all was quiet and the groups had packed away, Reg drove home in shock. He made no conversation with his daughter but she heard him say over and over to himself, as if she were not there. "It could have been Susan. It could have been my daughter on the stairs. It could have been Susan."

When they reached Macbeth Close, Reg slumped on the settee. Susan, realising he wanted to be left alone, quietly picked up her cat and went to bed.

Dorothy was in a good mood when she returned from Kettering with Candy. Seeing Reg's face, grey with worry, she asked cheerfully, "What's up with you?"

Reg made no reply as she went into the kitchen to put the kettle on.

"Would you like a drink and something to eat? I've bought some gorgonzola and pickles."

"No thanks. How was your night?"

"Packed out. Everyone had a fantastic time." Dorothy paused as she observed Reg's expression. "Are you feeling all right? Are you going down with flu or something?"

"I'll tell you in a minute," replied Reg, beckoning for Candy to go to bed.

"Happy New Year," replied Candy, yawning.

For a few minutes, Reg did not speak and when he did, his voice was cracked and almost inaudible.

"There was an accident. A terrible crush. I had to stop the dance. They kept pushing and pushing and I couldn't pull them off." Reg paused to clear the lump in his throat. "It could have been Susan. It could have been our daughter. I'm sure some of them were badly injured. I saw them on stretchers as they carried them out. It could have been Susan on those stairs and it's all my fault."

Realising the seriousness of the situation, Dorothy gently asked, "Start from the beginning. Tell me what happened."

Collecting his thoughts, Reg explained how he had sung the Wooly Bully and the laugh he got.

"If I hadn't started the competition just when the bar was closing, maybe there wouldn't have been so many people on the stairs. It was a stupid thing to do with kids wanting to go up for a last drink and others coming down for the competition. It was my fault Doe Doe. Do you know, I prayed to a God I don't believe in. I prayed it was a dream. I kept trying to turn back the clock, trying to work out in my mind why it had happened.

You can't blame yourself. You weren't to know."

"I should have known. It feels like a bad omen. A bad way to start 1966."

After a sleepless night, Reg tuned the radio to the BBC Light Programme and waited for the early morning news. What he feared most had happened. Four young people had died on the stairs, Joseph (Peter) Peare, aged 22, David Greenway, 19, Pauline Swingler, 16 and Keith Harding, 15. Others were badly injured and in hospital.

Reg lay back down with his eyes wide open and stared at the ceiling. A moment later there was a loud knocking on the front door. Dorothy automatically jumped out of bed and put on her quilted dressing gown. The knocking continued as she ran downstairs. Opening the front door, a shower of flash lights went off in her face.

"Can we speak to Mr Calvert? Is Mr Calvert in?" called the mob.

Dorothy, shocked to see a crowd of journalists, immediately shut the door and shouted, "Go away."

All day, Reg sat disconsolate while Dorothy shielded him from unnecessary callers. The hall manager phoned, very concerned about the tragedy and after some discussion, Reg agreed to say there were 926 teenagers in the hall that night, fewer than the actual 1,200 tickets sold.

SUNDAY MIRROR, January 2, 1966 PAGE 5

There were 926 people in hall for 900, says organiser

TEENAGERS FACING A QUIZ AFTER HORROR AT DANCE

Sunday Mirror Reporter

THEATRICAL agent Reg Calvert, 37, promoter of the New Year's Eve dance at which three young men and a girl died, said yesterday: "It is a disaster. I wish I knew what caused it."

Mr. Calvert was speaking after spending two hours with police investigating the cause of the accident at the Co-operative Hall in Nuneaton, Warwickshire.

It happened during a crush of people passing up and down a staircase leading from the balcony to the dance floor.

A section of the handrail was torn from its bolt.

Chief Superintendent Leslie Marlow said later that there was no rowdyism.

He added: "When the police got there there was a hell of a crowd and they had a job to get the dead and injured out through the crush and into ambulances."

Scores of teenagers are now being questioned by police to try to find out what caused the panic on the stairs.

INJURED
Colin Graham, 18: "Girls were screaming. Then I collapsed."

Pauline Swingler, 16 —died in the crush

Jack Buckby: manager of the dance hall.

Handrail broke

the stairs and going down and no one would give way.

"I collapsed and nearly suffocated as I was trampled on, and girls were screaming because they were getting crushed.

"I don't remember any more because I became unconscious."

VALERIE GRIMES, 18, of Tryan-road, Nuneaton, who was treated for cuts and ... shouting and scrambling to get over me."

THOSE WHO DIED were Joseph Brian Peare, 25, of Constance-close, Bedworth; David Greenaway, 19, of Eastfield-road, Nuneaton; Keith Harding, 15, of Barton-road, Nuneaton, and 16-year-old Pauline Swingler, of Fife-street, Nuneaton.

INJURED
Valerie Grimes, 18: "People scrambled to get over me."

Top: Nuneaton Co-op Hall. Below: Daily Mirror feature 2nd January, 1966

19. JANUARY 1966

Reg had booked Pinkerton's Assorted Colours to do a short tour of Scotland, appearing at the Lido Ballroom, Balloch, with the Sensational Alex Harvey Band. Unlike the Nuneaton dance, there were sturdy bouncers on the door to manage the crowd. On Sunday 2nd January, Pinkerton's were to be filmed at the BBC Stramash studio in Glasgow and Reg flew up to be with them. He did his best to put on an appearance of being relaxed and made no mention of the tragedy at the Co-op Hall.

It was to be the last of the weekly Stramash shows which had been running for over a year. While performers waited to be filmed, Reg chatted to various artists, including Adam Faith, who complained that the business was not how it used to be. In the dressing room were three attractive girl singers and seeing their potential, Reg suggested he could manage them.

"I'm the only person outside of the Jewish fraternity who can give you a hit record," joked Reg. "Think about it. If you decide to accept, you can call me at King's Agency in London and we can discuss it further."

Filming was over by 9p.m. and after a late meal and a few hours' sleep, the next day they awoke early to catch a 5 a.m. flight from Glasgow to Heathrow airport. With moments to spare, they were ushered straight onto the plane, each carrying a guitar and most of the drum kit. From Heathrow they caught a taxi and arrived at the BBC studios in Lime Grove, London, to be filmed for Blue Peter.

Dorothy drove to the office in London with her daughters. It was the day she and Reg had planned to be together to start their new lives in the city but when Reg returned from Glasgow, after only a few hours' sleep, he was brusque and irritable. With the stress of the New Year's Eve trauma combining with the collapsed Caroline merger, he was mentally and physically drained. In the evening, the family ate in a small, inexpensive café and afterwards, Reg and Dorothy caught a taxi to meet Tony Clarke at the Old Father Thames pub to discuss Pinkerton's next recording session.

It was rare for a new group to make it into the top twenty and everyone was thrilled when Pinkerton's, *Mirror Mirror*, reached number 8 in the charts but finding a new song to follow was proving difficult.

Pinkerton's were booked into the Decca Studios, West Hampstead, and given a ground floor office to rehearse prior to the recording session. In an adjacent room, Tony Hancock was trying to hear his tapes and became irritated when he heard them practicing and complained, "I can't get any peace with yobos in the next room." Each time the group started to play, he sent someone round to ask them to be quiet, which for a pop group, was an impossible request.

The songs Reg and Tony Clark agreed should be on Pinkerton's next record were, *Don't Stop Loving Me Baby,* written by Tony Newman and on the B-side, *Will Ya?,* composed by Reg.

The family were sleeping in Reg's flat above the Phoenix Theatre. It overlooked the busy Charing Cross Road and the living room was cheaply furnished with single beds, small table and chairs, and a black-and-white television set. In one corner was a partitioned kitchen area with a fridge, cooker, sink and several cupboards. Next to the kitchen was a small internal hallway leading to a double bedroom and a toilet cubicle. There was no bathroom to wash, other than the kitchen sink. At the windows, instead of curtains hung dark brown Army & Navy Store blankets.

Traffic noise and hubbub of the city permeated the flat and it was difficult to sleep. Susan and Candy had never experienced the seedier side of city life and the first time they heard a girl screaming, they jumped out of bed to peer out of the window. Running down the centre of the road was a scantily dressed young woman being chased by a man wielding a knife. In the street, people were waiting at bus stops and others were walking by. No one looked at the girl and no one went to help. Two nights later, the same episode was repeated. The third time, the girls stayed in bed, pulling blankets over their ears to block out the screams. When they asked their mother why no one helped the girls, she shrugged her shoulders and explained they were prostitutes.

Dorothy was spending her days searching for somewhere to live and soon realised that to find an apartment in central London was going to be difficult.

"We could buy a house?" suggested Dorothy.

"Could do, if you can find one somewhere near the office."

"You know very well there's nothing we can afford around here. But we could live a little further north of the centre so it's easy to return to Rugby. Most of the apartments are asking several thousands in key money and we could put that towards a deposit on a house."

"Mm," replied Reg, not committing himself either way, his mind elsewhere.

Letters had begun to arrive in the office, requesting that Reg pay the debts Atlanta/Caroline South had incurred during their merger. In response, he dictated a standard letter for Jill to send to suppliers, explaining that Radio City was taken over by Radio Caroline on 1st October, 1965 and they should forward their invoices to Atlanta Projects Ltd, 6 Chesterfield Gardens, W.1. From 1st January, 1966, King Music Limited, would assume responsibility for all amounts due on behalf of Radio City.

John drove Reg to Whitstable on Monday and during the sea crossing, Phil Perkins and Chris Cross (Mulloch), explained they had set up their own limited company, 'Offshore Maintenance' and would in future be invoicing Reg for their services. The idea was to reduce income tax by being self-employed and Phil had asked other members of Radio City staff if they would like to join him, but did not, however, ask Paul Elvey, as Phil mistrusted him.

Reg was astonished. "I'm sorry, you'll have to resign your position and leave Radio City on Friday."

"Let me explain," said Chris.

"No, let me make it clear, you can't start your own company and work against me."

"But we're not working against you," protested Phil. "We'll work just the same, the only difference is that you will pay the company directly."

"I've said no and I don't want to discuss it any further."

None of them wanted to leave Radio City and Tony Pine and Ian West, who were not company directors, were reinstated. Letters were sent on 26th January, to Chris Cross and Phil Perkins, giving them notice and wishing them every success with their Servicing Company. He also sent a letter to Paul Elvey, explaining the situation, asking him to act on his behalf and inform Phil Perkins on Friday that he should collect his personal belongings and see that they are taken off the station on the Friday boat.

On receiving Reg's letter, Chris Cross replied the following day, explaining he was Company Secretary as no one else felt willing, or able to take on the position. Realising it was unacceptable to Reg, he intended to resign and take no further part in the company.

Chris hoped that Reg would re-instate him, but this was not to be. Reg had already offered a week's trial to an Australian, Ian MacRae, who had just arrived in England and was looking for work.

The inquest into the tragedy at Nuneaton had been called for Wednesday 19th January.

Reg, who had no experience of these sort of proceedings, realised he would have to face the families of those who died that fateful night. Although it had not been his direct fault, Reg felt responsible for the tragedy and it weighed heavily on his mind. The Co-op management were also anxious. They employed the cashier and stewards and were responsible for providing adequate staffing, which on the night, had been badly lacking. The Co-op was not going to admit this, or acknowledge that if Reg had not acted so quickly, many more young people could have died.

The Coroner, in his summing up, said, "We have heard the story of this shocking tragedy which brought sorrow to the town at the end of last year. "*.... Four young people died of asphyxia due to compression of the lungs. The accident did not lie in any one factor or any one person. It was a mixture of small irregularities. ....*"

As soon as the inquest was over, Dorothy drove Reg to the BBC Television studios in Shepherd's Bush where Crackerjack was being broadcast live at 5 p.m. with an audience of children. Pinkerton's were the stars of the show and after filming, for fun, the group asked the presenter, Leslie Crowther, if they could have a Crackerjack pencil each as a souvenir. Apologising, Leslie explained that the BBC didn't provide any spare pencils as they were only given out to prize winners.

Dorothy arranged a second viewing to show Reg and her daughters an attractive, three-bedroom apartment in St John's Wood Court she had found. After viewing, Dorothy was happy and smiling.

"I really liked that apartment. Shall I make the arrangements to rent it?"

"No."

"Why not?"

"I don't want to live in St John's Wood. It's too far from the office."

"It's only a couple of miles and you can travel on the underground or catch a taxi. It's the best apartment I've seen and it's spacious. It won't take long to get to the office and it's the right side of London to drive back to Rugby."

"I've said no. I'm not interested and that's it."

"I've had it Reg Calvert. I'm going back to Rugby. If you want me to live in London, you can find us somewhere to live," stormed Dorothy.

At the weekend, Dorothy, in a mood, made a point of showing her displeasure and hardly spoke to Reg when he returned with their daughters. On Sunday morning, Pinkerton's were being filmed for Thank Your Lucky Stars at the Alpha Studios in Birmingham and Reg went out to spend the day there with Terry King.

Jim Dale, the compere of the show, tottered around in a pair of high-heeled boots he was wearing-in for his part in a pantomime and having a problem balancing himself, much to the amusement of everyone. Sandie Shaw, who always sang in bare feet, arrived, complaining about the new 70-mph speed restrictions on the motorways. When it was her turn to perform, Jim Dale rehearsed her introduction as the cameraman focused on her feet.

"Where else in the business would you see a pair of feet like these?"

Barry Bernard, Pinkerton's bass guitarist, could not help himself calling out, "Mike Nelson," and then began to laugh uncontrollably. Mike Nelson was famous as a frogman, (diver), and starred in the American action adventure series, Sea Hunt. Barry's laughter was contagious and soon everyone on set was laughing except for Sandie Shaw.

When Reg arrived back at Macbeth Close with Terry, they were pleased to find that Dorothy had prepared a meal for them.

"Are you coming back to London?" asked Reg, politely.

"No."

"I've found another flat. You could catch a train down and we could view it on Tuesday."

Tuesday, Dorothy caught the train to London and as she entered the office, saw immediately that Reg was in a bad humour. He nodded his head at her in recognition of her arrival but then, ignored her. With no idea of the problems her husband was experiencing, she waited impatiently and could barely control her temper until he finally said, they could catch a taxi to view the flat. By this time, Dorothy was in a very bad mood.

Reaching the apartment block, Dorothy took an immediate dislike to the unattractive front entrance. Following Reg into the flat, she proceeded to criticise everything she saw. After the viewing, Reg hailed a taxi and as they sat together in the rear seat, they argued vehemently, each as bad tempered and obstinate as the other.

"What do you think?"

"I don't like it."

"Why not?"

"It's not where I want to live."

"You're just being difficult."

"I'm not being difficult. I liked the apartment at St John's Wood and I'll only move to London if you find somewhere nice, otherwise, you can stay on your own. I don't want to live in that flat so there's no point in renting it because I won't come," shouted Dorothy.

Saying a curt goodbye to Jill, Dorothy returned to Rugby, leaving Susan and Candy to stay with their father.

Jill observed everything but said nothing. John, who had previously shared the Phoenix House flat with Reg, was now 'resident' on the office floor and Jill often saw him having a shave in the morning. Kenny Bell, who worked with Terry King, was more fortunate as he had the benefit of staying in a little flat on the top floor above the offices.

At the weekend, Reg's heart sunk when he saw Dorothy's car wasn't parked on the drive. Opening the door, he called out, "We're back," but there was no reply. The house was deserted, except for the two cats. This was the final straw in a very bad week. He had given some of his best Radio City staff the sack and his wife had left him, again. Weary, he went to bed to rest for a while. On the bedside cupboard Reg observed a black, leather bound diary with the page open on Tuesday's date. He read what Dorothy had written and mulled it over.

Tuesday, 25 January 1966.
Caught 8.31 to London. Reg very rude, as usual. Had quite enough of his resentment so caught the 7.30 train back to Rugby. Girls went ice skating. Candy worked switchboard of Agency, managed quite well. Reg supposed to have got a flat – surprise for me – surprise for him, I'm not interested.

Picking up a pen, Reg decided to continue the entries.

Friday, 28 January 1966
Went to Nuneaton. Came home early very tired, grateful for bed.
Candy arrived back 12 p.m.

Saturday, 29 January 1966
Went out shopping with the girls, bought Susan shoes, Candy wants to get some in London. Went with Susan to John Collier where she ordered a smart two-piece suit. My car would not start. Went in taxi. Amplifier not ready, went to Clifton Hall, brought equipment here to fix. Candy knows where Mum is but has promised not to say. Susan drove me to the dance and back. Tired, good to sleep.

Sunday, 30 January 1966
Wake 12.30. Susan has got the dinner ready, gone out in bubble. Candy is finishing off the cooking, eating about 2.30 then Susan will drive us to London. Candy and I going to the radio station Monday 6.30 a.m.
Hope to have flat soon. Present living conditions very bad but girls do not complain much. I am tempted to take a fabulous mansion flat, £1,400. Have not much time to find flat. Too much work. Must have better bed to sleep on. Susan made tea and now it's off to London 7 p.m. for another turbulent week – Would be nicer to stay in Rugby but there's something inside keeps pushing me on and on.

The following weekend, Reg was relieved to see Dorothy had returned to Macbeth Close and an uneasy truce reigned between them. Dorothy knew she had the upper hand and Reg accepted he could not make his wife move to London without first finding accommodation she approved of. Sunday evening, Reg returned to London with Susan while Candy remained with her mother and went back to School.

The family settled into a new weekly routine. Susan found a permanent job working as a receptionist for oil consultants, just off Sloane Square and after work each day, she met her father in his office. He was always happy to see her and they went together for a meal, usually to an inexpensive café or pizza place in Denmark Street and sometimes to film and recording studios to watch the Fortunes or Pinkerton's.

Susan disliked living in London. Not only was the flat uncomfortable, the walk to it was intimidating. Denmark Street was fine but as soon as she entered Charing Cross Road, seemingly respectable looking men would call out. "How much are you?"

The first time it happened, Susan was shocked and indignant. With her head held high, she ignored the men as they stared after her. Entering Phoenix House, there was no protection as more men loitered in the hallways or by the lifts and enquired, "How much are you?"

After several weeks, Susan decided it was time for her to find somewhere else to live. When she saw her father, she explained she was leaving. Instantly, she could see by his expression that he was angry.

"I've been to view a flat in Enfield and I'm going to share it with a teacher."

"Why?"

"I don't like living here. Every time I go out, men ask me how much I am."

"You can't go."

"I can. I'm old enough and I don't want to stay here any longer."

"I've told you, you can't go," insisted Reg, quietly.

"I can and I am," retorted Susan, defiantly. "You can't make me stay."

Involuntarily, Reg's hand went out and with force, he slapped his daughter across the face. Susan fell back and cried out with pain and shock. Reg stood motionless for a second, seeing the red marks he had made on her cheek. Furious with himself, he walked briskly to his bedroom and lay on the bed. He hadn't meant to lose his temper or hit his daughter. Almost certainly, she would leave him now.

Susan sat on her bed, even more resolute. When the pain eased, she went to the table and picked up her sketch book and began to draw. After an hour, Reg came out of his bedroom and sat next to her at the table.

"I've been thinking. I know it's difficult for you living here and if you agree to stay until the end of February, if I haven't found a decent flat, I'll pay for you to stay in a hotel. Would that be all right?"

Susan looked at her father and smiled. She realised he wouldn't apologise but could see by his expression, he was sorry.

"Yes, okay. I'll stay until the end of February."

"Good," replied Reg, relieved. "Let's go out and celebrate. I'll take you to a little French restaurant I know."

In high spirits, Reg and Susan walked from Charing Cross Road and into the Soho district. Susan had not entered Soho before and it was unlike the London she had seen. There were bright neon lights, nightclubs with uniformed doormen standing guard and girls lingering in dark doorways.

Even as they walked as a couple, arm in arm, girls stepped out of the shadows and tried to coax Reg to go with them.

Stopping outside the modest entrance to a French restaurant, Reg opened the door and ushered his daughter in.

"When a restaurant is good, it doesn't need to be showy," whispered Reg, as a waiter took their coats and led them to a table.

"What would you like to eat?"

"I'm not sure what anything is. It's all in French," replied Susan, smiling.

"Why don't you start with some escargots cooked in garlic butter?"

"What are they?"

"Snails," chuckled Reg.

"Uck, that sounds disgusting."

Reg ordered their meals and the waiter presented ten large snails, bubbling hot and prettily arranged in a silver dish. Susan looked at them in horror and began to giggle. Her laughter was contagious and soon, Reg was giggling too.

"I can't eat those."

"Of course, you can. This is how you do it." Picking up a little fork, Reg tugged the mollusc from the shell and popped it into his mouth. "Easy. Mm delicious."

Susan copied and closing her eyes, swallowed.

The two of them laughed and giggled as they had never done before. Reg noticed the other diners watching them and whispered to his daughter, "They think I'm your sugar daddy." This made them giggle even more and play to their audience. The earlier incident was forgotten and forgiven.

Above left: Hoist lifting luggage (RC) Right: Lifting crew (SC)

20. STORMY WEATHER

Radio City Aerials (EJ)

The Labour government received a lot of criticism about the 95 per cent supertax imposed on the 'super' rich which included the Beatles. George Harrison wrote the song, *Taxman,* which was to be released later in the year on the Beatles Revolver album.

If you drive a car, I'll tax the street.
If you try to sit, I'll tax your seat.
If you get too cold, I'll tax your heat.
If you take a walk, I'll tax your feet.

The consequence of high taxation meant there was an exodus of wealthy people going to live abroad or arranging to have money paid into overseas accounts. Reg, too, decided to save tax and made a trip to Switzerland to open an account for Radio City's overseas earnings, giving Dorothy the secret code, just in case something happened to him.

Phil's attempt to save income tax had failed and the saga of the Offshore Maintenance Company rippled on. Reg was sorry to lose him and wrote asking if he could design and develop a 'radio' microphone. Reg recognised the need for musicians and singers to be able to move about on stage while they performed. A wireless radio microphone was something that needed to be developed.

Reg had been hasty in giving his staff the sack and when Phil called into the office, he made his peace with him and was reinstated. However, the idea of radio microphones remained in Reg's thoughts and he decided to contact a company in Oxford to develop the concept instead.

Tom Edwards had been promoted to Senior Deejay and with the recent departure of Ricky Michaels, Alex Dee and Chris Cross, he was looking for more good disc jockeys.

In Australia, Ian MacRae had heard news reports of British pirate radio stations and how Allan Crawford had set up Radio Atlanta. In a quest for adventure, Ian had sold his car to pay for the passage to England on the Oriana. During the sailing, he met a group of girls and one of them offered to let him sleep on a settee in her flat when they arrived in England. With what little cash he had left, he bought a transistor radio to listen to the 'pirates'. Someone borrowed it and tuned it to 299 metres and hung it on the bathroom door. When Ian found it, he switched it on and heard the voice of an Australian deejay presenting the Dennis the Menace show. He thought the station sounded remarkably good and when Dennis gave out the address to send in competition entries, 7 Denmark Street, he decided to visit the office the next day.

Reg was in the office when Ian arrived and happy to chat to the young Australian about the station, explaining it was not on a ship but a wartime fort. He offered Ian a week's trial as a deejay and asked him to go to the Record Centre in Whitstable to see Eric Martin, the station manager. A short time later, he was on the Harvester with the change-over crew.

Arriving at Shivering Sands, he was shown around and gazed in wonder at the studio and transmitter room. It was not how he expected a radio station to be. The broadcasting equipment looked as though it was straight from the ark, held together with chewing gum and bits of string, but it all seemed to work surprisingly well.

The accommodation was on the first floor of the central tower. Reg had forewarned him it was basic, and it was. The bedrooms had bunk beds with thin mattresses and no one thought to take the bedding home to wash. With all men together, cleaning wasn't high on anyone's list of priorities. Ian, however, soon accepted life on the tower as homely, like a cosy slum. At the end of the week's trial, Reg approached him and asked how he'd got on?

"It was fine," smiled Ian. "But no one knows how to cook and the food was bloody awful."

Alan Clark regularly called into the office and often saw Jill to ask if he could go again to the station as a volunteer disc jockey. Sometimes he was lucky. He needed more experience and endeavoured to improve by listening and imitating other disc jockeys. Tom Edwards was not flattered at being copied and the other crew tactfully explained that he needed to develop his own on-air personality. Practice and persistence paid off and Alan was delighted when Reg offered him a permanent position. Surprisingly, it was his ability to imitate that was to make him an unusual deejay when he teamed up with Ian MacRae.

Ian soon established himself on the station by producing his own 'Monstrous Macca's Music Show'. Meeting up in a Whitstable pub with Alan Clark when off duty, the two of them began to bounce ideas off each other and discussed how they could produce a satirical show. They imagined an obnoxiously large woman who drove an E-type Jaguar and kept a bottle of gin in the glove box. Laughing at the idea, they named her Mabel and decided to call the programme the 'Auntie Mabel Hour'.

Ian and Alan went ahead with a trial broadcast without informing Reg. Fortunately, the programme received such good feedback, he encouraged them to develop the idea. Each day, Ian and Alan listened to BBC news broadcasts and they discussed together how they could put their own slant on events. They were both good at ad-libbing and over time, they became more outrageous. Sometimes, other deejays would join them in producing a programme, parodying songs, comic sketches, mimicking other programmes and with camp voices, doing a send-up of their rival station on Red Sands towers, Radio 390, and Eve Radio Magazine.

Fred Downs did not attempt to take his boat out during severe storms and sometimes the crew were left for a week, or more, with no new provisions and had to improvise. In a gale, the walk from the living accommodation to the studio took courage as the catwalk creaked and swung precariously from side to side as if it were ready to collapse. If it did, they knew they would not survive the drop to the raging sea. Even with the hardships, they preferred life on the forts and considered it infinitely better than being on a ship.

One very stormy night, the towers juddered and creaked more than normal with stormforce gales howling. Asleep in their bunks, the crew were abruptly awoken and feared the worst, believing the structure of the forts was disintegrating and collapsing into the sea. Outside, they could hear the terrifying sounds of clanging and banging. Switching on torches, they stood on beds to peer through windows. It was a black, starless night and they could see nothing of what was making the noise and crashing into the sea. The engineers agreed it was far too dangerous to risk going out to investigate and with a nervous sense of humour, everyone resigned themselves to the fact that this could be their last night together and tried to go back to sleep.

By morning, the clanging had ceased and at first light, the crew tentatively made their way outside. Laughing with relief, they saw the cause of their night-time terror. The towers had survived the beating of the storm and stood unscathed but Reg's improvised aerial had collapsed. The scaffolding poles had rained down, landed in various odd places, but most of them had fallen into the sea.

Disappointed his aerial had collapsed, Reg decided to investigate the possibility of having a proper one constructed and contacted Alan Arnold who ran a company called Arnold & Harris Ltd, at Dicker Mill in Hertford. Alan agreed to meet Reg at Whitstable quay and arrived in his E-Type Jaguar. He was a tallish man with a beard, of similar age to Reg and as they shook hands, they took an immediate liking to each other. On the sea crossing, they talked about their interests. Alan explained he had a heart condition but he enjoyed fishing and rough shooting and owned various shotguns and firearms.

"Do you mind if I do a bit of target practice while I'm on the towers as it's an unrestricted area."

"That's fine," agreed Reg. "I used to enjoy a bit of target shooting myself when we lived at Clifton Hall but I've got rid of my guns now."

After being shown around the forts and the makeshift aerial, Alan surmised that the station was being run on a shoestring.

"The aerial is dangerous as it hasn't been earthed. The problem with installing an aerial in this location is that the towers are high out of the water. With the rise and fall of the tide, it makes them 15–20ft above ground. The transmitter hasn't been properly grounded and is in effect, floating, causing it to go off frequency."

"That explains it," smiled Reg. "We get all sorts of whistling and strange noises and have to retune every couple of hours. Do you think you can build me an aerial?"

"I'm not sure. It'll be technically difficult and I'll need to check our legal situation. I'll let you know."

A few days later, Alan Arnold contacted Reg to say that he'd decided to take a gamble and build an aerial for him at a cost of £2,000. This was more than Reg wanted to spend and they came to an agreement. Reg could rent the aerial and pay £100 a month from his King Music account.

Reg was annoyed that Crawford and Smedley expected him to pay their debts when he had given them all Radio City earnings amounting to around £8,000. To try and sort the matter out, a meeting was arranged and Reg went to see Smedley at his office in Coleman Street on Friday 18th February. Smedley hedged around the problem of the debts and it was soon obvious, he would do his best to avoid paying them.

"You've got the transmitter we provided."

"Allan Crawford said it only cost about £700. Your engineers tried and couldn't get it to work and one of my engineers has spent the last three months working on it. Every time he tests it the transmitter breaks down within a couple of minutes. The only way we could manage to get it to function would be to power it with a much larger generator."

"I see," replied Smedley. "Perhaps we need to find you a generator."

"Even if we have a new generator, there's no guarantee it won't break down. The opinion of all our engineers is that the transmitter's too old and the wrong sort, it's a point-to-point transmitter and never going to be suitable for broadcasting."

Smedley was intent on having a radio station and with the demise of Atlanta/Caroline, had set his sights on Radio City. On the following Tuesday, Smedley invited Reg to lunch with a proposition.

"I have someone interested in buying Radio City. There's a businessman who's prepared to offer £10,000 for it."

Surprised, Reg shook his head, "I'm not thinking of selling. It's not enough. I wouldn't sell for that amount. I've already invested more than £10,000 in the station and as you know, we're making a profit."

"What about if we formed a substantial company?"

"There's no point in anyone buying a pirate radio station while the government are threatening to close us down. If the Labour Government are returned after the next election and Wedgwood Benn has his way, we'll all be out of business. It's pointless even discussing it until we know the outcome of the election."

"Radio City is outside British jurisdiction, so it'll be difficult to close you and it's a good offer. You should think about it," insisted Smedley.

The two men were from opposite ends of the social spectrum. Reg had come from nothing to make something of himself. Smedley, an ex-public schoolboy, had an air of superiority and was part of the establishment. He knew people in high places and had been Vice Chairman of the Liberal Party. His ex-wife, Eileen, remarried Harold Cassel, a criminal lawyer who one day, would become a judge and inherit a Baronetcy. Cassel had been a pupil of Hubert Parker, who was now Lord Chief Justice, responsible for the deployment of judges and President of the Courts of England and Wales.

Smedley, however, was not a wealthy man and his involvement with pirate radio was to make money and to free up the government's monopoly of information. He gave the impression of being a reputable chartered accountant and businessman, but his secretary, Pamela Thorburn, who was less than half his age, lived with him and for the sake of respectability, purported to be his housekeeper and children's nanny though both his children were teenagers. Smedley's personal assistant, Aubrey Boutwood, a 'retired' solicitor and company director, had been employed by Smedley for more than six years and they ran a charity for widows with no charitable account. Boutwood had a criminal record and had been to prison for committing bank fraud which resulted in a bank manager committing suicide. He had also failed to send in copies of company Annual Returns, carried on fraudulent business, induced a bank to give credit by false pretences, failed to keep proper books etc.

Reg was unaware of Smedley's other business dealings and when he received a further offer from him with a suggestion to start a company with capital in the form of 5,000 shares at one shilling each to be issued at £1 each, plus £20,000 in the form of 10 per cent unsecured loan stock, he was puzzled. He had never bought shares or dabbled in the stock market. When he showed the letter to Dorothy, she laughed.

"This doesn't make any sense. It's gobbledygook. A company with 5,000 shares at one shilling each issued at £1 is not a £5,000 company but a £250 company. And he wants you to take up half the shares. I told you he didn't ring true."

"He wants to be chairman and for me to be managing director."

"Has he paid the bad debts yet?"

"No, not all of them."

"I would tell him to pull the other leg."

Reg didn't like being pressurised but felt he had to listen and discuss Smedley's ideas while he waited for the debts to be paid. Reg had made it clear that he didn't want to sell Radio City so was surprised to receive another letter on 21st March, outlining a 'deadlock' agreement for this new company, proposing that in the event of any policy disagreement, one shareholder could offer to sell up, forcing the other man to accept an offer within 28 days. This meant that if Reg and Smedley held the two halves of the company, Smedley could offer his half to Reg at a stated price and if Reg did not produce the money, he would be forced to sell up to Smedley. It was more gobbledygook as far as Dorothy was concerned.

Dorothy had resigned herself to the fact that Reg had little time to go flat hunting and was surprised when he handed her details of a mansion apartment, 12a Welbeck House, Welbeck Street, London W1. The location was excellent, just off Oxford Street.

"Would you like me to ask Jill to arrange a viewing? "It's a lot of money and they also want £2,000 key money but it's the best I can find."

"That's enough to buy another house in Rugby," frowned Dorothy, as she scanned the details. "An evening would be good and I'll travel down by train and bring Candy with me."

All the family went to view the apartment and as they left, Reg tentatively asked whether Dorothy liked it.

"We'll need more furniture, new beds, bedding, more pots and pans and things," smiled Dorothy.

Reg gave his wife a hug, relieved at last to have found an apartment she approved of. "Okay, I'll give you some dosh to go shopping."

At the end of February, Reg kept his promise to his daughter and arranged for Jill to book her into the Carlisle Hotel. It was inexpensive and many of the groups who worked for King's Agency stayed there while they were in London. After eating her evening meal with her father, she caught an underground train to King's Cross Station and then made her way to Birkenhead Street. The roads were not well lit and her high heels clicked on the pavements, echoing in the dark. Susan felt nervous walking on her own in an area she was unfamiliar with and was relieved to find the hotel.

Mary Doherty, the Irish landlady, was expecting her and showed Susan to a clean but basic room, simply furnished with dark, old fashioned oak furniture. It was not a real hotel but a boarding house and Susan was disappointed. When Mary left the room, she hung her clothes in the wardrobe and then flopped disconsolately on the bed. Never had she felt so lonely. In the morning, she went to the dining room and sat on her own until a group of lively young men entered.

"We're the Geordies. Are you Reg Calvert's daughter?"

"Yes," replied Susan, shyly.

"Jill said you'd be staying here. I'm Billy Newton and we're staying for a couple of weeks. King's Agency are arranging our travel documents and contracts to work at a nightclub in Italy."

"That sounds exciting."

"It is. Can't wait to go."

Having the Geordies with their lively banter enlivened Susan's stay at the Carlisle and Billy Newton, their lead singer, immediately began to flirt with her. If they happened to be on their own, he did his best to kiss her but Susan resisted and always managed to duck away.

"Why won't you let me kiss you?"

"Because I don't want to," laughed Susan.

"Can I take you out? Would you like to go to the cinema?"

"No, thanks."

Susan was used to young men making advances and took it as light-hearted fun. She enjoyed Billy's company but was not interested in going out with him. She had grown up with musicians and singers and knew that most were fickle in their affections with a starstruck girl in every town they performed.

Reg arranged to take the lease of the apartment from 24th March, 1966, his 38th birthday. Dorothy began to make regular trips to London to go shopping to furnish their new home. There were three bedrooms, a spacious breakfast kitchen with a back door leading to the fire escape, two lounges and a large dining room.

As expected, the Labour Government called a snap General Election for the 31st March. David Sutch, excited by the prospect of more publicity, visited Reg in his office to discuss the campaign.

"I've decided to stand against Harold Wilson again," grinned David.

"Brilliant. You'll get fantastic publicity," chuckled Reg.

"Will you be my Campaign Manager?"

"I'd love to, but I've too much on. And you've never paid me for the previous expenses or 10 per cent commission for being your manager."

David was shocked. Reg had never asked for commission before although he had always paid for almost everything. That was the way it was.

"You wouldn't have Radio City without me starting Radio Sutch," retorted David.

"I think I would, but it wouldn't have been called Radio Sutch."

"I did a lot of work on the station and I paid for my men to stay on and look after it when you weren't there. I should get a commission out of the profits you're making."

Reg was quiet while he considered.

"I'll tell you what I can do. I won't charge you 10 per cent and I'll ask John Wileman if he'll be your Campaign Manager, providing you agree that Radio City belongs to me and you have no claim to it."

David accepted Reg's terms and Jill typed out an agreement for David to sign, stating he had no claim to ownership or part ownership, or any interest in the offshore Radio Station based on Shivering Sands.

Dorothy was angry when she heard that Reg had agreed to help David at the next election.

"I don't know why you do it. He's never appreciated the work you've done or paid you a penny. You're rushed off your feet and if you have any free time at all, you should be spending it in Loughborough, not with David Sutch. The nightclub is costing us thousands, all because you're too busy."

Reg shrugged his shoulders. "I'll get David to pay the expenses this time?"

"That'll be the day."

"I've persuaded John to be Campaign Manager and Jill will be the Election Agent. They'll go up to Huyton to organise everything."

"And who'll pay John and Jill's wages?"

Reg shrugged his shoulders in response and said he would get Jill to invoice. He would have relished the thrill of the election campaign if he hadn't been so busy. As it was, John travelled to Liverpool and found a suitable office to rent at 6 Derby Road, Huyton. It doubled up as an office and somewhere to sleep at night. It was a hectic two weeks and David continued his campaign for teenagers to get the vote at 18 and for free radio.

The family moved into Welbeck House on Sunday 27th March. The next day, Reg told Dorothy that he'd decided to go to Huyton on Thursday.

"That's not a good idea," frowned Dorothy. "You've forgotten it's my birthday. Not only that, you'll be up all night and you've arranged our housewarming for Friday lunchtime."

"I just want to see the count," smiled Reg. "I'll be back for lunch."

"Who's going to organise the party? Make the food, get the drinks in?"

Making no reply, Reg stood up and gave his wife an affectionate kiss on the cheek. He knew he could rely on her to do it, even though she was cross.

It came as no surprise that Harold Wilson retained his seat and David was elated to come third, with 585 votes. After the razzmatazz of the final day of the election campaign and staying up late to see the count, John, Jill, David and Reg returned to London to go to the flat-warming party which turned out to be a quiet affair with only a few people turning up. When everyone had left, Dorothy quickly tidied up and the family travelled to Macbeth Close for Reg to run the Friday night dance.

Shortly after the family's move to Welbeck House, John and Jill revealed that they had just married. No one had guessed about their relationship, not even Reg.

Jill had kept an account of the election expenses and forwarded it to the Huyton with Roby Urban District Council. It included the office rent, posters, a van as a mobile election office, printing of the manifesto, a drinks reception, and numerous other items. The total came to £233. 9s 9d. Other expenses not covered were invoiced to David, including paying Jill and John's wages at £20 per week each. David, of course, disputed them.

The Labour Party, gaining a 96-seat majority, were victorious. There was nothing in the Labour Party manifesto about bringing in commercial or local radio and the campaign for 'free radio' had fallen on deaf ears.

Mrs Garforth, Glen Dale's mother, telephoned the office from a phone box the day before the Fortunes were due to fly to Holland on 10th March. She was very distressed and asked to speak to Richard, (Glen). Her husband had been taken seriously ill and was in hospital. Jill explained that Glen wasn't in the office but she would ask Mr Calvert to get a message to him.

The following day, Mrs Garforth phoned again, to ask why Richard had not arrived. Reg spoke to her and explained that Glen had flown to Holland with the Fortunes.

"But he should be here, with me, and see his father," cried Mrs Garforth.

"I understand," replied Reg, sympathetically. "I'm sorry Mrs Garforth. He has a contract to fulfil and couldn't just cancel it. If important artists like the Fortunes, break contracts at short notice, they would be sued. The only excuse for not turning up is if the artists themselves are critically ill and unfit to travel. I can assure you he will be with you as soon as he can come."

Nothing Reg could say would placate Mrs Garforth. She wanted her son with her.

"You're only interested in making money, not in anything else."

Reg was upset by the outburst and tried to explain but Mrs Garforth was too distressed to listen. After pondering for a while what to do, he dictated a letter for Jill to post to her, explaining in more detail that he had contacted the hospital and understood that Mr Garforth's illness could end suddenly or continue for up to three months. Glen had had to make a difficult decision. Whether to go to the hospital and break his contract in Holland, which could cost the Fortunes many thousands of pounds in compensation, or, honour his commitments and take the terrible risk of not being with his family at a critical moment.

When Glen returned from his tour abroad, it came as a shock when he asked Reg to find a replacement. Glen had never wanted to be in a harmony group but Reg had thought he had settled down and was happy with the group's success.

"It would be madness to go now. The Fortunes are at the top of their game."

"My wife doesn't like me to be away."

"But she knew when she married you that you'd need to go on tour. Can't your wife put up with it while you're so successful?"

"No, she really doesn't like it."

"What do you plan to do if you leave the Fortunes?"

"Become a solo singer and make a record."

"You do have your own spot with the Fortunes so you're still a solo singer."

"It's not the same Reg."

"It may not be the same. It's better. If you go it alone, you'll find it hard. How many singers do you know that make it nowadays? Solo singers are out of fashion. It's all groups. You're earning fantastic money so surely your wife can put up with it?"

Glen shook his head in response.

"Does she realise that if you go solo, you'll still have to tour?"

"Sorry Reg. I've made up my mind but I'm not in a rush."

"Okay, I'll start looking and if you want to make a record, I'll help, but you need to find a good song."

Managing two top recording groups took a great deal of Reg's time and effort. Success came at a cost and one of Jill's responsibilities was to keep an account. Pinkerton's promotional advertising, December to January, amounted to £292. 10s 6d. By comparison, the Fortunes expenses, January to March 1966, amounted to nearly £4,000 and included new microphones, new suits, advertising, photographs, printing and various other items plus the travelling costs to the USA, Amsterdam and Scotland. Reg paid the accounts in advance of the groups repaying him from the bookings they received.

Pinkerton's second record, *Don't Stop Loving Me Baby,* was slow to go up the charts and received less publicity than *Mirror Mirror.* Knowing how important it was to keep the momentum going, Reg pondered on the song's lack of success. Whenever possible, he tried to come up with zany ideas to attract attention and get free publicity.

"What do you think of Pinkerton's colouring Trafalgar Square fountains?"

"Don't be ridiculous," replied Dorothy. "Pinkerton's will be prosecuted."

"That's the idea. It won't cost much and it'll be worth it for the publicity. Just wait till I tell them."

Not surprisingly, Pinkerton's were reluctant but Reg's laughter was contagious. He ordered dyes and had boxes of them delivered to his office. One fine sunny day, with Pinkerton's wearing their bright coloured jackets, they strode out together down Charing Cross Road and to Trafalgar Square. The group felt very conspicuous as they walked through the throng of tourists and headed for the fountain. To Reg's dismay, and Pinkerton's relief, the fountain had been turned off for cleaning.

"Never mind boys," said Reg, cheerfully. "Let's find a park and dye some fountains there."

The group walked down the Mall and into St. James's Park. There was plenty of water in the lakes, but no suitable fountain. They continued walking and passed by Buckingham Palace and into Green Park. By this time, everyone was weary, except for Reg, who considered the situation.

"Not a fountain in sight. If we keep walking, I think Hyde Park is in that direction. There must be one in there."

Pinkerton's, tired of walking across London, carrying boxes of dyes and cynical of ever finding a suitable fountain, joked between themselves as they trailed behind Reg. Reaching Hyde Park, they saw the canal and Serpentine but no fountain. Reg stopped and shook his head in disbelief.

"Shall we go back now?" asked the boys, relieved.

“Do you think that might be a fountain over there? I think that’s Park Lane,” said Reg, enthusiastically as he walked in the direction of his sighting. Reaching it, he smiled. It was a splendid fountain. Two bronze figures holding hands, seemed to dance above the spray of water in the centre of the pool and four bronze children danced around them. Pausing for a moment, he read the sign.

“They’ve named it the Joy of Life Fountain. What do you think boys, maybe some red will make it very joyful?”

Seating himself on the low wall around the perimeter, he began to unpack a box of dye. Resignedly, the boys joined him. It wasn’t a busy park and there were few tourists.

“What do you want us to do Reg?”

“Make a bit of a kerfuffle to attract attention and then throw the dye into the water,” grinned Reg.

Pinkerton’s looked guiltily at the passers-by but no one seemed to be at all interested. They threw the dyes into the water and began to laugh nervously as it changed to a pink colour. They waited, expectantly for their crime to be exposed but there was not a policeman in sight to report their dastardly deed to. When no one came, they felt a mixture of relief and disappointment. This was one publicity stunt that had flopped, but for Reg, it was all in a day’s work.

“Ah well. Can’t win them all. We’ve plenty of dyes left and we can do it another day when they refill the fountain in Trafalgar Square.”

Left: Platform hoist lifting crew: ?Alan Clark, Adrian Love and RWB Ross Brown. (EM)

RADIO CITY CREW

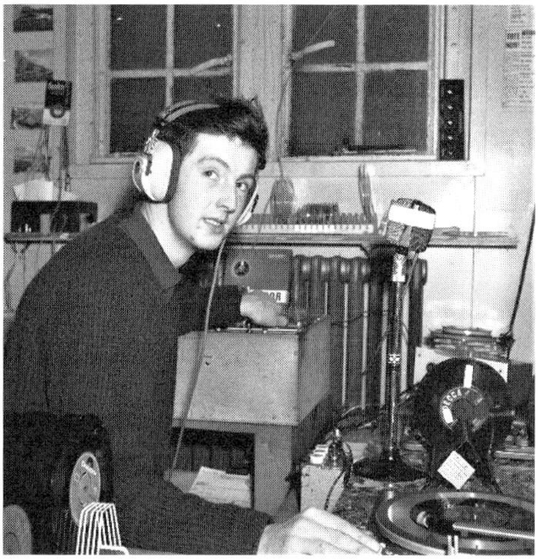

Top left: Chris Cross (Mulloch). One of the first disc jockeys on Radio Sutch/City (EJ)
Top right: Engineer Phil Perkins, nicknamed the 'Wizard' by some of the crew (RC)
Bottom left: Disc Jockey Eric Jay, a keen photographer (EJ photo taken by Chris Cross)
Bottom right: Johnny Flux (Edwards). He played in the Mannish Boys with Davie Jones who later became famous later as David Bowey

THE HARVESTER

Above: Dorothy Calvert with William wrapped in a scarf on the Harvester (RC)
Below: The Harvester, owned by Fred Downs. Fred provided a tendering service, ferrying crew and provisions twice weekly to Shivering Sands (EJ)

21. NEW PROGRAMME CONTROLLER

Dorothy Calvert on the Harvester going out to Shivering Sands
Behind: Engineer Paul Elvey and Station Manager Eric Martin (RC)

After moving into Welbeck House, Dorothy tuned into Radio City every day, making notes about the various programmes, how they sounded and the music played. The deejays were informed that Mrs C was now Programme Controller and it was reported back that one Australian disc jockey had remarked, "I'm not having a bloody woman telling me what to do."

Reg chuckled as he told his wife. "If he doesn't like it, he knows what he can do."

Dorothy was ready for a challenge. She had become bored with living a quiet life at Macbeth Close and on Easter Friday, Reg persuaded her to go with him to Shivering Sands, taking William and Candy with them.

Fred welcomed them aboard the Harvester. "Come and shelter in the cabin if you get cold on the crossing."

"William seems a bit subdued," observed Reg, as he got his camera out and took a photograph of his wife with William all wrapped up in her scarf.

"I don't think he's very well," said Dorothy, concerned. "He's been quiet for a few days. Do you think monkeys suffer from sea sickness?"

When the boat arrived at Shivering Sands, the wooden platform was slowly winched down to the boat deck.

"Ladies first," chuckled Reg. "Hold tight."

"I don't like this," muttered Dorothy, nervously. The platform started to swing, swaying from side to side as slowly, it was hoisted up. Dorothy began to scream. As it went higher, it swung more. Reg, who was watching from the boat, laughed as he saw her slide down to the floor while she continued to scream. Candy, unperturbed, held tightly to the ropes, enjoying the experience like being on a fairground ride. Reaching the landing stage, Candy stepped off as one of the engineers eased Dorothy from her seated position and helped her onto the tower. When Reg came up he put his arm around his wife.

"That wasn't funny Reg Calvert. I was petrified and so was William."

"Come and have a quick cup of tea and then you can see our new studio while I sort the engineers out."

Candy and Dorothy Calvert on platform hoist (RC)

“Uck. This kitchen needs a clean. In fact, everywhere looks as though it could do with a clean.”

“You can ask the guys to spruce it up a bit,” grinned Reg. “They might do it for you.”

“Is this the food they have to eat? No wonder everyone complains. You could buy better food from a supermarket and with the money you save, afford to pay a cook.”

“Good idea. I’ll get the deejays to advertise for one.” grinned Reg. “The studio’s over there on that tower.”

“You must be joking. You don’t expect me to go on that catwalk? It doesn’t look safe.”

“Come on, cowardy custard,” chuckled Reg. “Follow me.”

Dorothy walked as quickly as she dared, while grabbing hold of the rails. When she reached the studio, Dorothy tried to look confident as she sat down with Ian MacRae and Tom Edwards to learn how they produced their programmes. Reg left her and Candy while he went to see the engineers. Time on Shivering Sands was short and after an hour, Reg returned and hurried his wife and daughter to leave.

“I’ll use the toilet before I go.”

“I wouldn’t unless you’re desperate,” grinned Reg.

“I’m desperate.”

Reg waited outside and when Dorothy emerged, she was holding her nose.

“That toilet is revolting.”

“Just a bit,” agreed Reg, laughing. “The plumbing is iffy, so the engineers take it in turns to haul buckets of water from the sea to rinse them. It is funny though. If you’re quick after you’ve flushed, you can go outside and see your ablutions drop to the sea.”

“That’s even more revolting and really not funny.”

“Do you want to go down the ladder, or back on the lift?”

“What do you think?” retorted Dorothy, as she stepped onto the lift.

Within a few days of her visit to Shivering Sands, Dorothy had formulated how she wanted the station to work. Radio City would have a Top 60 Play List / Chart. The top five records were to be played every hour. Trays were made to stack records and once they were played they were to be filed into a separate tray, so each disc jockey could see at a glance which ones had been aired previously. They could stamp their personality on their programmes by playing their own choice of record in between the top 60, providing it was pop music. To ensure her instructions were being followed, Dorothy began to send memos to Tom Edwards.

Memo 12th April, 1966

Dear Tom,

This is my first memo to you on the station and I hope there will be many more. Firstly, I want the (advertising) tapes of Spanish Holidays returned to me. Also, the tape of Peter Jameson plugging 299 in name. The Cliff Pavilion is due for one plug a day. Swift Spray is due for four plus, a day. The disc of Call Me, an Instrumental, to be sent back to Denmark Street, no further plays.

I am also enclosing a list of records that Denis played this afternoon, I shall be logging all DJs by the way. I hope that when the list has been digested no further programmes of this kind will be put out. The station is POP, there is no room for a further 390 on the air, anyone who doesn't understand about the Top Twenty, please contact me and I will inform them as to what is currently required.

From now on, instrumentals must be beat and only leading up to the news, unless they are riding high in the charts. Anything resembling Jazz must be deleted. Beatles are favourite.

Also, please cut out any spiel or announcements after a plug, straight in with the next record, please keep it moving.

DENIS THE MENACE show, records played:

People. You Bring Me Down. Pied Piper. Call Me. Harlem Shuffle - Instrumental. Somebody Help me. When Evening Falls. One Track Mind. Why can't you come on home? Gurney Slade. Long Live our Love. I Fought the Law. You Baby. Shapes of Things. Working My Way Back to You. Substitute. Shake me, Wake me.

As you will see the ratio of top twenty records is very small, most of the records were dreary, particularly before I started taking notes. The records going up the top twenty must have priority, the ones going down are dead.

That is all now, will be listening,

Yours,

Mrs C.

MEMO 21st April, 1966

Dear Tom,

Enclosed disc for major plugging, six plugs a day for the next two weeks, starting immediately.

The Don is Don Charles and Pete is Peter Lee Sterling. Pete has one of the best voices in the record business today, as well as being a successful songwriter. The Artwoods B-side (I'm looking for a Saxophonist) is ideal for a play-off for 30 seconds or so.

Looking forward to hearing the bigger signal, have a lot of things lined up. We shall not require the new evening programmes to start until the generator has been supplied to the station.

The Southend Request Show can come off immediately but there are two adverts which are repeated in the Southend show from the Basildon Show and these adverts should be continued in the same time segment as the Southern Show would have gone out,

Yours,

Mrs C.

MEMO 26th April, 1966

Dear Tom,

Thank you for the letter which was received yesterday.

The Radio City Cook Vacancy has been filled so the ad can be dropped.

The Station promotion jingle beginning 'Music To Dream To', to be dropped, also the new jingle is weak. Do you think you could experiment a little with jingles, make them more 'with it'? I will listen out and let you know what is coming over good. We are trying to get some American jingles to help along.

Have spoken to Phil Jay, he apologises for any trouble over his tapes and asks if you could put a note with any further tapes which are faulty, giving approx. place so that he may rectify. His tapes are up-to-date and will be on the boat today. And check the other tapes supplies.

The evening programme tapes from Ed Moreno are coming out today so if you wish to commence evening programmes on Saturday, if everything is O.K., you may. The tapes are all numbered and an explanatory letter is enclosed.

Busily looking for more DJs, one very good possible.

Would you try the new schedules and let me know if they work out or if they need altering?

Yours,

Mrs C.

Reg ordered another large generator to power the station and the new aerial was installed in mid-April. It had to be tethered to all five towers and was a difficult and complex operation, taking several days to complete. Everyone was thrilled when they realised that Radio City was to become one of the top stations and would compete with Radio London and Caroline.

After the aerial had been installed, the crew dared Phil Perkins to climb up to the first set of lights. He accepted the dare with some bravado. With everyone cheering he started to climb, going higher and higher and not stopping until he reached the lights. Looking down, he waved to the crew who were far below. Suddenly, he saw just how high he had climbed and began to shake uncontrollably. Terrified, he hung on and tried to calm himself by staying perfectly still. After a while, he found the courage to climb back down. When he reached the roof, his face was white and he was still shaking.

"Never again. I'll never go up there again," said Phil.

Shortly after the installation of the new aerial, Reg received a telegram from the record producer, Joe Meek, congratulating him on the station. Dorothy was reluctant to go again to Shivering Sands and the weekly memos to Tom continued. Both Reg and Dorothy liked Tom and when he was off duty, he became a regular visitor to the office and Welbeck House.

Reg was delighted with the aerial. It had exceeded his expectations and Radio City could be clearly picked up in London and much further afield. Featuring the aerial, Reg designed promotional cards and posters, and had new jingles recorded with the catchphrase of 'Radio City, the Tower of Power'. To sell more advertising, the station boasted of broadcasting at 10kW although, in fact, they continued to use the 2kW Big Bertha transmitter. The old 10kW transmitter Atlanta had provided still did not work.

After all the struggles and heartbreak, Reg felt a sense of pride in his achievement that he had made Radio City a success. He had turned his life round and not only that, he had Dorothy back and they were happy.

"We'll be married for 20 years in June," reminded Dorothy.

"Twenty years. Who'd have believed it."

"Not my mother," laughed Dorothy.

"We should celebrate. I'd like to go to Spain and see where the oranges grow. A second honeymoon," smiled Reg.

Leslie Dunne lived in Ramsgate and had just completed a two-year catering course. While listening to Radio City, he heard an advertisement for a chef and decided to apply. A few days later, he was in the office at the Record Centre in Whitstable. Leslie looked very young for his age and Reg was concerned he wouldn't cope with the hardships of living on the towers.

"Life out at sea isn't easy. It's quite basic and there are few home comforts."

"I don't mind," assured Leslie. It was his dream job to work on a pirate radio station and he couldn't stop smiling when Reg offered him the position with one week on and one week off.

Leslie recommended his friend Barry Trice as the second chef on alternate weeks. They had both done the same catering course and learnt how to cook French cuisine but were relieved to learn that no French cooking was required. Dorothy joined Reg on his trips to Whitstable, taking the new chefs shopping at the Mass Supermarket. She advised them on the quantity and type of foods to buy and explained they should buy fresh meat and vegetables for the first couple of days, tinned food for the remainder of the week as keeping food fresh was difficult. If the boys on the station had any food preferences, they could buy it within reason, but alcohol was strictly prohibited. Once they knew what to do, the chefs went shopping on their own and organised their menus, which comprised mainly of full English breakfasts, stews and hotpots.

Leslie admitted he wasn't a good cook but his meals were better than the awful food the crew concocted and they were happy to have a chef on board. He was in teenage heaven and couldn't believe how lucky he was to work on a pirate radio station, with speakers in every room relaying all-day pop music. He quickly came to respect the crew and their various abilities and was in complete awe of the engineers. He thought Phil was like a wizard who seemed to be able to put his hand to anything. The disc jockeys were fun and Leslie considered Ian MacRae to be the best and Eric Martin, an intellectual type from a 'posh' family. The other Eric Martin from the Record Centre, was station manager. The crew respected Tom Edwards and although gay, he never made advances to the crew. Only when he was off-air was he over the top effeminate, camp and very funny.

Radio City Chef Leslie Dunne

Tom had a large fan club and often let it slip while on-air, what day and time he would be coming off duty and arriving in Whitstable harbour. Not surprisingly, there was invariably a crowd of people, mainly females, waiting to see him.

He suggested to Leslie that he should do a cooking request slot. They broadcast the programme and much to Leslie's surprise, he began to receive a small amount of fan mail and someone called Lydia Dustbin wrote in every day. The cooking programme developed and Leslie became the station's on-air chef and he regularly gave out recipes and answered cooking queries.

MEMO 5th May, 1966

Dear Tom,

Would you please put Cheeseman's' advertisement back on air this weekend, should not have been taken off. Louis Henson of Brighton to be postponed for now. Give the Language Course a repeat over the next four days. Will you give Wayne Gibson's record better promotion spots, please?

Now some criticisms. Tom, you are no Caruso, interrupting records is very bad unless it is very slick and this week it has been very slack. I have noticed from the correspondence that listeners object to records being 'hiccoughed' over, this goes for everyone.

Another point, you are all talking too much again. Denis did a Carmen plug on Tuesday and we wondered when he was going to stop. In future, if you can't keep to the point, tape it, listen to it back, make sure it punches and stop rambling. Denis, you sound as though you are talking to yourself and you are boring yourself to death. I know you can do better but you are letting yourself down badly, so please, and this means everyone, keep it swinging.

Our listening audience has increased, we are as powerful as the other stations so it is up to you as DJs to win and keep those listeners.

I have noticed your request for records, sorry NO Sinatra, will see to the others. Drop Pinkerton's plugging to normal for the position in the charts.

Now, Charts: We are going to publish the CITY 60, I hope you have done this week's as we want it on the Friday boat. Sorry if it is such short notice, but the only other way is for it to be read out after transmission on Sunday. If you have done it, let John have it or inform the boys to read it on Sunday. Let me know which it is please. Can you arrange to have the charts sent off every Friday in future.

Yours,

Mrs C.

Radio City staff were invited to Welbeck House for social evenings. The two sisters chatted to the various people and when Susan met Tom, he was sitting very relaxed in the lounge and her first impression was that he was the most handsome and debonair of all the disc jockeys. She also observed he was eyeing-up both her and her sister and realised he was calculating which of them to invite out. She was wary, guessing that disc jockeys would be of the same ilk as musicians.

Several days later, Candy was in raptures as Tom asked her out. She was only 15 and Jill was surprised that Dorothy permitted it.

"Don't you worry about Candy going out with an older man?"

"No, not really. He's a, you know, a …"

"You mean he's a … puff?" questioned Jill, shocked by the revelation.

"Yes, that's exactly what I mean," laughed Dorothy. "Have you heard his nickname on the station?'

"Tatty Tom, because he dresses so well."

Dorothy began to laugh. "His other name is Mother. Candy's perfectly safe with him. I think they just hold hands and talk."

Homosexuality was against the law and hidden in polite society. Few people mentioned it except to sometimes describe an effeminate man as a puff or a queer. Candy could hardly believe that Tom had chosen her and not her older sister. She and Tom immediately jelled and had much in common to talk about. They were both followers of fashion and passionately interested in pop music. Candy had always had crushes on various singers and popstars, her latest for Peter No one in Herman's Hermits. Sadly, Dorothy had not thought of the consequences of her vulnerable young daughter falling in love with Tom. Her only concern was to protect her virginity.

Major Smedley contacted Reg again, insisting on coming to his office to check the accounts before he paid the bad debts. It seemed to Reg, that Smedley's prime objective was to procrastinate about paying and to pressurise him into selling Radio City. Nevertheless, he asked Jill to type out an account and go through the files with him.

The accounts surprised Smedley. Whereas he and Allan Crawford had failed to make either Radio Atlanta or Caroline South a success, Radio City was thriving and making a profit of nearly £500 per week. The next day, he phoned Reg.

"I've got another businessman who's expressed an interest and may offer more money. He's asked if he could look at your Radio City accounts. How about we say, Monday 2nd May at 2.30 p.m.?"

"Okay," agreed Reg reluctantly, who felt he had been boxed into a corner and was uneasy about another request to see his accounts.

Gary Yablon made his way from his office at 2 South Square, Gray's Inn to Denmark Street. Reg was quietly spoken and businesslike at the meeting and explained about his expansion plans to buy a boat and start a second station near Lundy Island in the Bristol Channel. It was enough to have the desired effect. The following day, he received a letter from Gary Yablon, thanking him for his kindness and for an interesting discussion about his Radio City project.

I have told Mr Smedley that I do not feel able to recommend to my friends that they should proceed on the basis of the present Agreement. If, however, you should decide to alter your plans there might be a way in which we could work together.

The income from advertising amounted to nearly £1,000 per week, most of it from religious advertisers, including The A.A. Allen show, Voice of Prophesy, World Tomorrow, Sunday half hour Radio Bible Class and Wings of Healing.

The costs of running the station varied but came to about £220 most weeks, to include the boat tender service, generator hire, food, records, valves, diesel etc. Wages amounted to about £300 most weeks, depending how many crew were on duty.

Staff employed were Ian MacRae: £26. Phil Perkins: £26. Alan Clark: £21. Paul Elvey: £21. Eric Martin: £15. 10s. Tom Edwards: £26. Ross Brown: £16. Ian West: £31.10s. Bill: £21. Graham Bunce: £21. Leslie Dunne: £15. 10s. Barry Trice: £16. John Wileman: £20. Jill Wileman: £20.

Pirate radio stations were now broadcasting from waters all around Britain, some amateurish, others very professional with disc jockeys becoming celebrities. Millions of enthusiastic listeners of all ages, not just teenagers listened to the stations. On the seedier side, rumours abounded that some less successful fort-based stations were being used as a front for smuggling by a highly organised gang.

Manx Radio on the Isle of Man, commenced broadcasting in November, 1964 and was Britain's only licensed, land-based commercial radio station. Radio Caroline North broadcast off the Isle of Man, from a boat. Radio Scotland from a boat in the Firth of Forth, commenced in January, 1966. Radio 270, three miles off the Yorkshire coast from a converted Dutch lugger was planned to begin broadcasting in June, 1966.

Ship-based pirates anchored off Frinton-on-Sea were Radio Caroline South and Radio London. From the forts, Radio City and Radio 390 were both successful and popular stations. Radio Essex run by Roy Bates was continuing to operate with a weak signal from Knock John Fort. Radio Tower on Sunk Head, 14miles from Felixstowe, failed in its ambitious plans to broadcast both radio and television.

Swinging Radio England and Britain Radio began broadcasting in May, 1966. Don Pierson, who had masterminded Radio London, had formed new business partnerships and purchased the Olga Patricia, renaming it the Laissez Faire. The ship had two studios, one for Swinging Radio England and the second for a sweet music station, Britain Radio. It was to be financed chiefly by religious broadcasts.

NEWSPAPER REPORTS (extracts)

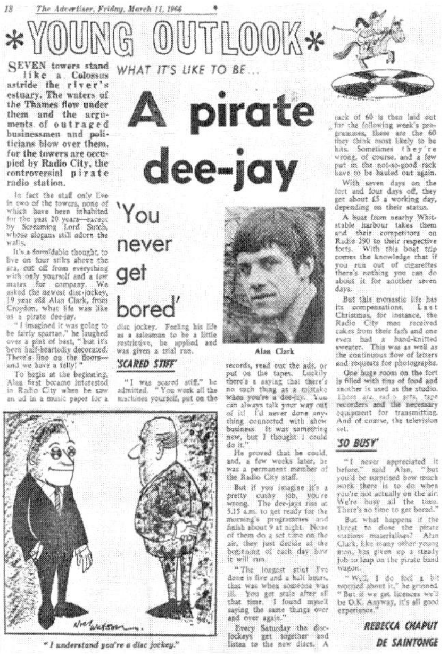

18 The Advertiser, Friday, March 11, 1966

YOUNG OUTLOOK

WHAT IT'S LIKE TO BE...

A pirate dee-jay

'You never get bored'

SEVEN towers stand like a Colossus astride the river's estuary. The waters of the Thames flow under them and the arguments of outraged businessmen and politicians blow over them, for the towers are occupied by Radio City, the controversial pirate radio station.

In fact the staff only live in two of the towers, none of which have been inhabited for the past 20 years—except by Screaming Lord Sutch, whose slogans still adorn the walls.

It's a formidable thought, to live on four stilts above the sea, cut off from everything with only yourself and a few mates for company. We asked the newest disc-jockey, 19 year old Alan Clark, from Croydon, what life was like as a pirate dee-jay.

"I imagined it was going to be fairly spartan," he laughed over a pint of beer, "but it's been half-heartedly decorated. There's lino on the floors—and we have a telly!"

To begin at the beginning, Alan first became interested in Radio City when he saw an ad in a music paper for a disc jockey. Feeling his life as a salesman to be a little restrictive, he applied and was given a trial run.

'SCARED STIFF'

"I was scared stiff," he admitted. "You work all the machines yourself, put on the records, read out the ads, or put on the tapes. Luckily there's a saying that there's no such thing as a mistake when you're a dee-jay. You can always talk your way out of it! I'd never done anything connected with show business. It was something new, but I thought I could do it."

He proved that he could, and, a few weeks later, he was a permanent member of the Radio City staff.

But if you imagine it's a pretty cushy job, you're wrong. The dee-jays rise at 5.15 a.m. to get ready for the morning's programmes and finish about 9 at night. None of them do a set time on the air, they just decide at the beginning of each day how it will run.

"The longest stint I've done is five and a half hours, that was when someone was ill. You get stale after all that time. I found myself saying the same things over and over again."

Every Saturday the disc-jockeys get together and listen to the new discs. A rack of 60 is then laid out for the following week's programmes, these are the 60 they think most likely to be hits. Sometimes they're wrong, of course, and a few put in the not-so-good rack have to be hauled out again.

With seven days on the fort and four days off, they get about £5 a working day, depending on their status.

A boat from nearby Whitstable harbour takes them and their competitors on Radio 390 to their respective forts. With this boat trip comes the knowledge that if you run out of cigarettes there's nothing you can do about it for another seven days.

But this monastic life has its compensations. Last Christmas, for instance, the Radio City men received cakes from their fans and one even had a hand-knitted sweater. This was as well as the continuous flow of letters and requests for photographs.

One huge room on the fort is filled with tins of food and another is used as the studio. There are radio sets, tape recorders and the necessary equipment for transmitting. And of course, the television set.

'SO BUSY'

"I never appreciated it before," said Alan, "but you'd be surprised how much work there is to do when you're not actually on the air. We're busy all the time. There's no time to get bored."

But what happens if the threat to close the pirate stations materialises? Alan Clark, like many other young men, has given up a steady job to leap on the pirate band wagon.

"Well, I do feel a bit worried about it," he grinned. "But if we get licences we'll be O.K. Anyway, it's all good experience."

REBECCA CHAPUT DE SAINTONGE

Alan Clark

"I understand you're a disc jockey."

Feature about Radio City and Alan Clark in the Advertiser. Alan Clark (RC)

NEWS OF THE WORLD: 17th April 1966

WAR ON THE RADIO PIRATES

Britain's pirate radio stations are already planning violent evasive action against Government legislation aimed at putting them out of business. .... But with 10 countries bound by a Council of Europe agreement signed 14 months ago to outlaw the pop pirate ships, the odds must weigh heavily against them being able to survive.

When the Queen's Speech is published next Thursday, it is almost certain to include a declaration of war on the pirate radio stations. Mr Anthony Wedgwood Benn, the Postmaster General is expected to fire two broad-sides. Making it illegal for any person to supply the pirate stations with food and other supplies. Banning all British companies from buying advertising time from them. ....

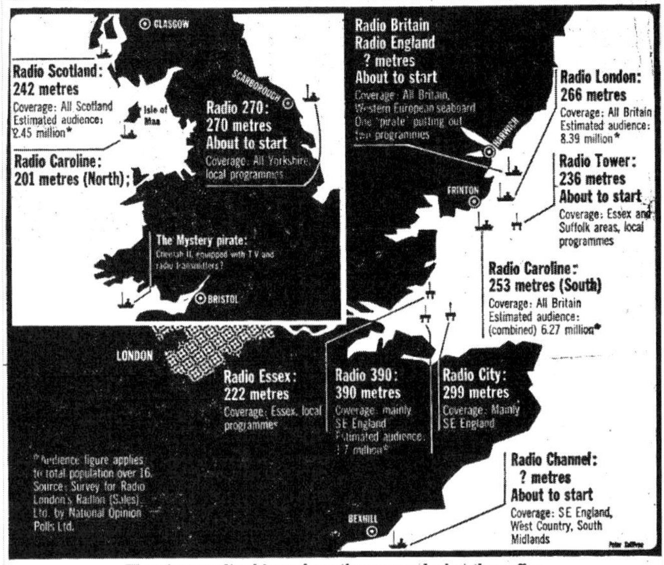

The pirate radio ships: where they are and what they offer

Offshore radio war widens with pirate TV expected this month

SUNDAY TIMES 1st May, 1966

By Dan van der Vat

The Swedish ship Cheetah II, equipped with a powerful TV transmitter, will soon leave the echelon of pop ships strung along the appropriately named Wallett Channel off the Essex coast. She is expected to make for the Bristol Channel, but test transmissions may be made before she gets there. The man associated with this scheme is Mr Philip Solomon, also a backer of Radio Caroline. Cheetah II took over from Caroline's South Mi Amigo when the latter ran aground earlier this year. Now Mi Amigo is back. As Cheetah II has inherited some of her radio equipment, the TV transmissions may be coupled with a local radio service.

A more immediate development in the booming offshore radio industry will be the start of transmissions from the most formidable entrant so far in the unofficial commercial radio stakes. This is the 480-ton Panama registered Olga Patricia, now renamed the Laissez Faire, which will open probably this week with two programmes simultaneously. Swinging Radio England, the first 24-hour-a-day pop programme and Radio Britain, 21 hours of non-pop light music a day. Wavelengths have not been settled yet.

Three other pirate radio transmitters hope to open within weeks. All this means fiercer competition but the general feeling in the business is that the advertising potential has barely been tapped, and the audiences are growing by the hour.

DAILY MAIL: 2nd May, 1966

PIRATE OLGA GOES INTO BATTLE

The latest and most powerful pirate radio ship was sailing up the Channel early today. ..... The ship is due to anchor four miles off the Essex coast near Harwich this afternoon. Tomorrow the first test signals for two pirate radio stations will be beamed from the Panamanian-registered ship to cover the whole of Britain.

Mr Benn has admitted in a Commons reply that he is at present unable to prevent the stations starting round the clock broadcasts. ..... He hopes to introduce the legislation in the Commons before the summer recess. It is planned to make it illegal to send food and water to the pirates, service transmitting equipment or act as agents for advertising.

Sixteen unnamed backers, made up of American, Canadian and British businessmen, have put more than £1 million into the Olga Patricia venture. ..... Two 55 kilowatt transmitters were installed making the stations potentially the most powerful operating around Britain. One transmitter will be used to send out 'pop' music on Swinging Radio England. The other will be used for non-stop romantic music on 'Britain Radio.' .....

DAILY MAIL: 27th May, 1966

The Musicians Union, prevented a show from being recorded at the Rainbow Club, Bradford. It had been organised by Ross Productions for Currys and would have been networked Friday lunchtime between Radio City, Caroline, Radio London and Radio Scotland. The musicians were threatened that they would lose their union membership if the recording went ahead as the Musicians Union were against pirate radio. The show was compered by Pete Murray and a reluctant compromise was reached. The Four Pennies, the Swinging Blue Jeans, Pinkerton's Assorted Colours, and Kenny Ball's Jazzmen, agreed to perform, but not to being recorded.

DAILY MAIL: 2nd June, 1966

BENN WON'T ATTACK POP PIRATE SEA FORTS

Postmaster-General Mr Anthony Wedgwood Benn has decided not to start legal proceedings under existing laws against three pirate radio stations operating from wartime forts in the Thames Estuary. Now he has been advised that there is doubt as to whether magistrates' jurisdiction extends to the forts.

GPO GREETINGS TELEGRAM

100 GTG 4.44 LONDON T 26 GREETINGS =

REG CALVERT RADIO CITY 7 DENMARK STREET W1 =

TO REG AND ALL CONCERNED CONGRATULATIONS ON THE
NEW HIGH POWER OF RADIO CITY SINCERELY = JOE MEEK +

Telegram from record producer, Joe Meek, congratulating Reg and all concerned on the new high power of Radio City. Reg and Joe had known each other for a few years and in the early days, Reg had introduced Joe to various musicians from the Southampton area including Heinz, Dowland Bros and Roy Phillips

Shivering Sands Towers showing new, very tall aerial (SC)

22. PLANTING A ROSE

Reg and Dorothy on the Harvester, Shivering Sands behind (RC)

Friday afternoon, the family joined the mass exodus of people leaving London for their weekend retreat. When they arrived at Macbeth Close, the two cats were waiting for them and Katy came running to Susan, who swept her up in her arms and stroked her.

"It's not good to leave the cats all week on their own," murmured Dorothy to Reg, as they entered the house.

"They look all right to me," replied Reg.

"And it's not fair on the neighbours."

"Margaret doesn't seem to mind feeding them, but you could try bringing them to London," suggested Reg.

"They'd hate to be locked up in the apartment."

Reg made no reply and began to get ready to go to the Nuneaton dance. Since the tragedy, fewer people were attending and the earlier session for young teenagers had closed.

"See you later, alligator," smiled Reg, kissing his wife.

"In a while, crocodile," replied Dorothy.

On Saturday morning while her daughters were out, Dorothy decided to take the cats to the vet. When Susan returned home, she parked her bubble car on the drive and called for Katy. Entering the kitchen, she called again, and then went outside to the garden and kept calling. Dorothy stayed in the lounge and shrunk from the moment she would have to confront her daughter with the truth.

"Have you seen Katy?"

Dorothy shook her head in response. "There's no point calling her."

"Where is she?" asked Susan, alarmed, intuitively knowing by the look on her mother's face that she had done something dreadful.

"I've had the cats put to sleep."

Susan stared at her mother with large, disbelieving eyes, as she comprehended her words.

"How could you?"

"It wasn't fair to leave them on their own each week."

"It wasn't fair to kill them. Katy was my cat. I didn't want to live in London and I could have stayed here and looked after her."

"Don't be ridiculous. You know you can't stay here on your own," snapped Dorothy.

There was nothing else to say. The cats were dead. Susan, her face crumpling, burst into tears and ran to her bedroom where she lay on her bed and sobbed. Dorothy returned to the lounge with William perched on her shoulder, chuntering accusingly.

"She loved Katy," said Reg, thoughtfully. "I remember when I brought her home as a little kitten in Southampton. They were like best friends and they've grown up together."

"I know, but she'll get over it. I don't know what else I could have done," replied Dorothy.

Susan stayed all day in her bedroom until she was called down for the evening meal. Her face, red and blotchy, she sat tight-lipped, saying nothing.

"What's up with her?" remarked Candy.

No one responded. Candy hadn't noticed the cats were missing and no one was going to tell her.

Reg, to break the silence, commented, "The Nuneaton dances are picking up a bit."

"Have they finished the other staircase yet?" asked Dorothy.

"Just about, but the Co-op management are so fuddy-duddy, they insist we leave lights switched on in the ballroom. It's mad. The kids like it dark and it's spoiling the atmosphere. The stairway and hallway were always well lit and that's where the accident happened. Not on the dancefloor."

The Nuneaton Saturday night dance continued with smaller crowds than before with Susan running the dance most weeks. One evening, when she was walking around the ballroom, a tall, dark haired young man who had just entered, put his hand around her waist and asked her to dance.

Lyndon had been on the stairs New Year's Eve with his best friend, Peter. His ribcage was still misshapen but Peter, who had been married with a young child, died in the crush. The memory of that evening and the loss of his friend was something he tried to forget. It had taken several months before he'd returned to the Co-op Hall and when he did, the first girl he saw in the ballroom was Susan. Since then, he had asked her to dance every Saturday and became a regular visitor at Macbeth Close, spending his weekends with her.

William's health became more of a concern. Dorothy couldn't coax him to eat and he lay listlessly in her arms, looking abjectly at her with his large brown expressive eyes.

"I'm sure he's ill. He's got no energy and he just wants to be cuddled."

"I wouldn't mind being cuddled all day," said Reg, as he gently stroked William. "He must be ill to let me touch him. Why don't you arrange to take him to the vets at London Zoo?"

"That's a good idea," smiled Dorothy as she stroked her monkey.

William was examined and diagnosed as suffering from congenital heart disease. He was small for a Capuchin and there was nothing the vet could do to save him. Reg and Dorothy were heartbroken. It was like being told they were about to lose a child. As William's energy sapped, Dorothy carried him around like a baby, snuggled in a blanket. He died quietly in his sleep and when Dorothy found him in the morning, she sobbed as she gently laid him in a shoe box. At the weekend, Reg dug a small grave in the garden and the family, with tears running down their faces, watched as Dorothy ceremoniously knelt and placed him into the ground. Reg, holding the spade, began to refill the hole as Dorothy planted a rose bush above him.

William loved jelly babies (RC)

The family could always hear Reg whistling merrily before he opened the apartment door and announced cheerfully, 'I'm back'. One evening, he returned not whistling but quietly. Dorothy, hearing the click of the door closing, found him ashen faced, sitting on the bed gazing into space.

"What's the matter? You look as though you've seen a ghost."

"Nothing," replied Reg, abruptly, as he began to take off his shoes.

Dorothy sat down next to him and waited for him to tell her what was troubling him. In the end, she broke the silence.

"Dinner won't be long. Susan's offered to cook tonight."

Reg nodded his head in understanding and took a deep breath.

"How d'you fancy moving abroad with the girls?"

"What for?" frowned Dorothy, surprised by his question.

"No reason."

"Yes, there is. I can read you like a book. We've only just got this apartment and now we're back as a family you want me to move abroad?"

"There's enough money in Switzerland to last a year or two."

"No Reg. I'm not going away without you, unless you give me a reason."

"No reason, but you could go abroad until our holiday in June."

"No Reg."

Dorothy knew that whatever her husband was concerned about must be so serious, he would not tell her until he'd found a way to resolve it. When they awoke next morning, Reg had come to a decision. He got up, grim faced and dressed. Dorothy could see by his expression that he was still troubled and later, when they were eating breakfast together in the kitchen, he broke the news.

"I've decided to sell Radio City."

"Sell it?" queried Dorothy. "To that Major Smedley? Has he made a better offer?"

"Not him. I'm going to approach Radio London to see if they'd like to buy it."

"Why Reg? Why, when you love it so much?"

"It's time to move on."

"I don't understand you. I'll never understand you. Just when you're making it a success, you want to sell."

Tentatively, on 12th May, Reg arranged a secret meeting in his apartment at Welbeck House with Philip Birch from Radio London. After the failure of the Atlanta/Caroline merger, Reg wanted to ensure that this time he would deal with a reputable company and get proper contracts signed.

Philip Birch was a very tall man, intelligent and honest, with a good understanding of the radio business. The two men got on well together and Birch was interested in Reg's proposal. It had come at the right time as he was concerned about the impact on Radio London's advertising revenue from the new, more powerful, Swinging Radio England and Britain Radio which had recently taken to the airwaves.

A few days after their meeting, Philip Birch contacted Reg to say his directors were interested and they'd put forward an idea. The new station would be called Radio UKGM, United Kingdom Good Music and registered in the Bahamas. It wouldn't compete with Radio London but target mature listeners, similar in style to the popular Radio 390, managed by Ted Allbeury. Reg agreed to everything in principle; the initial contract was to be drawn up and signed by the beginning of June, with a completion date at the end of the month.

Relieved and elated by their response, Reg, when he saw Dorothy, picked her up and swung her around, making her squeal.

"We can really start living again. Mm, I do love you. I'm so glad I married you."

"You're sloppy," laughed Dorothy.

'Sloppy ya doo dah, sloppy ya day," sung Reg, as he danced his wife around the lounge in a funny type of waltz, until out of breath, they flopped together onto the settee, laughing.

"Radio London personnel are coming out to Shivering Sands next week to look at the station, and if the agreement goes through okay, we'll be able to take our holiday in Spain at the end of June."

"I still don't understand why you're selling it."

"Mm, I love you, I love you, I love you. Let's go to bed," said Reg, kissing his wife.

"You always want to go to bed when you're happy," laughed Dorothy.

"I should earn double the amount I'm earning now," teased Reg, his eyes sparkling.

"How much?"

"And I'm going to set up a new company."

"How much will you be earning?" asked Dorothy, again.

"I've decided to call it Tarpon."

"That's an odd name. How much? Tell me."

"About a thousand pounds a month," laughed Reg. "The one problem I have is to get that transmitter working."

"I thought you said it was too old," replied Dorothy. Reg signed an initial agreement with Radio London on 1st June and sent a memo to the station the next day. Disc Jockey Alan Clark read the memo from 'Uncle' but was puzzled about what it could mean.

"Ian got it to work for about two minutes but it needs a much larger generator. I might have to hire one but first I'll see if I can persuade Phil to take an interest. He's a bit of a whiz kid."

Reg and Philip Birch agreed to keep the proposed partnership confidential while letters about the agreement went backwards and forwards. The new company was to be called Sweet Music Association with Reg receiving 45 percent of the shares and £1,000 per month (in US dollars) for 6 months, offset against any dividend. It was also agreed that Radio London could transfer to Shivering Sands and Sweet Music be broadcast from the ship, Galaxy. Equipment on the station was included in the deal:

1: 50 kilowatt 6 cylinder Diesel alternator
1: 6 cylinder 47 kva alternator
1: 15 kva Diesel alternator
1: Transmitter 2QY 500 output
1: Transmitter 2 type 892 output (RCA design)
1: 1 ton crane 3 phase electric
1: 2.5 ton crane 3 phase electric
3: VHF FM communications transceivers
2: VHF AM communications transceivers
1: Shipping band transmitter
2: Communications transmitter, plus other items.
OTHER ITEMS: 6: Turntables. 4: Tape machines. 2: AKG Studio microphones etc. 5ton Chain block and tackle. Acetylene welding and cutting equipment. Calor gas cooking equipment. Refrigerator.

MEMO 2nd June, 1966

TO: RADIO CITY STAFF
To: The D-J in Charge.

The bearer of this letter has authority to land on the landing stages – and will explain to you what it is all about. Please rehearse your interview and write down points before transmission.

Uncle

Alan Clark was broadcasting the afternoon show and was surprised to see Keith Skues and Duncan Johnson from Radio London, walk into the studio.

"Please don't say anything. Our coming has to be kept confidential," said Duncan.

Alan nodded his head. He now understood what the mysterious memo meant from Uncle, guessing Radio London were to become involved with the running of Radio City as they took an interest in looking around the station and meeting staff.

Reg never stood still and began to plan his future, knowing he'd have more time once he relinquished control of Radio City at the end of June. He decided to develop his new publishing business, King Music, and to take on the management of more groups. To help him, he asked Brian Harvey, who was in his 30s, if he would like to come and work for him. Brian was a music journalist who often called into the office to enquire about the Fortunes. He liked Reg and was pleased to accept. Brian respected the fact that Reg was forthright and straightforward in his dealings with the groups he managed, unlike other impresarios he had met.

Management: REG CALVERT - KINGS AGENCY (Variety) LTD., 7, Denmark Street, London, W.C.2.

PINKERTON'S (ASSORTED) COLOURS — Sole Representation : King's Agency (Variety) Ltd., 7 Denmark St., W.C.2. Management : Reginald Calvert TEMple Bar : 6303/4 6332/3

Above: Promotional cards for The Fortunes and Pinkerton's Assorted Colours King's Agency. Management: Reg Calvert

Radio City Poster

23. CONSPIRACY

Shivering Sands Towers one-man entry hatch (RC)

Disappointed that Gary Yablon had decided not to invest in Radio City, Smedley began to formulate a plan to take over the station without Reg's knowledge and set up a new company, Seagull Publicity Ltd, making himself chairman and Reg, managing director. Smedley began to send letters to his contacts offering shares at £1 each and cheques were to be made out to his own company, Investment and General Management Services. This was the way he operated, finding investors for small companies and making himself chairman in the process.

One of Smedley's contacts was Commander Horsley, an experienced Trinity House Pilot who was nearing retirement. He worked from the Royal Terrace Pier at Gravesend and had previously advised Allan Crawford on the best mooring place for the Mi Amigo. Horsley declined the offer but remained enthusiastic about pirate radio. He had imprudently purchased £2,000 of now worthless shares in Project Atlanta on behalf of his aunt's pension fund and had no intention of being cajoled into buying more shares in pirate radio.

By the beginning of June, Smedley considered himself ready to takeover Radio City and he called the office and spoke to Jill, explaining he'd found someone else to invest in Radio City. When Reg returned, Jill told him of the call.

"Mr Smedley sounded very excited."

"Did you mention anything about Radio London."

"No, I thought it better not to," replied Jill.

"Good. I need to ask him why he's not paying the overdue accounts. Can you phone him back in about 10 minutes and I'll speak to him?"

When Jill connected the call, Reg and Smedley chatted pleasantly for a few moments.

"I've some excellent news. I've found you a new investor."

"Ah," replied Reg, thoughtfully. "I'm sorry, I'm not looking for an investor. While you're on the phone, can you tell me why you're refusing to pay the overdue accounts?"

INVESTMENT AND GENERAL MANAGEMENT SERVICES
80a Coleman Street, London E.C.2.
Tel. Monarch 1661
Licensed Dealers in Securities.

24th May 1966

Captain A.C. Horsley M.C.
Meliora, Bowesden Lane,
Shorne.

Dear Sandy,

Seagull Publicity Ltd

I enclose a set of the draft documents in this case. I dare say there will never be a final edition as people are subscribing already, on the basis of the drafts, and with promises already made it looks as though we shall be over-subscribed.

If you want a participation, send us a cheque made out to Investment and General Management Services Limited and I will see you get what you apply for when we go to allotment.

As the station is already on the air and doing good business the risks involved are considerably less than in some other cases we have known.

I expect you saw the bit in the Times about the P.M.G. not taking action against the pirates.

Yours sincerely,
Oliver Smedley.

"What do you mean, you're sorry?" asked Smedley, indignantly.

"We sent you a letter listing the outstanding accounts and I've just received a reply from your office querying these and refusing to pay."

"I was phoning to tell you I've found an investor who wants to put money into Radio City."

"I've already said, I'm not looking for anyone to invest."

"What do you mean? You're not looking for anyone? I've got it all arranged."

"I've found someone myself."

"I thought we had an agreement? I was finding investors for you?"

"Since Mr Yablon came and looked at the accounts a month ago and decided not to invest, I have made my own arrangements."

"You've gone and done the dirty on me," bellowed Smedley, in response. "You knew I was looking for investors. I've being doing a lot of work on your behalf and you've gone and done the dirty behind my back."

Jill, who was sitting at the other side of the office could hear Smedley shouting down the line as Reg held the receiver away from his ear.

"Not at all," replied Reg, trying to be reasonable. "You didn't find anyone suitable and I don't remember there being any agreement that I couldn't find my own investors. My secretary has written to your office about the unpaid accounts and Mr Boutwood has replied querying them."

"That's beside the point. There's no way we will pay off the accounts now. You knew I was trying to find investors and you've gone behind my back. Who is this person you've found?" demanded Smedley, angrily.

"I've made an arrangement to go into partnership with Radio London," explained Reg, reluctantly. "It's all agreed. We'll be part of the Radio London network in a couple of week's so there is nothing else to be said about it."

"That's what you think," stormed Smedley, slamming the phone down.

Furious, he'd lost his opportunity to invest in Radio City, Smedley decided to take alternative action. He was short of capital and needed to make his man, Boutwood, redundant. He'd lost money with the collapse of the Atlanta/Caroline merger and pinned all his hopes on making money out of Radio City. He arranged a meeting with Horsley and Kitty Black and then telephoned Allan Crawford to inform him that he had taken the liberty of calling a meeting in his office.

"With the Atlanta Board?" questioned Crawford.

"No. Just us with Kitty Black and Sandy Horsley."

When Smedley arrived at Crawford's office in Dean Street, Crawford could see by his face that Smedley was angry.

"What's happened?'

"I'm furious. I happened to phone Reg Calvert to say I might have interest from a new investor and he'd the cheek to tell me I was too late. He's teamed up with Radio London."

"What do'ya expect?" replied Crawford, in his Australian drawl.

"I expected to make some money out of pirate radio," replied Smedley, angrily.

"It was a gamble that didn't pay off. Wish I'd thought about taking over a fort earlier. If I had, I might still be in broadcasting today," replied Crawford, thoughtfully.

"You might still be able to. He's supposed to be in partnership with us and I've seen the Radio City accounts and they're making good money."

There was a knock at the door and a slim, middle aged woman entered, neatly dressed with her hair smoothed back in a French roll.

"Kitty, come in. Nice to see you again," said Smedley, kissing her cheek.

A second knock at the door and a smart upright man entered.

"Ah, Sandy. Pleased you could come," said Smedley, as the two men shook hands. "I've arranged this meeting because I've bad news. Are you aware that Radio City's going into partnership with Radio London?"

"No, I hadn't heard," replied Horsley.

"For months, I've been trying to set up a new company, Seagull, to go into partnership with Calvert. I've written a prospectus and have been looking for investors."

"Yes, you sent me a copy."

"But Calvert has pipped you to the post," commented Crawford, dryly.

"The partnership with Radio London will be worth a lot of money," continued Smedley. "So I want to contest the deal and repossess my property. We have a transmitter out there he hasn't paid for. I need your help Sandy. I'm thinking of a boarding party."

"Do you think that's legal?"

"I'll take legal advice before we do anything. The trouble is, I can't issue a writ or take out an injunction as the towers have no known law English law."

"You won't get on the towers during the daytime. The doors would be shut against you," replied Horsley, thoughtfully.

"When do you think the best time to do it?"

"About two in the morning."

"This sounds very exciting," said Miss Black, laughing.

"It's not a good idea. It'll give pirate radio a bad name," said Crawford, irritably. He had heard enough of the conversation and could see where it was leading. He had come to know Smedley and taken a dislike to him and his tactics, wishing in hindsight, he could have set up the Atlanta Project without him.

"We need to organise boats and men for the boarding party," continued Smedley, ignoring Crawford's remarks. "And we need to do it quickly before Radio London personnel are on the tower."

"I know where there are some out-of-work riggers we can employ for the boarding party," replied Horsley. "We would need to hire a tug, maybe two. And we'll need provisions."

"That sounds just the thing," said Smedley, slapping Horsley on the back.

"Any idea of how much it will cost?" asked Miss Black.

"Quite a lot, depending how many days the men stay on the tower."

"I'm game. We can go four ways. I'll put in £250. It'll be quite an adventure," said Miss Black, enthusiastically.

"Why don't you ask the Atlanta Board to finance this?" queried Horsley.

"You can count me and the Atlanta Board out," said Crawford, abruptly. "I've no money and I don't agree with you boarding the station. I've already told you it will give pirate radio a bad name when we are trying to make it legal and I don't want the Radio Atlanta name involved in this operation. I would like to make it clear. I do not agree with what you are proposing to do."

"Thank you, Allan," said Smedley, impassively. "I agree. Perhaps you're right. It could give pirate radio a bad name."

Crawford, irritated by the meeting, had heard enough and left the room. As the door closed behind him, Smedley continued with his planning.

"Once we've boarded the station, I'm going to present them with a fait accompli. We should make quite a bit of money out of this deal and we'll each have a third share of any agreement that Reg Calvert or Philip Birch may come to."

"A third share?" repeated Horsley, astonished. "I just want to give money back to the shareholders. I invested £2,000 of my aunt's money into Project Atlanta and I managed to sell on £200 worth of shares, but I still have £1,800 and I feel responsible for my investment."

"You know Sandy, my elderly Aunt has invested practically all her money in Project Atlanta at my suggestion. If anything comes from this, all I get will go to the Project Atlanta shareholders," agreed Smedley.

"I entirely agree. But I don't want to be out-of-pocket doing this."

"No problem, you'll be reimbursed for any expenditure," assured Smedley, smugly, realising, he had successfully managed to get the gullible Horsley to foot the bill without having put in any of his own money. "This enterprise should be fun. All agreed?"

"Hear hear," smiled Miss Black. "And we should get some money back against our losses."

"Shall we set a date for the boarding party for Sunday 19th June?" suggested Smedley. "Do you think you'll be able to organise everything by then?"

"Yes. I think it'll be fine. I'll set the ball rolling," agreed Horsley, with some hesitation, not quite understanding that he had been duped.

The next day, Horsley contacted Max Hamilton, managing director of Ship Towage, and asked if he could provide a tug to go to the Nore, a sandbank in the Thames Estuary marking the point where the River Thames meets the North Sea. No mention was made of Shivering Sands. Hamilton said he could and the cost would be £90 per day weekdays and £120 per day weekends, for an eight-hour period.

The preparation to hijack the towers was like planning a wartime espionage expedition and everyone involved built up a web of subterfuge to ensure secrecy. Horsley invited two Trinity House Pilot colleagues to meet Smedley. Like him, they had bought shares in Project Atlanta and when they realised they might recoup some of their losses, they agreed to help.

Neil Buckland, one of the Trinity House Pilots, spoke to Fred Brandish, a Master Rigger and asked if he could find seven men for Captain Horsley. Brandish confirmed he could and quoted £2.7s 9d per day plus £4.18s a night, plus double rate on Sundays. The total pay for a seven-day week would be £54.16s per man plus Brandish's commission of 25 per cent.

"What will they have to do?" asked Brandish.

"They'll be going down river for three to seven days," replied Buckland, evasively.

"Will they be on a ship?"

"No, they'll be protecting some stuff for Captain Horsley. He's arranging it for the Major."

"I see," replied Brandish, still none the wiser who Captain Horsley or the Major were.

On Wednesday, Horsley contacted Henry Maxwell, another Trinity House Pilot and asked for his help. Wisely, Henry had not bought shares in Project Atlanta but was still eager to take part in the operation.

"Major Smedley has put £35,000 worth of equipment on the tower which hasn't been paid for," exaggerated Horsley. "We're going to take over the radio tower on Shivering Sands on behalf of the shareholders. Major Smedley wants the radio station off-air until he's been paid or some other arrangements made."

"Okay, count me in. Sounds a bit of a lark."

"Can you meet me and Don Jones on Friday morning, to discuss in more detail the boarding plan? It's top secret, so don't tell anyone."

Planning the hi-jack had become like a game of Chinese whispers and most of the people involved could only guess what they would be doing or where they would be going.

News of the impending boarding party reached Ted Allbeury. He worked with Smedley's cousin, the actor and disc jockey Mike Raven. Allbeury decided to forewarn Reg and rang his office on Wednesday afternoon, 15th June. Jill answered the phone and as Reg was out of the office he gave Jill a message about it, asking her to get Reg to call him back urgently on Victoria 9852. Reg returned to the office several hours later, and realising the gravity of the situation, he immediately dialled the number.

"Hello Ted. It's Reg Calvert."

"Hello Reg. Thanks for calling me back. I thought I'd let you know that I've heard on the grapevine that someone is organising a boarding party to take over Shivering Sands."

"Is it Roy Bates?"

"I'm sorry, I can't say," replied Ted, evasively, not wanting to reveal his source.

Reg realised he had to take the threat seriously and asked Jill to send a memo out to the station to tell the crew to keep a look out and tighten security. He then phoned Paul Elvey who was due back on the station on Friday, giving him instructions to keep all the hatch's locked.

"A Peter Dolphin called into the office while you were out," said Jill, looking at her other messages. "He's asked if he can go to Radio City for a week's trial. He's an actor and lives in Dolphin Square. He said he's between jobs and would like some experience as a disc jockey."

"Okay, he can go out with the boat on Friday," replied Reg.

"And Mr Boutwood phoned. He'd like to have a meeting with you on Monday. I've made an appointment for 11.30 a.m. He says he'll be leaving Mr Smedley's employment and there's a few things to tie up."

"That's fine. Hopefully he'll clear the debts before he leaves. I should be able to get there okay, but I'm going up to Manchester on Sunday to see a new group and may be late back."

Reg tried not to show his anxiety to his wife, but the threat of a boarding party was constantly at the back of his mind. On Friday morning, they went to have smallpox vaccinations in preparation for their second honeymoon. At the weekend, Reg helped his wife in the garden of Macbeth Close and did various odd jobs around the house she had been asking for.

"What's up with you?" smiled Dorothy, appreciatively.

"Nothing," replied Reg, putting his arm around his wife. "I want to make sure you can handle everything when I'm gone."

Dorothy looked at him quizzically. He was only going to Manchester on Sunday.

"Let's go and buy you a poodle," suggested Reg, impulsively. "I can see you with a poodle. What colour would you like?"

"I've never thought about a poodle," hesitated Dorothy.

"It'll keep you company when I'm not here."

"I'll have nowhere to walk a dog in London. There's no green areas or parks in Welbeck Street."

“Suppose not,” agreed Reg. ‘You can’t train a poodle to use the toilet like you did with William.”

Saturday night, father and daughter talked as they always did in the snug space of the car as they travelled together to Nuneaton and back. Reg was interested in her new boyfriend and tried to prise information from her without seeming too inquisitive.

“I’ve decided to finish with him next week.”

“Why?” asked Reg, surprised.

“We’re getting too serious and I don’t want to be serious with anyone. I want to travel, maybe work abroad next year.”

Making no comment about her decision, Reg replied, smiling, “The world’s your oyster. You can do anything you want to.”

After a late Sunday lunch, Dorothy drove Reg to Rugby station to catch a train to Manchester.

“See you later, alligator,” waved Reg.

“In a while, crocodile,” answered Dorothy.

At 10 p.m., Reg telephoned from Manchester to say he was tired and staying in a hotel for the night and would catch a train back to London on Monday morning.

The plans for the boarding party had gone smoothly. With everything in place, Smedley delayed giving final instructions until he was sure he had an ‘inside’ man on the station to leave a hatch open. Friday morning, after the Harvester had left Whitstable harbour, he contacted Horsley to give the all-clear to book the tug and increase the riggers from seven to ten men.

Horsley arranged the tug from Max Hamilton for one minute past midnight on Sunday, 19th June, taking advantage of the lower weekday rate. He also requested the use of a 20ft ladder, heaving lines and the tug’s smaller power boat, making up a story that the craft they were going to had a certain amount of overhanging super-structure and it would be safer to go alongside in a smaller craft.

“Can you tell me what it’s about or where we’re going?” asked Hamilton.

“I’ll let you know on the night but don’t worry. Everything is quite legal,” assured Horsley.

Neil Buckland phoned Fred Brandish to increase the number of men to ten, and for everyone to meet at the Royal Terrace Pier, Gravesend, at 11.30 p.m. on Sunday night.

“The men will want to know where they’re going.”

“Don’t worry. We’ll be going out to one of the towers.”

Fred Brandish had arranged with Alf Bullen, known by his friends as ‘Big Alf’, to find 10 men to do a job. Alf contacted his work mates who were all on strike and they were pleased to have employment, even though it was a bit of a mystery. One of Alf’s friends, Fred Law, worked at the

Tilbury Power Station and while they were having a drink together at the Chase Pub in Gravesend, it was suggested he might like a job afloat for at least 10–14 days.

"It should be a laugh and a giggle. We'll be paid about £54 a week," grinned Big Alf. "So you need to get your wife to let you go. We're meeting at the Old Comrades Club in Gravesend tomorrow night, about 10.30 p.m."

The Vanquisher moored alongside the Royal Terrace Pier, Gravesend on Sunday evening. Percy Smith, the skipper of the tug, asked Horsley what the job was for, but Horsley avoided answering, saying he would give details later. Percy Smith was curious and asked Dan Blackman, a local waterman whose small boat they had hired to tow behind the Vanquisher if he knew what they were going to do at the Nore.

"No idea, mate. I heard it was going to be a film stunt and there were film stars going," replied Blackman, shaking his head.

"I've spent all day preparing the Vanquisher for passengers and no one will bloody well tell me what's going on," retorted Smith, irritably.

"I can't imagine anyone hiring a tug at one minute past midnight unless it's for a film," replied Blackman.

Eleven men, most of them riggers, had gathered in the Old Comrades Club to have a few pints. At 11.30 p.m., they were loud and very merry as they made their way to the quayside and waited for instructions. Smith and Blackman looked at them with obvious disappointment. They had expected film stars, not a gang of rough, thickset riggers.

"Do you know what job you're doing?" asked Percy.

"No idea mate," replied Big Alf. "It's a mystery. No one's let us know anything."

"I was told it was just for a few days," replied one of the men.

"They said it could last for 10-14 days," said another.

Horsley checked his watch and at midnight, he nodded. Buckland instructed the riggers to load the Vanquisher with provisions that were stacked on the quay. Kitty Black arrived, dressed in dark slacks, dark coat and headscarf. She said hello to the riggers and laughing, told them that she was coming along as their cook.

The boat was hastily loaded and when they were underway, the riggers began to play cards and Miss Black settled down to do her knitting. With the lights of Gravesend shining in the distance, Smedley called Alf Bullen into the cabin.

"Can you tell me what the jobs about mate? No one's told us anything."

"What I want you to do is perfectly legal," assured Smedley. "I own the Shivering Sands towers and a lot of property on them. I want you to help me get it ashore. When we get there, we'll check to see if there are any trapdoors open and if there isn't, we'll wake them up and ask to come on board."

"Okay mate, I'll tell the men."

There was a good wind blowing and the tug, with the small power boat in tow, was buffeted about as it navigated its way through the inky black waters. It took nearly three hours to reach the towers and everyone was relieved to see them rising out of the gloom. As quietly as possible, the power boat was unhitched and boarded by the four pilots. Reaching the leg of the south-east tower, they took it in turns to jump off and climb up the ladders to the belly of the tower. Calling down, they confirmed the trapdoor had been left open. Soon, all the boarding party were shuttled to the tower leg and climbed up.

Miss Black, Smedley and Horsley, were first to make their way across to the living accommodation on the centre tower. Smedley opened the door to the first dormitory and shone his torch.

"What the hell's this?" asked Paul, sitting up. Recognising the man, he responded more politely, "Hello Mr Smedley."

"I've been sent by Mr Calvert with some people to prevent the possibility of a takeover. Please don't make a fuss. If you're calm, all will be okay."

"We mean you no harm," explained Horsley, as he shone his torch around the room and saw the frightened faces. "There's a dispute between managements. If you'd like to come and see Mr Calvert, we'll be happy to take you."

"You'd better know that Ian has an air rifle under his bed," beckoned Paul, as he quickly pulled on his clothes.

"Thank you for your advice," replied Smedley.

"I'll go and turn the generator on so we have lights," said Paul, and left the room with Smedley.

Phil Perkins was awoken by someone pushing what he thought was a gun in his face. He could hear voices and people calling to each other and realised it was a boarding party. With all the confusion, he immediately made his way to the transmitter tower and took the crystal out of Big Bertha and hid it in his pocket. The crystal was small and black, about one and a half inches long. He had spent hours working on it, grinding it down on a glass and wasn't prepared to let anyone take it from him.

Once the generator was working and the lights were on, Paul went with Smedley and Miss Black to the transmitter tower to talk.

"That's your transmitter over there," pointed Paul. "It's no good. The rest of the equipment is ours."

In another bedroom, the disc jockeys were woken by voices and Ian MacRae stood on his bed and looked out of the window.

"There's a boat out there with an engine running and lights. We'd better get dressed and see what's happening."

Leslie Dunne was sleeping in a room on his own and was roused by a man who stuck a gun in his stomach just as the lights came on.

"You. Get up and go to the sitting room and wait," said the intruder, gruffly.

Leslie did as he was told, terrified he was going to be killed. In the kitchen, he found Ian West in his pyjamas making mugs of tea.

"I think I've got appendicitis," groaned Leslie. "I've got terrible cramping pains in my stomach."

"Sit down and relax," replied Ian, as he passed mugs of tea to the crew.

Most of the Radio City staff had congregated in the kitchen area, wondering what was going on as men rushed about with torch lights.

The trial disc jockey, Peter Dolphin had brought a camera with him and as soon as he heard the kerfuffle, he got it out and began to take photographs of Smedley and the other boarders. Surprisingly, no one seemed to mind.

When Paul returned from the transmitter room with Smedley and Miss Black, Ian handed them a mug of tea.

"I want the crystal," demanded Miss Black. "I've heard that without it, you can't broadcast."

"It's all up mate. They want the crystal," said Paul loudly to Ian, so Smedley and Miss Black could hear him.

Reluctantly, Ian went to the transmitter tower with Smedley, Miss Black and Neil Buckland. Ian had recognised Smedley from a previous visit to the station when he had travelled back to Whitstable with him.

"I'm associated with the Atlanta Project and we're registered in Liberia," explained Smedley.

"Do you know who I am?" asked Miss Black.

"Yes," replied Ian, as he handed her a crystal from one of the transmitters, which she put into her handbag.

"We're concerned because we understand, in fact we know, the station has been sold to Radio London, but the transmitter which Radio Caroline supplied has not been paid for," explained Smedley. "The reason for removing the crystal and taking you off-air is so we'll have a good lever against Mr Calvert to get what we want."

"That's your transmitter over there," pointed Ian. "It doesn't work well and we don't use it."

"Can you give me the small black box with the butterfly thing in it?" asked Miss Black.

"I don't know what you're talking about"

"I want the small black box with the butterfly thing in it," she repeated, several times.

"I've no idea what you're talking about," repeated Ian, shaking his head.

"I'm putting a strong-arm guard to stop you doing any broadcasting," said Smedley. "And if anyone tries anything, I've given them instructions to smash everything and break up the aerial."

Ian could see through the studio window that someone had already gone in and torn the microphone from its fixing on the desk, turntables had been lifted, the mains leads cut and records were strewn all over the place. The only persons to have been in the studio tower just before him were Paul Elvey, Smedley and Miss Black.

When everything had settled down and the provisions stowed, the Vanquisher left the towers at 5.30 a.m.

Peter Dolphin stood on the catwalk with Paul Elvey to watch and take a final photograph of the tug sailing away in the dusky morning light.

"You should be able to take photographs without flash with that sort of camera," commented Paul, who was interested in photography.

"Yes, I'll take another one," replied Peter.

Several of the riggers had seen the flash and began to make their way menacingly across the catwalk towards them.

"Quick. You hide the camera for me while I keep them talking," whispered Peter, handing the camera to Paul.

"Okay, I'll hide it on the roof under the gun platform."

Peter faced the riggers and explained he was a photographer from the Daily Mirror and was recording the boarding party. An hour later, when Peter thought it was safe, he found Paul and asked him to return the camera.

"Okay. I'll go and fetch it."

"After Paul had searched the roof, he returned to Peter to say they camera was missing.

"It has to be there. That's where you left it."

"I've told you, I've looked and it's gone."

Don Jones and the riggers now occupied the studio tower and Peter went to see them and ask if any of their crew had taken the camera.

"No one's been over there," confirmed Don Jones.

"Someone must have been because my camera's missing."

Big Alf went off to search all the boarder's belongings and returned a short while later to say that he had not discovered the camera in anyone's bag.

Phil Perkins decided to send a radio message out and went to fetch the communications radio. Searching the room, he realised that someone had been in before him and removed it. He was puzzled as he knew the boarders wouldn't have known what to look for. Returning to his bedroom, he secretly made his own radio from a 'ham' radio kit he kept with his belongings. When he got it to work, he managed to communicate briefly with Eric Martin in the Record Centre.

"It's very dangerous out here," explained Phil. "There's been a boarding party and they've got guns."

24. BLACKMAIL

As the Vanquisher arrived back at Gravesend, the conspirators were jubilant, congratulating each other on a successful night's work. Smedley's next plan was to personally see Philip Birch at his home in Meopham and Henry Maxwell offered to go with him to show him the way.

"This should be fun, four of us in a Mini," laughed Miss Black, as she got into the rear seat with Horsley. When they arrived outside their destination, they waited for a few minutes until a quarter to eight when the front door opened and a tall, middle-aged man with dark hair emerged.

"That's him," said Smedley, opening the car door, he stepped out and greeted the man.

"Good morning Mr Birch. I'm Major Oliver Smedley. Could you attend a meeting at Allan Crawford's office at 47 Dean Street, for twelve noon today?"

"What's it about?" asked Philip Birch, looking puzzled.

"It's about Radio City and we're holding an urgent meeting."

"Okay, I'll be there."

Returning to the car, Smedley smiled smugly. "So far so good. He's agreed to come to the meeting but we could do with someone else being there to back us up. Do you know anyone who may be available?"

"I could ask Horace Leggatt. I'll give him a call," replied Horsley. "He's a Trinity Pilot and has some shares in Project Atlanta."

"Good man. Tell him it's important and ask him if he can come to the Dean Street office for 11.30 a.m."

"Good morning Allan," greeted Miss Black, yawning as she entered Crawford's office accompanied by Horsley. "Oliver will be here shortly. I hope you don't mind but we've arranged to meet here at lunchtime with Philip Birch from Radio London and Reg Calvert. Is it okay if we have a coffee while we wait? We've been up all night."

"And we're also expecting Horace Leggatt. I've asked him to come. He's one of the shareholders and he's coming to witness the meeting," added Horsley.

"Yes, I remember him," replied Crawford, uncomfortably. He could see by their faces they were in a state of excitement and guessed what they'd done.

Horace Leggatt then arrived and shortly afterwards, Philip Birch.

"We're waiting for Mr Smedley to arrive," explained Miss Black as she greeted Birch. "He shouldn't be long."

A few minutes later, Smedley came bustling into the office, holding a document in his hands.

"Good morning Mr Birch. I'm pleased you could come and I'm sorry to have kept you waiting. I've called this meeting to discuss a business proposition and inform you that we've taken over the Radio City fort during the night."

"You've done what? The station belongs to Mr Calvert," exclaimed Birch.

Crawford shook his head in disbelief. All he had said about giving pirate radio a bad name had been ignored. Standing up he apologised. "I've got other business to attend to so I'll leave you to it." He didn't agree with what they had done and left the room in disgust.

As the door closed to, Smedley continued.

"We're connected with Project Atlanta and an organisation called C.B.C."

"And what's this to do with me?" asked Birch, annoyed.

"As a businessman, I thought we could do a deal. If you would like the fort back, it will cost £5,000 plus 50 per cent of the advertising profit or 30 per cent of the advertising revenue."

"Why have you taken over the fort?"

"We put some valuable equipment on there and have been messed about by so many people in the past. This is the only way we can protect our interests."

"It really doesn't concern me. My deal is with Mr Calvert and I'm not interested in your financial proposition."

"In this case, possession is ten points of the law. I have the document here, if you would like to read it?"

"You have no moral, legal or other right to be on that fort. The whole thing is very underhand and you're using blackmail. If you have an agreement with Mr Calvert, it should be shown to solicitors and sorted out legally," replied Birch, angrily.

"Major Smedley has a valuable transmitter on the fort that hasn't been paid for," added Horsley, in defence of his colleague.

"He has a right to protect his equipment," insisted Miss Black.

"This is outrageous," replied Birch, losing his temper.

"That's up to you Mr Birch. But possession is ten parts of the law in a case like this. The forts are outside legal jurisdiction," repeated Smedley, smugly.

"I would never do business with people who've acted like you. How much longer will Mr Calvert be?"

"He's on a train from Manchester. His secretary said he should arrive at Euston by 12.30."

"I'll wait for him a little longer and then I have to go," replied Birch, impatiently.

Reg, on his arrival at Euston railway station, stopped at a telephone kiosk to call the office and Jill explained that she had received a message from Mr Boutwood, saying the meeting had been changed and was now at Mr Crawford's office in Dean Street with Mr Smedley at 12.30 p.m.

"It's 12.30 now. Can you call him on the other line and ask him if I'm too late?"

Reg waited in the telephone kiosk for Jill to make the call and after a few minutes, she came back with the answer that Mr Smedley would wait.

By the time Reg arrived at the Dean Street office, Philip Birch had left.

"Hello Reg," greeted Smedley, shaking his hand cheerily. "Let me introduce you. This is Miss Kitty Black, Sandy Horsley and Horace Leggett. Have a seat. I've called this meeting today to discuss a business proposition with you and to let you know that last night we took over Radio City"

For a moment, Reg was speechless.

"If you want the station back, we want £5,000 plus 50 per cent of the advertising profit or 30 per cent of the advertising revenue."

Reg couldn't quite believe what he was hearing and in a pretence to appear unconcerned, replied that the partnership deal with Radio London had gone through, so it was out of his hands and didn't affect him.

"You've got valuable equipment on the tower that belongs to Mr Smedley and Project Atlanta. You shouldn't have gone into partnership with Radio London without paying for the transmitter," accused Horsley.

"That transmitter is old and doesn't work."

"That's your problem. You shouldn't have let it drop in the sea," replied Horsley.

"It wasn't the transmitter that fell in, only the power pack and that was retrieved and dried," replied Reg, quietly. "As far as I'm concerned you can collect the transmitter at any time. We've never used it."

"I think you should seriously think about signing this agreement if you want your station back," smiled Miss Black.

Reg looked at the woman and tried to assess her as he looked her in the eye. She was aged about 50, elegant, tall, slim and cultured.

"What you've done is wrong. Radio City has nothing to do with Project Atlanta. Your transmitter is useless. It's sitting there doing nothing and you still owe me money for the transportation costs and the time when we were supposed to be in partnership. I thought the meeting today was with Mr Boutwood to clear up the remainder of the debts, which amounts to £322."

"You'll have to sign this agreement if you want to get Radio City back," said Smedley, firmly.

"If you try to board the towers to get the men off, they've been instructed to destroy all the equipment and render it useless," threatened Miss Black.

"We're outside legal jurisdiction so there's nothing you can do about it. Possession is ten parts of the law," said Smedley, smiling smugly.

Reg was visibly shocked. He couldn't believe what he was hearing. He clenched his fists tightly then released them as he tried to maintain a calm persona and find words to talk his way out of the problem. He would never have expected a respectable businessman and an educated woman to be so underhand. As nonchalantly as he could, he began to talk about his holiday in Spain.

"We'll have been married twenty years this weekend and we're having a second honeymoon to celebrate."

Ignoring Reg's holiday plans, Smedley pointed to the document. "You can have your station back if you agree to our terms."

"I do want Radio City back."

Reg was beginning to feel like a cornered rat as the seriousness of the situation became clear. His mind quickly turned over ideas of how he could remove the intruders from Shivering Sands. He knew it was almost impossible if the hatches were locked down so he would need all his ingenuity to get them off.

"You'll give me an opportunity to experiment," said Reg, thinking aloud. "I've always been interested in chemistry and I've been experimenting with a new nerve gas."

This wasn't true and no one in the meeting believed him, realising it was a bluff.

"I carry this gas pen around with me for my personal protection," explained Reg, as he took out the small pen he carried in his breast pocket. "You see, in here is a small amount of gas. I will make more and drop bombs on the towers and the boarders will be screaming to come off."

"Well you better make the bombs out of sticky bomb plastic, otherwise they won't stick to the towers," joked Miss Black.

"You must be mental," exclaimed Horsley, who seemed to believe everything said to him.

"I know I'm most unusual," replied Reg, trying to be cheerful. "My wife can do nothing with me when I've made up my mind."

"The station can quickly be returned to normal," smiled Miss Black, turning her head towards the document that lay on Crawford's desk.

"If you agree to draw up an agreement giving my company a half share, we can negotiate a deal right here and now," repeated Smedley.

Reg shook his head slowly. "I'll take steps to regain control of Radio City in whatever way I have to."

His anger was bubbling under the surface but he controlled himself and continued to talk very quietly. Reg could see they were inwardly laughing at his puerile attempts to warn them off.

"What you've done is totally wrong. Radio City belongs to me and no one else. I've come up the hard way and I know some strong-arm boys who'll sort your men out."

"If you want the station back, you can have it peaceably by signing this contract," reiterated Miss Black.

"I have another business I want to start. I'm thinking about having a station in the Bristol Channel. There's no one broadcasting to the West Country. If you're interested, we can talk about that as a new business proposition?" suggested Reg, trying a different tactic.

"No, we're not interested in new schemes," replied Smedley. "Just this one. And I seriously recommend that you and Mr Birch come to a decision to sign this agreement quickly."

"What you've done is wrong and I will find some way of getting your men off," repeated Reg, as he stood up to leave.

"I think there has been a good deal of talk and it would be better if everyone forgets what has been said," smiled Smedley, also standing up.

When Reg left the office, Horsley was subdued and muttered, "That didn't go well."

"Don't you worry," replied Smedley, condescendingly, as he patted him on his back. "Let's all go for lunch."

"I didn't like Mr Birch saying it was blackmail," added Horace Leggett, thoughtfully.

"I think we should take our men off as we haven't got a deal," frowned Horsley.

"No. We're in possession of the tower and looking after our own equipment," assured Smedley, confidently. "We'll keep our nerve and see if they crack."

"The longer the riggers stay on the towers, the amount will go up so I think we should call our men off today. It's already cost about £500 for the tug and supplies," explained Horsley, worried, as neither Smedley or Miss Black had offered to pay in advance for the boarding party and soon, the amount would exceed the £250 each they had said they'd contribute.

"Don't you worry old man. I've got another little plan up my sleeve. You'll be reimbursed when it's all over," replied Smedley, cheerfully.

Reg returned to Denmark Street in very sombre mood saying nothing to Jill or anyone else about what had happened. The phone rang.

"Ted Allbeury for you," said Jill.

"Hello Ted," greeted Reg, politely.

"I've heard Radio City's off-air."

"Yes. Some technical problem. We should sort it out soon."
"Someone said you've been boarded."
"No, it's just a technical problem," denied Reg. "Even if we were, it's up to Radio London as they're taking over."
"Ah, okay. Hope you're keeping well?"
"Yes, I'm fine. Looking forward to a holiday in Spain next week," replied Reg, trying to appear cheerful.

Ted Allbeury was a clever and inquisitive man who had worked in the Intelligence Service during the war. It was in his nature to keep his ear to the ground and after his conversation with Reg, he made a call to Radio London and spoke to Philip Birch's assistant, who confirmed the rumour was true. His next call was to Mike Raven, Major Smedley's cousin, guessing he might know more about what was going on.
"Yes," confirmed Raven. "Oliver has taken over Radio City and he'd like a meeting with you to discuss it."
"Okay, ask Oliver to meet me at my club for lunch tomorrow."

Reg went to the Radio London offices and had a meeting with Philip Birch who confirmed he would back Reg and have nothing to do with Smedley. This eased Reg's mind and he felt a little happier. All Radio City employees had been invited one by one, to be interviewed by Radio London about their future employment. As Reg was leaving, he happened to see Tom Edwards and they hailed a taxi together to return to Denmark Street.
"How did you get on?" asked Reg.
"Okay. I've just been discussing the format of the new programmes with Duncan Johnson. He's going to be Senior Disc Jockey when Radio London takes over."
"That's good. Would you like to come for dinner this evening?"
"That'd be great, thank you."
"I'll phone my wife and let her know you're coming."
Reaching the office, Reg asked Tom if he could go and order an ice cream cake for the evening. While Tom was gone, Reg broke the news to Jill and then phoned Dorothy to let her know what had happened. Replacing the receiver, he asked Jill what she thought he should do.
"What did Mrs C say?"
"Not much. I think she's as shocked as I am."
"What did Philip Birch think?"
"He said he won't do business with a person like Major Smedley. He thought it was outrageous to blackmail us into giving him £5,000 and 50 per cent of the profit. We're sitting tight and hoping that if they can't get either of us to pay, they'll take their men off. We're keeping it quiet so it doesn't get into the press."

"Can you go to the police about it?"
"I'm not sure. The trouble is the station is outside British jurisdiction."
The remainder of the afternoon, Reg spoke to various people on the phone. Fred Downs had been out with Tony Pine to see why the station was off-air and reported back that it had been boarded in the night by eleven men. Phil Perkins managed to get a message through to Eric Martin in the Whitstable office, saying it was dangerous and Kitty Black had taken a crystal.
"Can you try and find Kitty Black's telephone number," asked Reg.
"I'll look it up," replied Jill, picking up a telephone directory.
"If she has the crystal and we can prove theft, I suppose the police might be able to prosecute."

By the time Reg arrived home from the office, he was very subdued. Halfway through his meal he pushed his plate aside and stood up.
"Sorry Doe Doe. I'm not hungry. I've got a phone call to make."
"What's the matter with Reg? He doesn't seem his normal cheerful self," asked Tom.
"Hasn't he told you? The station's been boarded by a load of armed thugs. Major Smedley from Radio Atlanta has taken it over. They're blackmailing him," explained Dorothy.
"Will he want me to go out to the station tomorrow? I'm due back on."
"I don't know. You'll have to ask him."
"Reg asked me to order an ice cream cake. I'll go and fetch it."
"I'll come with you," said Candy, smiling.
Later, Tom and Candy returned with the cake and Reg came into the kitchen and sat down. He looked grey in the face and downcast. Dorothy cut the cake into slices and put the remainder in the freezer.
"Do you want me to go out to the station tomorrow?" enquired Tom.
"Not sure what to do," pondered Reg. "I've a feeling I ought to take all my men off for their own safety and then we can have a real go at removing the boarders. We know quite a few wrestlers and boxers that steward our dances we can call on. It's tricky. The boarders have been instructed to smash all the equipment if anyone goes near. And if we abandon the towers, Smedley can claim possession."
"Maybe I should go out as normal?"
"Yes, I think that's best."
The doorbell rang and Reg stood up, wearily. "I'd forgotten. I've agreed to see a singer who wants an audition and he's coming with his manager. I won't be long."
Tom stood up to go and after thanking Dorothy for the meal, he left with Candy who accompanied him to Victoria Station for his return journey to Whitstable.

At night, Reg tried in vain to sleep. His mind turning over all that had happened and whether he could have done anything differently. Somehow, he had to find a way to get the men off the towers. If he did nothing, he would lose everything. If he sent his own boarding party out, the men on the towers would smash everything. Do nothing and risk losing everything. Do something and risk losing everything.

"Can't you sleep?" murmured Dorothy, turning to lie in his arms.

"No. I'm tired but I feel so angry and helpless at the same time."

"You need to sleep. There's nothing you can do tonight."

In the morning, Reg felt awful, his left arm had become stiff from the smallpox vaccination and he felt he too was going down with flu. Slowly, with difficulty, he began to dress, using his left hand as little as possible.

"I don't know how I'm going to get through today. When I started the station, it was fun and exciting."

"Don't do anything mad. You need to keep calm."

"I will, but it makes my blood boil to think they can take over Radio City as if they have a right to it telling me that "in this case, possession is 10 per cent of the law." Major Smedley was so smug and self-righteous. Everyone believed him, except for the woman. I'm sure she knew the transmitter was worthless. The other two men seemed to be taken in by him."

"Just as you were. I told you he didn't ring true. My sixth sense."

"You and your sixth sense."

"You should take more notice of it," smiled Dorothy. "Did you speak to Allan Crawford?"

"I have and he told me he didn't agree with what they were doing but he wouldn't say much else. They all stick together like glue. "

"What about going to the police?"

"I might go later. I'm waiting for more information and I should get feedback this afternoon with the change of crew."

"How did the boarders get on?"

"What do you mean?"

"I thought all the hatches were kept battened down."

"They should have been. I spoke to Paul myself and told him to tighten up security."

"That's very strange," replied Dorothy. "Someone on the station must have let them in."

Different people were calling the office to enquire why Radio City was off-air and Jill told them it was a technical fault. Alan Arnold rang, wanting to know whether there was a problem with his aerial. Reg replied, cautiously, that the last time he had heard, it was fine.

"What's wrong then?"

"We've a bit of bother on the fort. There are some people who are stopping me transmitting."

"What do you mean?"

"They're trying to force me off-air," answered Reg, not wanting to give out more information.

"Can you keep me in the picture?" asked Alan, concerned about his aerial.

"Of course, I'll keep you informed."

Gradually, news filtered through to the office from the crew coming off the station and Reg learnt more of the night's activities. He caught a taxi to Bow Street Police Station and had a meeting with Detective Sergeant Colin Rutter who explained that the law was very complex with regard to jurisdiction."

"Something needs to be done," said Reg, as he explained more about the boarding party.

"It's outside our jurisdiction," repeated Rutter. "But I'll make enquiries at New Scotland Yard and see if anyone there can help you further."

"Is it possible that the police can prosecute Major Smedley and Miss Kitty Black? They've stolen equipment worth about £105 from the station and we can't go back on-air without it."

"You should speak to Major Smedley yourself to try to come to some agreement."

"My secretary's been trying to contact him all day but he's not answering our calls. What would happen if I take action myself to forcibly eject the boarders?"

"Sorry, I cannot advise you legally on that, but now you've brought it to my attention, you should await the outcome of our investigation."

Jill had been unable to find Kitty Black's phone number so when Reg returned to the office he called Crawford who told him that her real name was Dorothy, not Kitty. When Jill spoke to her, she denied having the crystal but said that Major Smedley knew where it was.

Reg deliberated over what to do and went to discuss things with Brian Harvey in the next office. It was his first day working for Reg.

"I've no intention of giving into their demands," explained Reg. "Philip Birch thinks we should just sit tight and not be blackmailed. At my meeting with Major Smedley, I felt like picking up a chair and smashing it over his smug head," laughed Reg.

"Your police contact sounds more hopeful," said Brian, optimistically.

"Not really, we're outside of jurisdiction. Could you do me a favour? Find out the cost of hiring a helicopter to the fort? We could get some actors, hire police uniforms from a theatrical costumier, and when we're outside the three-mile limit, they can put the uniforms on and board the fort and take the invaders off."

"That's an idea," smiled Brian. "Do you think it'll work?"

Reg grinned as he thought about it. "Don't know. It's worth a try."

Returning to his own office, Reg decided to send a note to the boarders explaining he had been to the police. He then phoned Tony Pine and asked him to take it out to the towers and read it to the men and do his best to try and stop any damage and pacify them.

The crew on Radio City were outnumbered two to one and realised it would be hopeless to try and regain control of the station. An uneasy truce followed. The boarders were tired after being up all night and had nothing to do other than prevent staff from going into the studio or transmitting room. They took to sitting around, snoozing and playing cards to pass the time. They had no blankets, nowhere to sleep, and not enough provisions. Once the enmity had subsided, the crew took pity on the boarders, giving them the extra things they needed. They realised they had to accept the situation and hope it would be resolved quickly.

John drove to Whitstable with the note and Fred took Tony to the station. As they arrived, a tug came alongside the towers with a party of about 15 men, two of them pilots with more provisions for the riggers. Tony showed the boarders the memo and tried to persuade them it was in their interest to leave. After the men briefly discussed it, they rejected the idea as they were being paid very good money for doing nothing and decided to stay put. When Fred returned to Whitstable, he phoned the office and spoke to Reg to explain the situation and that the memo had not had the desired effect.

The blackmail threat Mr Smedley and Company arranged has failed and Mr Calvert has approached Scotland Yard to deal with it. We send this letter as a caution to all people who have taken part in the subterfuge so that they might know the severity of what they are doing.

This boat will undertake to convey you to the mainland if you wish to come off, the alternative you should be aware of. We have photographs of the majority of your crew so that the availability of your addresses is only a matter of time.

Any damage to Radio City property will only ensue with the men responsible being directly charged with sabotage. I beg you take heed of this note as this is your last and only chance to leave peaceably.

Reginald Calvert

For Radio City.

Tuesday lunchtime, Smedley met Allbeury at his club and he put forward the same proposal as he had done the day before. Allbeury listened with great interest. He'd heard that Radio London was about to start a 'sweet music' station in competition to Radio 390, and was concerned it would seriously affect his profits. Another consideration was that Shivering Sands were outside the three-mile territorial limit, while Red Sands were not and could easily be closed by the government. Taking all things into account, £5,000 for Radio City seemed very reasonable.

After the meeting, Allbeury phoned the Radio London offices and spoke to Philip Birch.

"Hello Philip. I thought I'd let you know that I've had a meeting with Oliver Smedley today and he's offered to sell me Radio City."

"What are you going to do?"

"I'm going to hold a meeting with our directors to discuss it."

"It's not Smedley's station to sell. It belongs to Reg Calvert," replied Birch, shocked.

"It seems a good deal to me. I'll let my directors decide."

Philip Birch phoned Reg to let him know that Radio City was being put up for sale to other stations. It came as a blow. Suddenly, the boarding party took on a new characteristic. Sitting tight and waiting for the boarders to leave was no longer an option. Reg was incensed and picked up the phone to warn Allbeury off.

"Hello Ted, I understand you've had lunch with Mr Smedley?"

"Yes, that's right."

"I'm told he made you an offer?"

"Yes, he has."

"What do you intend to do about it?"

"I'm going to have a meeting with my board and discuss it," replied Allbeury, amiably.

"Let me make this clear," said Reg, quietly. "I want to warn you that I will personally take action to get every boarder off the station."

"What will you do?" asked Allbeury, provocatively.

"You have a very nice little business. If I lose my business and if you have anything to do with it, I'll see you lose yours," replied Reg, as he put the receiver down, white faced and grim.

Allbeury thought for a moment then phoned Birch and told him of the conversation.

"I've just spoken to Reg Calvert. He's a dangerous man."

"Reg has never seemed dangerous to me," replied Birch, calmly. "Mr Smedley's organisation has started this off with violence. He must expect these sort of things to happen. You can't just take over someone's Radio Station with force and expect the man to sit back and not be angry."

"I think he's psychotic. It would be a good idea to give him some Vegemite to make sure he gets a good night's sleep," joked Allbeury, who was in his element. He enjoyed conspiracy and detective work and when he finished speaking to Birch, he phoned Smedley.

"Hello Oliver. I've some news for you. I've just spoken to Reg Calvert. He's hopping mad and threatening all sorts of things."

"What sort of things?"

"He says he's going to kill all the boarders on the station. I told him not to be so absolutely ridiculous."

"Whatever in the world will he get up to next?" laughed Smedley. "Thanks for phoning and I hope you and I can do business together soon."

"I'll let you know shortly when I've arranged a meeting with our board," replied Allbeury.

Smedley spent most of the day in his office, except for lunching with Allbeury but each time Reg or Jill rang, his secretary, Pamela Thorburn, would politely say that Mr Smedley was out of the office but she could take a message. It was obvious to them that Reg was becoming more anxious.

"Could you tell Mr Smedley that I have brought written charges to bear on him for theft to the CID. However, if Mr Smedley contacts me in the next few minutes, I'll get the whole thing hushed up."

"I'll do that," replied Miss Thorburn, smiling at Smedley as she put the receiver down.

A little later, Reg telephoned again.

"Could you let Mr Smedley know we've sent a boat to the Tower to inform the men who have been left in charge that all their photographs are in Police possession and that if they don't come ashore immediately and surrender, they will be arrested whenever they do."

Each time Miss Thorburn put down the phone, she and Smedley laughed at Reg's futile bluffs and threats. Smedley knew the law. The towers were outside British jurisdiction and he was confident there was nothing the police or anyone else could do to remove the boarders.

As the afternoon drew on, Reg was feeling heavy with exhaustion and his arm became stiffer. He spent time discussing options, over and over, with both Brian Harvey and Jill, as he tried to formulate some sort of plan.

"I could go to Mr Smedley's home this evening and try and get him to see reason."

"Do you want John to go with you?" asked Jill.

"No thanks. When he gets back from Whitstable, can you ask him to go to Oxford University. The Fortunes have phoned to say that their PA system isn't working and they've a gig there tonight."

"Okay. Is there anything else you want me to do before I go home?"

“You could try Mr Smedley’s office again. See whether he’s back. I’m really worried about my crew on the station. It’s a very dangerous situation for them to be in.”

Jill dialled the number and Miss Thorburn answered it.

“I’m sorry. Mr Smedley is out of the office. Would you like to leave a message?”

“Do you want to leave a message?” asked Jill, with her hand over the mouthpiece.

“Yes, can you say that the situation is getting very dangerous.”

During the day, Alan Arnold had become increasingly worried by the threat that the boarders might cut his aerial down and phoned the office regularly to find out more about what was happening.

“What are you going to do about it?” asked Alan.

“I’m not sure,” replied Reg. “I’ve a few ideas. Do you think I can borrow one of your shotguns?”

“No. They’re far too valuable to take out to the station as it might get dropped in the drink. Have you thought about going to the police?”

“Yes, I went earlier this afternoon. It’s unlikely they can help. We’re outside jurisdiction.”

“What about recruiting a crowd of men from a local gym to take with you? They’re strong.”

“I don’t think we’d get onto the station. The hatches would be locked and we don’t want the boarders to smash up the equipment.”

“No, definitely not.”

“I’ve been trying to contact Mr Smedley all day. My secretary has found his home number and tried to call him but there’s no reply. I’m thinking I might go to see him at his home this evening. The trouble is, I had my smallpox vaccination the other day. I’m not feeling well and I can hardly move my left arm. Do you think you could drive and come with me for moral support?”

“Yes, I should be able to,” replied Alan, cautiously.

Before Reg left the office, he mulled over the day’s events with Brian Harvey, explaining that he’d like a peaceful settlement but didn’t know what to do for the best.

“I can’t get hold of Mr Smedley so I’ve left messages. Jill’s got his home address so I may go and see him there.”

“Would you like me to go with you? So long as it’s a peaceful discussion and no violence, I’d be pleased to come.”

“No, it’s okay thanks. I don’t feel well and I’m tired. If I decide to go and see Mr Smedley, I might telephone and ask you to arrange to pick me up in my car. Can you stay by the phone until about midnight?”

“Yes, I’m not planning to go out anywhere late,” replied Brian.

When Reg arrived home, Dorothy was in bed feeling unwell and he sat down next to her.

"I feel awful too. I think I'm going down with flu."

"You look all in. Have a rest while I cook a meal."

"I'm not hungry," replied Reg, as he caught hold of his wife's hand and held it tight.

"You have to eat, and I've got some filet steak."

"I don't know what to do. I can't believe what's happened. It's my worst nightmare and I feel so helpless. He must be short of money as he's given his man, Mr Boutwood, notice to leave. Since my agreement to go in with Radio London, he's refused to pay the bad debts and it makes my blood boil to think he can make money out of me by selling my station."

"Calm down. It's no use being angry. You have to stay calm."

"He's so sure of himself and what he's done. He knows he can get away with it and no one can stop him."

"Being angry won't help."

"Someone's told the press about the boarding party and I had to fight my way into Welbeck House. There's a load of photographers camped by the front door."

"There goes the phone again. I'll answer it," said Dorothy, picking up the receiver. "Detective Sergeant Rutter for you."

"Good evening," said Reg. "Have you heard any more?"

"I've made an appointment with Detective Inspector Barker at New Scotland Yard for 10 a.m. in the morning."

"I'm not sure whether I'll get there," replied Reg. "I'm thinking about going out to the fort to eject the men."

"That's not very wise, Sir, you'll be outnumbered ten to one."

"Not if I'm suitably armed and pepper them with lead," joked Reg.

"It would be a serious offence to carry a fire arm."

"I know and I don't even own a gun," replied Reg, seriously. "I'm actually thinking of going out and paying them off."

"You'd be better off discussing this with Major Smedley first. Try to get some resolution."

"I've been trying to contact him all day so I may go to his home this evening."

"You could wait until after you've had your meeting with Inspector Barker and see what he can do."

"They're trying to sell my business to someone else so I need to act quickly," explained Reg.

"So, you're intending to see Major Smedley this evening?"

"Yes, I think so. I'll tell him I've put this in the hands of the police and try and get him to see reason to take the men off."

"And you'll be at the meeting tomorrow morning?"
"Yes, I should be there. Thanks for your help."

There was no chatter or lively banter while the family ate their evening meal. An ominous air of anxiety hung over them and as soon as Reg had eaten, he left the kitchen and went to the bedroom. A few minutes later, Dorothy joined him and sat on the bed.

"I don't feel well, I think I've got flu," said Reg, shivering.

"It must be the side effect of the smallpox vaccination."

"I'd better get ready to go. I really don't want to but I've got to sort this out before he sells the station to someone else."

"I'll get dressed and go with you."

"No, I don't want you involved. I'll be okay to drive to Alan's house in Hertford and he's agreed to drive me to Mr Smedley's house in Saffron Walden. Alan is really worried about his aerial. If we can't make Mr Smedley see reason, then I'll go out to the station and pay the men off."

"You'd better have this," said Dorothy as she opened a bedroom drawer and handed him a brown envelope. "There's £440 in there that I'd saved for our holiday."

"Thanks Doe Doe," replied Reg, kissing her on the cheek. "We can have a holiday some other time when this is all over. Can you call Mr Smedley's house to see if he's in. Say it's the wrong number?"

When Reg was ready to leave, Dorothy, dialled the number and confirmed Smedley was there.

"I'll go out by the fire escape to avoid the reporters by the front door," said Reg, as he put on his warm winter's coat and black leather gloves.

"Be careful and stay calm."

"I will."

It was a cold midsummer's night and as he left the apartment he called out, "Good bye," but no one answered. A minute later he was gone.

The apartment was still and airless. Dorothy went back to bed and could not shake off a sense of foreboding as she waited anxiously, her head throbbing and her body aching. They had never had to face anything so serious in their lives before but she trusted Reg. He was good at talking and negotiating his way out of trouble and if he didn't succeed with Smedley, she knew he would be able to reason with the boarders and pay them off.

Her daughters occupied themselves quietly, sensing the gravity of the situation. Candy stayed in her bedroom, she worried about Tom, who had gone out to Shivering Sands as relief crew. Susan, to calm her nerves, sat at the kitchen table drawing a bouquet of flowers that Tom had given to Candy the day before.

The telephone rang at 9 p.m.

"I've arrived at Alan's house in Hertford. We'll be leaving in a few minutes."

"Take care," replied Dorothy.

Sandy Horsley lived in Shorne, about three miles between Gravesend and Rochester. He'd organised a gathering at his bungalow with the Trinity House Pilots who were involved with the boarding party and they were all very excited. Henry Maxwell and Neil Buckland were late arriving as they had just returned from taking more provisions out to Shivering Sands.

"How are the negotiations going?" asked Neil Buckland.

"Why don't you speak to Oliver yourself," replied Horsley. "I'll ask the operator to get his number for you."

For more than half an hour, various men talked to Smedley. At 10 p.m., Smedley explained he couldn't talk anymore as he was waiting for a visitor to arrive.

"Who is it you're expecting?" asked Horsley.

"A Press Association Officer," replied Smedley, mysteriously.

Horsley guessed who Smedley meant.

"Can you phone me back later after your visitor has called and let me know what he said?"

Alan Arnold and Reg set off in Reg's Zodiac towards Saffron Walden. It was an area that neither of the men knew and during the journey, the two men chatted amiably. When they reached Newport, Alan stopped outside the Railway Inn so Reg could ask directions. Fortunately, one of the locals knew exactly where to go and after buying a bottle of cider and some butterscotch sweets, Reg returned to the car.

"Wendens Ambo is not far now," confirmed Reg. It's a couple of miles before Saffron Walden and quite close to Audley End."

It was dusk and just getting dark as they drove into Wendens Ambo.

"It's a very pretty village," commented Alan.

"I think that must be Duck Street over there," pointed Reg.

Alan parked the car and waited while Reg walked up to the front door of a cottage and knocked. A moment later, a woman appeared.

"Is Mr Smedley in?" asked Reg, politely.

"Sorry, this is the wrong cottage. He lives three doors up," pointed the woman.

Turning, Reg beckoned to Alan where they had to go and together they walked toward a thatched cottage with roses growing around the door. The sitting room window was open and Smedley's voice could be heard as he talked to his companion who was in the dining room. Reg knocked the door and Pamela Thorburn got up to answer it.

"Can I see Mr Smedley please?" asked Reg, politely.

25. IN THE SILENCE OF THE NIGHT

Smedley, on hearing Reg's voice, walked quickly to his ground floor bedroom behind the lounge and reached up for a shotgun stored on the top of his wardrobe in a canvas case. He hastily unzipped the cover, loaded it and as he clicked the barrels shut, the telephone rang.

"Hello. Sandy Horsley here. Is that Oliver?"

"Yes, my visitor has just arrived."

"What are you going to do?"

"I've loaded my gun. Got to go," answered Smedley, replacing the receiver.

Stealthily, Smedley made his way out of the double French doors that led from the sitting room to a conservatory at the rear of the property. Across the way was Garden Cottage. A young man was stood in the doorway chatting to a lady who rented it from Smedley and did his cleaning.

"Is Mr Pithers in?" enquired Smedley, in a rush.

"No, he's away," replied the young man.

"Can you ring the police. Tell them to come. I have big trouble."

Neil Warden and Mrs Pithers looked at each other, wondering what the problem could be. They could hear no noise and thought he may have burglars. They went into the hall and Neil Warden dialled 999 and spoke to the police.

Pamela Thorburn had opened the cottage door and realising immediately who it was, answered sharply, "He's not in," and pushed the door closed in Reg's face.

Just before the door slammed, Reg put his foot in the door.

"I know he's in. I heard him talking to you."

"I've told you, he's not in," lied Miss Thorburn, as she tried to force the door closed.

"I want to take him to the police station so we can discuss what he's done," insisted Reg, quietly, as he pushed his way over the threshold and looked about. The cottage had a very small entrance hall with stairs opposite. On the left-side was the dining room and on the right-side, was the sitting room. Pamela Thorburn blocked the way and began to shout as she obstructed Reg in whatever way she could as he tried to make his way to the sitting room.

Reg could hardly move his left arm and kept it down as he tried to deflect her blows with his right arm.

"Alan, go and look upstairs and see if he's there," instructed Reg.

Alan went upstairs and after checking the rooms, returned a minute later.
"He's not there."

"He must be somewhere," said Reg, standing by the entrance to the empty sitting room.

Miss Thorburn had stopped pushing to bend down and stand up an electric fire she'd kicked over. Standing up, she shouted at Reg, "I've told you, he's not here. Now get out."

"If I can't speak to him, perhaps you'd like to come with me? I can take you to the police station," said Reg, looking at the woman.

On a coffee table, next to the settee was a telephone. Seeing it, Miss Thorburn rushed over to call 999. Reg, realising, pulled the telephone from her. Standing up, she began to wrestle with him again, making her way to the entrance hall where she picked up a bronze statue of Nelson to hit him with.

"Get out, get out," she yelled, raising the statue above her head.

She had fought like a cat and Reg was bleeding above his left eye where she had clawed him. He had not expected to be greeted like this and realised that Smedley must have made his escape to avoid him. Reg was ready to leave and Alan was already outside, waiting for him while he pondered what to do. Alan hadn't expected there to be a struggle and didn't want to get involved as he had a heart problem.

Before Miss Thorburn had a chance to hit Reg, he grasped her arm, forcing the object from her, he threw it across the hallway where it landed under a sideboard.

Smedley had not escaped. He was ready to confront Reg with his loaded shotgun. Walking briskly, he returned through the conservatory to the other side of the cottage and stood by the doorway of the dining room. He saw Reg wrestle the statue from Miss Thorburn and throw it away, under the sideboard. Without saying a word, he lifted his gun and pulled the trigger.

Alan heard the explosion. He pushed the front door open and as he stepped back inside, saw Reg's shocked expression as he toppled forwards from the sitting room doorway to fall onto his face in the hallway. Reg was hunched up with a blood red-rimmed hole in his chest.

Glancing to his left, Alan saw a man holding a double-barrelled shotgun in firing position with the barrels pointing towards the floor. He presumed it must be Smedley.

"My God this is murder," exclaimed Alan.

Smedley looked at him coldly and lifted the gun. Alan, very alarmed, saw the barrels move in his direction. He ran for his life, out of the cottage and towards the car. When he had collected his wits, he decided to get help from the nearest cottage. He ran along the passageway and found the door open and inside, Neil Warden was sitting by the telephone and speaking to the police.

"Get help, quickly. A man's been shot."

"I'm onto the police now."

"For God's sake, get help quick, a man is bleeding to death."

Alan waited for the man to pass the message onto the police and while he stood there, Smedley came and stood alongside him, still carrying his gun. He beckoned Alan to return with him. Nervously, he followed. As he entered the hallway, he saw that Reg was now unconscious and lying on his back covered with a bedspread. His face had turned grey. Bubbles of blood were between his lips and he was breathing with the sound of a death rattle.

"I need a drink?" said Alan, in shock.

Smedley nodded and Miss Thorburn poured a glass of whisky from a bottle on the sideboard near the front window. Alan drank it quickly. He could see that Reg's condition was getting worse. Every minute seemed like an hour as they waited for the ambulance.

"What sort of shot and bore is that gun?"

"12 bore. Number 12 shot," replied Smedley, coldly.

"Perhaps it isn't too serious then as it's only a small shot," replied Alan, hopefully, although he could see that was not the case.

Miss Thorburn poured Alan a second whisky which he drank while the three of them talked. All the while Smedley held onto his gun.

"I'll go outside and wait for the ambulance," said Alan, as he looked at Reg. But he could see it was too late.

Smedley returned to the Garden Cottage and made another phone call to the police.

"Who's calling?" asked the police officer.

"Mr Smedley, of Duck Street, Wendens Ambo. Newport 529. Are the police and ambulance coming? The man is very ill. I think he's dead."

"Yes," replied the Police officer. "The police and ambulance are on their way. What has happened there?"

"A very violent man knocked at my door and it was answered by my companion. He forced his way past her and I went to fetch my gun. When I came back another man was there. An argument developed and I let fly at him," replied Smedley.

"What sort of weapon was it?"

"A shotgun."

"What distance did you fire from?"

"Only a few feet."

"What part of the body did you hit him?"

"In the right side of the stomach. I think he's dead."

The ambulance arrived first and Smedley was standing by the body still holding his loaded shotgun in the crook of his right arm.

"Have you phoned for a doctor?" asked one of the ambulance men as he removed Reg's glove from his left hand and felt his pulse.

"No."

"Could you do so."

Smedley made no move, so one of the ambulance men asked if he could use the telephone and was told to go upstairs and use the one in the bedroom. Before he could get to the phone, Doctor Hunter arrived. He had received a call from Neil Warden to attend to Mrs Eileen Pithers who had become hysterical when she realised that Smedley had killed someone.

It had taken 20 minutes for the ambulance to arrive at 11.30 p.m. During that time, the cottage had been mysteriously strewn with various objects, mainly statues of Napoleon.

The local police arrived shortly after the ambulance and Constable Kearney took the gun from Smedley and placed it against a wall. He picked his way across the debris of statues and asked Smedley what had happened.

"I shot him," replied Smedley, starkly.

"Do you live in the house?" asked the constable, looking at Alan Arnold.

"No, I came with him," replied Alan, pointing to the lifeless body on the floor.

"What happened?" asked the constable again.

"I don't know. We came to the house and this man went mad and shot him."

The police constable took Smedley into the dining room and sat him down.

"Can you tell me what has happened?"

"Yes. It's a long story. I know the man and I know him to be violent. I was not surprised when he came here tonight. You see we had an expedition the other day. It was to do with pirate radio stations. I am the man who started it all off. He had the towers in the Thames and the other day we took it from him."

Miss Thorburn entered the room and the constable asked if she lived with Smedley.

"No. I'm just a friend," she lied.

"Would you like to sit with Mr Smedley?"

"Yes."

"Were you present at the time of the shooting?"

"Yes."

"What happened?"

"There was a banging on the door. I went to open it and a man burst in. He appeared to be mad and I realised it must have been Calvert. He said "Where's Smedley? I've come to take him to the Police." He had something in his hand. I think it was a statue of Napoleon. He shouted, "Where's the bastard? I have come for him and I'll get either you or him." He then jumped at me and we struggled. I told him Mr Smedley was not here but he attacked me. We struggled from one room to another. The fire got knocked over and I switched it off in case it caused a fire. He hit me and we continued to struggle back into the hall. He was just going to hit me on the head with the Napoleon when he looked up and saw Mr Smedley. He threw the statue at Mr Smedley and then made a dive at him. It was then the shot was fired. The man moved about a bit but fell where he is now. I tried to help him but there was nothing I could do."

"There was a hammering on the door," emphasised Smedley. "I knew it must have been him and he had threatened me harm and to kill me and all the others. I went out of the French windows in my bedroom and got my shotgun. I loaded it. I knew he came here to kill me. When I went back to the hall, he was about to hit Miss Thorburn on the head with a heavy thing. I could see he was mad and I knew he carried arms. I got to the hall and he looked up and made a dive at me. I had no choice but to fire. I didn't think to aim at his legs. I just fired."

The police began to take photographs and write down a description of the objects that lay scattered about.

On the hall floor, a heavy stone bust of Napoleon lay with its stone plinth near the stairs.

In front of a side table, a small statuette of Napoleon was in pieces on the floor.

On the table, a small statuette of Napoleon had been broken off its base. Above the table, a picture was hanging askew on the wall.

To the right of the front door, a statuette of Napoleon was lying on the floor at the foot of a column.

A paraffin heater was lying face down on the floor and beside the fireplace, the electric fire Miss Thorburn had put upright was now lying on its back.

In the centre of the sitting room the telephone lay on the settee, its long cord which trailed across the room to a table against the front wall, now had its junction box hanging loose.

The bronze statute Reg had thrown under the cupboard was picked up and placed by his un-gloved left hand. Some of the photographs which were shown in court, taken after his death, made Reg appear in a violent mood, in a position ready to throw the statute.

In the silence of the night the telephone rang. It was ten to four. Dorothy awoke with a start and reached out her hand to answer, expecting to hear Reg's voice.

"Is that Mrs Calvert?"

"Yes."

"This is Saffron Walden Police Station. I'm afraid I've some bad news. Your husband's been shot."

"Shot? Where?"

"At Major Smedley's cottage in Wendens Ambo."

"Is he alive?"

"No, I'm sorry to tell you that he died at the scene. Do you think you could attend the Saffron Walden Police Station and answer some questions?"

"Yes, I'll come as soon as I can."

Replacing the receiver, Dorothy sat stunned, not believing what she had heard and thinking she must be in a nightmare. Was she asleep? Was she dreaming? No. It was real. Reg was dead. Reg always walked away from trouble so how was he shot? How was she going to get to the police station? She couldn't call John as he was in Oxford with the Fortunes. Then she remembered that Reg had left a piece of paper by the bed with Brian Harvey's phone number. Picking it up, she dialled the number.

"Brian?"

"Yes."

"This is Mrs C. Can you come and fetch me?" asked Dorothy, tremulously, as she tried to hold herself together and not break down. "I've just had a call from the police at Saffron Walden. Reg has been shot. Major Smedley has killed him and I don't think I'm in a fit state to drive."

"Shot! How?"

"I don't know."

"Okay. I'll be with you as quickly as I can."

Wrapping herself in her dressing gown, Dorothy went into Susan's bedroom and gently woke her. Susan sat up and looked at her mother realising by the bleak look on her face that something was seriously wrong.

"Go and wake Candy and bring her into my bedroom. I have to get dressed."

Together, the girls went barefoot into their mother's bedroom. She had dressed and seeing her daughters, came over and put her arms out to encircle them and hold them close.

"I've just had a telephone call from Saffron Walden police station." Dorothy hesitated, searching for the right words but there was nothing she could say to soften the truth. "I have to go there. Your Dad's been shot. He's dead."

Candy immediately broke down, her body shaking as she sobbed. Dorothy held her daughters to her even more tightly before gently pushing them away. Looking at her eldest daughter, she appealed to her.

"Susan, you have to be strong for me. If you're not strong, I won't be able to cope. Take care of your sister. I have to go."

"How did it happen?"

"I don't know. I don't know anything. Brian will be here soon. He's going to take me."

The police at Saffron Walden were very kind and thoughtful as they gently questioned Dorothy. She told them all she knew, about Reg, the aborted merger with Radio Atlanta and Caroline, the shock of the boarding party and being blackmailed by Smedley and Kitty Black for money and 50 per cent of the business. She described how Reg had tried to contact Smedley all day to speak to him to get some resolution and why he had gone that evening to talk to him.

In the adjoining room, Dorothy could hear Smedley. He sounded so cool and calm it sent a shiver through her body. As she listened, she couldn't dispel the thought that he knew he was going to get away with murder.

After several hours of questioning, Dorothy and Brian were escorted to a hotel so they could rest before going on to identify Reg's body.

Reg's body was taken to the mortuary at Herts and Essex Hospital at 5.15 a.m., and the post-mortem was carried out in the presence of Detective Superintendent Brown and other officers.

The pathologist described the external injuries as a circular hole approximately 1.25" in diameter with a ragged edge in the right chest. The gunshot wound was discharged at close range, the main charge passing horizontally backwards with extensive destruction of the right lung and liver.

"In addition to the firearm wound, there were fresh linear abrasions just over 1" long below the left eyebrow, an abrasion 3/8" of an inch long on the inner side of the left lower eyelid, tiny abrasions behind the outer end of the left lower eyelid, tiny abrasion over bridge of nose, tiny abrasion beside the left nostril. The abrasions, mainly around left eye, suggestive of finger nail scratches. There were no marks on his back and none on the arms or hands. Recent vaccination mark left upper arm."

On leaving the hotel, press photographers were waiting outside for Dorothy. Brian drove, following a police escort to Bishop's Stortford hospital and as they walked to the mortuary, Dorothy had the sensation that her legs were disconnected from her body and at any moment, she would lose consciousness and faint. With supreme inner strength, she kept walking, supported by a police constable and a police woman.

The mortuary was in a building that reminded Dorothy of a wartime mizzen hut. As they showed her into a room, she was shocked to see Reg lying there, his body, not properly covered. Blinking tears from her eyes, she saw the ugly open wound where he'd been shot and the post-mortem they'd carried out on his stomach.

The man she loved was now a corpse, laid stiff on a table. His natural wavy hair was swept back away from his face and had turned completely straight. On the left side of his face was bruising and a jagged cut over his eye.

"Oh, my God. They've blinded him," gasped Dorothy, stunned, as she turned to face the police officers.

"Is that your husband, Reg Calvert?"

"Yes, that's my husband."

"Would you like a cigarette?"

"Thank you," replied Dorothy, her hand shaking as she took the lit cigarette and put it to her lips and inhaled deeply. She had not smoked for several years but was now grateful to start again.

26. AFTERMATH

Jill Wileman was awoken by a loud banging on her front door. Opening it, she was surprised to see her father, holding a newspaper.

"Have you heard the news?"

"No," replied Jill, puzzled.

"Where's John? Is he with Reg?"

"No, he went to Oxford last night to sort out the Fortunes PA system."

"Thank God for that."

John stayed all night at Oxford University and heard the early morning news on the radio. In shock, he went to the dressing room to tell the Fortunes. The other group performing were Geno Washington and the Ram Jam Band. They all knew Reg. He had been the person to give the Demons, a Nuneaton group, their opportunity to turn professional and they had reformed themselves into the Ram Jam Band.

Pinkerton's Assorted Colours had a week-long booking at the Greasbrough Social Club and were staying at the Queens Hotel in Barnsley. Their roadie, Roger Forrester, heard the early morning news and telephoned the police to confirm it was Reg who had died. Pinkerton's couldn't believe it. Reg played such an important part of their lives and he had been responsible for making their career a success. Without him, they were at a loss what to do.

Leslie Dunne's mother heard the news on the radio. "Radio City Chief was shot dead last night." She misheard and thought they said, Radio City Chef. Immediately, she became very distressed, believing it was her young son who had been killed.

Sandy Horsley was horrified. After his brief phone call to Smedley the night before, he had worried but had not expected the outcome to be murder. When Smedley did not call him back, he had asked the operator to keep trying Smedley's number until well after midnight. He now felt a sense of responsibility. Horsley was not a wealthy man and with the boarding party running into a third day, the costs were escalating. With Smedley in prison, he realised he might never be paid. He phoned Smedley's office and left a message to be passed on to both Kitty Black and Aubrey Boutwood, informing them that he didn't want to do anything that might prejudice Oliver Smedley's defence, but he needed money. He would only keep the men on Shivering Sands until Friday. He then telephoned Mr Deterding, a member of the Atlanta board and asked for financial assistance.

"I'm sorry, I know nothing about a boarding party," answered Deterding, surprised.

"I thought Mr Smedley was going to have a meeting with you and inform you about our plans to take over Radio City."

"No, he hasn't contacted me or, to my knowledge, anyone else on the Atlanta board," replied Deterding.

"The trouble is, if I take the riggers off Radio City, it may prejudice Mr Smedley's defence and I don't want to do that."

"I can see it's a problem for you but there's nothing I can do today. We're having a board meeting on Monday 27th June, and I can bring the matter up then."

A boat arrived at Shivering Sands at 10 a.m. with Michael Housego and a photographer from the Evening Standard. They shouted up that Reg Calvert had been murdered and were allowed on board. Peter Dolphin asked if he could return with them to Sheerness and they agreed. He was keen to sell his 'inside' story to the press but angry he no longer had the camera with the photographs and reported it missing to the police.

The boarders on Radio City had heard the BBC news and were concerned in case they were implicated. Paul Elvey took charge of the situation and the next boat to arrive with more press photographers was greeted by Paul shouting at them aggressively, telling them to go away or he would throw scaffolding poles at them. A press helicopter flew overhead, taking aerial photographs of the disc jockeys on the roof. Later, Sergeant Brown arrived with six police officers in a launch and Paul allowed them on board to take statements.

The riggers were feeling very uncomfortable and unsure what to do. When their supply boat came they were told to remain on the fort and continue to protect the equipment.

Pamela Thorburn telephoned Dr Hunter on Wednesday evening and asked if he could come and examine her at the cottage in Duck Street. She explained how she had struggled with Calvert on the previous night and showed him some bruising on her left upper arm and complained of a slight pain in moving her right knee. The doctor agreed that, in his opinion, her injuries were consistent with her story. She did not disclose that the bruising had occurred when she had tried to hit her opponent with a brass statue.

<<<<<>>>>>

After visiting the mortuary, Dorothy returned to Denmark Street. She was ill, exhausted and in shock.

"What are you going to do?" asked Jill, who was in tears.

"Carry on."

"No one expects you to," said John, quietly.

"That's the whole point. No one expects me to. Major Smedley knows he's going to get away with killing Reg. He's going to walk free. He wouldn't have shot him if he didn't know in advance he could get away with it."

"He can't Mrs C," replied Jill, shocked by Dorothy's prediction.

"You didn't hear him talking in the next room. The police said they had never seen anyone kill in cold blood before and neither he, nor the woman with him, had a mark on them. He knows he can get away with it. If you wear the right tie and know the right people in the right places, you can get away with anything. He must have thought, with Reg out of the way, he could take over the station. But I want it back. I'm going to carry on for Reg."

"I should have gone with him," said John, distressed. "I should have been there."

"No John, I'm glad you didn't go. I'm sure he'd have killed you too."

They all sat in silence until the telephone rang.

"It's been ringing all day," said Jill, as she answered the call. "It's the press. Do you want to make a statement?"

"Yes. But not now. Tomorrow."

John took Dorothy back to the apartment and as they walked to the car they passed a newspaper stand. The headline was 'Pirate Radio Chief on Murder Charge.'

Susan and Candy were waiting anxiously for their mother to return and as Dorothy unlocked the door, she called out, "I'm back." The two girls immediately came out of their rooms and Dorothy put her arms around them. They stood for several minutes in a silent circle, holding onto each other for strength.

"I'm cooking a meal," said Susan.

"I'm not hungry."

"You have to eat. You have to keep strong."

Dorothy nodded. "I'll have a rest first."

Susan had tried to remain strong for her mother and continue as normal. After the meal, Dorothy lit another cigarette and beckoned her daughters to sit with her. She knew she couldn't shield them from the pain and had to disclose the way their father had been killed. Slowly, she described what had happened.

"He must have known your Dad was coming. The police said that as soon as he arrived, he loaded his shotgun and went to a neighbouring cottage to tell them to call the police as there was going to be trouble. Your Dad had only been in the cottage three or four minutes when he killed him. I should

Where Radio City chief was found shot

THE 17th-century thatched cottage in Duck Street, Wendens Ambo, near Saffron Walden, Essex, where Mr. Reginald Calvert, 38, head of Radio City, a pop pirate station at Shivering Sands in the Thames Estuary, was found shot dead early yesterday. The cottage belongs to Major Oliver Smedley, 54, a company director and former member of the Liberal party executive, who was later charged with murdering Mr. Calvert.

● Major Smedley on his way to Saffron Walden magistrates' court where Mr. A. S. Tee, appearing for him, said that Smedley completely denied the charge.

Daily Telegraph 23rd June 1966

have gone with him. I should have been there for him. He was left to die on his own and I wasn't there for him."

Dorothy paused. A lump in her throat had grown so large she could barely speak. Looking at her daughters, she realised she had to protect them. It was just the three of them now. Dorothy talked on quietly, preparing them for what was to come. Susan, burst into tears. All day she had been strong for her mother but could contain her grief no longer. In her mind, she could see the vision of her father, lying bleeding on the floor. Running to her bedroom, Susan threw herself on the bed and wept.

Dorothy did not cry.

The sound of her daughter weeping cut through her like a knife. Lighting another cigarette, Dorothy resolved to stay strong. She must not break down. She would not cry. The pain would go on and on. Next, she would have to attend an Inquest, then the Court Hearing and then a Trial.

Thursday morning, a crack of daylight glimmered through a gap in the curtains. Dorothy turned over and put her arm out to reach for Reg. His side of the bed was cold. Immediately, her mind flashed back to the happenings of the previous day. A sense of grief so overwhelming engulfed her and she wanted to die. The pain was too much. Opening her eyes, she knew she had to get out of bed and face whatever she had to do.

Walking barefoot to the wardrobe Dorothy stared at her brightly coloured summer clothes. It was traditional to wear black when you were a widow in mourning but it was a colour she disliked intensely. Recollecting her childhood in Huddersfield, in every street there had been widows who wore black for the remainder of their lives. Her own widowed mother had chosen instead, to wear dark grey. Sliding the coat hangers along the rail, Dorothy pulled out a light-blue suit. It would have to do until she could buy black.

After eating a little toast and drinking coffee, Dorothy caught a taxi to Denmark Street. As she walked up to the office door, a man bumped into her.

"If you carry on with Radio City the same will happen to you as your husband."

She looked up at the man to get his description but he was gone. He had melted away into the crowd. Shaking all over, she climbed the two flights of rickety stairs to the office.

"Are you all right Mrs C? You look like you've seen a ghost."

"I've just had a man threaten to do the same to me as happened to Reg."

"Shall I call the police?" asked Jill, concerned.

"There's no point," replied Dorothy, taking a packet of cigarettes from her handbag. "There's nothing they can do. I didn't see his face."

The telephone rang relentlessly and Jill dealt with as many calls as she could. Dorothy was now responsible for all of Reg's businesses, Radio City, the nightclub, the dancehalls, the groups and King Music.

"I've told the press you'll speak to them this afternoon and ITV want to do an interview."

"That's fine,"

"And a trial deejay, Peter Dolphin called in. He's an actor between jobs and Mr Calvert said he could go out last week. He said he took his expensive camera with him and photographed the boarding party. Apparently, he gave the camera to Paul Elvey for safekeeping but Paul didn't return it. He's asked if you can get it back for him."

"Yes, of course. I expect Paul kept the camera for evidence of the boarding party. We can print the photos and return his camera."

There was a knock on the office door and two men entered who Dorothy had not seen before.

"I'm Timothy Hardacre and this is counsel, Ronald Shulman. We heard the awful news and called in to see Mr King yesterday to ask if we can represent you and he suggested we should see you today."

"How can I help you?"

"Your husband used our services in 1964. I am a solicitor and he asked me to get counsel's opinion on the legality of remaining on Shivering Sands. We would like to represent you and we've a plan to remove the boarders and prosecute them."

Dorothy listened to their proposal and after some discussion declined to accept their services.

"I'm sorry, but I don't want any more violence and I've already got my own solicitor."

In the afternoon, Dorothy spoke to various reporters and explained what had happened on the towers. ITN television news filmed her and from somewhere deep inside, she found the courage to speak directly to the cameras and confirmed she would be taking over the running of Radio City and wanted the boarders to leave.

"I have always been the brains behind the business. If my husband had just been wounded I would have sold it. But now I intend to keep it going. My prime aim is to get it back on air as soon as possible and we are sending out a boat from Whitstable to Shivering Sands to ask the boarding party to leave. I hope they will do so. Surely, they will have had enough by now."

After filming, Timothy Hardacre phoned to tell her he had taken the liberty of giving out press statements saying he was representing Mrs Calvert and they were going to Radio City to physically remove the boarders.

"I've been trying to find out our legal position at the Towers and I think I've found something in Section 15, which could be used," claimed Hardacre.

"I'm sorry, but at this stage, I'm not interested," replied Dorothy, firmly.

"It really is very urgent. We must have your authority to go ahead."

"I've told you, I'm not interested."

"If you were Mr Calvert, he would take advice."

"I am Mrs Calvert. You will not find me so easy to put pressure on."

Later, Hardacre telephoned the apartment and Susan answered the phone.

"I don't want to speak to him. Tell him I'm not in," said Dorothy, irritated.

Susan was cooking the meal and when she had served, she saw her mother staring blankly into space.

"Come on Mum, please try to eat."

Dorothy nodded and stubbed out her cigarette in the glass ashtray.

"I want Radio City back," said Dorothy. quietly to her daughters. "I hope the boarders see the television news and realise they should come off. They've nothing to gain by staying on. I don't understand why they're still there. He knows he's going to get away with murder."

"He can't Mum," replied Susan, trying to reassure her mother.

"That's what everyone says but you didn't hear him that night. Everyone knew I was against the station to begin with. Maybe he thought that if he killed Reg he could keep it."

The phone rang again and Candy went to answer.

"It's Auntie Ada."

"Okay, I'll take it in the bedroom," replied Dorothy.

The two girls cleared the table and Susan washed the dishes while Candy dried. A few minutes later their mother returned and looking distracted, lit another cigarette.

"Ada has heard the news on the radio and is coming to stay with us until the funeral." Dorothy paused and frowned. "She's very upset. There's something I need to tell you before she comes. Something you need to know. Ada is your grandmother."

There, she had said it. It was a skeleton in the family cupboard, a shadow which had hung over Reg's life he never mentioned but had emotionally scarred him.

"Your Dad's dad was Edward Pearce, a violinist, but he and Ada never married. In those days, most girls had their illegitimate babies adopted. Ada was different. She decided to keep her baby and continued to work as a professional musician. She was earning enough, travelling the world and playing in orchestras and women's bands. He stayed with his grandparents and they brought him up. They became his Mam and Dad. Ada promised to take him home. Promises. Always promises. Even after she had married and had more children, she didn't take him."

"Why didn't you tell us before?" asked Susan.

"Your Dad was so ashamed he didn't want you to know. When he was growing up they told him he was a ne'er-do-well. The neighbours would say, 'where's the bastard' and not call him by his real name. After we were married and he was successful and drove a big car, we went back to Huddersfield. He wanted to show them he had done well. The family and neighbours were so pleased to see him." Dorothy paused, her face softening with just a hint of a smile. "They really loved him and it didn't matter he'd made a success. He didn't need to prove himself. They loved him as he was."

The phone rang and Dorothy went to her bedroom to answer it, returning a little later to sit with her daughters in the lounge, her eyes flickering with exhaustion as she tried to stay awake.

"That was your Granddad. He was in a phone box, crying. He heard it on the news. He couldn't understand why anyone should want to kill our Reggie. He said he's getting a gun and coming down on the train to shoot Major Smedley. I told him not to be so stupid as he would be imprisoned. He told me he doesn't care. He said he's old and it didn't matter about his life. I've tried to reason with him. I just hope he takes notice. That's all I need, for him to try and kill Major Smedley."

There was no time for Dorothy to rest. The doorbell rang at 10 p.m., and Detective Chief Inspector Barker and Detective Woods asked if they could come in to ask some more questions. Intuitively, Dorothy felt she could trust Inspector Barker. He was a man of integrity and she told him everything he wanted to know and explained about the offers she had had regarding the removal of the boarders.

"Today I've had different security firms and people offering to go out to Shivering Sands to remove them. I've told them I don't want anyone to go out as it might involve violence and someone may get hurt. And there's a solicitor and counsel who want to represent me. They told me that my husband had asked for counsel's opinion on the legality of occupying the towers in 1964."

"That's interesting. Do you think you could ask for a copy of counsel's opinion?" asked Barker.

"Yes, I'll call him now."

The police officers were still in the apartment at 11.30 p.m. when the doorbell rang. Dorothy was surprised to see Hardacre and Shulman standing there, and as they entered, were taken aback to see police officers in the apartment with her.

"Do you think we can speak to you on your own?" asked Hardacre.

Dorothy nodded and showed the police officers to another room.

“How can I help you,” asked Dorothy.

“What we want you to do is go out on a boat with us tomorrow and we’ll tell the boarders that unless they leave the fort, you will go straight to Court to swear information for their arrest. The police have agreed to this action and they have backed up Mr Shulman’s legal opinion.”

“What will it cost?” queried Dorothy.

“The initial legal fees for the operation, including going out to the fort will be £250. It will be a private prosecution so there will be more costs.”

“I’ll think about it,” replied Dorothy, cautiously. “Have you brought a copy of the document I asked you for?”

“No, sorry. We haven’t had time to make you a copy.”

It was nearly one in the morning before all of Dorothy’s visitors had left and she was exhausted but sleep was almost impossible. The day’s events churned around, and around in her mind.

In the morning as she was preparing to go to the office she received another phone call.

“Mrs Calvert?”

“Yes.”

“If you continue with Radio City the same will happen to you as happened to your husband.”

It was beyond Dorothy’s comprehension as to why she was receiving death threats. Why were the boarders still on the towers? None of it made any sense. Was Smedley able to arrange death threats from prison or was there someone else who was interested in the towers? Shaking, Dorothy lit a cigarette and sat in the lounge for a few minutes to calm her nerves. Her daughters could see her fear and sat silently with her.

“I’ve just had a phone call threating to kill me if I carry on with Radio City.”

“What are you going to do?” asked Susan.

Dorothy was desolate but with steely determination, she smiled wanly at her daughters and stood up.

“I’m going to the office. I’ve got to carry on.”

“I don’t want you to go,” said Candy, tearfully.

“I’ll be all right. I’m not giving in. I won’t give in. I shall run Radio City for your Dad. I’m determined that Major Smedley will not have it.”

Dorothy stretched out her arms and encircled her daughters, holding them tightly before leaving them. As she left, the two girls looked at each other, terrified, knowing that someone might try to kill their mother.

Friday lunchtime, Dorothy had to attend New Scotland Yard for more interviews with Detective Chief Inspector Barker. While she was there, Dorothy told DCI Barker that she had decided not to have Hardacre or

Shulman represent her and he offered to let her use his phone to inform them. When Dorothy spoke to Hardacre, she informed him of her decision and instructed him to assist the police by supplying the document with counsel's opinion about the occupation of Shivering Sands Towers.

POLICE STATEMENTS Extracts

JAMES BARKER – DETECTIVE CHIEF INSPECTOR

On Thursday 23rd June 1966, following newspaper publicity given to the 'take over' of a fort in the Thames Estuary, I was making enquiries accompanied by Detective Sergeant Woods to ascertain relevant facts.

At 10 p.m., I went with Detective Woods to 12a Welbeck Street to see Mrs Dorothy Calvert. This lady was obviously unwell and told me this was owing to a recent vaccination. She was also grieved over the death of her husband, but she was calm and quite rational.

We had some conversation with her during which she told us much of the conditions at the fort and the persons employed there. I asked Mrs Calvert if she had any document of title to the fort.

Her husband and David Sutch had obtained counsel's opinion to the legality of their station before the business was commenced. Mrs Calvert believed a document to be in possession of Mr Timothy Hardacre, a solicitor who acted for her late husband. At my request, Mrs Calvert telephoned Mr Hardacre and asked him about the document.

At about 11.30 p.m. that evening Mr Hardacre called at the flat and was shown into the lounge where I was waiting with Mrs Calvert. I heard Mrs Calvert instruct Mr Hardacre to hand to myself a copy of the 'counsel's opinion' obtained by her late husband. Mr Hardacre asked to speak to Mrs Calvert alone.

I went to another lounge where we met Mr Shulman of counsel. Mr Hardacre joined us a few minutes later. Mr Shulman then told us in detail of the various offences of piracy, conspiracy, larceny, and wilful damage committed by the persons who had occupied the fort at Shivering Sands.

Mr Shulman told me he intended to visit the fort at 3 p.m. the following day, 24th June, to dump into the sea all the supplies left there for the 'invaders' and to inform them that Mrs Calvert intended to supply to a Court in Kent for warrants for their arrest for the offences disclosed.

I told Mr Shulman that I did not agree with him. I told him that such provocative conduct would undoubtedly cause a breach of the peace on, or in the vicinity of the fort, and I warned him of the possible consequences should persons be injured as a result. He agreed to abandon the idea of dumping supplies into the sea, but stated his intention of addressing the men on the fort, pointing out the error of their ways and informing them that Mrs Calvert would apply for warrants for their arrest unless they left the fort.

Mr Shulman told me he was satisfied the fort could be classified as a ship and therefore came within the provisions of Section 15 of the Larceny Act 1916. Mr Shulman spent a long time expounding his reasons for coming to this decision and I eventually left the address at 12.45 a.m. on 24th June.

Saturday 25th June, Mr Hardacre and Mr Shulman called at New Scotland Yard. I had not requested their attendance but earlier that day, I had sent an officer to Mr Hardacre's office with a document signed by Mrs Calvert, authorising him to hand to police any document relating to the tenure of Shivering Sands Fort.

They did not want to give the police the document, but gave a copy of their recent opinion by Mr Shulman with the possibilities of action against the men in possession of the fort. Mr Hardacre said, "You must understand we have to protect our client's interests. She may say, hand over a document, but I am still responsible. Some documents may be prejudicial against her. In the event of any subsequent government action, I don't want to hand them the defence on a plate. This is why Mr Shulman is here."

CENTRAL OFFICE – NEW SCOTLAND YARD REPORT: 24th JUNE, 1966

I was sharing an office with Inspector Barker so I was aware of enquiries.

Friday lunchtime 24th June, 1966, Mrs Calvert came into the office. I knew she had made a written statement suggesting that a solicitor named Hardacre was acting without proper instructions.

At about 4.20 p.m. that day, I received a telephone call from a gentleman who said he was Mrs Calvert's solicitor asking for an interview with Detective Inspector Barker. He was out of the office. "I have Counsel with me and would like to come and see you. Where can I find You?" I said, "At New Scotland Yard." He said, "Whereabouts." I said, "If you come to one of the entrances and see one of the uniformed officers and ask for me I will come and see you." He said, "No, tell me where you are and we will come straight over. It's important that we see you." I said, "Where are you?" He said, "In the Flying Squad Office." I said, "Wait there, I will come across."

In view of the information received, I did not go to the Flying Squad but telephoned Mr Bacon, an ex-CID officer. I told Mr Bacon of the two gentlemen and to accompany them to my office and remain with me throughout any interview.

Mr Bacon brought them to the office. I asked them for their admission slip which callers usually collect. Mr Shulman said, “We have none.” I said, “Well how did you get in?” Mr Shulman said, “We walked in. We come often, we went to the Flying Squad.”

I kept both men standing in the doorway and said, “I don’t like this. What do you want?” Mr Shulman said, “Is Mrs Calvert here?” I said, “Not so far as I know.” Mr Shulman said, “What we want is a copy of her statement.” I said, “Why, may I ask?” Mr Shulman said, “We are entitled to a copy of our client’s statement.” I said, “If you have her instructions and obviously, you have not. Let us get details of who you are.”

I brought both men into the office and asked Mr Bacon to make a note of the names and addresses. Mr Shulman said, “Where is Mrs Calvert’s statement? ...... This is terribly important and urgent.” ......

I asked for their telephone numbers. Mr Hardacre, “Mayfair 8853 and I am on 24 hour call.” Mr Shulman appeared reluctant to give any further information. I asked him again for his address or telephone number. He said, “I am Mr Shulman of Counsel.” I said, “And your address please?” He said, “Brick Lane, Temple E.C.4.”

DUTY OFFICER: J. Minors FRIDAY 24th JUNE, 1966

6.05 p.m. Received a telephone call from a young woman who announced herself as ‘Mrs Calvert’s daughter.’ She said, “My mother has told me to ring you. The two men are here. Mr Shulman and the other one, they are demanding to see my mother. She does not want to see these men, what shall I do?” I told Miss Calvert to inform the men of her mother’s wishes and ask them to leave.

She returned to the telephone about a minute later and said, “The two men must have heard me on the telephone to you as they have left.” As the caller seemed worried and upset, I instructed Miss Calvert to inform me if the men returned and I later passed the message covering my conversation to Detective Chief Inspector Barker.

27. THE BOARDING PARTY

Police on the left with men from boarding party and Radio City crew. Ian MacRae looking out of top window. Phil Perkins centre, under 'R'. Big Alf wearing a cap. Leslie Dunne on right

On Thursday evening, the boarders watched the ITN news and became uneasy when they saw Dorothy appealing for them to leave. There were also rumours of security men coming out to force them off. It was an anxious time on the towers as everyone waited for something to happen.

The boarding of the station and shooting of Reg had made headline news and Horsley had taken it upon himself to keep the men on the station without being able to speak to Smedley, Miss Black or the directors of Project Atlanta about the best course of action. After hearing about the murder, Kitty Black left London for a holiday without providing a forwarding address. Horsley tried to contact her, leaving messages with her maid and at Allan Crawford's office. On Friday, she returned and agreed to meet him.

"Did you have a good holiday?" asked Horsley, politely.

"I thought I'd have a few days away. Poor Oliver, locked up in Brixton prison."

"It's terrible news. We've a problem with keeping the men on the towers."

"Yes, I realise," replied Miss Black.

"I don't want to prejudice Oliver's case by withdrawing the men."

"I agree. We need to keep them on there."

"The trouble is, I need some money to pay them," explained Horsley.

"Sorry, I've no money with me."

"What about a cheque?"

"I forgot to put a cheque book in my bag today," replied Miss Black, apologetically.

Horsley was not a wealthy man and it was apparent that Miss Black was reluctant to contribute to the mounting costs and that he may never get payment from Smedley who was in prison.

"I'm only prepared to pay for them up to midnight. We need to come to some arrangement. I cannot carry on financing everything."

"I understand. Poor Oliver. It's a difficult situation."

"Can you pay me some of the money?"

"Sorry."

Horsley looked at her in disbelief. In desperation, he rummaged around in his inside pocket. "I have my cheque book. We can alter it and you can make a cheque out to me."

"Can we do that?" asked Miss Black, incredulously.

"Yes, even if you only pay me the £250 you agreed to, that would help," replied Horsley, handing her a blank cheque. "With the men staying on so long, it's going to cost far more than I estimated. And you understand, I'm not prepared to pay for the men to stay any longer than tonight. From now on, you have to agree to pay for everything yourself."

"Yes, I understand," answered Miss Black, as she signed the cheque

Dorothy asked Fred Downs to go to Shivering Sands on Friday morning with provisions and a change of engineers. Tony Pine and Ian West were to replace Paul Elvey, Phil Perkins and Leslie Dunne. As they arrived back in Whitstable Harbour, the press were waiting. Paul, throughout the incursion, had acted as spokesman for the intruders and described them as being quite reasonable until Thursday evening. A motor barge had delivered supplies to them and after that, they had turned hostile. Paul reported that it was now dangerous on the forts and Big Alf had warned that if Mrs Calvert, or any of her officials or unauthorised callers set foot on the fort, they were ready to demolish equipment, the aerial, and sever catwalks.

Paul Elvey caught a train to London and went first to the office but as Dorothy wasn't there, he made his way to Welbeck House with his girlfriend to pay his condolences. Dorothy opened the door and Paul, smiling, presented her with a large box of chocolates. Dorothy, incensed by his insensitivity, pushed the door closed in his face leaving Paul and his girlfriend standing in the communal hall.

Dorothy was tense and gave Jill instructions to notify Paul that she had terminated his employment.

Detective Inspector Brown (right) investigates the shooting and boarding party on Shivering Sands. Ian MacRae, Paul Elvey, Leslie Dunne, Phil Perkins, Tom Edwards

Ultimatum by Shivering Sands inva

PIRATES STAND REPEL BOARDERS!

Threats to cut down radio mast

Evening Standard Reporter

The invaders who took over Radio City, the pirate station on a Thames Estuary fort, threatened today to chop down the radio mast and destroy other equipment if there was any attempt to board the fort.

WEATHER—Dry.—

24th June, 1966 Evening Standard feature. Above Right: Hoisting up police officers

"I thought he would have brought me the camera for evidence but instead, he brought me chocolates. If he'd been loyal to Reg and done his job properly and made sure the hatches were locked, Reg would be alive today."

Not surprisingly, Radio London withdrew from their partnership deal and promptly paid any due accounts. There was one small piece of good news which gave Dorothy hope that the boarding party would soon depart. All the pirate radio stations had come together to make an agreement; none of them were prepared to take over Radio City and pay the ransom money to Smedley.

Late on Friday evening, Dorothy and her daughters returned to Macbeth Close and as soon as Dorothy opened the door, she felt Reg was there. That night, he came and lay by her side. In the morning as she awoke from her dreaming, she put out her hand to touch him. Fleetingly, she saw him go, like a breath of air in the cool light of day.

Susan could also sense her father's presence and it troubled her. On Saturday, she began to feel ill with flu and stayed in bed most of the day. In the evening, her boyfriend came and drove her to the Nuneaton dance and when they arrived at the dancehall, Mrs Thomas was waiting to see her.

"I'm so sorry," said Mrs Thomas, her voice quivering as she put her arms around Susan. "Your Dad was so good and kind. I don't know why anyone would want to kill him."

Susan nodded, too full of emotion to speak with tears flowing down her cheeks. For a moment, they held each other tightly as they stood in the empty ballroom. The groups were on stage assembling their equipment and soon, crowds of happy teenagers would be filling the dancefloor.

By Sunday, Susan had flu and was too ill to return to London and instead, stayed at her friend's house where Mr and Mrs Lamont took care of her. Dorothy and Candy returned on their own to the apartment where they ate a quiet supper before going to their bedrooms. Candy tuned her radio into 299 metres and left it running quietly to crackle and hiss while she got ready for bed. Without warning, the hiss stopped and she heard music. Turning up the volume, Candy listened. Yes, it was music and coming from Shivering Sands. In great excitement, she burst into her mother's bedroom.

"Radio City's on-air."

"I can't believe it. I've got it back," laughed Dorothy, triumphantly, as she hugged Candy.

With no prior notice, a tug had arrived on Sunday evening and the riggers were told to pack their bags and leave immediately. Jubilantly, the Radio

City crew waved them off, then debated amongst themselves what to do next as they feared the studio and transmitting tower may have been booby trapped. They waited nervously for half an hour and when no explosion occurred, they dared to cross the catwalk. As soon as they reached the studio, they began to put everything back together. The engineers found a crystal and got the transmitter up and running and by 10 p.m., they were on-air. Ian MacRae selected the first record to be played. *Strangers in the Night* by Frank Sinatra.

Drawing received by Tom Edwards from a listener signed Lydia Dustbin.

Reg Calvert 1928 – 1966

28. SO MANY FLOWERS

The last photograph of Reg on the Harvester going to Shivering Sands

Ada caught a train from Lancaster to London on Monday and made her way to Welbeck House. She was a small, plump woman with large bosoms, overly affectionate and very distressed. For the next few days she followed Dorothy like a lost lamb, even into the bathroom, frequently crying and wiping her eyes in what Dorothy considered to be an exaggerated display of grief.

Friday was the day of the funeral. In the morning, the curtains were kept drawn in the house at Macbeth Close. Relatives and friends began to arrive, most wearing black and speaking in hushed voices. Dorothy was edgy and nervous, determined not to break down. She occupied herself, making teas, coffees, and polite conversation as she chain-smoked and clock-watched.

The time seemed to be interminably slow as she waited for the funeral entourage to arrive at 1.30 p.m.

The hearse stopped outside the house carrying the light oak coffin, covered with flowers. So many flowers. Grim faced, Dorothy sat in the plush comfort of the first limousine with her daughters and Ada. They all began to cry, except Dorothy. She was determined to stay strong. She had to stay strong.

The limousine moved sedately in slow procession behind the hearse. As they reached St Peter's Church at Dunchurch, the bells began their slow, mournful peal, one strike for each year of Reg's life. By the entrance were crowds of mourners, television crews and photographers.

With dignity, Dorothy supported her daughters, one each side, as they walked slowly behind the flower clad coffin held aloft by ushers. With tears veiling their eyes, they ignored the intrusive flashing of the press cameras and entered the tranquillity of the ancient church. Dorothy composed herself as she sat in the front pew and focused on the multitude of shimmering colours in three beautiful stained glass windows. Reg had liked this church. It was odd, she recollected, he'd often spoken about the mystery of life. He had lived each day as if it was his last, sensing he would die young. But not like this. No one should die like this.

The service was a formality, to give peace and finality to Reg's days on earth. As Dorothy sat there, half listening to the prayers and seeing her daughter's trembling with silent sobbing, she knew she would not find peace unless his killer was brought to justice.

"We have but a short time to live.
Like a flower, we blossom and then wither.
Like a shadow, we flee and never stay.
In the midst of life, we are in death."

A deep hole had been dug in a grassy area of the churchyard that was still empty of graves. The sun was shining and the air, very still. In a field next to the graveyard, ponies idly grazed on lush grass and golden buttercups. This was a good place for Reg to lie, but Dorothy knew he would not sleep. He would keep coming back to haunt her.

With only the sounds of birdsong, the coffin was gently lowered into the ground. Dorothy picked up a handful of soil and sprinkled it onto the coffin and beckoned her daughters to do the same.

"... we therefore commit his body to the ground; ashes to ashes, dust to dust; in sure and certain hope of the Resurrection to eternal life, ..."

Mourners, many people Dorothy did not recognise, stood in clusters away from the grave as the final prayers were said. Afterwards, they introduced themselves as they gave their condolences and told her how Reg had affected their lives.

David Sutch was there, angry and upset.

"If I'd still been involved in the station, this would never have happened. I would have got strong men in straight away. They'd have known that and not tried to take the station. Reg was too soft. Everyone knew he was soft."

After the funeral, when family and friends had said their goodbyes, the house in Macbeth Close was quiet. But Reg had not gone. He was still there.

The grave at Dunchurch covered with flowers (DC)

Saturday night, the show must go on and the dances were run as usual.

Sunday, the family returned to London. Shortly after they arrived at the apartment, Ada phoned from a coinbox.

"Hello love," said Ada, in her warm Yorkshire lilt. "How are you?"

"I'm coping."

"I've something to tell you. I went to a spiritualist meeting this evening. There was a woman clairvoyant on stage. She was going around the room and stopping to tell different people messages from their loved ones. She went past me. And then she turned and came back."

Ada began to cry, sobbing loudly as she continued.

"She went through it all. Of our Reggie being shot and she collapsed on stage."

Shocked, Dorothy did not know what to say and tried to hold herself together.

"He sent you a message," continued Ada. "You need to go and see someone, a clairvoyant. He wants to tell you something."

"I don't want to."

"But you should," insisted Ada, still crying.

"I'll think about it," replied Dorothy, kindly.

Two weeks had passed since that fateful phone call in the middle of the night. The finality of death had not fully registered with Dorothy or her daughters. Each evening, they expected Reg to return, to hear him merrily whistling as he came through the apartment door and call, 'I'm back'.

The days following the funeral, Dorothy invited Jill and John to the apartment for a meal. Tom sent Candy a bouquet of red roses and came to London to take her out. Dorothy, on impulse, suggested to Susan they go to the cinema to see a comedy starring Doris Day in The Glass Bottom Boat. For the first time since losing Reg, they found themselves laughing.

Throughout her married life, Dorothy had maintained a form of normality in their topsy-turvy world. Now, more than ever, she realised she needed to provide stability for her daughters.

Outwardly, Dorothy gave the impression of being in control. Inwardly, she could feel herself sinking into the fathomless deeps of mourning. She had not cried. She would not cry. Dorothy knew she could not allow herself to wallow in grief and had to remain strong. She could easily drown. What made her stay on the surface was her determination to run Radio City. Disturbingly, different clairvoyants began to contact Dorothy and it unnerved her. In the evening, in the quiet of the apartment, she would sit with Susan at the kitchen table to try to make sense of it.

"They keep saying your Dad is trying to contact me. He has a message. They want me to go to their meetings."

"Are you going?" asked Susan, concerned.

"I don't know," muttered Dorothy. "I don't know, I don't know."

"You might find out what happened."

"I'm frightened. I don't understand. Whether to believe them. The state I'm in now, I might easily get hooked into that sort of thing."

Susan patiently listened while her mother related the day's events, repeating over and over, her fears and anxieties. When she was on her own with her sister, Susan suggested that they take over the running of the apartment between them.

"What do you mean?" asked Candy.

"I've been thinking. If I do the food shopping, cooking, and washing-up, you could do the tidying, hoovering and drying-up."

Candy disliked her older sister making suggestions and at first refused.

"I don't see why I should. You're so bossy," snapped Candy.

"If you don't want to do anything, that's up to you," retorted Susan.

After a few minutes, the two girls stopped bickering and became friends again, with Candy agreeing to do her share of the household chores. When they told their mother in the evening she was pleased her daughters had come together to share the work and it was one less thing for her to think about.

More than anything, Dorothy dreaded the weekly sea crossing to Shivering Sands. Braving her fears, she went out to the station, expecting most of the crew to give notice and leave after the dreadful experience they'd been through. To her surprise, they all said they wanted to stay.

Sitting at Reg's desk in the office, Dorothy realised she had to consolidate the various businesses and piece together the jigsaw of his life.

The rent was settled to the end of June on the nightclub at Loughborough and Dorothy gave notice that she would make no further payments. The owners of the Essoldo tried to force her into honouring the contract Reg had signed but Dorothy would not be pressured. She did not want to run a nightclub and instructed her solicitors to fight their action.

The Fortunes and Pinkerton's both asked Terry King to be their manager. Glen Dale was replaced in the Fortunes by Shel Macrae. Glen made his debut as a solo singer and recorded *Good Day Sunshine*, written by Lennon and McCartney.

When Terry suggested she exchange her shares in the agency for his shares in King Music, Dorothy agreed. They both preferred to be independent and at the back of Dorothy's mind was the future prospect of expanding the publishing side of the business.

Jill took down a telephone message that startled her and when Dorothy returned to the office, she did her best to soften the blow.

"I've had a request from a French film crew. They want to do a film on pirate radio and have asked permission to visit Radio City next week."

"That's okay. They could go out on the boat on Tuesday if they want to."

"I'll let them know. And you've had more people offering to provide security on the station."

Dorothy frowned. "I don't want to speak to them. They're becoming a nuisance. If anyone calls again, ask them to send details in writing and explain that for the time being, I'm not looking for extra help."

"And I've had a message about the Court Hearing. It's arranged to be held at Saffron Walden Assizes, 18th to 20th July. They've cancelled me as a witness," said Jill, quietly. "And they've cancelled you. It seems they've cancelled everyone. No one from Radio City is being called."

Dorothy was incredulous. "How can they arrange a Court Hearing without any witnesses? I told you, Smedley knows people in the right places and he's going to get away with it."

"He can't Mrs C. British justice isn't like that."

Dorothy took a deep breath and tried to calm herself as she stubbed out her cigarette.

"Can you telephone everyone and let them know they've been cancelled."

"Yes, I'll do that. The only person I won't be able to speak to is Ian West as he's on the station this week. I'll include it in this week's memo to the station?"

Dorothy, in the office, picking up the pieces and carrying on after Reg's death

MEMO 14th July 1966

To Radio City staff

Note: ***NO*** *VISITORS:* So called Insurance or Security men may try to call.

1. IAN WEST: You are **not now required** to go to Court on Monday
2. Possibility of getting new Ford kva (generator).
3. NEW DJs: I class as unprofessional conduct, singing and interrupting of records. Anyone who must sing, please tape it and I shall be only too pleased to audition you for recording contract!!!
4. TOM: It was the day-to-day programme schedules I required – could you please oblige?
5. ALL STAFF: We are now advertising programme times as being from 6 a.m. until midnight EVERY DAY.
6. Any technical problems, please relay to Fred.
7. There should now be a sufficiency of DJs and Ed Moreno tapes will be coming out next week to make this possible. There are four DJs this weekend, so continue till midnight as from Saturday.
8. If opportunity arises, GENERAL TIDY UP PLEASE as French TV cameras will be coming out on Tuesday's boat.

All the best for now,

See you Tuesday,

Mrs C

POLICE REPORTS

The police worked quickly and efficiently, taking statements from everyone, including Radio City crew, Philip Birch, Ted Allbeury and those involved with the boarding party and murder. The whole sordid affair gradually unravelled and it was obvious that some witnesses were less than candid in telling the truth as they tried to defend their position. Detective Superintendent George Brown from Essex Constabulary carried out most of the investigations and reported back to Detective Inspector J.A. Barker, Criminal Investigation Department, New Scotland Yard.

By 23rd June, Inspector Barker had compiled an accurate three-page summary from witness statements and forwarded it to the Home Office.

"I am sending you this report, which was prepared over the weekend to enable the Home Office to deal with some parliamentary questions. The Essex and Kent Police Forces take the view that these 'pirate radio stations' are nothing to do with them. The Commissioner takes the view that as nobody else appears to be willing to show interest in the matter, the Metropolitan Police must do so."

By 27th June, a further 29-page report was sent to P.E. Brodie, OBE, who forwarded it to Sir Norman Skelhorn, QC, Director of Public Prosecutions.

ESSEX COUNTY CONSTABULARY

Report by G.T. Brown, Detective Superintendent.
6th July, 1966 (Extracts)

Miss Dorothy Black. She is Director with Crawford of C.B.C. (Plays) Ltd, which is connected with Project Atlanta. She is a very shrewd woman, very forthright, and could well have been the person pushing Smedley in the boarding party. She feels completely justified in the action taken.

Alexander Clark Horsley. Known variously as Captain Horsley, Commander Horsley, and Major Horsley from his wartime activities. He appears apparently honest but is easily confused and has difficulty in keeping to the point. He claims only a personal interest and thought the whole thing a bit of a lark.

Mrs Jill Vivian Wileman. Secretary. She speaks of her employment by Calvert and the various negotiations between him and Smedley.

Aubrey Nicholas John Boutwood. Personal Assistant to Smedley. He describes business affairs of Smedley and Calvert. He is C.R.O. No. 12622/57. He has two convictions in 1954 and 1956 for minor Company offences and a third in Oct 1956 when he was sentenced to 12, 12, 6 and 6 months imprisonment for offences of fraud in relation to a company. He is an undischarged bankrupt. He and Smedley are involved amongst other things in the 'National Benevolent Fund for the Aged,' A charity organisation, which I understand is not registered anywhere.

Lilian Elizabeth McDonnell. Licensee of The Railway Inn Public House, Newport. She speaks of Calvert calling into the Public House about 10.35 p.m. asking for directions. She describes Calvert's manner as perfectly normal.

Dorothy Calvert. The widow of the deceased. She should make a good witness and is obviously a shrewd business woman. She will say that Calvert was not a violent man but he was a man full of ideas and of an inventive nature. He carried a gas fountain pen which was found in his pocket after his death and never produced by him. She will say that he carried this for protection in the Dance Hall business.

Pamela Gail Holdsworth Thorburn. She has since complained of injuries inflicted by Calvert. She has shown me two bruises on her left upper arm. Thorburn is obviously biased in favour of Smedley and will say that she feared for her life. She is a very intelligent young woman.

Detective Constable Frank Eric Mann. Photographer. Found gas fountain pen, and £440 in £10 notes, mentioned in Mrs Calvert's statement as money she gave her husband to use to bribe the 'Riggers' on the fort into leaving.

Detective Sergeant Colin Godwin Woodford. Has been present with me throughout this enquiry and can corroborate all my evidence.

"I anticipate that this case will be fought on lines of 'justifiable homicide'. The shotgun is in good condition and there has been no suggestion by Smedley that it went off accidentally and in fact his whole demeanour has been that he deliberately fired the shot. He will obviously say that he feared for the life of himself and Miss Thorburn and she will definitely say so.

Miss Thorburn says that Smedley was in the dining room and getting himself a drink when Calvert knocked at the door. Arnold says he heard voices in the sitting room. These two rooms are divided by the hall, and front door. From each room, there are a pair of French doors giving access to the conservatory at the rear, at one end of which is Smedley's bedroom. It seems likely that Smedley went direct from the sitting room to his bedroom on hearing Calvert at the door. ..... His only part in the proceedings was to return to the dining room from the conservatory being already armed with the gun and to at once deliberately shoot Calvert without a word having been spoken between them.

The cost of the eleven Riggers for one week on basic Rigger salary at 24 hours a day plus the commission of Brandish, the Master Rigger, amounted to £735. 10s. I believe the actual cost was £200 in excess of this. I understand that the total cost, including payment for the boats and supplies, is something in the region of £1,700. Much of this has been met initially by Horsley but presumably Smedley and Miss Black will foot the bill.

I anticipate the Preliminary Hearing will take about three days. I have provisionally arranged the hearing at Saffron Walden on Monday, Tuesday and Wednesday 18 –20 July, 1966."

27th June, 1966. Dorothy Calvert, escorted by Supt. G. Brown, Essex CID to the Inquest at Chelmsford, Essex. The police had been kind to her and outwardly, she gave the impression of being in control. Inwardly, she could feel herself sinking into the fathomless deeps of mourning but she would not cry. Dorothy knew she had to stay strong to face all that was to come (AL)

29. THE HEARING

Dorothy put complete trust in the police officers who had been kind and considerate to her on the night of the murder and afterwards in their questioning. John drove her to Saffron Walden where she was met and escorted into court by Detective Superintendent Brown who had done most of the police investigation. Nervously, Dorothy took her seat next to John. She had never attended a court before and had little knowledge of the legal system or how a Hearing was conducted. Her sixth sense told her that Major Smedley was going to get away with murder but she was unsure how he would do it. During the court proceedings, Dorothy listened intently and quickly began to understand.

There were only three main witnesses: Kitty Black, Pamela Thorburn and Alan Arnold. Supplementary witnesses included: Horace Leggett who was at the meeting on 20th June; Lilian McDonnell from the Railway Inn where Reg had asked directions; Neil Warden who had phoned the police on the night of the shooting; plus police and medical officers.

Kitty Black had been puzzled by the choice of witnesses and queried why she had been called for the Prosecution, explaining she was a friend of Major Smedley and should be a Defence witness.

Kitty Black spoke of the Dean Street meeting and claimed Reg allegedly owed Major Smedley a lot of money. He had threatened gas bombs and various other ways he might remove the boarders but omitted to mention she had lightheartedly joked with him about it and that no one had believed him. Nor did she explain that Allan Crawford had refused to have anything to do with the boarding party and that at the earlier meeting, Philip Birch had accused them all of blackmail.

Pamela Thorburn gave a graphic image of Reg attacking her, of being mad, very violent, red in the face and using bad language saying, "Where's the bugger Smedley?" Smedley stared at her the whole time she was in the witness box as she enlarged and exaggerated every detail of the struggle. How she had fought with Reg from room to room as he searched for Smedley. Reg had knocked her down and thrown statues at her and her bruises had only just gone. Miss Thorburn, when asked, admitted she and Smedley sometimes shared a bed although they had separate bedrooms. She said he was a gentleman and she had known him since she was eight years old.

Alan Arnold was nervous and easily manipulated in his responses by suggestions put to him by both the Prosecution and Defence Counsel. He explained how Reg had been calm upon his arrival at the cottage. Arnold had been surprised by the struggle but had not thought to intervene as he had a bad heart. No questions were asked about the actual shooting or how he had run for his life when Smedley raised the gun at him. Nor did the Prosecution ask about his initial police statement: “We came to the house and this man went mad and shot him.”

Smedley gave his evidence with the self-assurance of an innocent man. Calvert owed him £10,000 for a new transmitter. He had peaceably taken over the radio station to look after his equipment until a settlement could be reached. Calvert had threatened gas attacks to remove the men on the station and he carried a gas gun. Smedley knew that Calvert was a violent man and had come to kill him and all the others. He was completely justified in shooting him and had saved the life of his housekeeper.

Dorothy wanted to scream out, ‘he’s lying, it’s not true’, but she kept her nerve and stayed calm. When she returned home she was distraught. After their meal, Dorothy sat at the kitchen table with her head in her hands, going over and over the day’s events.

“He’s going to get away with it. He’s going to get away with murder. I know he is. I’m sure the magistrate knows him. Not only has Major Smedley killed your father, he’s destroying his reputation and there’s no one to tell the truth. Alan Arnold was sitting behind me. At lunchtime, I asked him what had really happened. He looked at me, and without saying a word walked out. He was terrified. I could see it in his eyes. He was like a frightened rabbit. I don’t understand what’s happening. No one believes me. They keep saying British justice isn’t like this. That no one can get away with murder and walk free. But I know he will. I just know it.”

Tuesday, the headlines in the press portrayed Reg of being a violent man who carried a gas gun and was threatening a gas attack. Dorothy held her head high as the Hearing continued with more shocking revelations. In the evening, she went over it again as she tried to fathom what was happening.

The family retired to bed early and Dorothy tossed and turned as she tried to sleep. Never far from her conscious mind was the dreadful image of Reg lying dead on the mortuary table. She understood now how Smedley was going to get away with murder. The Prosecution Counsel were not going to call her, or anyone else who knew Reg, to give witness in court and tell the truth.

Dosing fitfully, Dorothy was abruptly awoken. From the family bathroom came the sound of loud banging. Glancing at the clock, she saw it was half past midnight. The bathroom and kitchen windows had a grill on them and someone on the fire escape was trying to force their way in. Terrified, she jumped out of bed as her daughters, shivering with fear, ran into her bedroom.

“I’ll phone the police. You call the porters,” instructed Dorothy.

Susan ran out of the apartment in her nightdress and pressed the lift bell for the concierge. She knew it would take a little while for him to come, so ran back to her mother, leaving the apartment door ajar. The loud banging and levering of the grill continued.

Dorothy felt more scared and vulnerable than ever before. Logic told her that any normal thief would be quiet when trying to break in and leave as soon as the lights were switched on. The banging continued. Putting her arms around her panic-stricken daughters, she tried to remain calm.

Within a few minutes of her telephone call, five policemen burst into the apartment from the central lobby and ran through each room. Relieved, Dorothy opened the back door to the fire escape where the intruder would have been. Policemen clattered heavily down the metal steps to the area behind the building and ran up to the roof. Whoever had been there had timed their escape perfectly and was nowhere to be seen.

Dorothy thanked the police for coming and lit a cigarette. Looking wearily at her daughters, she hugged them.

"Go back to bed, you'll be safe now. They won't try again tonight."

It was another warning meant to frighten her, but why?

Wednesday was the last day of the Hearing. Dorothy and John took their seats to listen to another catalogue of exaggeration, half-truths and lies. To their amazement, Peter Palmes for the Prosecution, stood up and announced to the court that he had been to Major Smedley's cottage that morning and discovered it had been broken into during the night and half a pillowcase of silver had been stolen.

During the lunch adjournment, John went to a public telephone kiosk to call Jill. As he waited his turn, he could hear a young man in front of him booking a celebration dinner for Major Smedley. John realised that even before the case concluded, they knew Smedley was going to be released on bail.

The newspaper reporters were very supportive of Dorothy. Many of them had known Reg and realised the Hearing was prejudiced and apologised they were unable to tell her side of the story as it was sub judice. She told them about the attempted break-in. To verify her statement, they phoned the police and they denied any record of her call or of sending officers.

When the Hearing concluded, as expected, Smedley was released on bail and Inspector Brown could see by Dorothy's face that she was angry but he had been powerless to influence the Prosecution Counsel's legal reasoning or their choice of witnesses. Dorothy complained bitterly to him that the Hearing had not been carried out correctly.

"There's Mr Palmes, why don't you speak to him directly?" suggested Inspector Brown, taking her gently by the arm and walking her over.

"Hello Mr Palmes. This is Mrs Calvert. She would like to ask you a few questions."

"How can I help?" asked Mr Palmes, politely.

"I don't understand why no witnesses have been called on our side. You've called Miss Black as a witness when it's obvious she's on Major Smedley's side. Why didn't you call Mr Birch who was at the earlier meeting?"

Mr Palmes looked at Dorothy and smiled wanly. It was obvious to Dorothy that he was not going to answer her question, so she continued.

"You seem to be acting for Major Smedley and the Defence, rather than my husband? You're reinforcing everything they're saying."

She was now in full swing and her pent-up frustration poured out.

"My husband was not a violent man. He never went around hitting people and beating them up. He always walked away from trouble and would talk his way out of anything. He'd been trying to contact Major Smedley all day and he went there to talk to him. If they couldn't agree a settlement, he was going to the station to pay off the boarders with more money than they would have earned. When Reg was angry, he went chalk white in the face and became very, very quiet. He did not go red in the face. He did not shout and he never swore. What Miss Thorburn said about him swearing and being red in the face was untrue. I have never heard him swear in twenty years. Even when he was angry he did not swear. He never picked up objects and threw them about. He had a bad arm from his small pox injection and could hardly move it. And the transmitter. It was old and did not work. It wasn't worth anything. Major Smedley could have taken it away at any time. It was a complete lie when he said it was worth £10,000. He took over my husband's radio station with force and then tried to blackmail him and Mr Birch. When he didn't succeed, he tried to sell the station to other people. He has made out that he was justified in taking it. Had you called the engineers, you could easily have proved his story was a lie. He owed my husband money. The police took the evidence to prove it. Where are the letters and accounts they took that proves Major Smedley owed Reg money? Radio Atlanta were the ones who couldn't afford to pay the bills and my husband had to take control of the station again. And the gas gun? What gas gun? My husband had a little pen that gave out a very small amount of tear gas that is legal and easily available in Germany. It was less dangerous than carrying a perfume spray. My husband was the person who had been injured. Not Miss Thorburn. The police said on the night that she had not one bruise or mark on her. Reg was scratched and cut above his left eye. He was the one who had been hit. He was probably blinded at the time he was shot. Why didn't you say anything about that in court?"

When Dorothy had finished her barrage of questions, Peter Palmes said very politely, "Thank you," and walked away.

Dorothy looked at Inspector Brown and shook her head. "He's acting for Major Smedley, I know he is."

LIST OF WITNESSES included

Dorothy Black
Pamela Thorburn
Horace Leggatt
Alan Arnold
Neil Warden – back cottage
Lillian McDonnell – Railway Inn, Newport
Police and medical officers

LIST OF WITNESSES NOT CALLED

Theodore (Ted) Allbeury – Radio 390
Philip Birch – Radio London
Allan James Crawford – Project Atlanta
John Boutwood – Smedley's Personal Assistant
Commander Alexander Clark Horsley – Organised Boarding Party
Det. Serg. Colin Rutter – Police, Bow Street Station
Dr Donald Hunter
Dorothy Calvert
Jill Wileman – Reg Calvert's secretary
Brian Richard Harvey – King Music
Leslie Dunne – Radio City Chef
Thomas Edwards –Head deejay
Peter Dolphin – Trial deejay
Paul Elvey –Engineer
Ian MacRae – Deejay
Phillip Perkins – Engineer
Ian West – Engineer

Boarding Party included:

Neil Peter Buckland
Alfred Pullen
Henry Cyril Charles Collier
Kenneth Field
Harry George Fereman
Basil Michael Fowler
Raymond Jarvis
Alfred Law
James McKnight
William Park
David Henry Pipcin
Alfred Reader
Ronald Walters

'My God! You've shot

CALVERT 'LIKE A RAVING MANIAC'—GIRL

Evening Standard Reporters: Saffron Walden, Tuesday

Dark-haired Miss Pamela Thorburn, housekeeper at the Essex country cottage where "pop pirate" Reg Calvert was shot dead, was suddenly called into court during the evidence of a prosecution witness in the shooting drama at Saffron Walden court today.

He had described bursting out with the words: "This is murder," to her employer, Major Oliver Smedley, as his business friend, Mr. Calvert, fell dying in front of him.

Then the witness, bearded company director Mr. Alan Arnold, of Greenways, Hertford, agreed that Calvert had been grappling with her before the fatal shot was fired, but that the situation took him so by surprise that he never lifted a finger to intervene.

He denied knowing that Calvert, who is said by the prosecution to have dramatically threatened to use nerve gas to get a "boarding party" off the Radio City fort in the Thames Estuary, had a tear-gas gun with him when he went to the cottage

MAJOR SMEDLEY today
He is accused.

A kaleidoscope

The story, which Mr. Arnold called a "kaleidoscope of events," was told when the hearing against Major Smedley, who is accused of murdering Mr. Calvert, 38-year-old head of Radio City, entered its second day.

The accused man, who won the MC in Normandy and has many business interests, is alleged to have killed Mr. Calvert when he called at his home in Wendens Ambo, near Saffron Walden, to discuss a quarrel over the Radio City pirate station.

Major Smedley, who had been concerned with a firm called Project Atlanta, had mounted a boarding party on Radio City two days previously and closed it down, according to the prosecution.

Mr. Arnold, who said that he had met Mr. Calvert earlier this year, gave evidence of erecting a radio mast on the fort for him.

On June 21 he noticed that the station was off the air, and later that day had several telephone talks with Mr. Calvert.

That night he drove him to Major Smedley's house, where Mr. Calvert pushed his way in.

He continued: "A struggle broke out with a young woman there. She was trying to push him out, and he was trying to push his way past her. The whole thing was a bit of a surprise to me.

'Out of hand'

"The young woman broke away from Calvert to get to the telephone, but he snatched it from her and jerked the cord from the wall.

"I decided the thing was getting out of hand and the best thing I could do was to try to find Mr. Smedley. But I could not find him, and when Calvert was struggling with the young woman again I became extremely apprehensive and went outside into the street to get help.

"Then I heard a shot, and went back inside the house where I saw Mr. Calvert falling forward with a hole in his chest. I saw Mr. Smedley with a shotgun in his hand.

"It was a tremendous shock to me. I don't remember my first words to Mr. Smedley, but I did say that 'This was murder.'

"I can't remember his reply, but I went to the house next door to get help.

Sat in lounge

"The young woman was still there. Mr. Smedley still had the gun when I returned. We sat down in the lounge until the ambulance arrived.

"I took no part in the fracas. It all seemed to happen very quickly."

Mr. Peter Palmes, prosecuting, asked if Mr. Calvert's actions on entering the house came completely as a surprise, and the witness agreed.

Defence counsel Mr. John Gower asked him: "Did you know Mr. Calvert had a gas gun on him and ammunition for it?"

Mr. Arnold: "No."

He did not feel it was at all odd to have a business talk at that time of night.

When Mr. Gower asked if his own words to Major Smedley were: "My God! My God! You've shot him," and if he added: "My wife said I should never have come. Please give me a drink. For God's sake give me a drink," he replied it was difficult to remember what he said.

But he agreed that Calvert forced the door open and burst in.

Mr Gower asked for Miss Thorburn, housekeeper-secretary to Major Smedley, to come into court. She did so, wearing a black pill-box hat and a black and grey costume.

Mr Arnold agreed that it was she with whom Calvert had been struggling.

Mr. Gower: "She was obviously trying to stop him coming in and he was using violence on her to try to force his way in?"

Witness: "That is true; he was resisting her attempts to push him out."

Mr. Gower commented: "But she was the housekeeper and there lawfully. You never raised your voice or lifted your finger to try to stop him."

Mr. Arnold replied: "No, it was a situation that took me completely by surprise."

Cross-examined, Mr. Arnold said he was obsolutely flabbergasted at what was going on.

Asked about Calvert's manner during the struggle, Mr. Arnold said he was furious and he became extremely apprehensive.

Pressed on this point by counsel, Mr. Arnold said: "I became alarmed for the safety of the young woman and Mr. Calvert's behaviour."

Counsel: "If you were alarmed for the safety of the girl why didn't you physically intervene and restrain Calvert?"—"It may be because I didn't think of it, or it may be because I didn't like to be involved in excitement myself.

'A distortion'

Mr. Arnold said that Calvert was furious and he could see by his flushed appearance that he was in a temper. He had the manner of a man in a rage.

Counsel: "In an uncontrollable rage?"—"Not knowing him very well I could not say whether it was uncontrollable."

Counsel: "Would it be fair to say that you didn't know Calvert sufficiently well to risk physical intervention?" — "I think that would be a distortion."

Re-examined by Mr. Palmes, Mr. Arnold said he didn't like to get involved in excitement and tried to lead an ordered life. He had heart trouble and had twice had heart attacks.

Then 23-year-old Miss Thorburn was brought into the witness box to give evidence against her employer.

She said that on the night of June 19 she saw Major Smedley leave from Audley End Station, near Saffron Walden, after telling her that he was

A bust of Napoleon is carried to the court today. A witness told the court it was thrown.

Smedley, reading: "Calvert says he had notified the CID and lodged a formal charge of theft against you, and Kitty, and they are coming to get you.

"He has sent a boat out to the tower with a message that they have photographs of them. If they come off in his boat no further action will be taken, but if not as soon as they come ashore they will be picked up."

(The prosecution case is that the shooting occurred after a boarding party had been placed on the fort by Major Smedley, and that it included one of his business associates, Miss Dorothy "Kitty" Black, a theatrical impresario.)

Miss Thorburn said she spoke to Major Smedley about the note.

She added: "We all laughed about it because there was no question of there having been a theft."

She went home with Major Smedley, arriving there about 7.45.

She went on: "About 11 o'clock there was a knock at the front door. They were two firm knocks. Major Smedley was in the dining room and I was in the sitting room.

"It was possible that we were talking across the hall but I can't remember. I went to the front door and opened it. I saw a man standing there who I later learned to be Calvert.

"Within a split second I knew who it was, because it was obvious he was not paying a social call. He was extremely furious.

'Ran under arm'

"I immediately tried to close the door but he pushed it violently open and pushed me backwards. It happened in a split second and as he came through the door he was shouting: 'Where's Smedley?'

"There were a lot of swear words as well.

"He then said: 'I am going to take him to the police.' I said something like 'Do be sensible. If you've got a charge to bring, why don't you get a policeman and bring him here.'

"We were then in the hall. We were struggling. He was trying to get into the sitting room, I think, and I was trying to stop him. There was more or less a permament struggle between the two of us.

"I had seen the other man behind him when I opened the door (she was referring to Mr. Arnold).

"Calvert said to him: 'You go and look upstairs,' which he did. As he spoke to Mr. Arnold, Calvert looked upstairs. I took the opportunity to run under his arm to go to the telephone in the sitting room.

"I ran into the sittingroom and got as far as dialling one 9. He wrenched the phone out of my hand and pushed me, so that I fell through the door leading to the bathroom.

"I fell backwards onto the floor, but going down I caught the wall so I did not fall very heavily. I came rushing back out.

"He hit me on the shoulders with the handset. I think he was trying to hit me on my head.

"I said to Mr. Arnold: 'Why don't you help me?' or 'Help me, for goodness sake.'"

'Desperate man'

Miss Thorburn said that during her fight with Calvert he knocked over an electric heater, hurled the telephone set down when it was no more use, and tried to throw a heavy bust of Napoleon at her. But she dodged it.

He claimed that he was going to take Mr. Smedley to the police and said: "I am a desperate man. I don't care what happens. I am going to get him alive or

MISS THORBURN today.
Called into court.

get him I'm going to take you.' I had no idea what he meant; I had no idea where he wanted to take me.

"He continued by saying: 'If you don't come willingly, I will take you dead' or something like that. I didn't move. I said something like, 'Don't be stupid. I am certainly not coming willingly.'

Reeling back

"It was while I was saying this that he said: 'There is the bugger.' He pushed me back towards the dining room and went past me.

"It happened so quickly. Before I could even straighten up he was reeling back into the sittingroom doorway. I have no recollection of the shot at all.

"I didn't know what had happened, I was just feeling relieved that he was no longer attacking me. It must have been after I first saw him stagger."

When she first noticed Smedley she said that she saw him in the hall outside, beside the body. He was still holding the shotgun.

She was handed a shotgun which she identified as belonging to Smedley. Asked about the statuette, she said she saw Calvert pick it up but she didn't remember what happened to it. She later found it in the dining room.

'Give me a drink'

Miss Thorburn said that after Calvert had collapsed on the floor she went to see how he was, and Mr. Smedley kept saying: "Where are the police?"

Both she and Mr. Smedley

19th July, 1966 Evening Standard

30. THE STORY AS TOLD BY THE PRESS

'Pop pirate' planned 'nerve gas' attack on fort, murder court is told

'HE CAME TO KILL ME . . . I SHOT HIM'

—ALLEGED STATEMENT BY SMEDLEY

Evening Standard Reporters: Saffron Walden, Monday

Wealthy Major Oliver Smedley sat in court here today and heard prosecuting counsel tell what he is alleged to have said to a police officer who arrived at his home shortly after Radio City pop pirate chief Reg Calvert was shot dead.

When asked what happened, he is said to have replied: "I have shot him." Asked for more details, he went on:

"Calvert had threatened to do me harm, to kill me and all the others. I went to get my shotgun and loaded it. I knew he came to kill me. I could see he was mad. I knew he carried arms."

"I had no choice but to fire. I did not think of aiming at his legs. I just fired. I feel morally right. I knew he was a violent man and he came to kill me."

Counsel told the court that what the accused had said about Calvert being armed was true. He was carrying something that looked like a pencil or a torch, but was, in actual fact, a gas gun which squirted a stream of tear gas.

18th July, 1966 Evening Standard

EXTRACTS

Tuesday 22nd June, 1966. Daily Mirror

SEA RAIDERS CAPTURE POP PIRATE RADIO

A boarding party of ten men and a girl have captured a pop pirate radio station in an amazing commando style raid. Last night the station's staff of ten engineers and disc jockeys were said to be held as hostages. The station is Radio City, based in a wartime fort on the Shivering Sands in the Thames Estuary twelve, miles from Whitstable, Kent.

It went off-air on Sunday night and did not resume broadcasting.

Mrs Dorothy Calvert, 38, wife of Radio City's owner, Mr Reg Calvert, said last night that her husband was later told he could have the fort back – in return for half the profits.

"We have no intention of being blackmailed like this," she said. Mr Calvert had a phone call from a man earlier this week asking him to go to a meeting in a London Office. Also asked was Mr Philip Birch, managing director of Radlon, the organisation handling advertising from Radio London and Radio UKGM which was due to take over Radio City next month....

Wednesday 23rd June, 1966. The Guardian

CITY MAN ACCUSED OF MURDERING PIRATE RADIO DIRECTOR

Oliver Smedley, a City accountant, and a former vice president of the Liberal Party Executive, was charged at a special court at Saffron Walden, Essex, Wednesday 22nd June, for the murder of Mr Reg Calvert, head of the radio station Radio City. He was remanded in custody until 1st July. The proceedings lasted about four minutes. Smedley sat in a leather upholstered chair at the head of the council table, about a yard from the chairman of the court, Lord Braybrooke. ...... Smedley's solicitor, Mr A.S. Tee, said "He has asked me to say that he completely denies the charge. The only application is one for bail." The application was refused.

Mr Smedley had resigned in 1959 as Liberal candidate for Walthamstow West because of the party's attitude to joining the Common Market. He fought four elections, two against Mr R.A. Butler and twice at Walthamstow. He is a director of a variety of companies dealing with investments, breweries, a distillery, fruit farming and the entertainment world. He is connected with the Cheap Food League. For 16 years, a partner in the London firm of Ford, Rhodes, Williams & Co who have firms in India, Ceylon, Australia, Pakistan and South Africa. He was educated at Monkton Combe School, near Bath. During the war he served in the Royal Artillery and attained the rank of major. He became a parachutist, was twice wounded and awarded the Military Cross.

Wednesday 23rd June, 1966. Daily Telegraph

POLICE SAIL TO SEE POP PIRATES

Police investigating the death of pop pirate radio chief Mr Reg Calvert sailed out to his Radio City in the Thames Estuary last night. Detective

Superintendent George Brown, head of Essex CID with a team of six, went in a launch from Tilbury to the string of forts at Shivering Sands.

Statements were taken from the five men on Radio City's staff – and from ten men who boarded the station early on Monday. ....

On the forts, earlier in the day I talked to the men involved in that boarding. Their leader known as 'Big Alf' said: "You don't need our names. All I can say is that we were carrying out instructions in good faith. We came here to collect transmitters."

Only one man among the 10 would give his name. Electronics engineer, Mr Don Jones, 38, said: "I'm here to make sure no damage is done." The other men said they were riggers. The radio men provided beds and blankets for the boarding party, and while I was there, they all shared a pot of tea.

Paul Elvey, electrical engineer in charge of the station, said: "The crystals were taken from the two transmitters. We have been off the air because of this."

Senior disc jockey Tom Edwards, 22, said: "There is nothing to do but eat, sleep, and watch TV until the trouble is sorted out."

Thursday 23rd June, 1966. Evening Standard

MP: 'POP PIRATES ANARCHY' BILL TO BAN THEM

The Government is ready to act to prevent further operation of pirate radio stations around the shores of Britain, the Postmaster General, Mr Anthony Wedgwood Benn, told the Commons early today. He said that the Bill which will arm the Government with necessary legal powers is now ready. Its introduction only awaits a place in the congested Parliamentary timetable. Mr Benn's announcement at the end of the Commons second successive all-night sitting on the committee stage of the Finance Bill, came within 36 hours of the shooting of Radio City pirate chief, Mr Reg Calvert.

Mr Hugh Jenkins (Labour Putney) pressed him, in view of the events at the Shivering Sands fort, to give the legislation top priority. Said Mr Jenkins: "These extraordinary and tragic events serve to impress on everybody that piracy is piracy in whatever aspect it occurs. We have seen the hijacking of one of the stations and the invasion and taking over of this illegally occupied area by another group equally illegally occupying it. ......"

Friday 24th June, 1966. Daily Mail

SHOT MAN'S WIDOW PLANS TO CARRY ON

From her London office, yesterday Mrs Dorothy Calvert said she had taken control of Radio City. She said: "We will ask the people who grabbed our broadcasting base to leave."

Today the Radio City tender will leave Whitstable, Kent, with a replacement crystal. Mrs Calvert hopes to go with them. Said Mrs Calvert: "The engineers will soon have the equipment repaired when they get to the station."

Her secretary, Mrs Jill Wileman, said: "There is no question of us using force. The pirates will be invited to leave in our tender." ....

The boarding party was put on the station to guard a £10,000 transmitter, which a company called Project Atlanta claims as its property. Last night Mr Peter Buckland, who led the boarding party, said: "As far as I am concerned the men stay put. I am shortly going out to take them provisions. Until everything is cleared up they are staying."

Radio City disc jockey Mr Peter Dolphin who came back to the mainland on Wednesday, said yesterday that he had been given police protection after receiving a threatening phone call.

Friday 24th June, 1966. Evening News Night Special

POP PIRATE RIVER ALERT

London's river police were ordered this afternoon to stand by their launches ready to send a boarding party to Radio City on Shivering Sands in the Thames Estuary. The order came from Scotland yard after they had been told of alleged threats to people connected with the pirate radio station. High speed police launches stood by at Wapping police station – headquarters of the Thames police division. Meanwhile Yard chiefs made urgent inquiries regarding police jurisdiction over the fort which is ten miles off Whitstable."

WIDOW FIGHTS FOR PIRATE STATION

Dark Haired Mrs Dorothy Calvert, widowed four days ago, launched her own battle last night to restart Radio City. ..... Mrs Calvert has taken over her husband's role. And last night in her London office she said determinedly: "The station will be on the air this weekend and I'm prepared to put up a big fight to make it succeed." ..... Stormy weather stopped a bid yesterday to take new crystals to the transmitter.

A radio Caroline spokesman stated yesterday that all connections between Radio Caroline and Project Atlanta of which major Oliver Smedley is a director, were severed in December 1965.

Friday 25th June, 1966. Daily Telegraph

FORT STANDS BY TO REPEL BOARDERS

The boarding party who seized Radio city .... Stood by yesterday to wreck the 240ft high transmitting mast and to repel raiders. ..... Mrs Calvert, 38, is considering legal action against the boarding party. She cancelled a proposed visit to the station yesterday after seeing her lawyer, Timothy Hardacre.

ARREST SOUGHT: Mr Hardacre said Mrs Calvert has instructed her lawyers to issue proceedings against persons who have forcibly taken possession of Radio City. ..... Mrs Calvert said she received a threat after her television appearance on Thursday. "I cannot say any more at this stage."

Friday 25th June, 1966. Daily Express:

BOARDERS THREATEN TOWER

Legal action is to be taken against the boarders who closed down pirate radio station Radio City. This was decided yesterday after Mrs Dorothy Calvert, whose husband Reg was shot dead on Tuesday, had consulted with her lawyer.

But at the same time the raiders who took over the station replied with a threat to chop down the radio mast if any one tries to board the fort. They warned that 'there will be trouble' if anyone, including Mrs Calvert herself, attempts to board the station. .....

After seeing her lawyer, Mr Timothy Hardacre yesterday, 38-year-old Mrs Calvert was said to be "not too well" following the shock and strain of the past few days. Mr Hardacre said he had been instructed "to issue legal proceedings against the persons who have forcibly taken possession of Radio City and against those who have aided and abetted them."

The boarders – comparatively friendly until yesterday – were described by a Radio City spokesman as now being 'very hostile.' As two Radio City supply boats approached the fort, grim-faced men stood by with oxy acetylene burners to cut the cables and send the aerial toppling into the waves. The invaders' leader – burly ship's rigger 'Big Alf' Bullen – watched as new food supplies for the six Radio City men were winched on board. On the catwalks, other members of the boarding party stood guard at the doors of the locked transmitter building. Big Alf allowed two relief engineers onto the fort and three Radio City men were lowered to the boats to be taken ashore on leave.

One of them, engineer Paul Elvey, 30, said: "The boarding party has suddenly become more hostile towards us. We were kept to our own quarters most of the time and they have a 24-hour patrol round the catwalks. There has been no violence yet – but there would be if any one they didn't want tried to set foot on the fort."

Earlier Big Alf told me. "All I can say is we came here in good faith to collect some transmitters. We came here as instructed by our governor – but I'm not saying who that is."

A dispute over the ownership of a transmitter, said to be worth £10,000 is the reason that Radio City was put off the air.

Saturday 25th June, 1966. Evening News

PIRATES: SEND IN NAVY SAYS SIR ALAN

Sir Alan Herbert, Chairman of the British Copyright Council, today urged that the Government should send the Navy at once to the Shivering Sands towers pirate radio station. .... Sir Alan said: "Since Ministers seem to be speechless as well as paralysed, I take it on myself to send a friendly warning to the latest trespassers of the Shivering Sands towers."

It is reported today that an executive of the company behind them said: "The Fort is outside the territorial limits. You tell me to which court anyone is going to take the case?"

"This is a dangerous delusion. The towers (and the Red Sands towers as well – Radio 390) have been in territorial waters since 30th September, 1964, under an Order in Council specially made for the purpose by the last government. Moreover, they are in the area of the Port of London and all the criminal laws apply. If anyone cuts down the mast they will be doing malicious damage to private property and if they destroy the gangway, it is Government property: and if energetically used, the law will get them. If they start broadcasting without a licence they are clearly liable to be searched and prosecuted by magistrates of Kent or Essex. ......"

Saturday 26th June, 1966. The Observer:

SEIZED POP STATION FOR SALE

Attempts by a group of businessmen and women to sell the still silent Radio City – taken over by a boarding party ... were revealed yesterday. The moves came after the raiders landed on the rusting wartime anti-aircraft station. ..... The negotiators first approached Mr Philip Birch, managing director of Radio London which claims the largest (12 million) commercial radio audience in Britain. Mr Birch said: "They stopped me at my garden gate just as I was leaving for work. There was a woman among them arguing their case. They were asking for £5,000 and 50 per cent of the advertising profits or 30 per cent of the advertising revenue. I was absolutely astonished. I couldn't believe my ears. I turned them down flat because I took a pretty poor view of the whole affair. The whole idea was preposterous."

The group then approached Mr Edward Allbeury, managing director of Radio 390, which claims a four million audience. He said: "They asked us if we were interested in operating the fort. It came right out of the blue and was almost unbelievable. ..... I told them it would have to be discussed with the board. But so far we have not considered it."

A Radio City spokesman, Mrs Jill Wileman, said yesterday at the station's business office: ..... "We have asked Scotland Yard for help in regaining possession of the Shivering Sands fort. Mrs Dorothy Calvert has given orders that no violence is to be used on her side."

Monday 27th June, 1966. The Guardian

RADIO CITY BACK ON-AIR AFTER BOARDERS LEAVE

.... Eight members of the party arrived at Sheerness in the motor barge, Kethole, early today and a Customs vessel put off from the harbour to intercept it. Asked by Customs officials where they were from, the men answered: "Shivering Sands." ..... Shortly after the party had left, the station came on the air. .... An emergency crystal was being used in the transmitter. It had been hidden by the staff after the raiders had taken away the two main crystals to immobilise the set.

Mr Ian MacRae, at the microphone, dedicated the first tune to the boarders – the song: "Strangers in the Night."

Mrs Calvert said last night: "I have not negotiated at all. They left without any payment. They knew it was no use. I hope this is now the end. My lawyers are advising me whether to sue."

A business associate who acted for Mrs Calvert in the dispute gave this version of why the raiders left: "All the radio stations agreed they should not give any money to the company that sent the boarders. We also agreed that we would help Mrs Calvert legally."

ORIGINS OF DISPUTE:

Mr Philip Birch, ... He said that a company which had lost many thousands of pounds in radio claimed that it had some equipment on Radio City. "But since the equipment does not appear to be worth a darn, there is no logic in the takeover by the boarding party." Mr Birch explained that this company had formerly owned one of the ships with a radio station on it. But because it was thought that the Government was to take action, the company had in practice written off its interests in Radio City. Its attitude changed however, when Radio City signed a deal with UK Good Music, who were to broadcast 'sweet music' from Radio City beginning in July. The group then demanded payment. ....."

Tuesday 28th June, 1966.The Sun

MORE EXCITING THAN TV, SAYS PIRATE RAIDER

'Big Alf' Bullen, leader of the boarding party who captured and held Radio City for a week, declared yesterday: "I wouldn't have missed it for anything. The nearest you get to adventure these days is on the telly. But this was much more exciting than The Man from U.N.C.L.E."

Early yesterday, eight members of the boarding party arrived off Sheerness in the motor barge, Kethole. The barge moved into one of the berths off Sheerness harbour and the eight men carrying cases came ashore where three cars were waiting for them.

"The job is now finished," one of them said, adding that for him and the other men it had been a "week's holiday."

Later, another of the men, Jim McKnight, from Liverpool, said: "A launch came out and a letter was handed to 'Big Alf' Bullen, who led the boarding party. He read it, tore it up, and said: "You can all go home. There was no rough stuff. We were told to keep the disc jockeys away from their equipment and this we did without trouble. ..... No attempts were made to board the fort while we were there and it would have been easy to repel boarders. All we had to do was batten down the hatches."

Tuesday 28th June, 1966. Morning Star

MURDER CHARGE MAJOR DEFENDS POP PIRATES

Major Oliver Smedley – charged with murdering pirate radio chief Mr Reginald Calvert – defends the existence of radio pirates in an article published yesterday.

"The pop stations might be thought to have served a purpose by making dents in the monopoly positions of the BBC and the record companies," he says in New Outlook. A Liberal magazine.

Major Smedley writes: "The belief is growing that the Government will not take action to put the pirates out of business until compatible facilities have been provided for the considerable volume of advertising business they are now carrying." He adds that investors in the stations stand a good chance of getting their money back, and perhaps a great deal more.

He stipulates that the activities of Radio Atlanta, now known as Radio Caroline South, should not be in breach of the law in any country. Groups and musicians who would never have had a chance if they were not on the 'monopolists' labels were not being heard by a wide public. That the offshore stations had prised open the market to new entrants was surely in their favour. ...

He also comments: "If more people are listening to the pirates than to the BBC it is at least prima facie evidence that, despite its enormous revenue from licences, the BBC are not providing a service which a large part of the population require."

Tuesday 28th June, 1966. Evening Standard

RADIO CITY DISC JOCKEY TELLS OF 'BOGUS DETECTIVES' AND SAYS I WAS KIDNAPPED

Radio City disc jockey, Peter Dolphin, told today how he was driven from his home in Victoria to a flat in the East End by two men posing as Scotland Yard detectives. ..... "I was kept in a room somewhere near Mile End Road the whole weekend with nothing to eat and just a glass of water. ..... "

Monday 18th July, 1966. Evening Standard (later edition)

HE CAME TO KILL ME

Wealthy Major Oliver Smedley sat in court here today as prosecuting counsel told how the major had led a boarding party to Radio City. ..... Then two nights later the pop pirate chief, Reg Calvert, called at Mr Smedley's home at Wendens Ambo. ... When a police constable arrived at the house and asked what happened Smedley is said to have replied: "I have shot him."

Asked for more details he went on: "Calvert had threatened to do me harm, to kill me and all the others. I went to get my shotgun and loaded it. I knew he came to kill me. I could see he was mad. I knew he carried arms. I had no choice but to fire. I did not think of aiming at his legs. I just fired. I feel morally right. I knew he was a violent man and he came to kill me."

Prosecution Counsel told the court that what the accused had said about Calvert being armed was true. He was carrying something that looked like a pencil or a torch but was in actual fact, a gas gun which squirted a stream of tear gas.

The first witness, Miss Dorothy Black, a business associate of Major Smedley, told of a business meeting in Soho which was attended by Calvert. "He said he was an amateur chemist and an expert in explosives and poison gases and had discovered a nerve gas. He had not been able to use it on anything except animals and wanted to try its effect on human beings. He said he would lob shells of it with mortar into the fort. Two of our party at the meeting were horrified at his apparently callous attitude."

Earlier the court had been told by Mr Peter Palmes, Prosecuting, of the nerve gas threat in the dispute over the Radio City Fort in the Thames Estuary. Mr Palmes said it was possible that they were extravagant threats which were not meant to be taken seriously but they led up to the events which ended in the shooting drama.

The court is being asked to send Major Smedley, who won the MC in Normandy in 1944, and was once a Liberal candidate in parliamentary elections, for trial.

Mrs Dorothy Calvert sat in the back of the court as the story of the dispute over a transmitter at Radio City was told.

Mr Palmes said the fort at Radio City on the Shivering Sands in the Thames Estuary cast a long shadow over the events but he did not propose to go into the whole background in detail except for the last two days before the shooting. ..... "The prosecution are not concerned with the rights or wrongs of that particular event but only with the shooting which arose from it."

Major Smedley was concerned with a firm called Project Atlanta a considerable time ago. This amalgamated with Radio Caroline, which was approached by Calvert for financial assistance over the installation of a stronger transmitter. There was no real financial agreement and the deal fell through but nevertheless a transmitter was put on the fort. It was estimated that the transmitter was worth about £10,000 and it was alleged that Major Smedley had an interest in its ownership. ...... Major Smedley claimed that it was his and had apparently not been paid for, or at least the royalties for it had not been paid for by Calvert.

Mr Palmes continued:

"The result was that a decision was come to by the accused and by his colleague, Miss Black, and by other persons involved in Project Atlanta, to protect their equipment by putting a party of men on board Radio City and in fact closing it down. ..... Arrangements were made for Mr Birch, the third party, to meet them at Project Atlanta's office in Dean Street. Major Smedley made a proposition regarding Radio City in the hope of also becoming a party to the deal which was going through between Mr Calvert and Mr Birch. ..... Mr Palmes said that Mr Birch turned this down. Mr Calvert had also been contacted and arrived at the meeting later. The same proposition was put to him but he also turned it down. Mr Palmes told the three magistrates hearing the allegations: "Calvert was obviously disturbed by the turn of events. He made a number of extravagant threats." They were directed more to the boarding party than towards Smedley. He made these threats very extravagantly. In the circumstances, possibly nobody took him seriously. In the course of them he said he had access to a number of strong-arm men he would use. He talked about nerve gas that would be used. When he really got going he said that those on the fort would wish they had never gone there in the first place. Undoubtedly, he was angry over Radio city when he made these rather wild threats. .....

Tuesday 19th July, 1966. Evening Standard

MY GOD! YOU'VE SHOT HIM
CALVERT LIKE A RAVING MANIAC – GIRL

Dark-haired Miss Pamela Thorburn, housekeeper at the Essex country cottage where 'pop pirate' Reg Calvert was shot dead, was suddenly called into court during the evidence of a prosecution witness in the shooting drama at Saffron Walden court today. She had described bursting out with the words: "This is murder," to her employer, Major Oliver Smedley, as his business friend, Mr. Calvert, fell dying in front of him.

Then the witness, bearded company director Mr. Alan Arnold, agreed that Calvert had been grappling with her before the fatal shot was fired, but that the situation took him so by surprise that he never lifted a finger to intervene.

He denied knowing that Calvert, who is said by the prosecution to have dramatically threatened to use nerve gas to get a 'boarding party' off the Radio City fort in the Thames Estuary, had a tear-gas gun with him when he went to the cottage. The Story, which Mr Arnold called, a "kaleidoscope of events," was told when the hearing against Major Smedley, accused of murdering Mr Calvert, 38-year-old head of Radio City, entered its second day.

20th July, 1966. Staffordshire Evening Sentinel

SMEDLEY'S COTTAGE RAIDED DURING THE NIGHT

The cottage at Wendens Ambo, Essex, belonging to William Oliver Smedley, the city accountant and former vice-president of the Liberal Party, who is facing a murder charge, was broken into during the night.

This was disclosed by Mr Peter Palmes, prosecuting, when Smedley was brought into the dock today at the beginning of the third day of the hearing. Smedley, aged 54, is accused of the murder of Pearce Reginald Hartley Calvert. ...

Mr Palmes told the magistrates that a police inquiry would be started. He had been down to the cottage to visit the scene. It was apparently then that the break-in was discovered. He told the magistrates taking the committal proceedings that the break-in might necessitate Smedley's secretary, Miss Pamela Thorburn, going back to the cottage to see if anything was missing.

First witness today was Constable Christopher Kearney who said that after receiving a radio message, he went to the cottage in Duck Street at 11.30 p.m. He saw the accused standing in the hall in his shirt sleeves. He asked him what had happened, and Smedley replied, "I shot him." Mr Arnold was standing near the door in the living room. When he asked him what had happened, Mr Arnold, pointing to Smedley, said, "I do not know. We came to the house and this man went mad and shot him."

The body of Calvert was in the house. He took Smedley into the dining room and asked him to tell him what had happened.

Smedley relied, "Yes, it is a long story. I know the man and I know him to be violent. I was not surprised when he came here tonight. You see, we had an expedition the other day. It was to do with pirate radio stations. I am the man who started it all off. He had the towers in the Thames and the other day we took it from him."

Constable Kearney told the court that Smedley had said in an alleged statement to him, "There was a hammering and I knew it must have been him, and he had threatened to kill me and all the others."

After Prosecution had asked the Magistrates to say there was a prima facie case of murder, Mr John Gower, QC, defending, said he would be making a submission to the effect: "That there is no evidence upon which you can properly commit Mr Smedley to stand trial upon any offence at all."

The magistrates at Saffron Walden, Essex, yesterday decided that William Oliver Smedley, a 55 year-old City accountant and a former Vice President of the Liberal Party, ... should not face a murder charge at the Assizes. They committed him to Chelmsford Assizes on October 11 on a charge of manslaughter and the Chairman of the Bench, Mr J.H. Wiseman said, "We have decided that no jury could convict on a charge of murder."

31. MISSING EVIDENCE

The Police spent time investigating the 'mysterious' case of Peter Dolphin the temporary disc jockey who arrived at the station the Friday before the boarding party. They called him in for interviews on 28th June and 1st July, 1966 and strongly suspected that he had sought employment on the fort at the instigation of a newspaper who had prior information that Oliver Smedley intended to 'take over' the fort by force. He had not produced the camera until the boarding party arrived and he told the boarders and others that he was a Daily Mirror reporter and was seen typing out reports on his own typewriter.

On the Wednesday morning after the boarding party had arrived, a boat came out with two journalists from the Evening Standard and he returned with them to Sheerness. The police suspected that the camera was loaned to him by the press and the police report stated:

'In my opinion, the circumstances of the disappearance of the camera and Dolphin's possible part in this could be examined a little closer. Dolphin, who is a professional actor, did not appear to me to be a particularly trustworthy sort of fellow. He denied emphatically any knowledge of press men. I then produced two letters signed by him on his own headed notepaper typed and written on the fort, instructing the person to whom they were addressed, to contact Tom Mervin of the Daily Sketch, and Martin Jackson of the Daily Express, and claim £5 for the use of the story of the boarding party.'

The police questioned Peter Dolphin further and he reluctantly accepted authorship of the letters, but denied being employed by a newspaper. He also denied prior information of the boarding party's intentions before they took over the fort. He also denied being supplied with the camera by the press.

Newspaper articles appeared after Peter Dolphin's first police interview, stating that he had been kidnapped by two men and he was under police protection.

The police called him in for a second interview on 1st July. Dolphin insisted that he had been kidnapped but when questioned further, he was unable to describe the men concerned, the vehicle in which he was removed, the final destination, or the room he alleged he had been confined against his will. Dolphin finally agreed that the newspaper statement was inaccurate and reluctantly admitted he had not been kidnapped.

Nothing was making sense to Dorothy's analytical mind. Who had let the boarders on the station? Why was her life threatened? Why did Major Smedley want Radio City so much? Who was behind him? Who was making the threats? Her daughters listened to her fears and did their best to console her. They were all living in a nightmare and the girls constantly worried for their mother's safety.

"No one believes me. No one. He's going to walk free. I know he is," Dorothy often repeated.

"Major Smedley must know people in the right places. Why did the Prosecution Counsel not call witnesses on your Dad's side? They've allowed witnesses to say things without proof. The police took evidence which proved Smedley owed your Dad money. Why didn't they use it? Why?"

Susan wanted to help her mother and made an appointment to see their member of parliament, Quintin Hogg, on Tuesday 26th July. He had relinquished his title of 2nd Viscount Hailsham and was both an MP and a lawyer. Taking her sister with her, they entered the bustling central lobby of the House of Commons. The building was expansive, like a cathedral, with wall paintings, statues of Kings and Queens all around and a very high lofty ceiling. Their prearranged meeting point was at the bottom of the wide stone stairway. After a few minutes, a small, rotund man who reminded the girls of the Charles Dickens's', Mr Pickwick, made his way down the steps and greeted them.

"Are you the Miss Calverts?"

"Yes," they replied.

"Would you like to talk to me in the tearoom or in my office?"

"Your office," suggested Susan.

"Come this way then."

They followed, up the stairs and along a series of corridors until he opened a door and ushered them in. After the magnificence of the central lobby, his office was a disappointment. A small, dingy room that needed decorating, simply furnished with a desk, cupboard and numerous books and journals lining the shelves.

"Have a seat. How can I help?"

The sisters explained who they were and why they had come.

"Yes, indeed, I have heard of this case."

"Our mother is very worried," explained Susan. "Nearly all the witnesses were cancelled and no one is telling the truth about what really happened. She is sure that Major Smedley is going to get away with murder and walk free."

"I see," replied Quintin Hogg, looking over the top of his half-rimmed spectacles as he considered the matter. He was a very experienced lawyer and Queen's Counsel. After discussing it further with the girls, he smiled at them.

"Tell your mother not to worry. No man could do what he had done without going to prison. He will get at least the minimum sentence and it could be a lot more."

The two girls thanked him and went home reassured, proudly telling their mother what they had done. Dorothy, amazed that her daughters had sought advice from their member of parliament, shook her head sadly.

"Quintin Hogg doesn't know what's going on. That may be the law but somehow, he's going to get away with it."

The press didn't linger on the case as there were new and more exciting stories to be printed. England was hosting the Football World Cup and they had reached the final and were to play against Germany on Saturday 30th July at Wembley. Everywhere, there were Union Jacks flying and the excitement in the country was mounting. The match was a nail biting draw, two two. And then, in the closing minutes of extra time, Geoff Hurst scored two more goals. England four. West Germany two. England had won the World Cup.

The dances on Saturday were like party nights, with everyone celebrating the victory. Football, however, was of no interest to Dorothy or her daughters and on Sunday evening, they packed their cases and made the return trip from Rugby to London by train. As they opened the apartment door they were greeted with the sound of the burglar alarm ringing. Dorothy called for the concierge and he went with her to check that no one was there. When he left, Dorothy looked startled.

"I don't understand," said Susan.

"I don't understand either. Someone's trying to frighten me. I'm trying to work it out but I can't."

With the Hearing over and the Trial booked for October, time was short. Somehow, Dorothy needed to challenge the Prosecution Counsel into calling more witnesses and she sought advice from her solicitors, Nockolds & Son. After much discussion, they agreed that the best way forward would be to state her concerns in a letter to the Director of Public Prosecutions.

The Director of Public Prosecutions
12 Buckingham Gate
London SW1

4th August, 1966

Dear Sir,

We are acting for Mrs Dorothy Calvert the widow of Pearce Reginald Hartley Calvert who was killed by William Oliver Smedley on 21st of June, 1966.

As you will be aware Smedley has now been committed to the next Court of Assize for the County of Essex on a charge of Manslaughter.

Our client is aggrieved, in our view justifiably, at the manner in which the Prosecution has been handled so far which has resulted in the impression being given that the criminal in this case is not Smedley but our Client's husband; and, moreover, has enabled Smedley, without calling any evidence, to avoid committal on the charge of murder which offence he was originally charged with.

We think that not only in the interest of our Client who is concerned to see her husband's name and character are properly protected but also in the public interest we are justified in referring you to the following matters which have given rise to our Client's disquiet:

Firstly, why did the Prosecution's case begin with evidence of a previous day's meeting between the deceased and Smedley and his three associates? The result has been that two of Smedley's colleagues who were called (and who are naturally disposed in Smedley's favour) have given evidence apparently designed to show that Smedley was justified in fearing the deceased.

In this connection, why were Mr Leggett and Miss Black (whose account incidentally of the meeting was much more extravagant than that given by Mr Leggett), neither of who had met the deceased before and only saw him for about half an hour, encouraged to give their opinions of the deceased's character when no further evidence was called as to the sort of man the deceased really was. Miss Black, for example, was allowed to give evidence of the feelings of two of the members at the meeting who she said: "were horrified at the callous attitude anyone could adopt to human life". We do not see this statement supported by Mr Leggett in his deposition and for some reason or another, the other man at the meeting, namely Captain Horsley, was not called as a witness.

Mr Birch was at a prior meeting .... and thought Smedley and his associates were "underhanded or highhanded and even referred to the whole thing as blackmail". Why was Mr Birch not called as a witness?

Secondly, why was it decided that the Prosecution should not concern itself with the boarding party put upon Shivering Sands by Smedley? The Defence have been at some pains to elicit from Smedley's colleagues that the boarding party was a peaceful one and was sent to the fort to protect equipment the Prosecution said was worth £10,000. The result of the Prosecution's omission is that unchallenged evidence has been admitted to show a state of affairs which we believe is contrary to the truth ......

Even on the evidence given in the depositions, questions come to mind which throw doubt on whether Smedley's expedition was a peaceful and legitimate one. If so why had Smedley not first asked for the transmitter back? Why was it necessary to send seventeen men against six on the fort? Who did the transmitter belong to? (Miss Black did not seem to know – see depositions – Mr Leggett thought it belonged to Radio Atlanta). Why did the boarders eventually leave?

We believe that the boarding party was not sent to the fort to protect the transmitter but had an ulterior motive in trying to get the deceased into a business deal with Smedley by exerting pressure on him through putting his station off the air. We say this for the following reasons: -

- *a) The transmitter which Smedley alleged belonged to him or his companies was not used for broadcasts from the fort. It was a 1940 three phase 10kW transmitter and was inadequate for broadcasts from the station. Its value is probably more like £500 than £10,000. ...... When Smedley's party came on board they obtained the crystals not only of the transmitter which is alleged they owned but also the crystals of the G.E.C. set which did not belong to him. Why should they do this?*
- *b) The transmitter had been at the fort from October 1965 until June 1966 and no communication had been received by Radio City about it. Out of the blue, Smedley's boarding party went to the fort in June allegedly to take possession of the transmitter. The transmitter is still at the fort and no request had been made for its return.*
- *c) The crystals which Miss Black said were given to her freely were given up because Mr Ian West, an employee of Radio City who was on the fort at the time was told by Smedley: "Mr Calvert has sent me with a party to protect you from a possible takeover". It was a little later that it became apparent that Smedley was in fact the takeover. ......*
- *d) The third major matter we wish to raise is the decision that was made not to call Mrs Calvert as a witness. Mrs Calvert was in a position to give an account of the dealings between Radio City and Smedley and as to her husband's actions and state of mind on the*

night he set out to see Smedley. We have particularly in mind that the deceased took £440 with him (which was later found on him) with the object of going on to Kent to buy the men off the fort if his talks with Smedley failed. This seems to us a most relevant matter.

e) *Other matters which Mrs Calvert has mentioned to the Police but which were not mentioned at the preliminary hearing are that the deceased was almost blind in his right eye and that if the scratches inflicted on him by Miss Thorburn over the left eye were serious they would effectively have blinded Calvert; also, that her husband made a complaint at Bow Street Police Station on the morning of his death about the illegal nature of Smedley's boarding party.*

It is in our view regrettable that the evidence about the so called "gas pistol" has been allowed to be introduced without any explanation as to why the deceased carried one.

Mrs Calvert has told the police that it was carried as a means of defence if attacked. The deceased ran dance halls in the Midlands and had to deal with large amounts of cash. He therefore sought to protect himself if attacked. ...... Despite the impression given at the preliminary hearing, these pens are not lethal weapons and are very limited in their application.

It will no doubt be a matter for comment by the Prosecution at the trial as to why Smedley, as soon as there was a knock on the door, should rush out to collect a gun and go to phone the police leaving his housekeeper alone with what is alleged to be a violent man. Further, when he returned to the house without uttering any words at all he fired at the deceased's stomach thus killing him.

It would appear to us that in the interests of justice and of our client's husband, who is now dead and cannot speak for himself, that the foregoing matters should be thoroughly investigated and steps taken to ensure that such further evidence as is necessary should be heard when the case goes to trial.

We should therefore be grateful for your assurance that this will be done.

Yours faithfully,
Nockolds & Son. Solicitors, Bishop's Stortford.

Dorothy asked the police to return documents and correspondence they had taken relating to the debts owed by Radio Atlanta/Smedley as they had not been used in evidence at the Hearing. These proved Smedley and Miss Black were lying when they said that Reg owed them money, but the reply came back from the police that they had been misplaced.

Knowing Smedley had greatly exaggerated the worth of the old transmitter by saying it was worth £10,000, Dorothy contacted RCA Great Britain Ltd for a quote to supply a new RCA transmitter. They replied it would be £6,310. Dorothy sent a copy of the quote to the Prosecution Counsel as more evidence.

The details of the case were forwarded from Peter Palmes to Mr Hora with his response to the letter received from Dorothy's solicitors. There was also a question raised as to whether the charge of murder should be reinstated.

Note: To: Mr Hora.

Re Smedley –
I have dealt with the few matters discussed at the court. I have recorded our proceedings sheet of jacket telephone conversation with Defence Solicitor.
Would you keep an eye on the pathologist angle in case we have to have Dr Johnson at the trial? Otherwise hope the case gives you no trouble !!!!
Many thanks,
(Peter Palmes)

OBSERVATIONS by the Prosecution Counsel:

"This is a case where the main prosecution witnesses are sympathetic to the accused in varying ways. Even Arnold, who is an objective witness, does not help the prosecution very much as he was thinking primarily of his own position. Miss Thorburn is an excellent witness for the accused and will impress the jury with her honesty, though she probably has exaggerated the fury of Calvert's attack and her own fears.

The photographs of the inside of the cottage are rather misleading as to the amount of space. In fact, it is all much smaller than appears, and the hall, for instance, is quite crowded with three people in it.

The defence have been given the name of ALLBEURY (in the second bundle of not called statements) ....

In the light of the evidence of the happenings at the cottage, the Magistrates stated that it was most improbable that a jury would convict of murder, and so committed for manslaughter.

The defence, however, will make a determined effort to obtain an acquittal on grounds of self-defence.

Counsel is particularly asked to consider whether or not Mrs Calvert should be called. It should be borne in mind that she is very bitter over the whole matter and will try to introduce a lot of the background dispute concerning Radio City, which will give the impression that Calvert was in an even more violent mood than has already emerged.

In spite of the committal charge, Counsel is asked to consider whether the evidence upon the dispositions justifies reinstating the murder charge? Counsel is sent herewith information a letter received from Mrs Calvert's Solicitors.

What it comes down to is that they would have liked the evidence to go far more deeply into the business transactions of Smedley to show that his methods left much to be desired. However, such evidence would not have been relevant as support for an allegation of murder. If admissible, this evidence more likely would tend to show that Calvert had reasons for wishing Smedley some harm or that the latter had cause for fearing for his safety on the night of 21st June.

Other matters that are complained of in the letter arose in perfectly proper cross-examination.

Counsel has already been asked to advise whether Mrs Calvert should be called. The extent to which she can speak as to her husband's intentions on the 21st is of course limited to his actions, and Arnold, a witness later in point of time, and also independent, has given evidence regarding this aspect."

Smedley's solicitor asked for a police search to discover whether Reg Calvert had a criminal record. The report came back that there was a minor offence, 18 years previously for £5 when he worked on the markets, plus eight carparking offences in Southampton. They also made a request to the police for a copy of the witness statements and this was approved.

As further evidence of Reg's threatening and violent behaviour, Miss Thorburn found a scrap of paper with her scribbled note on it with the final message Jill had given her and she presented it to the police as proof and the police requested a second interview with Jill to check the authenticity of the note.

Jill Wileman:
Police Statement 7th October, 1966

On 21st June, I was in the office the majority of the day with Mr Calvert. He instructed me to try and contact Mr Smedley on approximately three occasions at Monarch 1661, Investment and General Management Services Ltd, 80a Coleman Street, London EC2. In the morning, I rang the number and a woman answered.

'May I speak to Mr Smedley please.'

'Who is it calling?'

'Mr Calvert.'

'Mr Smedley is not here.'

'When do you expect him?'

'I'm not sure if Mr Smedley will be in the office before evening but I will pass on my message if he phoned.'

Left another message later.

The final conversation in the afternoon. Mr Calvert sat opposite me. As it was getting late in the afternoon I put my hand over the receiver and asked Mr Calvert if there was anything specific he wanted to say. As we had been talking together prior to this call about the fact that the boarding party were still on the station and we had received messages from our people in Whitstable to the effect that these men were getting hostile, Calvert said, 'Yes, you can tell her things are getting dangerous.'

The lady said she would write the message on a pad and leave it on Mr Smedley's desk for him to see if he arrived.

"I have been shown a piece of blue note paper on which there are various writings and it appears that my final message for Mr Smedley via his secretary is written there. In addition, there is a paragraph with regard to outstanding accounts from Radio City. This was not included in any conversation I had with this lady and it would have been prior to 21st June.

There is nothing else on the paper which refers to the conversations I held with the lady.

Left: John Wileman on the Harvester going to Shivering Sands. Man behind, probably worked for Fred Downs (RC)

With Reg's failing eyesight, he needed a driver and John became his righthand man. After Reg's death, John continued to work for Dorothy. He had married Jill, Reg's secretary, and without Jill and John's support at her time of need, she would not have been able to carry on.

Postcards were printed so disc jockeys could personally reply to their fan mail

32. LIFE GOES ON

Eric Martin and Dorothy Calvert in the new studio (Powell, Broadstairs)

Tuesdays became a day Dorothy dreaded. Whatever the weather, unless Fred cancelled the trip, she went to Shivering Sands. Dorothy had never expected to pick up the pieces and take control of a pirate radio station but she quickly learnt what needed to be done. She spent time talking to her engineers and disc jockeys, learning how everything worked so she could improve the station. With members of staff who she disliked or mistrusted, she could be curt, but to most, she was kind and considerate.

At the end of July, just five weeks after Reg's death, the government brought in a Bill to suppress pirate radio. Prior to Reg's death, there would have been public uproar. Now, there was hardly a whimper as everyone accepted the inevitable. The new law was planned for August, 1967, would make it illegal for British subjects to broadcast from a pirate station, install equipment, supply tapes, records or advertise on the programmes and there would be fines with up to two year's imprisonment for offences.

Realising time remaining to run Radio City was short, Dorothy decided not to invest in a new transmitter but to keep Big Bertha. Instead, she asked her engineers to make an improved studio. Previously, there had been a lot of unnecessary equipment ordered and Dorothy suspected that some of the engineers may have been selling it on. Under her management, if engineers wanted a component, they had to show her exactly where it fitted and what it was used for. Very quickly she began to understand the technical side and requests for new equipment were greatly reduced.

Most were happy to work for Dorothy but there were a few disgruntled members of staff. Paul Elvey complained bitterly about his dismissal, not accepting that he had done anything wrong. Tony Pine had lost his lucrative provision order and didn't like Dorothy's authoritarian management style. After a while, he became unreliable and was asked to leave. The Australian disc jocky, Dennis the Menace, gave notice and was replaced. New disc jockeys recruited included Australian, Ross Brown who called himself RWB and Adrian Love, a knowledgeable musician and the son of band leader, Geoff Love.

Woolf Byrne approached Dorothy for a position as a disc jockey and she offered him a week's trial. He had good musical knowledge and had been a member of the Manish Boys until they split up. Their guitarist, Johnny Flux, was a former Radio City disc jockey before moving onto Radio London. Their singer, Davy Jones, was later to become better known as David Bowie.

Not knowing what to expect, Woolf made the sea-crossing to Shivering Sands but became terrified when he saw provisions and crew being winched up on a wavering platform. With some encouragement and bravado, he managed to cling to the ropes as he was hoisted up. Once aboard, Phil Perkins explained how to use the studio equipment and asked if he could stay up late and do a test transmission after the station closed.

The Radio City crew were a happy team and had fun, often playing tricks on each other. Tom Edwards was the focus of many of their pranks and he took it all in good humour. He was slow to get up in the morning and timed, to the minute, the crossing from the living accommodation to the studio. The news had to be transcribed from the on-the-hour BBC broadcasts, then rewritten in Radio City style and read out at half-past-the-hour. If it was Tom's turn to read the news, the crew sometimes added embarrassing errors to the script. Tom blithely read them out, only realising what he had said when it was too late, his face blushed pink. Regardless, he continued to read on to the end, making a point of not looking at the crew as they laughed at him.

Leslie liked to share provisions equally but Tom ignored him and often sneaked into the storeroom and helped himself to biscuits or chocolate bars just before he was due on-air.

"You haven't to take the biscuits or we'll run out," reprimanded Leslie.

Tom smiled cheekily in response and continued to help himself.

Anticipating that Tom would enter the storeroom just before he was due to read the news, Leslie filled a bucket with seawater and carried it to the roof and waited. On cue, Tom quickly entered the storeroom and came out holding his 'stolen' goodies. Leslie tipped the bucket and water sploshed down and drenched its target. Tom glanced up and Leslie burst out laughing. Frowning and letting out a lot of expletives, Tom shook the water off like a wet bedraggled sheep dog and hastened across the catwalk to the studio. With water dripping from him he sat in the office chair and read the news as if nothing had happened.

Keeping the station clean and tidy was not on the crews' agenda even though Dorothy regularly reminded them. Leslie kept the galley and the main living area clean and tidy but the disgusting state of the toilets, even with Mrs C in charge, did not improve and was a regular source of amusement.

To produce an advertisement with reverberating sound, the disc jockeys would take a microphone down on a long cable and do the recording while in the toilet. For a bet, Alan Clark agreed to read the news while sitting on the seat. On another occasion, to try and make Tom break-up and laugh, the sound of a flushing toilet was spliced to the end of a news item. Tom, however, was too professional and remained straight faced until the microphones were switched off.

To be a good disc jockey was hard and did not come easily to Woolf who realised he was only acting at it. Dorothy, not impressed, complained about his style and selection of records so did not offer him a permanent position. Woolf was charming and good looking and Dorothy had a soft spot for charming and good looking young men. Week after week, she agreed to give him a second chance in the hope he'd improve. Woolf, however, disregarded her instructions, purchased his own choice of records and played them without her permission. When Dorothy heard his programme, she was furious. As far as she was concerned, he had committed a cardinal sin and she gave him no more second chances.

The record companies continued to provide free copies of their new releases in the hope that they would be played on Radio City and Candy began to help compile the Top Sixty Chart.

Everyone suspected that telephones belonging to Radio City staff, including the office and Dorothy's home, were being intercepted. Little clicks could be heard as the police operator tapped into the line and listened. Phil Perkins was annoyed by this and arranged for Leslie Dunne to call him from a public coin box. They hatched a plan for a hoax boarding party and discussed launching it from West Beach in Whitstable. Within 10 minutes, there were large numbers of police in the area searching for the boarding

1966 RADIO CITY DISC JOCKEYS

Top left: Tom Edwards (SC) Top right: Adrian Love (SC)
Bottom: Australians, Denis the Menace - Denis Straney and 'RWB' Ross Brown

1966 RADIO CITY DISC JOCKEYS

Top left: Paul Kramer (SC) Top Right: Ian MacRae (SC)
Bottom left: Eric Martin - Richard Lee (SC) Bottom right: Woolf Byrne

After Reg's death, Dorothy gave Susan her father's camera.
Her photos are acknowledged (SC).

party. Phil and Leslie stood back and watched. They thought it hilarious as they knew that only a small rowing boat could launch from the gently sloping shingle beach.

Religious advertisers, and others, began to withdraw their custom after reading the sensational newspaper reports.

Dorothy observed how people Reg had helped to establish, such as the Fortunes and Terry King, were beginning to dissociate themselves from ever knowing Reg. Peter Jameson, who worked as a Sales Director of RaCity Sales, gave notice and left the company. Dorothy was now left in a difficult financial position as she endeavoured to carry on.

The Atlanta transmitter remained unused and Dorothy sent an invoice to Smedley for storage and asked for its immediate removal. The letter was not responded to.

One of Reg's sayings had been, "No publicity is bad publicity." Although Radio City's income had reduced, its following greatly increased with a very loyal listenership. The disc jockeys replied in person to their fan mail and played most of the requests. The Auntie Mabel hour with Ian MacRae, Alan Clark and others chipping in, had developed into a satirical sketch show and was one of the most popular pirate programmes on the air. In defiance to the threats to her life, Dorothy was enjoying the challenge of running Radio City, and like her husband, was determined to make it a success.

Owning a radio station meant Dorothy was in a unique position to explain on air, the truth behind the sensational headlines and disprove what had been said in court. Dorothy was in a quandary. Should she break the law? Should she broadcast the truth? Was it a risk worth taking to air her concerns on radio? Would the police be able to prosecute as Radio City was outside British jurisdiction? Could she be imprisoned for contempt of court?

33. THE TRIAL

The trial was arranged for 11th October, 1966 not at the Old Bailey as originally thought, but at Chelmsford Assizes. Dorothy was dreading it. Her sixth sense told her that the outcome was a foregone conclusion. Smedley would walk free. But, much to her surprise, the day before the trial, she was notified that she was to be called as a witness. Maybe her solicitor's letter to the Prosecution Counsel had made a difference? She could only hope. The judge was to be the eccentric Lord Justice Melford Stevenson.

On the morning of the trial, Dorothy dressed quickly and carefully, sweeping her hair from her face into a French roll and to brighten her pale face, put on a red lipstick and blue eye shadow. That would have to do. The press would be out in force and she would have to smile at the cameras and put on a brave face.

Both her daughters had taken time off work to accompany her to the trial with Susan's boyfriend, Lyndon, who had come down from Nuneaton to be with her. The girls had not attended the previous court hearing or inquest but Dorothy felt it was important for them to be there. When they arrived, press photographers flashed their cameras as they walked into the building. Taking their seat outside the courtroom, they waited for the proceedings to commence. Opposite, sat Major Smedley. Dorothy ignored him. Susan stared at him with contempt. This was the first time she had seen the man who had murdered her father. Taking her sketchbook and pencil from her handbag, she began to draw his portrait.

As they entered the court, Dorothy was informed that Peter Palmes would not be the Prosecution Counsel and been replaced by Hugh Griffiths, Q.C. She hoped, against hope that he would present the facts better than Peter Palmes had and that the trial would be fair and just. That he would have read the letter sent by her solicitors and received the evidence the police had taken which proved it was Smedley who owed Reg money.

As the court proceedings commenced, Hugh Griffiths outlined to the jury the 'facts' of the case. That Smedley had shot and killed Calvert on the night of 21st June, with a 12-bore shotgun at Smedley's home at Wendens Ambo, Essex. That the gun had been discharged at point-blank range, something like one to two feet."

Immediately, Dorothy stiffened, becoming tense as she continued to listen. Already, the evidence was wrong. How could he get it so wrong? The gun had not been fired at point-blank range. Reg had been shot while standing in the hallway by the sitting room door.

Griffiths continued, describing how Calvert had gone to Smedley's house, forced his way past Smedley's housekeeper and fought with her, and when Smedley appeared, Calvert leapt towards him.

"If a man breaks into your house and he offers violence towards you, you may stand your ground and you may meet violence with violence, but in the submission of the Crown, the violence used must be commensurate with the accused's towards you. Outrageous though Calvert's behaviour was that night, there was no warrant for the accused to go to the extreme measure of shooting and killing. It is possible you may have to consider in this case, that Smedley not only in his own defence killed, but to save the life of a young woman."

Dorothy shook her head in disbelief. The knot in Dorothy's stomach grew tighter as she sat motionless and tight lipped. Surely, the Prosecution Counsel should be acting for Reg and not Smedley? He must know from all the witness statements that Reg was not a violent man. Why was he distorting the truth?

Next, the Prosecution Counsel began to describe the merger and business transactions, saying that "Calvert had been in touch with Smedley and that Smedley agreed to help Calvert with finance for purchasing a more powerful and efficient transmitter on the fort. This was bought and installed."

"There were also negotiations between them about a merger of interests but apparently, these negotiations broke down, or at least, Calvert chose to regard them as having broken down, because he entered into negotiations with the man named Birch, who had an interest in yet another station known as Radio London. This came to the attention of Smedley who was concerned because of the transmitter in which he had been instrumental in providing the money."

"To preserve his position and those with whom he was associated, the accused conceived the plan of going out to the fort with a number of men; of boarding the fort; possessing themselves of the crystals which are the vital parts of the transmitters, so that the station would be off the air and thereafter negotiating from a position of strength with Mr. Birch and Calvert."

Dorothy was incredulous. Reg had never approached Smedley for finance. It was Allan Crawford who had suggested a merger with Caroline South and provided the old transmitter. It had all gone wrong because the transmitter was no good and Crawford had run out of money.

"They got in touch with Birch and Calvert and invited them to come to the offices in Dean Street, London. The accused offered a deal, the broad outlines of which were that they would be interested to talk if he put up £5,000 cash and cut them in for a share of the interest or 30% of the profit. Birch said he was not interested."

Dorothy stared at Hugh Griffiths. Surely, he must know the deal had been blackmail?

"When Calvert arrived, the situation was put to him in the same terms. His immediate reaction appeared to have been that he could not care less because he had already concluded a deal with Birch whose financial position was secure. The broad outline of the rest of Calvert's attitude was this: They had chosen to put people aboard the fort, he would make it his personal business to see that they came off and he elaborated upon his background, how he had been born in the slums of Huddersfield and come up the hard way, how he ran a number of dance halls and had a call on some of the toughest fighters in London. Calvert also threatened to used nerve gas to get the people off the fort and had produced a small object looking something like a pen."

Hugh Griffiths described how Reg and Arnold had arrived at the cottage in Duck Lane, Wenden's Ambo and how Reg had seemed perfectly calm and in an ordinary frame of mind.

"The door was opened by Miss Thorburn, who acted as dual role of housekeeper and secretary and looked after the children. When she opened the door, she saw Calvert and though, apparently, she had not seen him before it seemed she knew who he was because she went to close the door. Calvert pushed open the door and thrust her back into the hall. Calvert shouted out. "Where's Smedley?" and used bad language. Calvert said that he was going to take him to the police. Miss Thorburn tried to persuade him that Smedley was not there and she said, "If you have got a charge to make be sensible and bring the police here."

"You will hear that Calvert laid hands on her and was violent, and the court might think that he was trying to force her to tell him where Smedley was. Arnold would say that he went upstairs to find Smedley. Miss Thorburn would say that Calvert suddenly said, "There's the bastard?" and thrust her aside and made a dive forward. She did not hear a shot but saw Calvert stagger backwards."

"A gas gun was found on the dead man. It was not in the cocked or firing position. It was the Crown's case that although Calvert's conduct was clearly outrageous it was not of such a character that would justify shooting him down at point-blank range."

By now, Dorothy was ready to burst into tears but she held herself strong. She had to get through today and listen to the lies and half-truths. Dorothy knew Reg had been wrong to enter the cottage but he had not been violent toward Miss Thorburn. He had only gone to talk to Major Smedley before he sold his station to someone else. Reg never shouted when he was angry and he never ever used bad language and to describe the small pen he carried as a gas gun was ridiculous.

Kitty Black was the first witness. Looking very smart and business-like, she described how the boarding party was peaceful. She claimed that the transmitter had cost £10,000 to bring to the fort and that Major Smedley had lent Calvert money to pay the wages.

Mr Molony, the defence lawyer for Smedley, cross examined her about the legal position and Miss Black explained they had discussed it. From their study of the maritime laws governing international waters, they were certain there could be no normal redress in British law that would give them a right to distrain on the property or otherwise enforce their position.

At the meeting in Dean Street, Miss Black described how Reg Calvert had threatened that he would use things against the people on the fort which would have them "screaming to come off." He had produced a gas gun pen and said that if he did not get the party off, he would drop ammonia bombs onto the fort. He would make it his personal business to get them off. He had a fortnight's holiday due and this would give him some fun and he knew some of the best fighters in the country. She hoped that she need not take what Reg Calvert had said seriously, although some fellow-shareholders in Project Atlanta who were at the meeting, did take them seriously.

When Dorothy was called, she stood calmly in the witness box answering questions put to her, quietly and honestly. She told the court that she was controller of programmes on Radio city and last saw her husband alive at 7.30 p.m. on 21st June, before he left to see Major Smedley.

"He was worried about the boarding party and for the safety of his men. But he was calm."

Mr Molony questioned her about the agreement between her husband and Major Smedley and Dorothy explained that there was a tacit agreement between him and her husband. "Had anyone asked him for the transmitter, he would have said, please take it."

"So far as you are concerned, this transmitter was of no interest to Radio City and was always available to its true owner?"

"Yes," replied Dorothy and she went on to explain that, "the transmitter provided by Major Smedley had not been used for broadcasting. It was nearly 30 years old and component parts were not available. It would have cost thousands of pounds to make it serviceable. I have written to Major Smedley on 26th July, sending him a statement of accounts for storage of the transmitter and asking him when it would be removed."

"My husband went to talk to Major Smedley and if he would not agree to take the boarding party off the fort, my husband was planning to go the next day and pay them off. He had a boat available at 6 a.m. I had £440 at home for a holiday. He would have used that to pay or buy the men off."

"What were your husband's reason for the boarding party being put on the fort?" asked Hugh Griffiths.

"He told me they wanted him to sign an agreement giving them half of the profits of Radio City."

The time Dorothy had in the witness box was short and she returned to her seat, angry, knowing the only reason she had been called as a witness was to placate her. Surprisingly, Major Smedley's lawyer had been the person to ask the most questions. The Prosecution Counsel had asked her very little and seemed to dismiss her answers as inconsequential.

Pamela Thorburn was questioned about her relationship with Major Smedley and admitted there was a "considerable attachment". She told the jury at length about the struggle and that Calvert looked extremely angry as he forced his way into the cottage and shouted he was going to take Major Smedley to the police. He had thrown a heavy statue at her and when she had tried to dial 999 he wrenched the phone from her and shouted, saying, "Don't you realise I am a desperate man. I am going to take him dead or alive and if I can't get him I'll take you. Are you coming willingly or do I have to take you dead?" When Major Smedley entered the dining room, Calvert had said, "There's the bugger" and pushed her aside and went past her. "In absolutely no time at all he was reeling back. It took her several seconds to realise he had been shot."

The more Dorothy listened, the more furious she became. How could they say what they said and look the jury in the eye? The whole trial was built on fabrication and hearsay. Where was the evidence and why hadn't they called more witnesses?

The trial followed a similar format to the hearing except that the piece of paper Miss Thorburn had found with her scribbled note was given as new and important evidence of Reg threatening violence. Inexplicably, Jill Wileman was not called as a witness to counter this with the truth.

When Alan Arnold took the witness stand, Dorothy could see he was nervous and easily manipulated by both the Prosecution and Defence Counsel. His answers were careful so as not to implicate himself. He described how Reg had been perfectly calm on their journey to Wendens Ambo. When the door was answered by a young woman, Reg had pushed it open. About the struggle, he described it as a shoving match, "all arms and legs." He was asked why Reg had wanted to borrow a gun and Arnold explained he had wanted to protect himself when going out to the station to ask the boarders to leave. Arnold had refused to loan him a gun and they had no gun with them that night. Again, he was not questioned about his entry into the cottage immediately after the shooting or how Smedley had pointed the gun at him and how he had run for his life.

During Smedley's evidence, Susan was in tears, realising her mother had been right all along. This man was going to get away with murdering her father. Taking a deep breath, she shouted to the court that he was telling lies. The judge, looking up to the visitor's gallery, demanded the woman be removed and two policemen escorted her out.

The trial continued.

Dorothy remained where she was, shocked and surprised by the outburst. It was the first time anyone had referred to her daughter as a woman. What was more shocking was Major Smedley's demeanour. He gave the impression of being a wealthy, law abiding member of the community and his testimony was convincing. He was completely innocent of any crime. It was obvious now, he was going to get away with murder.

In response to questioning, Smedley said that Mr Calvert had made threats against him at a lunch with another pirate radio chief. "He said he had killed before and he would be prepared to kill again. The talk was of a violent man who knew ways of doing things."

"When I heard the knock at the door and saw Calvert kicking his way in, I went to a neighbouring cottage to phone the police. On the way I collected my shotgun and loaded it with two cartridges. I did not intend to use the gun. After speaking to a neighbour, I returned and saw my secretary, Miss Pamela Thorburn and Mr Calvert struggling."

"Mr Calvert had something in his hand which I assumed was a fire arm. I thought Miss Thorburn was in great peril. As soon as Mr Calvert saw me he brought down his right hand. I thought he was going to fire at me. He followed it up by coming towards me with the whole of his body, his eyes were protruding. He looked off his head. I fired the gun as something either hit me or whizzed past me. I didn't know it was a statuette which Mr. Calvert was holding. I did not actually fire at the man. He sort of ran onto the gun. If he had not moved he wouldn't have been hit."

Dorothy stared disbelievingly at Smedley. No one, especially Reg, would charge at a man holding a gun.

Smedley's defence lawyer, in his summing up, expounded to the court. "It must be almost unique for a man charged with homicide or any other crime, to go in advance of the moment that the killing occurs and take steps to get the police to the scene as soon as possible. The evidence tendered by the prosecution could not justify any charge of murder or manslaughter. The entry of Calvert, on the night he met his death was technically a burglary. It was quite clear that Calvert went into the house meaning to do harm of a grievous sort to Smedley. Calvert had executed a violent felony and in the circumstances, a person within the house was entitled to take extreme measures to resist it."

The judge reiterated that Mr Calvert and another man had forced their way into Mr. Smedley's house in Duck Street, Wendens Ambo, Essex. "It is not long before the man Calvert embarks on a sequence of acts which, you might think, is very much like the conduct of a lunatic." Waving his hand at the jury, he said they need not go out to discuss the evidence as there was no case to answer, the accused should be acquitted of unlawful killing.

Outside the court, Dorothy was furious but tried to hide her anger and paused to speak to the press. The reporters, who were experienced in court cases, sympathised with Dorothy and her fight for justice.

"Do you have any comments Mrs Calvert?"

"What's the point of having a jury when they're not allowed to go out to discuss the evidence."

"I've never been to a trial like this one, but at least they called you as a witness," commented one reporter.

"One small voice against so many. I was the only person to speak up for Reg and they asked me hardly any questions. There was evidence with the police which proved Major Smedley and Kitty Black were lying when they said Reg owed them money. It was the other way around. But they lost it. Reg wasn't a violent man. He went to talk. Everything he said and did was built up out of proportion. Major Smedley had taken his radio station over with force and then he killed him. It was all wrong."

"What will you do now Mrs Calvert?"

"Carry on."

"Will you continue to run Radio City?"

"Yes, of course. I have always been the business brains – my husband was never a violent man, and it was his gentle nature that prevented his being a success in business. He always needed me to do the pushing."

"You said before that you were thinking about taking out your own legal action."

"Yes, I have instructed my solicitors to issue a writ against Major Smedley for damages and the loss of my husband. And I shall sue his associates in Project Atlanta for trespass and loss of business. They put Radio City off air and not only did we lose income then, but it affected the deal with Radio London."

"Is business any better now Mrs Calvert?"

"It has suffered tremendously. We should have been earning between £5,000 and £10,000 a month but it is picking up now."

"I've heard on the grapevine, Major Smedley has sold his story to the Sunday People,"

"Nothing surprises me," replied Dorothy.

"What about the gas gun?" asked another reporter.

"You mean one of these?" Dorothy pulled out the small pen she carried in her handbag. "It's less dangerous than a perfume spray. Major Smedley was the one who was dangerous. He was carrying the real gun."

When Smedley walked briskly from the court, the cluster of reporters soon turned their attention to him.

"Have you anything to say, Sir?"

"Yes. This case has done a tremendous damage to my business career."

"Will you be continuing in pirate radio?" asked another reporter.

"No, I think my interest in pirate radio will be less active now. … I would just like to say that this whole affair has been a tragedy. An appalling waste of a very brilliant man's life. Calvert was the sort of man I regard highly and on whose side I would normally be. But he was out of his depth. I think we all were."

SMEDLEY IS CLEARED—AND GETS COSTS

By DON CASSELL

MAJOR OLIVER SMEDLEY was cleared yesterday of the manslaughter of Reginald Calvert, the pop radio chief.

Major Smedley, holder of the Military Cross and former vice-president of the Liberal Party, was awarded 250 guineas costs from public funds by Mr. Justice Melford Stevenson after the jury's verdict at Chelmsford Assizes.

Now 55-year-old Major Smedley faces the possibility of a High Court action by Mrs. Dorothy Calvert.

Mrs. Calvert, who took over the Radio City pop station after her husband's death, said last night: "I have contacted solicitors about claiming damages from Major Smedley for the loss of my husband."

SEIZED

Mr. Calvert, who was 38, was shot dead after he burst into Major Smedley's cottage at Wendens Ambo, Essex, on June 21.

Less than 48 hours before, Major Smedley had led a boarding party who seized Radio City, on a disused fort in the Thames Estuary.

The court was told that Major Smedley wanted to "protect the interest" of his own Project Atlanta, which had financed a new transmitter for Radio City.

Major Smedley said that his secretary, Miss Pamela Thorburn, struggled with Mr. Calvert when he entered the house. He believed Mr. Calvert had a firearm in his hand.

"I believed he was going to fire," Major Smedley told the court. "Something came whizzing past me. He came at me and at that moment I fired my gun."

There was no question of an aimed shot, he added. His reaction was instinctive.

'BRILLIANT'

Major Smedley said he realised later that what Mr. Calvert had in his hand was a bronze statuette of Napoleon.

Mr. J. T. Molony, Q.C., defending, submitted that it was a case of justifiable homicide. "Technically," he said, "Calvert was a burglar when he entered the premises.

"He went into this house [illegible]

OLIVER SMEDLEY—last night's picture.

The Sun, Wednesday 19th October, 2016

34. LOOSE ENDS

This is where the Life and Death of a Pirate ends but for Dorothy, it was the start of a new chapter. She had been left to pick up the pieces and carry on but there were still loose ends and many unanswered questions.

After the trial, Dorothy spent sleepless nights trying to make sense of all that had been said in court. In her mind, she went over and over Major Smedley's account. He had changed his story and what he said was very credible except that it was wrong, wrong, wrong. Reg was shot in the hallway, not in the dining room. No one would have charged at a man holding a gun, least of all Reg. Why hadn't the Prosecution Counsel challenged his statements? Had he been in collusion with Smedley?

Dorothy was angry with the legal system and angry with herself. She hadn't managed to get a fair trial and everything had been distorted with no new witnesses called to tell the truth. Most of all, she regretted she hadn't broken the law and taken her opportunity to broadcast the facts on Radio City.

The police returned the documents that were apparently 'lost' during the court procedure which proved Radio Atlanta / Smedley, owed Reg money. More surprising was a visit from a police officer who requested that she reinstate Paul Elvey as he claimed he had been unfairly dismissed. This puzzled Dorothy. Why should the police be taking an interest in Paul Elvey? She refused, explaining that under no circumstances would she have him back on the station. If he had done his job properly and made sure the hatches were battened down, her husband would still be alive.

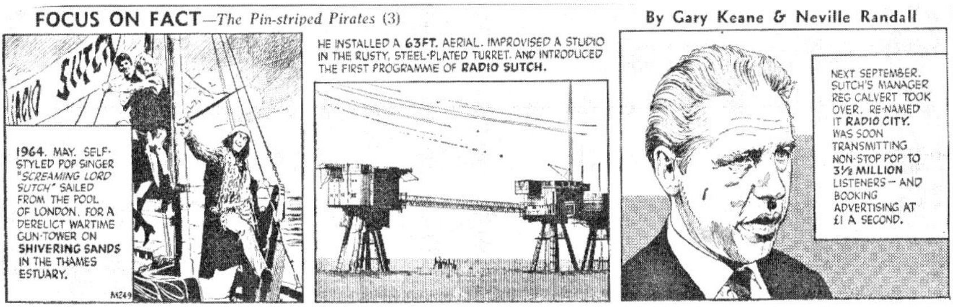

19th October, 1966. The Daily Sketch

NEWSPAPER HEADLINES Wednesday 19th October

Major Smedley is cleared after telling the jury:

RADIO CITY BOSS RAN ON TO MY GUN

By KEVIN HUNT

WARTIME hero Major Oliver Smedley was yesterday cleared by a jury of unlawfully killing Radio City boss Reginald Calvert, and was awarded 250 guineas costs.

Raid

Object

Major Smedley ... "Calvert was coming at me fast"

The night a girl and a war hero faced an angry intruder

SMEDLEY TELLS HOW HE SHOT RADIO CITY CHIEF

SUSAN CALVERT . . . escorted from the court in tears.

WAR hero Major William Oliver Smedley was cleared yesterday of the manslaughter of pirate radio chief Reg Calvert. A jury took less than a minute to reach the verdict without even leaving the jury box.

Mr. Justice Melford Stevenson ordered Smedley's release, and awarded him 250 guineas costs.

REG CALVERT

STRUGGLING

Calvert—the pirate dogged by disaster

RUSHED

2 WOMEN IN RADIO CITY COURT CLASH

By KEVIN HUNT

TWO women clashed yesterday in evidence in a court which heard of the link between an early morning raid on the Radio City pirate station on Shivering Sands and a midnight shooting in a country cottage.

Before the court was wealthy businessman Major Oliver Smedley, 55, a former vice-president of the Liberal Party, who is accused of the manslaughter of Radio City's boss, 38-year-old Reginald Calvert.

SMEDLEY—who pleaded not guilty—was said to have headed the boarding party which "captured" the broadcasting station on Shivering Sands last June.

CALVERT was said to have later driven to Major Smedley's country home in Duck-lane, Wendens Ambo, Essex, and to have been shot as he struggled in the hall with Miss Pamela Thorburn, 23, who was the major's housekeeper-secretary and looked after his children.

Sell

The boarding party's descent on Radio City, said Mr. Hugh Griffith, Q.C., prosecuting at Essex Assizes, Chelmsford, came after Calvert opened negotiations to sell out the station to another pirate broadcasting group.

The two women who gave evidence yesterday are theatrical impresario Miss Dorothy Black, known professionally as Kitty Black, and Mrs. Dorothy Calvert, widow of the shot Radio City chief.

Aim

Miss Black, of Brunswick-gardens, Kensington, said she was a shareholder in Project Atlanta, of which Smedley was chairman. The company was associated with Radio Caroline—another pirate station.

The aim of the seventeen-strong party, added Miss Black, was to prevent the sale under Calvert's negotiations of a £10,000 transmitter which had been provided with money raised by Major Smedley.

"As far as we knew the proposed deal did not include paying back the cost of our transmitter," Miss Black went on.

Miss Black told the all-men jury that she herself was in the boarding party—in which one group of men was led by a rigger called "Big Alf."

There was no violence, and a transmitter crystal—a vital part—was handed over to her on request.

About a dozen men, including "Big Alf," were left on Radio City to look after the transmitter until such time as its ownership and future use could be established.

Miss Black said that afterwards, at a meeting in a London office, Calvert said he had discovered a new form of nerve gas and it would be a good opportunity to try it out against the boarders remaining on Radio City.

Mrs. Dorothy Calvert

THE MAJOR

Major Smedley . . . on a manslaughter charge.

THE WIDOW

Mrs. Calvert . . . widow of Radio City chief.

Reasons for raid

told the court she understood from her husband that the boarding party wanted him to sign an agreement giving them half of the proceeds of Radio City.

The transmitter was not being used to send transmissions when the boarding party arrived, Mrs. Calvert added.

Bills

It was nearly thirty years old, and not serviceable, and component parts were not readily available. It would have taken thousands of pounds to make it serviceable.

"Its owner could have taken it away at any time without loss," said Mrs. Calvert.

Since her husband's death she had sent Smedley bills to cover the cost of storing the transmitter on board Radio City and asked him when it would be removed.

The trial goes on today.

Above left: Daily Mirror.
Above right: Daily Sketch.

Left: Daily Mirror

Extracts

The two women who gave evidence yesterday are theatrical impressario Miss Dorothy Black and Mrs Dorothy Calvert.

Miss Black said the aim of the 17-strong party was to prevent the sale of the £10,000 transmitter which had been provided by money raised by Major Smedley.

Mrs Dorothy Calvert told the court that the boarding party wanted her husband to sign an arrangement giving them half the proceeds of Radio City. The transmitter was not used. It was nearly 30 years old and not serviceable.

After the trial, various journalists contacted Dorothy to write her story but were unable to get it published. They were informed there was a D-Notice which prevented it. This, however, did not apply to Smedley or his associates.

D-Notice: A government notice issued to news editors requiring them not to publish certain information for reasons of national security.

SUNDAY PEOPLE feature
6th November, 1966
Right: Pamela Thorburn with Major Smedley.
Below: Kitty Black, knitting, with Major Smedley.

kill me... personally!

HE WAVED A 'GAS-GUN' AND THREATENED THE WHOLE CREW WITH MASS MURDER

had to cast off and anchor in the bay outside the harbour.

A gale blew up that night, and only supreme seamanship by the captain, Polish Mark Odalowski, saved the Mi Amigo from destruction.

The specially manufactured radio mast was mislaid in transit and eventually found in a storeyard.

Naturally, we were furious.

All kinds of things were done to try to slow down the preparations of our rivals.

SCUFFLES

During the war Allan Crawford had been a bomber pilot. As an Australian, he had always resented it if things went wrong. Now his blood was up.

Unknown to me, false information was fed into the radio room of the Caroline to try to create difficulties for them.

In the bars and taverns ashore there were constant

arrive from Galveston, Texas, was held up.

In the end, we had to watch O'Rahilly's boat steam out to sea—knowing she was almost certainly bound for the anchorage point off the Essex coast which we had planned to occupy.

When we got there some four weeks later, sure enough the Caroline was just where we had expected to find her. From her tall mast in the forepeak was rippling out the first of Britain's "pirate" radio broadcasts.

Radio Caroline — however bitterly we begrudged the fact—was first on the air.

Our own transmission began soon afterwards. The two ships were little more than half a mile apart. It became an obvious embarrassment to us both, as we were competing for the

where she broadcasts still as Caroline North.

LAST DECEMBER we gave up active control of our ship to O'Rahilly. By then we had realised that our original aims for commercial radio were unattainable—at least until legal circumstances changed.

We had not managed to use our "pirate" platform for any *useful* purpose. And we had *not* made money. In fact we had lost it in thousands.

A "pirate" radio station is a mighty expensive set-up to run.

You have got to pay and maintain a full ship's complement in addition to your broadcasting technicians and disc jockeys.

You have got to hire a foreign contractor to take

Dorothy wanted to take out her own court action against Smedley and show he had told lies about the ownership of the transmitter and its value. More importantly, she wanted to prove he was guilty of murder. Her solicitors, however, strongly advised her against this, explaining it would cost thousands and as Smedley had been acquitted in a court of law, she would undoubtedly lose the case.

Freelance reporter, Nicolas Travers, approached Dorothy before the trial to write her version of events.

"When the trial ends, everybody will be wanting to hear your side of things, I should imagine. Can you promise me not to give any big interviews? Obviously, you cannot refuse to answer questions, one at a time. But I do want to keep this exclusive."

After the trial, Nicolas approached various newspapers to see if they were interested in publishing the story and was shocked to find that no one would take it.

"I have tried a number of papers. None wanted to know. The News of the World is running a big feature (by Mike Raven, Major Smedley's cousin) on Sunday. This story is with the Sunday Times. I told them that if they don't want to pay, they can have it free – as long as they print. I think there has been a miscarriage of justice. I want to see it put right."

Nicolas Travers

Radio City Party at Welbeck House. Cousin of Leslie Dunne. (?) Jill Wileman, Eric Martin, (?girl) Adrian Love. (? Alan Clark) Dorothy Calvert. (?girl) Leslie Dunne, Candy Calvert. (?girl) Susan Calvert. (? Janice). Photo: John Wileman

Dorothy moved forward with her life and put all her energy into making Radio City a success. It was a happy station and this joy was transmitted over the airwaves. Disc jockeys were encouraged to stamp their personality on their programmes and the Aunty Mabel show won a top radio award. To Dorothy's surprise, she had come to love running Radio City and even enjoyed the weekly trips out to Shivcring Sands.

Above: The Harvester about to leave Shivering Sands. Platform hoist lift going down carrying crew to return to land.
(Photo from Woolf Byrne.

Left: 1966 Whitstable Harbour showing the Harvester moored up in the centre of the front three boats.
(Photo from Leslie Dunne).

With Reg's untimely death, the government worked quickly to put an end to pirate radio stations. In the autumn of 1966, the first court summonses were issued against Essex Radio and Radio 390. Both were found guilty of contravening Section One of the 1949 Wireless Telegraphy Act, by using a transmitter without a licence within British territorial waters. They were fined £100 each and ordered to close. Neither did. They were 'pirates' and determined to fight to the end.

Radio City was to be summoned in court on 8th February, 1967 although everyone knew, Shivering Sands was outside British waters. Two weeks prior to the summons, Dorothy received news that terrified her. She could hardly believe, after all that had happened, that anyone in their right mind would try to take over Radio City and organise another boarding party.

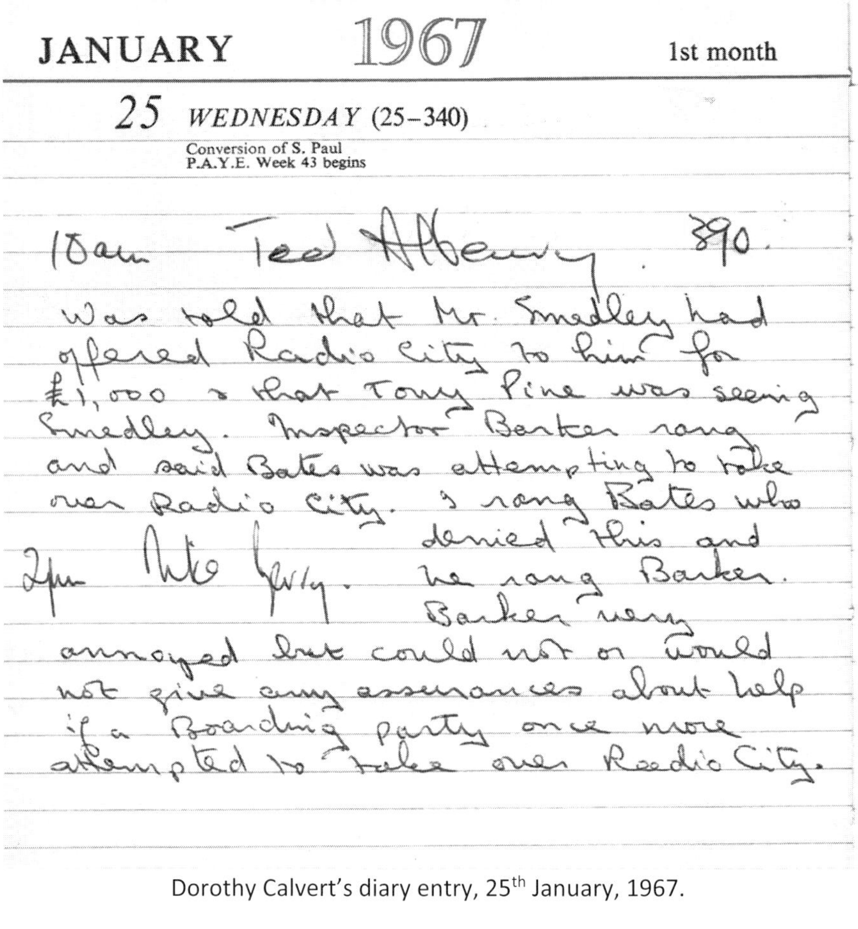
JANUARY 1967 1st month

25 WEDNESDAY (25–340)

Conversion of S. Paul
P.A.Y.E. Week 43 begins

10am Ted Allbeury 390.

Was told that Mr. Smedley had offered Radio City to him for £1,000 & that Tony Pine was seeing Smedley. Inspector Barker rang and said Bates was attempting to take over Radio City. I rang Bates who denied this and he rang Barker. Barker very annoyed but could not or would not give any assurances about help if a Boarding party once more attempted to take over Radio City.

2pm [illegible]

Dorothy Calvert's diary entry, 25th January, 1967.

Ted Allbeury telephoned Dorothy to say that Mr Smedley had offered Radio City to him for £1,000 and that Tony Pine was seeing Smedley. He was so angry, he told her that he had thrown Smedley down the stairs. Next, the News Editor of the Daily Express contacted Dorothy to warn her that someone had spoken to a Mr Bollen at Gravesend, making enquiries as to how much it would cost to take a boarding party out to Radio City.

Desperately worried, Dorothy called Inspector Barker to ask for his advice and he contacted a Mr Angell at the Home Office. Telegrams were sent to the various offices and departments regarding protection of Radio City. Kent police did not have a suitable boat to go out to the station, so Inspector Barker made arrangements with the Home Office for the Marines to stand by with a boat at Chatham.

None of this information was relayed to Dorothy and she was unaware of the protection they were apparently providing, but, she did hear a rumour that Smedley had been detained and held for three weeks to prevent him arranging another boarding party.

The police were still monitoring telephone conversations of Radio City personnel. On Wednesday 8th February, information was received from a D.I. Metcalfe, 'A' G.P.O., about a planned boarding party that would leave by boat in the area of West Beach, Whitstable. The police acted very quickly and within minutes of the message, they surrounded the beach. Very soon, it became obvious that there was no one on the beach and no boarding party. It had all been a hoax.

Phil Perkins and Tony Pine both knew there was no possibility of sailing a boat from West Beach and thought it hilarious to see the whole area swarming with police a short time after their telephone conversation. Phil was very loyal to Mrs C and had no intention of being part of a boarding party. He merely wanted to prove a point that the police were 'illegally' listening to his telephone calls.

Tony Pine admitted that he did have plans to take control of the towers and wanted to find a way of keeping the station running after the anticipated shutdown on 8th February. His efforts, however, were thwarted by the police who always seemed to know and be around.

Tony was interviewed by the police about the hoax phone call and was accused of wasting police time and resources. He was cocky in his response.

"It's your fault for illegally tapping peoples' telephones. I wonder what the court will think about that?"

The Home Office and Police knew that the Shivering Sands Forts were well outside British territorial waters. Regardless of the facts, Rochford Magistrates Court decided that Shivering Sands were within the limit and the station was ordered to close and fined £100.

For Dorothy, there was no British justice. She gave instructions for Radio City to close at midnight on 8th February, 1967. No one was expecting it, believing she would appeal as Radio 390 had done. Dorothy, however, was weary. The recent threats of a boarding party had made her decide that it was time to say goodbye to Radio City and Shivering Sands.

During the final hour of the station, disc jockeys broadcast a joint show telling of their life on Shivering Sands and Tom Edwards selected the last record to be played, *The Party's Over* by Shirley Bassey.

Candy tried to persuade her mother to keep Radio City and was heartbroken when the station closed and Tom stopped calling at Welbeck House.

It took a while to dismantle and remove the equipment. Dorothy sold what she could but the transmitter purchased by Atlanta was left behind. When everything was cleared, a generator was kept running and the lights remained glowing for three weeks until the oil ran out. Fred Downs, who kept an eye on the forts, informed Dorothy that when the lights went off, Smedley returned to the towers and stayed on for several weeks.

Dorothy did her best to find employment for her crew with other radio stations. Paul Kramer joined Caroline North. Alan Clark went to Radio 390 and used the pseudonym, Christopher Clark. Adrian Love went to the BBC and also worked with Ross Brown (RWB) on London 67 producing radio shows. Phil Perkins went to Caroline North and then transferred to Caroline South. Ian MacRae and Tom Edwards joined Caroline South.

Roy Bates changed Radio Essex's name to BBMS Britain's Better Music Station. He continued to broadcast from Knock John Fort only to be prosecuted again on 30th November. The station limped on until Christmas day when it ran out of funds. Bates decided to move the equipment to Rough Sands Fort which was of the same design as Knock John but further out to sea. He failed to start up a new station but in late 1967, he returned to Rough Fort, renaming it the Principality of Sealand. It was outside British jurisdiction and he gave himself the title of Prince Roy and later issued Principality of Sealand stamps, passports and currency.

Ted Allbeury appealed the court decision and continued to run Radio 390 on Red Sands Towers until July, 1967.

If Allbeury had not shown so much interest in buying Radio City and aggravating the situation with Smedley by saying Reg was dangerous, maybe the outcome to this story would have been different. Up to the point of Reg's death, the pirates were so popular that it would have been political suicide for any government to close them and they hoped that one day, they would be granted licences to continue broadcasting on land.

METROPOLITAN POLICE CRIMINAL INVESTIGATION DEPARTMENT NEW SCOTLAND YARD

REPORT: 27th January, 1967 (Extracts)

To: Chief Superintendent.

With further reference to the attached papers which deal with Pirate Radio Stations and in particular with Radio City at Shivering Sands, Thames Estuary.

On 25th January, 1967, I received reliable information that an attempt was being planned to seize control of the Radio City Forts and this attempt would be made before 7th February, 1967.

From information received it appears that Anthony Pine of 15 Island Wall and Philip Perkins of 106 Island Wall, Whitstable, are illegally operating a radio transmitter and a person known as 'Uncle' of Southend-on-Sea is involved. It appears that Pine and Perkins, who operate a company known as Offshore Maintenance Ltd from 15 Island Wall, are acting with Roy Bates of Southend to take possession of Radio City.

I have spoken to Mrs Dorothy Calvert, who assured me she had made no business arrangement for these people to take over her fort and any attempt so made would be contrary to her wishes and would have to be made by some form of subterfuge or force.

Mrs Calvert confirmed the information by telling me that within the last two days she had been told that Major Oliver Smedley, who was recently acquitted of murdering her husband, had offered to sell her fort to Edward Allbeury, the proprietor of Radio 390.

I reminded Mrs Calvert that my interests were solely in preventing a breach of the peace and sought her cooperation. She promised to check her security arrangements at the fort and to inform this office if an attempt was made to board Radio City. Mrs Calvert is going to send an extra man to the fort in order that an all-night watch can be maintained.

It appears, after my telephone conversation with Mrs Calvert she telephoned Mr Roy Bates and warned him not to touch her property. Bates denied that he had any intention of doing so, and he later telephoned me at this office. He assured me he did not intend to take over Radio City and that Major Smedley had an interest in these towers and suggested that he was the one to watch. I am not prepared to accept an assurance from Mr Bates, but he is well aware of police interest in his activities. At the same time, he is firmly convinced of his right to take over just what he fancies in the estuary.

It is believed that Bates is the man named 'Uncle'. If this is so the association between Pine, Perkins and 'Uncle' is sufficient to establish the intentions of Bates. I am told Bates is the type of man who would take over the fort and then defy anyone to do anything about it afterwards.

It must not be forgotten that Smedley maintains a claim to certain equipment on Radio City and it is quite possible that Bates and Smedley are acting together to take over this Radio Station. Bates, recently summoned and convicted, has now nowhere to broadcast. He recently took over a tower well out into the North Sea (Rough Tower) but was forced to leave it owing to its dangerous condition and he is now losing large sums of money from advertising revenue as a result.

It is more than coincidental that information about fresh activity in the estuary has reached me from three different sources on the same day.

When violence was threatened at this fort during the summer of 1966, it was accepted that if the necessity arose, Police would be sent there solely to prevent a breach of the peace and a Royal Marine vessel from Chatham was offered and accepted as a safe means of conveying police to the fort.

I have spoken to Chief Superintendent Davies, Thames Division, and a Sergeant and five men are available at short notice to proceed by road to Chatham if the services of police are required at the fort. ..... I have informed District Commander, East Kent Police, and he will make every effort, within his powers to prevent Bates and his associates leaving a Kent harbour for the purpose of taking over the fort.

Some difficulty may arise with Mrs Calvert if some form of police assistance is not forthcoming. This lady, who has always been helpful, has been summoned to appear on 8th February, 1967, to answer charges of transmitting from Radio City, contrary to the Wireless Telegraphy Act and a conviction, as with the other fort operators, is expected. To secure this conviction, the Court will need proof the fort is within British territorial waters and therefore within the jurisdiction of British law. .....

J.A. Barker
Detective Chief Inspector

METROPOLITAN POLICE TELEGRAPH'S (Telegrams)

(Telegrams were a means of communication. Most were short and to the point.)

From: DCI Barker
To: Mr M.W. Gibson, District Commander, East Kent Police.

We have received reliable information that Mr Roy Bates and two men from Whitstable, Anthony Daniel Pine of 15 Island Wall and Philip James Perkins of 106, Island Wall, are planning to take over the fort at Shivering Sands, known as Radio City. It is also suggested that Smedley is associated with this plan.

In June, 1966 when violence was then threatened at this fort, officers from this force were prepared to go to prevent a breach of the peace and a Royal marine vessel from Chatham was offered for this purpose. Would your force now be prepared to accept responsibility for maintaining law and order at the fort?

Reply: I am prepared to do anything within my powers to prevent these people leaving here to take over the fort but I cannot accept responsibility as I have no means of getting there.

From: DCI Barker
To: East Kent Police

I understand Kent police have a boat available.

Reply: There is one boat which is only suitable for work in the Medway and that is kept there. There is another boat, I have been on it, but I doubt whether it is suitable for work in the open sea. The boats are under the command of Mr Jennings of West Kent.

From: Mr Angell, Home office. 2nd February, 1967
To: Chief Superintendent. C.1.
Your report re. 'Radio City' has been passed to me for a decision. Unfortunately, this Fort is outside police jurisdiction, but it is obviously a matter which calls for urgent consideration. I cannot see that anything can be done without fresh legislation but I will have the matter looked into.

Action: Mr Gibson: Assist. Chief constable, East Kent, informed of above and he said he would telephone Mr Angell.
(Copy to Chief Inspector Barker)

From: Mr M.W. Gibson, Asst. Chief Constable, East Kent
2nd Feb. 1967. 4.15 p.m.
To: Chief Superintendent C.1.
I have been reading the report sent to this Force by you regarding Radio City. I have spoken to our legal department and it is their opinion that our jurisdiction ends at low water-mark and if we went to the Fort we should be outside our bailiwick and the position would be tricky. I have spoken to the Chief Constable, Essex, and he agrees that he is in the same position. In my view this is not our job and in fact, is not a police job. It is a job for the Navy, as I do not think that police officers are equipped to carry out this sort of exercise. I realise the matter is urgent and if you can let me know the name of the Home Office official dealing with this I will telephone him.

Reply: We have heard nothing from the Home Office but I will find out who is dealing with it and ring you back.
(Copy to Chief Inspector Barker)

From: Mr Angell, Horseferry House, Home Office. 2nd February. 6.35 p.m.
To: Chief Supt. C.1.
Further to our previous conversation about 'Radio City' it seems to me that we cannot stand by and do nothing if offences are committed on the Fort. Action will have to be taken and the matter sorted out afterwards. I think it is unnecessary to have a Royal Naval vessel standing by permanently and if you agree I will get in touch with the Admiralty and ask them to be ready to supply a vessel at short notice if needed. From what you tell me, it would appear that Kent and Essex are not prepared to send officers to the Fort and we must again look to the Metropolitan Police to supply men if action is required. Obviously, the present position is unsatisfactory and consideration will have to be given to regularising the position.
(Copy to Chief Insp. Barker)

From A.C.C. 2nd February, 1967. 7 p.m.
To Chief Supt. C.1.
I have been informed by Mr Angell of the Home Office that the Royal Navy are now prepared to provide transport to Radio City in the event of it becoming necessary for Police to attend there. If transport is required, Commander Davis of the Ministry of Defence is to be contacted and he will make the necessary arrangements.
(Copy to Chief Inspector Barker)

From: Chief Supt. Davies. 3rd Feb.1967. 2.30 p.m.
To: Chief Supt. C.1.
Chief Inspector Barker has been on to me about 'Radio City' and I have made arrangements that if a call is received six of my officers will meet at Wapping. If a call comes it will probably be during the night and it would be better for them to go to Chatham by road. I would be grateful if you would arrange transport and appoint a CID Officer to be in charge of the operation.

Reply: This will be done and I will ask Chief Inspector Barker to make necessary arrangements.

From: D.I. Metcalfe 'A' G.P.O. 8th February, 1967. 8.25 p.m.
To: Chief Superintendent C.O.C.1. D.S. Cooper.
I have received reliable information that a boat is going to West Beach Whitstable at 8.30 p.m., where it will flash its lights twice and pick up eight men and take them to Shivering Sands where they intend to take over Radio City.

Reply: Thank you, we will put the arrangements in hand.

~~~~~~~~~~~~~~~~~~~~~~~~~~

Wednesday 8th February, 1967. 11.10 p.m.
Chief Inspector Barker telephoned to say that the message was a hoax, that the person responsible was known to the Kent Police and they would deal with it.
A person whose surname is SMYTHE telephoned the information to a man whose first name is 'Barry' in order to test whether 'Barry's telephone was being tapped. It is not known whether they are connected with the press, but Smythe is a friend of PINE, one of the men strongly suspected of being concerned in the conspiracy to take over Radio City.

Thursday 9th February, 1967
From: Commander Davies, Duty Officer, Ministry of Defence:
To: Chief Superintendent C.1.
Re: Radio City
Can we take our vessel off permanent 'standby'? If this is done we can use it for essential matters at Chatham and it could be made available for your use within three hours or so of receiving a request.
~~~~~~~~~~~~~~~~~~~~~~~~~~

REPLY from J. Mannings: Yes. In view of recent developments and action now being taken, it is doubtful if the vessel will be required again. A delay of three hours will not seriously interfere with Police action as our men will have to be collected at Wapping and transported by road to Chatham. Thank you for your prompt assistance last night.

Car Sticker

RADIO CITY

Daily 06.00 to 24.00 Hrs. 1034 KC/S

TO:

FROM:

Confirming your most valued report on

SINCERE BEST WISHES
From all the Station Staff.

We hope you will continue to enjoy
our programmes.

REGGIE KRAY

Shortly after the station closed, a man came into the office asking to make an appointment with Mrs Calvert as his boss wanted to have a meeting with her. As Dorothy was not there, Jill arranged for him to come back at 6 p.m. The man, in his mid-40s, tall with a hooked nose, spoke with a cockney accent. When he returned, he explained to Dorothy that he had been a friend of Reg's but Dorothy knew this was untrue. He was not the sort of person Reg would choose to be associated with.

Dorothy was taken to a nightclub not far from Bond Street and introduced to his boss, Reggie Kray, a man she had vaguely heard of as a nightclub owner. There was quite a party going on and he had some girls with him. Dorothy felt on edge and decided to stay firmly businesslike. After a short while, Reggie Kray suggested they all go to the Astor Club and everyone squeezed into his Rolls Royce.

When they reached the Astor, they were ushered to a large table and different people came and went. On stage was a cabaret with an American female singer. Reggie Kray excused himself and spent some time in the office so while Dorothy waited, she sat back and watched the show. When he returned, he sat down next to Dorothy so they could talk. He was very polite and gentlemanly, but Dorothy was on her guard.

"Can I get you another drink?"

"I'm okay, thank you."

"Come on, I'll get you another."

"No, really. One martini is my limit," replied Dorothy, firmly.

"I understand you run Radio City?"

"Yes, I did, but it's closed now. We had a court action against us a couple of weeks ago."

"Yes, I heard, but I'd like you to carry on running it."

Dorothy, taken by surprise, shook her head.

"I can't. It would be breaking the law."

"You don't need to worry about that. You can start broadcasting whenever you like and you'll be all right. I'll make sure of it."

"No, I'm really sorry, I can't. I'd be fined £100 a week if I went back on-air."

"No, they won't prosecute you. I've got the government in my pocket."

Reggie Kray continued to try and persuade Dorothy to restart Radio City, assuring her she would be okay. No matter how persuasive he was, Dorothy was adamant, she would not give way and he eventually conceded defeat.

"I can see I'm talking to a lady who won't change her mind."

Dorothy smiled. "No, I don't often change my mind when it's made up."

"I'll drive you home," offered Reggie Kray, politely.

Dorothy accepted and at midnight, he drove her back to Welbeck Street in his Rolls Royce.

PAUL ELVEY AND THE KRAY'S TRIAL

During the summer of 1968, office and home telephones were again being intercepted and Dorothy, when she was out, kept looking over her shoulder as she had an unpleasant feeling she was being followed.

In July, 1968 the trial of the Kray twins was being held at the Old Bailey on conspiracy to murder. The judge was Lord Justice Melford Stevenson who had previously tried Smedley. Dorothy now realised that the Reggie Kray who was on trial was the same man who had told her he had the government in his pocket. Also on trial was Paul Elvey, formerly a Radio City Engineer.

NEWSPAPER REPORT

The Observer: 21st July, 1968 (Extracts)

"The Court at Bow Street, where charges for conspiracy to murder were being heard last week against the Kray twins and others. We have seen extraordinary contraptions in court. A neat hide attaché case was fitted up with clips and springs to hold a hypodermic needle that could be released by a cord to inject a dose of hydrogen cyanide through a hole in the side when swung against someone's leg.

There was the crossbow, a clumsy weapon of mahogany and steel with telescopic sights, bought at Lillywhites. The evil steel-tipped arrows, we were told, were used for killing deer and would, at the least, cause multiple haemorrhage in a human being at a range of up to 50 yards. We did not see the gelignite, though we were shown a cheap, sky-blue suitcase in which it was said to have been found. ......

The evidence grew more bizarre as the week progressed. With Thomas Cooper there was discussion of plans to kidnap the Pope and to release Tshombe, as well as the more immediate matter of killing someone involved in a case at the Old Bailey. Cooper was plump and pale, with long sideboards and an American accent. He was self-assured, and when counsel sneered at him he sneered right back.

All the evidence led up to Eugene (Paul) Elvey. He was a young man with a high domed forehead and sandy hair. His eyes behind spectacles were sandy and his voice was pale and colourless to match.

He talked about his experience exclusively in business language. He spoke about "my colleague and I" and how they "generally discussed the operation". Words such as "murder" were left to the lawyers; the witnesses spoke about "contracts" and "organisations".

Thomas Cooper claimed he was an agent for the United States Treasury Department investigating gold smuggling and links between the Mafia and the Krays. He explained, he was employed by the Krays in early 1968 and to test his loyalty, they asked him to carry out a murder. Cooper employed Paul Elvey to do the contracts for him and Elvey was sent to Glasgow to buy explosives for a car bomb. Police detained Elvey in Scotland and he confessed to being involved in three murder attempts.

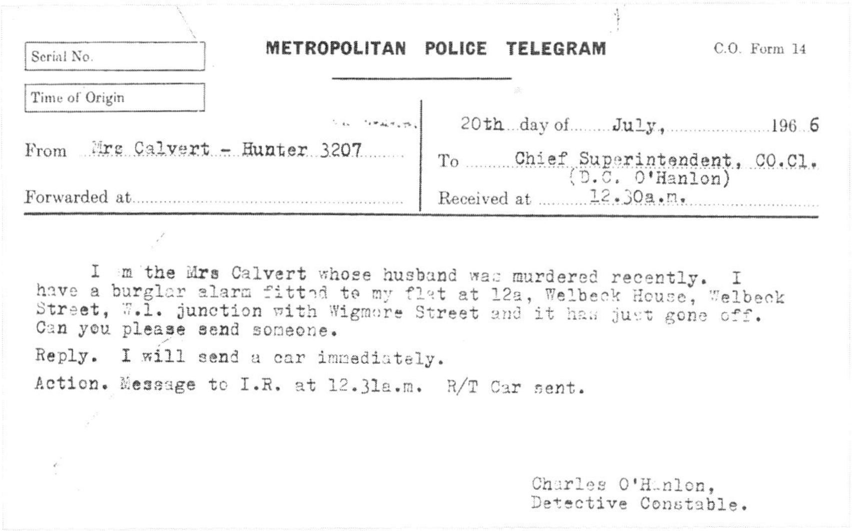

METROPOLITAN POLICE TELEGRAM C.O. Form 14

Serial No.

Time of Origin

From Mrs Calvert - Hunter 3207

Forwarded at

20th day of July, 1966

To Chief Superintendent, CO.C1. (D.C. O'Hanlon)

Received at 12.30a.m.

I am the Mrs Calvert whose husband was murdered recently. I have a burglar alarm fitted to my flat at 12a, Welbeck House, Welbeck Street, W.1. junction with Wigmore Street and it has just gone off. Can you please send someone.

Reply. I will send a car immediately.

Action. Message to I.R. at 12.31a.m. R/T Car sent.

Charles O'Hanlon,
Detective Constable.

Police record of phone call regarding attempted break-in (Released 43 years later).

Dorothy was never able to unravel the mystery of why Reg was shot or how his killer had managed to walk away as a 'free' man. So many pieces were missing from the jigsaw, so many lies, cover-ups and unanswered questions.

After the trial of the Kray Twins, Dorothy wondered whether the Krays had threatened Reg? Did they want Shivering Sands as a base for drug smuggling? Why did Reg decide to sell Radio City to Radio London when he loved running the station? Why did he want Dorothy and their daughters to live abroad for their safety until the station had been sold? Was the Radio City engineer, Paul Elvey, working for the Krays while he was employed by Reg?

Why, in January 1967, did Smedley want Radio City again? Was he involved with the Krays? Dorothy thought this unlikely but his office was in the East End of London and he employed a corrupt solicitor. He was also known for managing tax avoidance off-shore accounts.

How had the legal system been corrupted? Had the Krays 'pulled strings' with their government contacts? Or was it Smedley's associates in the legal profession? His ex-wife had married Harold Cassel, a barrister who had been a pupil of the Lord Chief Justice of England. Why did the Prosecution Counsel appear to be working on behalf of Smedley? Why didn't they call witnesses on Reg's side or use evidence which proved Smedley was lying in court? Why didn't the judge allow the jury to go out and deliberate the evidence? Why did he award Smedley 250 guineas for killing her husband?

Dorothy also pondered whether the government had been involved? Pirate radio was so popular they needed a reason to bring in new legislation. The shooting of Reg had given them that reason.

Why were telephone lines intercepted and why did the government put a D-Notice on Dorothy's version of events?

For what reason was Dorothy's life threatened when she continued to run Radio City after Reg's death?

Who was it who attempted to break into her apartment on the same night that Smedley had half a pillowcase of silver stolen? Why did the police deny being called out to her apartment that night?

The Marine Broadcasting Offences Act came into force on 14th August, 1967 and most of the pirates stopped broadcasting. Radio Caroline, however, avoided the law by operating from an overseas base and Ronan O'Rahilly was quoted as saying: "We were the first to broadcast and we will be last to close."

In September, 1967 the BBC transformed itself and did something it said it never would. It emerged with four new stations. Radio One: Pop music, all day. Radio Two: Easy listening music, all day. Radio Three: Classical music, all day. Radio Four: Talk radio, all day. There was also a promise there would be local and commercial radio stations. Reg's dream of 'free radio' had come about; but he had to die for it.

Within a year of Reg's death, Dorothy was living on her own. Lyndon asked for Susan's hand in marriage and she gave them her blessing. Candy went to work in Germany as an au pair, returning to England after several years and married in 1972.

After the station closed, Dorothy spent time establishing her publishing business, King Music, and helped, among others, a new young group called Fleetwood Mac.

Dorothy had a restless spirit, never settling anywhere for long. In 1970, she decided to move permanently from London and for a while, lived in Macbeth Close. For company, she bought a pretty, black-and-white Papillon puppy and named him Scampi. In the early mornings, she sometimes caught a glimpse of Reg sitting at the bottom of the bed playing with her puppy. Other times, she sensed him lying gently by her side. During bad periods, he came to her in vivid dreams where they vehemently argued, just as they had in life. Reg haunted her being and would never leave.

Dorothy Calvert and Shivering Sands, 1966 (AL)

Dorothy Calvert died in 2010 aged 81 and was laid to rest with Reg at Dunchurch. A few months prior to her death, she said to her daughter, "I know you'll be the person to tell this story." And I have.

THE END

CONTRIBUTORS include

CLIFTON HALL

Dorothy Calvert. David Jay (Hunter). David St. John. Pete Chambers. Laurie Hornsby. Sylvia Anderson. Jon Washington. Tanya Day (Mary Day). Roy Young. Tom Owen. Danny Storm (David Hurran) Roger James (Scarrott). Glen Dale (Richard Garforth). Chris Capaldi. Andy Brown. Gary Fletcher. Larry Reddington. Mike Richards (Hopcraft). John Wileman. Buddy Britten (Geoffrey Glover-Wright). Barney Peacock. Colin Angel (Wilsher). Geoff Chalke. Tony Burnett. Mike Everest (Banks). Johnny Neal - Starliners. John Roberts. John Allison. Bob Lawton. Freddy Were (Tony Rocco).

SHIVERING SANDS

Dorothy Calvert. Arthur Addy. Tom Long and Tony Newman - Liberators, Pinkerton's Assorted Colours. Ross Brown. Woolf Byrne. Cliff Cuttelle. Colin Dale. Chris Dannett. Leslie Dunne (Luc Dunne). Derek Diamond. Tom Edwards. Paul Elvey. Dick Dickson. Martin Green. Tamara Harrison. Mike Hayes. Printz Holman. Peggy Knight. Bob Le-Roi. Ian MacRae. Eric Martin (Richard Lee). Phil Perkins. David Phillips. Tony Pine. Norman St. John. Jill Wileman. Kenny Bell. Keith Skues. Hans Olof Gottfridsson. Jon Meyer. David Phillips.

HISTORY – RESOURCES

Life and Death of a Pirate is based on the memories of people who were there at the time. In addition, research documents include: Diaries of Reg and Dorothy Calvert. Radio City office files, correspondence, accounts, solicitors' letters, police records etc. The London Sound by Brian Long. Colin Nicol's interview with Allan Crawford. Newspaper editorials. The Monitor. National Archives. Witness statements etc.

ARIES PERSONALITY

Aries is the first sign of the zodiac. People born under this sign are independent and strongly project their personalities onto others, they can be very self-oriented but underneath may lie insecurity.

Arians do not like to take orders from others. They have an intense desire to succeed and put too much pressure on themselves. They venture into the world and leave impressions on others that they are exciting, vibrant and talkative.

Aries live adventurous lives and like to be the centre of attention, are natural and confident leaders. Impulsive, they do not always think before they act or speak, can be short-tempered and aggressive and may say whatever is in their head and regret it later.

They have a low tolerance for boredom and are notorious for not completing what they have begun before they go off in search of excitement elsewhere. Arians are activists and if a business idea comes their way, they tend to plunge right in and take a gamble and follow their dreams.

Aries Woman is hot-blooded and forceful, likes to be independent and can fend for herself. She has a great need for love and passion but will never let a man become her master as she considers herself to be his equal.

Reg and Dorothy Calvert, both Arians, born a week apart in March 1928

SHIVERING SANDS (RC)